Intercultural Reciprocal Learning in Chinese and Western Education

Series Editors
Michael Connelly
University of Toronto
Toronto, ON, Canada

Shijing Xu ⓘD
Faculty of Education
University of Windsor
Windsor, ON, Canada

This book series grows out of the current global interest and turmoil over comparative education and its role in international competition. The specific series grows out of two ongoing educational programs which are integrated in the partnership, the University of Windsor-Southwest University Teacher Education Reciprocal Learning Program and the Shanghai-Toronto-Beijing Sister School Network. These programs provide a comprehensive educational approach ranging from preschool to teacher education programs. This framework provides a structure for a set of ongoing Canada-China research teams in school curriculum and teacher education areas. The overall aim of the Partnership program, and therefore of the proposed book series, is to draw on school and university educational programs to create a comprehensive cross-cultural knowledge base and understanding of school education, teacher education and the cultural contexts for education in China and the West.

More information about this series at
http://www.palgrave.com/gp/series/15114

Yuhua Bu
Editor

Narrative Inquiry into Reciprocal Learning Between Canada-China Sister Schools

A Chinese Perspective

palgrave
macmillan

Editor
Yuhua Bu
East China Normal University
Shanghai, China

Intercultural Reciprocal Learning in Chinese and Western Education
ISBN 978-3-030-61084-5   ISBN 978-3-030-61085-2   (eBook)
https://doi.org/10.1007/978-3-030-61085-2

© The Editor(s) (if applicable) and The Author(s), under exclusive licence to Springer Nature Switzerland AG 2021
This work is subject to copyright. All rights are solely and exclusively licensed by the Publisher, whether the whole or part of the material is concerned, specifically the rights of translation, reprinting, reuse of illustrations, recitation, broadcasting, reproduction on microfilms or in any other physical way, and transmission or information storage and retrieval, electronic adaptation, computer software, or by similar or dissimilar methodology now known or hereafter developed.
The use of general descriptive names, registered names, trademarks, service marks, etc. in this publication does not imply, even in the absence of a specific statement, that such names are exempt from the relevant protective laws and regulations and therefore free for general use.
The publisher, the authors and the editors are safe to assume that the advice and information in this book are believed to be true and accurate at the date of publication. Neither the publisher nor the authors or the editors give a warranty, expressed or implied, with respect to the material contained herein or for any errors or omissions that may have been made. The publisher remains neutral with regard to jurisdictional claims in published maps and institutional affiliations.

Cover illustration: © WORDS AND MEANINGS / MARK SYKES / Alamy Stock Photo

This Palgrave Macmillan imprint is published by the registered company Springer Nature Switzerland AG.
The registered company address is: Gewerbestrasse 11, 6330 Cham, Switzerland

FOREWORD

Narrative Inquiry into Reciprocal Learning Between Canada-China Sister Schools: A Chinese Perspective is one of only a few scholarly books that I have read entirely in one sitting. This highly compelling volume addresses three phenomena well known to me—narrative inquiry, reciprocal learning, and the Canada-China Sister Schools Project—through a less familiar lens: the Chinese perspective. While learning about the latter, my knowledge of the former became broadened, deepened, and more keenly calibrated in cross-cultural ways (Craig, 2020). I especially commend Yuhua Bu and her co-authors for their even-handedness in researching and presenting their Canada-China Reciprocal Learning Project experiences. The project (and this book series!) originates with the doctoral work of Shijing Xu who came to Canada searching for western knowledge while carrying with her deep understandings of her Chinese culture and heritage. Under the direction of her dissertation advisor, Michael Connelly, Xu studied Chinese newcomer families in Canada—which was the first book in this Intercultural Reciprocal Learning in Chinese and Western Education Series. In her dissertation study, Shijing Xu interwove western narrative research methods and the Schwabian theory of "the Practical" together with school-based research and Confucianism. Her research eventually gave rise to the teacher education reciprocal learning program and sister school network in which Yuhua Bu and her team have played leading roles. That work subsequently morphed into this series of books cohering around experiences of reciprocal learning.

Like some books in this series, Bu et al.'s volume begins with historically rooted cultural practices in Chinese education settings, which many dynasties and multiple colonial forces have shaped. Concurrently, the author team remains open to their Canadian partners' perspectives and to learning reciprocally from their points of view. This is no easy feat. I urge readers to ponder the complexities embedded in this "deceptively simple task" (Connelly and Xu 2019) before beginning to digest this book.

From the beginning, I recommend that readers also keep in mind the extent to which the author team learned about themselves and their systems in relation to what they came to know about others and their systems—with the others, in this instance, being Canadians. For example, midway through this volume, a North American attending a U.S.-based conference declared, "They [the Chinese, the Chinese school] are a dictatorship. Do you [the Canadians, the Canadian School] take your democracy to them?" This query particularly caught my attention because I recall a Canada-China Reciprocal Learning meeting when a member of the Chinese delegation learned about the bureaucracy surrounding human subject research in Canada and remarked, "You are more communist than we are!" What is interesting in both of these cases is how the educators attempted to situate themselves in the partnership work while dealing with their own conceptions/misconceptions *and* deliberating their collaborators' conceptions/misconceptions as well. Later on in this volume, there is a discussion as to whether Canadian schools have any culture at all. Additionally, there is a comparative dialogue, which focuses on how mathematics is taught in both countries. These are incredibly rich and thought-provoking discussions. I will not preemptively give the authors' thinking away. Please read to the end of this volume and process the provisional "answers" that Bu, her co-authors, and other Chinese team members arrived at in their quest to reciprocally know.

Along the way, readers will recognize that reciprocal learning is not for the faint-hearted because so much of it takes place on the boundaries. In these in-between spaces, no one-size-fits-all answers hold for all time. However, what does prevail is the spirit of inquiry, which is evident in the plentiful questions posed throughout this volume. These begging questions call for attention and action as matters are visited and revisited, which is highly reflective of narrative inquiry's storying and re-storying process.

One other thing I would like to shine the spotlight on are the chapter titles that the authors have chosen. Chapter 2, "Friends from Afar," demonstrates from the outset the degree to which the Chinese respect foreigners and concomitantly seek to learn from them, while Chap. 3 metaphorically likens John Dewey's meeting of Confucian China to Michael Connelly's contemporary visit with Ye Lan in which he learned about New Basic Education Project at East China Normal University in Shanghai. The next chapters are ones readers would anticipate being a part of a book of this nature. We then come to "Society, History, and Interaction of Sister Schools," and "Circles and Straight Lines: Teachers' Life Worlds," with the latter being of particular interest due to its metaphorical implications. Three notable topics follow, "Leadership and Power," "Faith and Action," and "Future," which end this book. These titles—crisp and right-on-the-mark—provide a helicopter view of the content through which this volume becomes a highly coherent piece of scholarship. These stimulating titles invite readers to enter into the authors' worlds and to engage in reciprocal learning alongside them.

I now end with two interconnected points. First, Connelly and Xu (forthcoming) assert that the Canada-China Reciprocal Learning project is an exemplar of Schwab's Practical (Schwab 1969) in action. I would add that this book, *Narrative Inquiry into Reciprocal Learning Between Canada-China Sister Schools: A Chinese Perspective*, provides valuable practical knowledge gleaned through intercultural experience, which instantiates Connelly and Xu's claim (Craig in press). The fact that Chinese voices are now joining Canadian voices shores up their argument that "reciprocal learning as collaborative partnership" is an exciting new version of comparative education. It breaks through the crust of knowing this and knowing that to become "doing this and doing that and doing it this way and doing it that way with a sense of inquiry" (Xu and Connelly 2017, p. 17, emphasis in original). This brings me to my final point. Yuhua Bu and her collaborators, all writing in English as a second language, worked with narrative inquiry for the first time and let experience through the front door and theory in the back, sometimes against their best inclinations. Their sense of inquiry did not skip a beat. This made their explications of the experiences shared in this volume real, truthful, and worthy to be shared and acted on nationally and internationally. This book gives life and breath to reciprocal learning and will enormously help "reciprocal learning as collaborative partnership" become a viable counter-story to the dominant international narrative of measuring youth's knowledge of "this and that" in decontextualized settings cut off from the authentic, real-world experiences of their lives as lived.

Professor and Endowed Chair of Urban Education   Cheryl J. Craig
Texas A&M University

REFERENCES

Connelly, M., & Xu, S. (2019). Reciprocal Learning in the Partnership Project: From Knowing to Doing in Comparative Research Models. *Teachers and Teaching: Theory and Practice, 25*(6), 627–646.

Connelly, M., & Xu, S. (in press). Reciprocal Learning as a Comparative Education Model and as an Exemplar of Schwab's The Practical in Curriculum Inquiry. In M. F. He & W. Schubert (Eds.), *Oxford Encyclopedia of Curriculum Studies*. New York: Oxford University Press.

Craig, C. (2020). *Curriculum Making, Reciprocal Learning and the Best-Loved Self.* New York, NY: Palgrave Macmillan.

Craig, C. (in press). Joseph J. Schwab: Historical and Contemporary Impact on Education. *Oxford Encyclopedia of Education.*

Schwab, J. (1969). The Practical: A Language for Curriculum. *The School Review, 78*(1), 1–23.

Xu, S., & Connelly, F. M. (2017). Reciprocal Learning between Canada and China in Teacher Education and School Education: Partnership Studies of Practice in Cultural Context. *Frontiers of Education in China, 12*(2), 135–150.

CONTENTS

1 Introduction   1
Yuhua Bu
   1.1   *Origin and Background*   2
   1.2   *Our Learning and Growth in Projects as Researchers*   3
   1.3   *Objectives of the Sister School Project*   7
       1.3.1   *Objectives of the Sister School Reciprocal Learning*   7
       1.3.2   *The Research Purpose of the Sister School Project*   8
       1.3.3   *The Purpose of Writing This Book*   9
   1.4   *Structure and Main Ideas of the Book and Its Authors*   9
       1.4.1   *Structure of the Book*   9
       1.4.2   *Synopsis of Each Chapter*   10
       1.4.3   *Authors and Division of the Book*   13
   References   16

2 Friends from Afar   17
Yuhua Bu
   2.1   *Who Are We: Understanding Our Cultural Identity*
       from Both Sides of Chinese Traditional Culture   19
       2.1.1   *Looking Inward: Expressions of Love and*
            Consideration of Others   19
       2.1.2   *Looking Outward: Harmony Without*
            Uniformity, Loyalty Together with Consideration   23

ix

2.2		Repositioning Contemporary Chinese Cultural Identity: A Member of a "Community of Shared Future for Mankind"	26
2.3		A Century's East-West Dialogue About China's Education and Its Contemporary Appeal	28
2.4		The Two Contemporary Schools of Education Involved in This Project	33
	2.4.1	From Dewey and Schwab to Connelly and His Students: The Development of Empiricism Educational Theory	34
	2.4.2	Ye Lan and Her Academic Team: School of "Life-Practice" Educology and "New Basic Education" Research	39
2.5		Conclusion	45
References			46

3 Dewey Meets Confucius

53

Shan Qi

3.1		Introduction	53
3.2		Dewey's First Encounter with Chinese Education at the Beginning of the Twentieth Century	54
	3.2.1	Dewey to China: A Basic Judgment on Chinese Education	55
	3.2.2	China to Dewey: The Reaction of China to Dewey in the Modern Age	57
3.3		Connelly Coming to China: Another Meeting with China's Education at the Beginning of the Twenty-First Century	64
	3.3.1	Connelly to China: Basic Judgement About Chinese Education	65
	3.3.2	China to Connelly: The Reaction of Chinese Education to Connelly	69
3.4		Discussion and Conclusion	72
	3.4.1	A Century of Chinese Education: What Has Changed and What Remains Unchanged	72
	3.4.2	The Future of Reciprocal Learning Between China and Canada: Mutual Benefit and Symbiosis	77
References			80

4 Literature Review, Theoretical Framework and Research Method 87

Yuhua Bu

4.1 *Literature Review* 87
    4.1.1 *Reciprocal Learning* 87
    4.1.2 *Sister School* 89
    4.1.3 *Narrative Inquiry in China and in the World* 91
4.2 *Theoretical Framework and Methodology* 93
    4.2.1 *School of Life-Practice Educology* 93
    4.2.2 *Narrative Inquiry* 94
4.3 *Research Method* 96
    4.3.1 *Researchers of the Sister School Project* 96
    4.3.2 *Sister School Research Partners* 98
4.4 *Data Collection and Analysis Method* 104
    4.4.1 *Data Sources* 104
    4.4.2 *Research Tools* 105
4.5 *Ethical Considerations* 106
References 106

5 Society, History, and Interaction of Sister Schools 109

Yuhua Bu

5.1 *An Overview of the Sister Schools* 109
    5.1.1 *History of Minzhu Primary School* 109
    5.1.2 *The Landscape of Bay Street School* 114
    5.1.3 *Summary* 118
5.2 *The Process of Reciprocal Learning Between Sister Schools* 120
    5.2.1 *Exploratory Phase (September 2013–September 2014)* 121
    5.2.2 *Breakthrough Phase (September 2014–December 2015)* 121
    5.2.3 *Development Phase (March 2016–October 2019)* 123
    5.2.4 *Continuous Symbiosis Phase (March 2018– Present)* 125
5.3 *Basic Methods and Content of Cross-Cultural Reciprocal Learning Between Sister Schools* 126
    5.3.1 *Modes of Communication Between Sister Schools* 127
    5.3.2 *Contents of Communication Between Sister Schools* 132
5.4 *Summary* 137
References 137

xii CONTENTS

6 Circles and Straight Lines: Teachers' Life Worlds 139
Yuanyuan Zhu
6.1 *Introduction* 139
6.2 *Conceptualizing the Background* 140
    6.2.1 *Teachers and Teachers' Teaching in Different Contexts* 140
    6.2.2 *Reciprocal Learning Across Cultures in RLP* 143
6.3 *Research Methodology* 143
    6.3.1 *Data Collection* 144
    6.3.2 *Data Analysis* 144
    6.3.3 *Introducing the Teachers and the Researcher* 145
6.4 *Shanghai-Toronto Sister School Teachers Stories* 148
    6.4.1 *Heterogeneous Lesson: "The Tree's Shadow"* 148
    6.4.2 *Lesson Preparation and Discussion: "Brave Duck, Brave Me"* 153
    6.4.3 *Lesson Preparation and Discussion: "My School"* 158
6.5 *Findings* 162
    6.5.1 *Curriculum Structure* 162
    6.5.2 *Teachers' Teaching* 163
    6.5.3 *Teachers in Community* 166
6.6 *Conclusion and Discussion* 167
References 170

7 Interaction Between Teachers and Students 175
Yangjie Li
7.1 *Introduction* 175
7.2 *Literature Review* 177
7.3 *Theoretical Basis and Research Methods* 179
    7.3.1 *Theoretical Basis* 179
    7.3.2 *Research Method* 180
    7.3.3 *Research Participant* 181
    7.3.4 *Research Process* 182
7.4 *Findings* 184
    7.4.1 *Teacher-Student Interaction in Classroom Teaching Between Two Sister Schools* 184
    7.4.2 *Teacher-Student Interactions in Two Video Conferences Between Two Sister Schools* 197

7.5	*Discussion*	201
	7.5.1	*Comparison of the Characteristics of Teacher-Student Interactions in China and Canada*	201
	7.5.2	*The Factors Influencing the Differences of Teacher-Student Interaction in Two Countries*	204
7.6	*Conclusion*	207
References		209

8 Leadership and Power 213

Cheng Zhong

8.1	*Background*	214
	8.1.1	*The Trajectory of HE LE Culture in Minzhu Primary School*	214
	8.1.2	*HE LE Culture Met Bay Street School*	218
8.2	*Research Method*	221
	8.2.1	*Narrative Inquiry*	221
	8.2.2	*Introducing the Researcher and Research Process*	222
8.3	*Literature Review*	223
	8.3.1	*Image, Metaphor, and Experience*	223
	8.3.2	*Encounter of Teacher Leadership Images in Life-Practice Educology and the Ontario Leadership Framework*	226
8.4	*Story Constellations of Principals and Their Teacher Leadership Images*	232
	8.4.1	*Images of Principal Ting*	233
	8.4.2	*Images of Principal Darlene as the Lead Learner and Co-learner*	239
8.5	*Cultural Comparison and Analysis on Sister School Principal's Teacher Leadership*	241
	8.5.1	*Family Culture and the Power Structure Behind the Principal Images*	241
	8.5.2	*Principal Appointment System and the Principal-Teacher Relationship*	242
	8.5.3	*"Life Consciousness" Encounter Teacher Professional Development*	243

xiv CONTENTS

8.6 *Discussion: What Can We Learn from Each Other?*   244
  8.6.1 *Moral Leadership: Intersection of the East and the West*   245
  8.6.2 *The Integration of Technology and Technique Matters*   247
  8.6.3 *Autocracy or Democracy? From Dualism Misunderstanding to Cosmopolitan Learning Community*   248
  References   250

9 Faith and Action   259
Yuhua Bu
  9.1 *How China-Canada Sister Schools Understand and Locate Themselves and Each Other*   260
    9.1.1 *The Understanding of MPS about Itself and MPS in the Eyes of BSS*   260
    9.1.2 *The Understanding of BSS about Itself and BSS in the Eyes of MPS*   267
  9.2 *The Social Identity of Sister Schools Between Canada and China*   276
    9.2.1 *The Social Mission of Schools in Canada*   277
    9.2.2 *Identity Orientation of Schools in China*   281
    9.2.3 *Why China Understands School Identity in this Way*   282
  9.3 *Discussion*   283
    9.3.1 *Do Chinese Schools Need to Learn from Canada and Re-understand the Relationship between Schools and Society in the Future?*   283
    9.3.2 *Do Canadian Schools Need to Have Their Own Unique Culture?*   285
  References   286

10 Future   289
Yuhua Bu
  10.1 *Will the Sister Schools Continue Their Cooperation After the Project?*   289
    10.1.1 *Do Teachers Think the Project Beneficial? Will They Continue to Cooperate?*   290
    10.1.2 *Are There Conditions for Further Cooperation?*   297

10.2	*What Should MPS Learn from BSS if the Cooperation Continues?*	300
	10.2.1 *Learn to Leave More Space for Children's Individualized Growth*	301
	10.2.2 *Learn to Provide Students with the Structured Framework of Thinking to Support Independent Learning*	304
	10.2.3 *Learn to Provide Special Students with More Professional and Inclusive Education*	306
	10.2.4 *Learn to Become More Open-Minded and Positive in Reciprocal Learning*	308
10.3	*What Should MPS Stick To?*	309
10.4	*What Positive and Negative Experiences Has the Sister-School Cooperation Provided for Cross-Cultural Reciprocal Learning?*	311
	10.4.1 *Positive Experience in Sister Schools' Reciprocal Learning*	311
	10.4.2 *Reciprocal Learning Between Sister Schools Needs Further Improvement*	313
10.5	*Expectations: What Kind of Future Do We Expect?*	315
	References	316

Index 317

ABBREVIATIONS

BSS	Bay Street School
ECNU	East China Normal University
LPE	"Life-Practice" Educology
MDSB	Minzhu District School Board
MPS	Minzhu Primary School
NBE	New Basic Education
NI	Narrative Inquiry
RL	Reciprocal Learning
RLP	Reciprocal Learning in Teacher Education and School Education Between Canada and China Program
SSHRC	Social Sciences and Humanities Research Council of Canada
SSP	Sister School Project
TDSB	Toronto District School Board
UT	The University of Toronto
UW	The University of Windsor

Notes on Contributors

Yuhua Bu is a professor and Ph.D. Supervisor in the Faculty of Education, East China Normal University (ECNU); Deputy Director of Institute of "Life-Practice" Educology Research in ECNU; and Deputy Director of the Department of Education. Her main research fields include basic educational theory, teacher education, English teaching reform, and study on ethical education. From 1997 until now (20 years), she has been cooperating with Professor Lan YE on "New Basic Education." She has done a of significant number of research projects in various fields in Chinese school reform and has published several books, journal articles, and other publications, some of which have been awarded by the Chinese government. Her books *Research on Curriculum Ideology* and *Nurturing the Public Spirit in the Life of the Classroom* were awarded the National Education Science Third Prize and the Shanghai Humanity and Social Science Second Prize, respectively. Her books *Guideline of "New Basic Education," English Teaching Reform* and *Further Studies on "New Basic Education" Classroom Teaching Reform* were awarded Shanghai Social Science Second Prizes. She has also been honored with the titles "New Century Excellent Talent of the Ministry of Education" and a "National Excellent Supervisor of Graduate Students."

Cheryl J. Craig, Ph.D. is a Professor and the Houston Endowment Endowed Chair of Urban Education in the Teaching, Learning and Culture Department at Texas A&M University. She is an American Educational Research Fellow, a Division B Lifetime Achievement Award winner, and a recipient of the Michael Huberman Award for her Contributions to Understanding the Lives of Teachers. She was the secretary of the International Study Association on Teachers and Teaching for six years. She is an Executive Editor of *Teaching and Teacher Education*, Executive Editor of *Teachers and Teaching: Theory and Practice*, Associate Editor of *Frontiers of Teacher Education*, honorary professor at Northeast Normal University and a research collaborator with Dr. Yuhua Bu at East China Normal University, Shanghai. Cheryl Craig also is the Chair of the International Advisory Committee of the Canada-China Reciprocal Learning Grant, which is the largest Partnership Grant funded by the Social Sciences and Humanities Research Council of Canada.

Yangjie Li is a doctoral student in the Faculty of Education, East China Normal University. His main research field includes teacher education and basic theory of education. He has published several papers in Chinese Social Sciences Citation Index journals, such as the review and prospect of the study on teacher-student interaction in China during the 40 years of reform and opening up. He has also won the National Scholarship for Doctoral Students from the Chinese government in 2019.

Shan Qi holds a Doctor of Education and has graduated from East China Normal University. She is working at the Taiyuan Normal University, Education Academy. Her research focuses on basic education theory, basic education reform, and education ethics. Her representative papers include "How Foucault's Thoughts Affect Pedagogy Research in China" in *Knowledge Cultures* (2019), and "Why Did Herbart Pedagogy Take Root in China" in *Educational Theory and Practice* (2018).

Cheng Zhong is a Ph.D. candidate of education at the Chinese University of Hong Kong. His main research interests are sociology of education and basic education reform. From 2016 to 2019, he studied at East China Normal University. He was a research assistant in the Canada-China Reciprocal Learning Program in Teacher Education and School Education. His main responsibilities include collecting field data and assisting the sister school principals and teachers in communicating cross-nationally.

Yuanyuan Zhu is a doctoral student in the Department of Education, East China Normal University, Shanghai, China. Her research interests include teacher education, teacher professional development, and teacher learning in community. She has published several journal articles on topics like teacher identity and teachers' reciprocal learning across cultures. She has been an assistant, since September 2015, in the program "Reciprocal Learning Research on Teacher Education and School Education Between China and Canada."

List of Figures

Fig. 2.1	NBE's influence in China	44
Fig. 3.1	Statistics on the number of educational journal papers, dissertations and books on the theme of "narrative inquiry" from 2003 to 2019. (The data in this table are from CNKI, Chao Xing and Wan Fang database, and the retrieval is carried out under the theme of "narrative inquiry")	70
Fig. 5.1	All kinds of artistic writing methods of Chinese "water" written by BSS students on World Water Day	123
Fig. 5.2	Communication subjects and interactive relationship of sister schools	127
Fig. 6.1	Seat map of the lesson discussion	154
Fig. 8.1	The relation network between image, metaphor, and experience	225

LIST OF TABLES

Table 4.1	Paired teachers of the two sister schools	99
Table 5.1	Reciprocal learning between principals of sister schools (2013–2014)	133
Table 5.2	Themes of video conferences of sister schools in 2014	135
Table 6.1	Comparison of heterogeneous lessons by Hanny and Ding	164
Table 7.1	Important activities covered in this chapter	184
Table 7.2	Teacher-student interaction in important reciprocal learning activities between two sister schools	202
Table 7.3	Impact of reciprocal activities on Ms. Liu in teacher-student interaction	208
Table 8.1	The *Idea into Action* and the OLC	230
Table 8.2	The images in "Life-Practice" Educology and OLF	232
Table 8.3	The framework of LPE and OLF	232

CHAPTER 1

Introduction

Yuhua Bu

This book explores how Chinese school-based educators learn from others and attain consciousness of themselves and others in dialogue with the world in an era marked by increasing globalization and information exchange. Minzhu Primary School (MPS) in Shanghai and Bay Street School (BSS) in Toronto (both names are pseudonyms) have been sister schools engaged in cross-cultural exchange since 2008. In 2013, they became members of a China-Canada reciprocal learning program whereby they formally carried out reciprocal learning goals. Together they have practically explored ways to learn reciprocally in cross-cultural partnership while remaining grounded in their home culture and language. Our research on the sister schools project has been conducted over a period of more than 10 years. In this book, we explore how Chinese school-based educators view themselves, understand others, grow and develop as a consequence of a decade of cross-cultural reciprocal learning in the context of being sister schools.

Y. Bu (✉)
East China Normal University, Shanghai, China
e-mail: yhbo@dedu.ecnu.edu.cn

© The Author(s), under exclusive license to Springer Nature
Switzerland AG 2021
Y. Bu (ed.), *Narrative Inquiry into Reciprocal Learning Between Canada-China Sister Schools*, Intercultural Reciprocal Learning in Chinese and Western Education,
https://doi.org/10.1007/978-3-030-61085-2_1

1.1 Origin and Background

Professor Michael Connelly of the University of Toronto and Dr Xu Shijing of the University of Windsor visited Professor Ye Lan, founder of "New Basic Education" (NBE) of East China Normal University in Shanghai in 2007, and were warmly welcomed by the principal, teachers and pupils when they came to Minzhu Primary School (MPS), whose reform as an experimental school was led by Professor Ye. Professor Connelly was curious about and appreciative of the campus life of MPS and its unique Chinese-style educational and teaching activities, believing that "this school is exciting, open and innovative, and that we have a lot to learn from Chinese schools" (Xu and Connelly 2017). In 2008, Professor Connelly invited Professor Ye and the principals of six Shanghai experimental schools engaged in NBE research to Toronto for an educational tour. This visit further deepened the friendship between the two sides and increased their interest in each other's educational culture, so they established three pairs of sister schools based on friendship rather than on a project, an official promotion or a contract. One pair of schools was Bay Street School BSS in Toronto and MPS in Shanghai. Sister schools mainly communicate with each other through interested teachers who send greetings and small gifts during holidays, and occasionally interact with each other through videos. Although there was no further professional cooperation and exchanges, the friendship between sister schools has nevertheless been fruitful.

Dr Xu and Professor Connelly have long hoped to apply for a reciprocal learning program based on the vision of bridging the East and West dichotomy by harmonizing Eastern learning with Western knowledge. In 2013, Dr Xu and Dr Connelly successfully applied for a seven-year Canada-China Reciprocal Learning Partnership in teacher education and school education in 2013–2020 (RLP). The program "provide[s] an exceptional cross-cultural experience with international engagement … to broaden teacher candidates' horizons for a society of increasing diversity in today's globalized world" (Xu 2019). RLP has two infrastructure components: the Canada–China Sister School Network with Sister School pairs between Toronto and Shanghai, Beijing, and Changchun schools, and between Windsor and Chongqing schools, and the Reciprocal Learning Program (RLP) between the University of Windsor and Southwest University China in partnership with the Greater Essex County District School Board (GECDSB) (Xu and Connelly 2017).

In 2013, with the successful application of the China-Canada program, the Shanghai-Toronto sister schools naturally became important members of the project. This pair of sister schools' reciprocal learning experiences are the research focus of this book.

1.2   OUR LEARNING AND GROWTH IN PROJECTS AS RESEARCHERS

At first, we had no experience in researching reciprocal learning in cross-cultural sister schools. In addition, our cooperation experiences with MPS have always been in the form of "intervention research" studies. Yet Dr Connelly and Dr Xu, the co-hosts of RLP, proposed that we change this approach and reexamine our relationship with MPS to become collaborators, instead of giving guidance or being guided. Such cooperation meant that MPS would do what a sister school should do, and we researchers would only provide necessary help for communication between the two sister schools, such as language translation and information transmission. Of course, we would enter the field and collect qualitative research field texts through narrative inquiry. Unfortunately, we were somewhat confused by their proposal at the beginning and we kept wondering: Will sister schools independently carry out reciprocal learning? What is narrative inquiry? How can we enact this new research method?

As to the first question of whether sister schools will independently carry out reciprocal learning, to be honest it did not go well in the beginning. Although the principals and teachers of both schools were full of curiosity and were friendly and open-minded, there were too many differences when they exchanged topics or content that might lead to reciprocal learning. MPS teachers found that the barriers between the two schools were not time or language (which is what they initially envisaged), but the curriculum delivery system of teachers in both schools. There were major differences: MPS's teachers and curriculum are subject-based, the children's curriculum is taught by different teachers every day, and the schedule of each course is well divided, and can hardly be adjusted. Moreover, every course at MPS has a set of teaching materials, so teachers do not have to prepare a great deal of content other than when preparing for lessons. But BSS in Canada was different, with the curriculum being very flexible. Teachers can choose and process teaching materials creatively without having to use prescribed teaching resources.

Therefore, in the first year reciprocal learning did not progress smoothly for either school. Both sides remained cautious. Every time my graduate students came back to East China Normal University from MPS, they always complained to me of the difficulties and suggested that I give the schools some advice. It seemed that it was impossible for reciprocal learning to truly happen between the sister schools. As the host of the Chinese program, I was often confused at that time. I even wrote out some reciprocal learning suggestions for the sister schools and hoped they could actively carry out reciprocal learning on this basis. However, I later gave this up. I also complained to Dr Xu, who always told me that scientific research is just like this, that we do measure our research by whether the sister schools would successfully carry out reciprocal learning. Even if the two schools could not reciprocally learn, this would be a research conclusion, and we would of course need to explore why sister schools failed in the cross-cultural reciprocal learning endeavour. Of course, looking back now, the difficulties of the first year were only temporary. About a year and a half later, the sister schools began to learn reciprocally step-by-step. Today, the friendship between the sister schools has become even more firmly cemented.

The second question I had was: "What is narrative inquiry and how do we carry it out?" I earned my master's and doctoral degrees from East China Normal University in the 1990s. At that time, Chinese universities did not pay much attention to educational research methods in our academic preparation. Although we had also taken courses in educational research methods and knew that Western universities attach equal importance to qualitative research and quantitative research, we seldom used either kind of research method in practice. As my major was educational theory, I did research through reading and thinking. When we conducted NBE research in schools, we did not attach particular importance to research methods either, but paid more attention to how to explore reform experiences and strategies according to situations relating to education in the schools. We were often confused about how to elaborate such educational research issues as rich and complex reform events.

We were at a further loss when my graduate students and I were first asked by the RLP principal investigators to use narrative inquiry to carry out sister school research. From that point onward, we began to read books on narrative inquiry written by Professor Connelly and Professor Clandinin (Connelly and Clandinin 1990; Clandinin and Connelly 2000). Yet we still did not understand how to enact narrative inquiry in research. I remember that Dr Shijing Xu once explained to us how to make field notes. She told us to fold a piece of A4 paper into two parts. Two-thirds of the space was to be devoted to recording what we saw and heard in the study, and one-third to recording what we thought and felt. However, what puzzled me at the time was: "Was this a sociological approach?" "Perhaps even an anthropological approach?" "How can field notes be part of a narrative inquiry method?" Later, we learned while practicing. Every time we sent the field notes to the Canadian graduate students, Professor Connelly would add further suggestions on how to write field notes. At the same time, graduate students from the research group of the University of Toronto also shared their field notes, which helped us to learn through contrast and comparison. Eventually Professor Connelly offered less guidance to us. Perhaps he thought we were more and more able to write field notes. However, we still had a vague idea about the difference between narrative inquiry as a research method in sociology and anthropology. We still did not realize the uniqueness of narrative inquiry as a research method in the field of education.

In 2016, we invited Professor Cheryl Craig, who was a postdoctoral student of Dr Michael Connelly and Dr. Jean, from the Department of, Teaching, Learning and Culture of Texas A&M University, to deliver some lectures at East China Normal University. We hoped to learn more about narrative inquiry through developing a close collaboration with her. Dr Craig used her articles written using the narrative inquiry method to show us what narrative inquiry was. Although we still did not fully understand the research method, some important concepts, such as time, spatiality, relationship and context, attracted our attention. We began to understand that narrative inquiry and John Dewey's theory of experience are closely aligned. In 2017, ECNU invited Cheryl Craig again to give lectures to our colleagues and students every year and to guide us to write articles in the narrative inquiry research genre. At the same time, we also read more and more articles written by her and others in the narrative inquiry tradition. So narrative inquiry as a research methodology began to sink in. Influenced by Cheryl Craig, we used narrative inquiry to collect and analyze data more autonomously in the next two to three years. In fact, three graduate students chose this project as the theme of their graduation theses, and one of the important research methods of our book is narrative inquiry.

Later, we became more and more clear about the research fields and the research underpinnings of our partners, Dr Connelly, Dr Xu Shijing and Dr Cheryl Craig. Our initial impression of them had to do with narrative explorations. Thus, we thought that their research field was solely composed of educational research methods and wondered why Dr Michael Connelly was interested in NBE at the beginning. We found that narrative inquiry is related to Dr Michael Connelly's teachers' personal practical knowledge (Connelly et al. 1997) investigations.

Personal practical knowledge has also been described as a way to reconsider past experience and future expectation, and to address the demands of a present situation (Connelly et al. 1997). As a result, teachers' personal knowledge is about teachers themselves and their teaching, and develops throughout their professional lives (Johnson and Golombek 2002). Drawing on these concepts of personal practical knowledge and "person-centered education" (Cornelius-White 2007), professional development has increasingly focused on learning from practical experience and interpersonal sensitivity (Knezic et al. 2010). In other words, Michael Connelly believes that when researchers are engaged in teacher development research, they should first respect and grasp the practical knowledge of teachers. Hence, narrative inquiry is the most appropriate research method for the study of teachers' knowledge as shaped in context, because this kind of research methodology makes it possible for teachers' experiences to be presented in the form of stories, and the relationship between the researcher and the teacher is formed through such communications. The researcher is not completely outside the life experience of the research participant, as we imagined. When the researcher approaches the life world of the teacher, the researcher has already impacted the life of those being researched. In other words, Professor Connelly believes that the relationship between researchers and teachers is equal, and researchers should not interfere with teachers' educational practice. On this point, we have found Professor Connelly more like a spectator and an admirer on many occasions in BSS and MPS education activities. He always observed teachers' teaching quietly and attentively, and did not put forward his own suggestions and opinions. We once asked him to express some opinions on the observed classroom teaching but he discussed more how he appreciated the teacher's practices in the classroom he had observed. In this regard, we thought he did so out of politeness or because of his research position. But there is always a question that remains unsolved. That is, if he observes that a certain teaching method used by a teacher is not appropriate, and he also knows how to teach better, will he also insist on not speaking up? In contrast, when we communicate with teachers in China, we often appear as experts. We always feel that we should give some suggestions to teachers, and teachers also feel that experts must have some suggestions that are worth listening to. Of course, we also recognize teachers' independent status, which is not to be interrupted in their practice. So which is more reasonable? How do Professor Connelly and Dr Cheryl Craig understand us after they have been with us for such a long time? The above is what we thought about and learned as researchers in the seven-year research project. In fact, Professor Connelly never considered himself to be our mentor, nor did he force us to use the method of narrative inquiry or require us to change our way of communicating with Chinese teachers. Rather, I find that I have already learned a lot from him, and he has become my mentor. We have also learned a great deal from Dr Shijing Xu, Dr, Cheryl Craig, Dr Yishin Khoo and other graduate students of the University of Toronto, as well as the teachers at BSS. We have been growing into a new self. How wonderful reciprocal learning is. How great it is to learn from friends from afar (Confucius, Analect 1, p. 1).

As this book is about the process and growth of two sister schools in a cross-cultural reciprocal learning project, our discussion as project leaders will stop here. But we believe that the growth and change of our research team is also an important result of this research project and an important condition for the smooth unfurling of this practical research program.

1.3 Objectives of the Sister School Project

1.3.1 Objectives of the Sister School Reciprocal Learning

Although Minzhu Primary School and Bay Street School differ greatly in national and cultural backgrounds, they also have a lot in common. For example, both schools are models of green education and both pay special attention to the construction of students' wellbeing personally, psychologically and socially, in addition to the cultivation of students' good character. These common themes provide many possibilities for exchange and cooperation between the two schools. Later, we found that for Minzhu Primary School, its international exchange with BSS might have a certain representative significance, as it is a public school for the working class, and the income level of students' families is below the poverty level. If the existing international communication mode had been followed, cross-cultural communication would have been unsustainable. Therefore, in its process of effecting reciprocal learning with BSS, we set the following objectives for the sister schools (Bu et al. 2019):

- To bring the global vision to children in ordinary schools and promote students' cooperation and communication in the context of cross-cultural reciprocal learning;
- To determine how Chinese teachers can learn from the Canadian method of problem-solving and inquiry teaching;
- To determine how Chinese schools can integrate new ideas and new experiences of
  intercultural reciprocal learning into schools' philosophies, teaching management, curriculum provisions, student activities, teacher development practices and student evaluation, so as to promote modern school development with both Chinese characteristics and international features;
- To determine how Chinese teachers can position and understand themselves in the context of cross-cultural exchanges.

1.3.2 *The Research Purpose of the Sister School Project*

By participating in this international project, we hoped:

- To provide ourselves with an interactive perspective both from the external to the internal and from the internal to the external, so as to clearly understand the advantages and disadvantages of Chinese education by placing it in the framework of education all over the world;
- To understand how scholars from all over the world understand contemporary education and what views and attitudes of interaction they hold on education in different cultural backgrounds;
- To learn from the project directors how to carry out educational research guided by narrative inquiry methodology;
- To increase opportunities for international academic exchanges and for Chinese educational thought and practices to step onto the international educational stage, so that the world can better understand Chinese education;
- To explore the possibility and basic strategies of cross-cultural educational interaction between China and the world at the level of primary and secondary schools with low cost and high quality;
- To provide a platform for graduate students to participate in international academic research, and to train young scholars to understand and explore Chinese education issues from a global perspective.

1.3.3 The Purpose of Writing This Book

Through authoring this book, we hope to:

- provide scholars with a concrete understanding of the differences and similarities in education between China and Canada and their historical and cultural roots from a Chinese perspective by analyzing the example of the reciprocal learning between the sister schools;
- clarify the conditions, characteristics, process and rules of the development of the reciprocal learning between the sister schools in China and Canada, so as to provide examples for other similar cross-cultural cooperation between sister schools;
- To learn and conduct narrative inquiry by writing, thus deepening our understanding and application of this research methodology;
- To understand the requirements and rules of international academic publishers by cooperating and communicating with them, and to improve our ability to communicate with international education peers.

1.4 STRUCTURE AND MAIN IDEAS OF THE BOOK AND ITS AUTHORS

1.4.1 Structure of the Book

The structure of this book moves from the past to the present to the future, and from the outside to the inside. Chapters 1, 2 and 3 describe the multiple back drops of the Shanghai—Toronto sister school project: the historical and cultural thought and contemporary attitudes of China's foreign relations, and he background of Chinese and foreign exchanges in the past 100 years of Chinese education. We also consider the educational influence of Dewey, Connelly and others in the past 100 years and at present in China, the research of New Basic Education (NBE) pioneered by Chinese educationalist Ye Lan, as well as the meeting and communications that took place between Professor Connelly and Professor Ye Lan. Chapter 4 introduces our theoretical framework and research method. In Chap. 5, the new story about the sister schools' 10-year reciprocal learning emerges from 2008, in which we highlight the conditions and relationships that exist between and among contemporary Chinese society, education and school development. Then, from Chap. 6 through Chap. 9, we discuss important topics from a reciprocal learning perspective. These topics include school systems, power relationships, school cultures and leadership, faith and action. In Chap. 10, we return to the theme of the book and elaborate new possibilities, feasibilities and new hopes for the future.

1.4.2 Synopsis of Each Chapter

Chapter 1 and 2 address four topics, the first being the spiritual core of Chinese traditional culture, which centers around "benevolence" in Confucian culture. In treating "others", Chinese culture has always followed what Confucius says: "Is it not a delight to have friends coming from afar?" China has always continuously seen itself as part of the world, hoping to "integrate into the world", to be friends with the world, and to contribute to the development of the world. Therefore, President Xi Jinping (2018) articulated the vision of "a community of shared future for mankind". Second, we discuss the significance of contemporary globalization, the information age and cross-cultural and reciprocal learning, especially the dialogue between China and the world. Our third point of discussion is to explain the relationships between China's modern education and the educational thought of Japan, Germany, the US and the former Soviet Union (among other countries), and explain the development of modern and contemporary Chinese education under the influence of multiple cultures and bodies of educational thought. Fourth, we explicate the academic pursuits and impact of two influential educational schools of thought in China and the US in the transformation of modern society: the first being the development and spread of the Dewey school of experiential philosophy in the US and Canada, as well as its subsequent development and inheritance of core thoughts of several generations after Dewey—Schwab, Schwab's students Lee Shulman and Michael Connelly, Connelly's student Clandinin, Clandinin's student Cheryl Craig, and so forth; and the second being the construction *Life-Practice*, an educational school of thought pioneered by China's famous educator Ye Lan and her protégés through creating New Basic Education in China and establishing relationships between Minzhu Primary School and New Basic Education. The elucidation of the aforementioned topics explains and situates the main theme of this book—the sister school project viewed from a Chinese perspective—in the world and its history.

Chapter 3 describes two encounters. The first is the five lectures given by Dewey when he visited China in the first half of the twentieth century and the educational exploration by Dewey's Chinese disciple Xingzhi Tao. This chapter also elaborates thoughts and challenges experienced in China's exploration of education modernization in the first half of the twentieth century and the influence of Dewey on Chinese education. The second encounter involves the emergence, development and influence of New Basic Education in China, the spread and influence of Michael Connelly's version of narrative inquiry into the study of curriculum as lived in China, face-to-face meetings between Connelly and Professor Ye Lan and his knowledge of China's New Basic Education reform over a decade.

Chapter 4 introduces our theoretical framework and research methodology. China's Normal School tradition means that those working in the field of education in Chinese universities are not as estranged from teachers and principals in the schools as is the case in the West. This means that educational scholarship in China is distinctly different from that of the rest of the world. This chapter discusses the issue of China fitting into a global research community using indigenous approaches and orientations derived from different schools and philosophical traditions. At the same time, this chapter also introduces the researchers of the Shanghai-Toronto sister school project, the historical development of the sister schools, the participating teachers and the research methods we used.

Chapter 5 focuses on the sister schools and their communication process. This includes MPS's and BSS's narrative histories, their social environments, the origins of their students, the qualifications of their teachers, their school philosophies and the community cultures within which the two campuses are situated. The process of reciprocal learning between sister schools is introduced. At each stage, we incorporate stories of reciprocal learning between teachers, students and principals, and present some related cases. At the same time, this chapter also introduces the main content and methods of sister school communications.

Chapter 6 describes differences between Chinese and Canadian school life. In general, Chinese school life is marked by segmentation, and school life in Canada is comprehensive integration. Therefore, we use the metaphors of "straight lines" and "circles" to demonstrate the cultural differences. For example, in the structure of school curriculum, China employs subject-based specialization while Canada uses integrated learning. In the division of work, roughly six to eight Chinese teachers of various disciplines are jointly responsible for one class and each teacher communicates with students in his or her subject area. In Canada, one specific teacher is responsible for a class of students and all of their subject matter learning in the elementary grades. As far as the teaching schedule is concerned, Chinese classes are divided into sections due to the design of the curriculum, while the schedule for Canadian students is far more flexible.

Chapter 7 mainly explores how MPS teachers discovered differences and adjusted their behaviors in reciprocal activities with another BSS teacher in the context of classroom teaching and video conferences. We found that the differences in teacher—student interaction between the two countries are mainly manifested by the degree of control. Differences result from Chinese traditional concepts regarding the teacher—student relationship and teaching, and from the evaluation of teachers by the administrative department of education. In addition, cross-cultural reciprocal learning is affected by such factors as the teachers and their mentors involved in the reciprocal project, as well as the project itself. Based on the theory of expansive learning and cultural-historical activity theory, we put forward some suggestions for improvement.

Chapter 8 aims to explore and understand Toronto-Shanghai sister school principals' teacher leadership in the reciprocal learning context. The data include researchers' field notes, records of teachers' communication and cooperation, and interviews of teachers and principals in both countries. Principal Ting's (Shanghai) and Principal Green's (Toronto) teacher leadership images—Principal Ting as (1) big sister (parent) and (2) teacher master; Principal Green as (1) lead learner and (2) co-learner— are presented and revealed in their principal stories. Through cultural comparison and analysis, Principal Ting's images are nested in the traditional Chinese family culture, principal appointment system and "Life-Practice" Educology, while Principal Green's images are closely connected to the Ontario Leadership Framework and Ontario Leadership System. The encounter of these images, showing the different culture, history and reality in the Chinese and Canadian education worlds, highlights the potential of reciprocal learning through establishing common ground rather than being trapped in differences. Reciprocal learning is reflected in: (1) moral leadership at the intersection of the East and the West; (2) the integration of teacher leadership technology and technique and (3) building a cosmopolitan learning community.

Chapter 9 focuses on school identity approached from inward and outward perspectives. From the outward perspective, there is the notion of how China-Canada sister schools understand and position themselves in relation to local government, society and people. From the inward perspective, there is the question of how China-Canada sister schools' principals, teachers, students and parents think about such questions as "Who does a school belong to?" "What is the school's mission in society?" and "What is the relationship between the school and the individual?"

Chapter 10 discusses whether the sister schools will continue reciprocal learning when the project-based reciprocal learning initiative comes to an end, what MPS should learn from BSS, what MPS should stick to, and what should be expected in the future. In general, we believe that the sister schools will still carry out cross-cultural reciprocal learning even if there is no project, but will be filled with uncertainty. In the subsequent cooperation, MPS should learn much from BSS. At the same time, MPS should stick to its own culturally imbued practices. Our biggest expectation for cross-cultural communication in the future is to build a better "our" future within the "I-You" relationship.

1.4.3   Authors and Division of the Book

Five authors participated in the writing of the book.

Yuhua Bu is Professor and Ph.D. supervisor at the Faculty of Education of ECNU, Deputy Director of the Institute of "Life-Practice" Educology Research in ECNU, and Deputy Director of the Institute of Schooling Reform and Development. Her main research fields are philosophy of education, teacher education, school reform and ethics of education. Since 1997, she has been cooperating with Professor Lan Ye on NBE and has carried out a great deal of research in various fields in Chinese school reform, publishing numerous books, journal articles and other publications, some of which have won government awards. *Research on Curriculum Ideology* and *Nurturing the Public Spirit in the Life of the Classroom* were respectively awarded the National Education Science Third Prize and the Shanghai Humanity and Social Science Second Prize. Her book *Guidelines of NBE English Teaching Reform* And *Further Studies on NBE Classroom Teaching Reform* were awarded Shanghai Social Science Second Prize. She has also been honored with titles such as New Century Excellent Talent of Ministry of Education and National Excellent Supervisor of Graduate Students.

Shan Qi graduated from East China Normal University and works at Taiyuan Normal University. Her research focuses on basic education theory, basic education reform and education ethics. Some of her representative papers are "How Foucault's Thoughts Affect Pedagogy Research in

China" in *Knowledge Cultures* and "Why did Herbart's Pedagogy Take Root in China" in *Educational Theory and Practice*.

Cheng Zhong graduated from East China Normal University in 2019. He is a doctoral student at the Department of Educational Administration and Policy, Chinese University of Hong Kong. His research focuses on basic education reform and sociology of education. His articles have been published in top-tier Chinese Social Sciences Citation Index (CSSCI) journals such as *Journal of East China Normal University (Educational Sciences)* and *Global Education*.

Yangjie Li, a doctoral student from the Faculty of Education, ECNU, is mainly interested in research on teacher education and basic theory of education. He has published several papers in CSSCI journals and also won the National Scholarship for Doctoral Students from China in 2019.

Yuanyuan Zhu is a doctoral student from the Faculty of Education, ECNU. Her current research interests include teacher education, teacher professional development and teacher learning in the community. She has published several journal articles on topics such as teacher identity and teachers' reciprocal learning across cultures.

Acknowledgments Finally, we wish to express our thanks to many people. First and foremost, our thanks go to Dr Michael Connelly and Dr Shijing Xu, whose trust and friendliness have given us the opportunity to work with them in depth. We have learnt from them about how to conduct narrative inquiry and how to host a large complex project. Of course, how they have supported us encompasses more than that. The publication of this book is also closely related to their encouragement. They have always supported us without hesitation when we invited them to participate in our international academic conferences. Of course, the most important thing is that both of them have introduced us to international academia, and made us understand the thoughts and currents of the international academic community in general, helping us break through our original narrow academic research scope. Through this project, we have also met many excellent scholars.

The second person we would like to thank is Dr Cheryl Craig, who is also a mentor and a good friend of ours. It was through this project that we got to know Dr Craig. We were fascinated by her when we first heard her giving an academic speech. She is clear-minded, agile in her responses and beautifully expressive. We also felt her kindness and sincerity in our subsequent closer contact. As we have mentioned in this book, it is through her that we have a deeper understanding of the theoretical basis and specific application of narrative inquiry. At the same time, she has offered valuable suggestions on the structure of the book. Moreover, when the first draft of the book was completed, she was the first reader and reviewer. She read the whole book chapter by chapter, sentence by sentence, and carefully helping to revise it, which benefited us a lot. Her wisdom has inspired us to write this book.

Of course, we owe our heartfelt thanks to many other scholars: Ian Westbury, Ruth Hayhoe, Zongyi Deng, John Lee and Zongjie Wu. They are the international advisory board members of the Canada-China Reciprocal Learning Project, who participated in team meetings every year and gave us many insightful suggestions and opinions. For this, we would like to express our thanks.

Also, we would like to thank the two sister schools in Shanghai and Toronto. Due to ethical concerns, we cannot list their real names, but we appreciate them and pay homage to their sincere spirit of cross-cultural reciprocal learning.

Of course, we also like to thank the graduate students from the University of Toronto and ECNU who participated in the sister school reciprocal learning. In Toronto, we thank Dr Yishin Khoo and other graduate students there who must remain anonymous. Most of these graduate students or visiting scholars from the University of Toronto are Chinese students. They study in Canada, but they are able to focus on the educational exchanges between China and Canada, which we appreciate very much. In addition, their serious and excellent research work is also very valuable and worthy of studys. In fact, ECNU graduate students have already learned a lot from them. In Shanghai, I also would like to thank my graduate students, such as Dr Liu An, Dr Yang Qian, Dr Qi Shan, Liu Yanting, Sun Tong, Zhong Cheng, Zhu Yuanyuan, Liu Luxia, Dai Meng, Ding Wen, Li Yangjie and other students from ECNU, who have provided irreplaceable support for the promotion of this project and the exchange between sister schools. I particularly want to thank Dr Liu An for translating and proofreading most chapters of this book.

Most especially, I (Yuhua Bu) would like to thank my supervisor, Professor Ye Lan. Originally, she was the main person in charge of this project in Shanghai, but because she was overloaded with many other jobs, she entrusted me with full responsibility for the project. This is not only because of her trust in me, but also because she expects me to gain experience from this project. She has only participated in this project on certain occasions, yet these were key instances where her support gave me more confidence and strength.

Last but not least, we would like to thank Springer Palgrave Macmillan. Milana Vernikova, Linda Braus and Tikoji Rao made an enormous effort to publish this book. They have been tireless in giving us valuable information and answering our questions. Although we have not met them, we have felt their sincerity and friendship.

REFERENCES

Bu, Y., Qi, S., Zhong, C., & Zhu, Y. (2019). Cong 'Li Tu' Dao 'Zai Di': Zhong Jia Zimei Xiao Kua Wenhua Huhui Xuexi de Shijian Tansuo 从 '离土' 到 '在地': 中加姊妹校跨文化互惠学习的实践探索 (From 'Grounding Off' to 'Grounding On': The Practical Exploration on Cross-Cultural Reciprocal Learning in China-Canada Sister Schools). *Global Education, 48,* 62–73.

Connelly, F. M., Clandinin, D. J. (1990). Stories of Experience and Narrative Inquiry. Educational Researcher, 19(5): 2–14.

Connelly, F. M., He, M. F., & Clandinin, D. J. (1997). Teachers' Personal Practical Knowledge on the Professional Knowledge Landscape. [Article]. *Teaching and Teacher Education, 13*(7), 665–674. https://doi.org/10.1016/S0742-051X(97)00014-0.

Cornelius-White, J. (2007). Learner-Centered Teacher-Student Relationships Are Effective: A Meta-Analysis. *Review of Educational Research, 77,* 113–143.

Clandinin, D. J., & Connelly, F. M. (2000). Narrative inquiry: Experience and story in qualitative research. San Francisco: CA: Jossey-Bass.

Johnson, K. E., & Golombek, P. R. (2002). *Teachers' Narrative Inquiry as Professional Development.* New York, NY: Cambridge University Press.

Knezic, D., Wubbels, T., Elbers, E., & Hajer, M. (2010). The Socratic Dialogue and Teacher Education. *Teaching and Teacher Education, 26,* 1104–1111.

Xi, J. (2018). The Common Building of the Community of Human Destiny. Speech at the headquarters of the United Nations, Geneva, xinhuanet.com, January 19.

Xu, S. (2019). Reciprocal Learning in Teacher Education between Canada and China. *Teachers & Teaching,* (2), 1–27.

Xu, S., & Connelly, F. M. (2017). Reciprocal Learning between Canada and China in Teacher Education and School Education: Partnership Studies of Practice in Cultural Context. *Frontiers of Education in China, 12*(2), 135–150. https://doi.org/10.1007/s11516-017-0013-6.

CHAPTER 2

Friends from Afar

Yuhua Bu

Regarding the relationship between China and the world, the Chinese classical Confucians have thought long and hard about it, always maintaining an open attitude. They believe that China is a part of the world, but they hope to maintain an open dialogue with the world as well. But China has a history of more than 5000 years, and there was a closed era where China was put at the center, and as a result, it has lagged behind developing and developed countries in the world. But this situation has notably changed since the 1980s. China hopes to become a part of the world, to integrate into the world, and to develop and share the destiny of and with the world.

In the early 1980s, China began its policy of reform and opening up. In the early 1990s, the Chinese government firmly committed to a market economy. In 2001, the first year of the twenty-first century, China formally joined the World Trade Organization. These historic events all marked China's determination to participate more and be more open to the world. In 2017, the 19th National Congress of the Communist Party

Y. Bu (✉)
East China Normal University, Shanghai, China
e-mail: yhbo@dedu.ecnu.edu.cn

© The Author(s), under exclusive license to Springer Nature
Switzerland AG 2021
Y. Bu (ed.), *Narrative Inquiry into Reciprocal Learning Between Canada-China Sister Schools*, Intercultural Reciprocal Learning in Chinese and Western Education,
https://doi.org/10.1007/978-3-030-61085-2_2

17

of China summed up the nature of the development of current and contemporary social development, emphasizing that through its long-term efforts, China has entered a new era. "This new era is not only marked by the new changes taking place in all aspects of [China], but also by the historic changes in China's relations with the world, namely, [China] is getting closer to the center of the world stage and constantly making greater contributions to mankind", assessed Xi Jinping (2017). Meanwhile, the concept of "a community of a shared future for mankind"[1] was advanced as the basic principle of international exchanges.

The cross-cultural reciprocal learning program discussed in this book involves two sister schools from China and Canada. The program, which has a history of more than a decade, first began in 2007 and officially expanded in 2013 against the backdrop of China playing a growing role on the world stage. In this context, when we engage in dialogues across borders and cultural types, new directions of thinking are opened and new questions need to be answered:

1. How should we understand ourselves from the perspective of Chinese cultural traditions?
2. In the context of contemporary globalization, what cultural position should we adopt to engage in dialogues with our international counterparts?
3. In the course of 100-year modernization of China's education, what is the impact of past relations between China and the West and between the ancient and modern?
4. As for the current project, what are the questions asked and ideas put forward by the North American followers of Dewey's educational thoughts including Joseph Schwab, Lee Shulman and Michael

---

[1] A community of a shared future for mankind also means a community of common destiny. The concept first appeared in a report delivered by former Party General Secretary Hu Jintao to the 18th National Congress of the Communist Party of China in November 2012. In the report, Hu emphasized that "mankind has only one earth to live on, and countries have only one world to share" and called for the building of a harmonious world of enduring peace and common prosperity by raising awareness about human beings sharing a community of common destiny. Hu envisioned a new type of equitable and balanced global development partnership that would stick together in times of difficulty, both sharing rights and shouldering obligations, and boosting the common interests of mankind. President Xi Jinping first proposed the concept in an international arena at the Moscow State Institute of International Relations in March 2013, and raised it again in a speech to the World Economic Forum at Davos in January 2017, which "won him high credits at home and abroad".

Connelly (Schwab's students), D. Jean Clandinin and Shijing Xu (Connelly's students), Cheryl Craig (Clandinin's student and Clandinin's and Connelly's post-doc student), and by the school of Life-Practice Educology founded by China's Ye Lan as well as her colleagues and students? What are the similarities and differences between the two schools?

This chapter begins with reflections on these four basic questions.

2.1 Who Are We: Understanding Our Cultural Identity from Both Sides of Chinese Traditional Culture

Because we share the same cultural ecology, we usually do not reflect on who we are from the perspective of cultural identity. However, when we engage in dialogue with those representing another culture, we naturally look at ourselves from the dimension of cultural identity. We think: Which culture do we belong to and what are the characteristics of this culture? What cultural identity do we usually hold when we interact with foreign cultures? The former questions are concerned with our day-to-day cultural identity, while the latter query concerns the cultural identity we project when we interact with others.

The connotation of "culture" is rich and varied, but, on the whole, it expresses a kind of lifestyle and spiritual value that has become habit, with the final result being the collective consciousness of a group of people. As such, when culture is relative to a certain group, it has two faces, both inward and outward. With these understandings in mind, we will analyze some characteristics of Chinese culture.

2.1.1 Looking Inward: Expressions of Love and Consideration of Others

First, Chinese culture should be understood in view of the form of its society. In the history of Western civilization, China's transition from a primitive society to a civilized society has experienced a series of changes that broke the old clan ruling system, replacing the consanguineous (blood-relative) clan with the regional state and the political state. In China, however, historical accounts, myths, and legends of ancient China show that the ancient Chinese entered the class society by transforming clan leaders directly into slave-owning aristocrats, and later turning family slavery into clan slavery, thus establishing "families" and "band"-style states, rather than Western-style "city-states" (Hao 1993). The reason for this is that the Chinese Neolithic age, which was based on agriculture, lasted for a long time. The organizational structure of the clan society developed fully and firmly, the blood ties were stable and strong, and were not weakened and impacted by navigation, nomadism, or other factors. Although China entered the class society and went through the changes of the economic and political systems at all levels, the social life and social structure based on the production of agricultural small families characterized by kinship rarely changed. The essence of the reform carried out in the Western Zhou Dynasty (1122–771 BC), which is of great significance in the history of Chinese social development, was to turn the clan organization into a political organization and a state system. It made a breakthrough in the clan organization and initially formed the embryonic form of the state system, yet formally the system was bound to be established and maintained in terms of the patriarchal clan. Thus, a social pattern came into being with the integration of "family and state" as well as "home and country".

Fei Xiaotong described the structural characteristics of Chinese society that gave rise to the integration of "family and state" as a "differential pattern":

> Each family, with itself being the center, draws a circle around it, the size of which depends on how influential the power of the center is.
> Unlike the members of a group standing on a planar surface, the social relations with others center around oneself, resembling ripples after a stone is thrown into water. The further the ripples are pushed out, the thinner they become. In this way, everyone has a circle with himself as the center, belonging at the same time to another circle centering around someone who is superior. (Fei 2013)

This kind of family-state structure characterizes Chinese culture as strongly ethical, since the principles of a family fundamentally make up those of ethics, and the culture that grows out of this prototype is bound to an ethical standard, reflected specifically in the characteristics we will now discuss.

First, the ethical relationship features a differentiated social order and people treat others as they expect to be treated. As far as ethical culture is concerned, the differential society, as Fei Xiaotong suggested, is like putting the "self" in the center like a stone thrown into the water. Interpersonal relationships are similar in the differentiated social order: people treat others in the way they would like to be treated. What Confucius valued is the word "push" that occurs when water ripples are pushed outward. He said, "The superior man bends his attention to what is Essential. That being established, Tao naturally comes into being" (The Analects: On Learning). "The Essential" refers to the fundamental, while Tao refers to the principles of governing a country and being a man ([*sic*] woman). "Tao" has varied meanings in ancient Chinese thought. The "Tao" in "On Learning" refers to Confucius called benevolence or the moral ideological system with benevolence as the core and its embodiment in life. Therefore, the meaning of "establishing the Essential to effect Tao" is that when what is considered fundamental is established, the principle of governing the country and being a man will naturally come into being, which is reflected by "those who in private life behave well towards their parents and elder brothers, in public life seldom show a disposition to resist the authority of their superiors. And as for such men starting a revolution, no instance of it has ever occurred". Extending from oneself to the home, from home to the state, and from the state to the world is like a path pushed outward circle by circle. Just as Mencius (2004) observed, "It is simply that they knew well how to carry out, so as to affect others".

Second, reason, rather than truth, and the importance of life are valued. Admittedly, the universality of truth that should be sought in any culture falls into two categories, the extensional truth and the intentional truth. Extensional truths, on the whole, refer to the natural sciences, subject areas like mathematics, for example. They exist unaffected by people's subjective attitude. Take a flower, for instance. How aesthetically beautiful it is, is not scientific knowledge, but a subjective judgment made by a perceiver. If we speak of botany in a scientific manner, it is scientific knowledge associated with extensional truth. Intentional truth is knowledge related to the beholder and his/her subjective senses.

The East and the West perceive these two kinds of truths differently. Chinese culture is more concerned with individuals' true feelings of life, including joys and sorrows, partings and reunions, custom and rites, all of which are intentional truth, disregarded more often than not by Western cultures that attach more importance to the extensional truth. Chinese culture does not attach the same degree of importance to extensional truth but believes that life is a whole, with scientific knowledge only being a part of it. If life is only understood from a scientific perspective, life is incomplete and not fully truth worthy to the Chinese way of thinking. Hence, the Chinese culture values intentional truth more. From the perspective of rational type, Liang Shuming, a representative figure of contemporary Neo-Confucianism, believes that Chinese culture stresses "reason" or "common sense", with references to people's behaviors, which are dynamic rather than static. Westerners place a premium on physics, namely, the laws of nature or the principles of society, which is static and cannot show the direction of life until lived. Liang explained:

> In Chinese books, what is often mentioned is nothing other than sentiment and reason in the human world, such as fatherly kindness, filial piety, knowledge of shame, love of people, fairness and justice, faithfulness and honesty. In the Western books, however, what it discussed is reason in the sense of natural science, if not in the sense of social science, or in the sense of purely abstract mathematics or logic. (Liang 2005)

Reason, in Chinese people's eyes, shows the direction of people's action. It is often embodied in such powerful words as "I do not know how a man without truthfulness is acceptable!" "Don't covet possessions when you see them". "Don't escape when you are in trouble!" Such words are abstract, not referring to anything or anyone in particular, yet they are not static but dynamic (Liang 2005).

Profound differences in perceptions of truth between Chinese and Western cultures naturally affect our sister schools' project research. For example, we have found that, due to cultural differences, teachers' way of persuasion and reasoning is different when handling interpersonal conflicts in classroom teaching and routines, which leads to different effects. We address these matters in Chaps. 5–8.

As earlier suggested, from the inside view of Chinese culture, the Chinese way of handling matters is distinguished by differential love, which starts with "filial piety" on the basis of blood kinship. The differential nature of such feelings is in conflict with equal love upheld in modern society. Indeed, in the history of Chinese thought, the "benevolence" advocated for by Confucius never developed into the moral principle where everyone is equal, let alone an underlying principle of law. Kinship ethics and the situation of law giving way to sentiment when the two are in conflict have long been in existence, adapting to the stability of the family system and the feudal social system in China. People's treating others as they expect to be treated and their differentiated love are reflected in many aspects of Chinese social life. The same is true in the education sector. That is why we refer to the embodiment of Chinese culture in contemporary school life in other chapters of this book.

2.1.2 *Looking Outward: Harmony Without Uniformity, Loyalty Together with Consideration*

Chinese culture has a unique dual nature. Inside, its way of treating others with compassion and consideration is based on blood kinship and forms close or distant interpersonal relationships. Is it then more indifferent to foreign cultures? As a matter of fact, that is not the case. Chinese culture adopts a very kind and benevolent stance toward foreign cultures.

First, Chinese traditional culture regards "harmony without uniformity" (Analects of Confucius Zilu) as the basic principle of coexistence with others. The pattern of differential order not only recognizes but also maintains the existence of differences. However, if there is too much difference, there will be a risk of conflict. How does Chinese culture deal with the conflicts between differences so as to maintain harmony in social relations?

The reason why two subjects interact and coexist for a long time would simply be that the two "are attracted to each other by common tastes", "have a common goal", or "are birds of a feather". Obviously, this is a "seeking-common-ground" approach, which, however, was deemed inappropriate by early Chinese culture, as it is difficult for things to develop or last if they are carbon copies of one another. Instead, only through interactions with different ways of knowing, doing, and being can the existence of things become possible. Hence, "harmony without uniformity" became a foundational belief in Chinese culture. This view has been repeatedly confirmed in Chinese philosophy and is evident in such sayings as "Harmony begets development, while disharmony begets none" from *Guan Zi* (Liang Yunhua 2004, p. 945), "When Yin and Yang interconnect, all things grow", a belief held by Zhuang Zi (Guo Qingfan 1961, p. 712), "All things develop when in harmony" declared Xun Zi (Wang Xianqian 1988, p. 309), "Everything comes into being with the harmony of Yin and Yang," which is contained in the *Huai Nan Zi* (He Ning 1998, p. 44), "Development comes from the harmony of heaven and earth" (天人合一) asserted Dong Zhongshu (Su Yu 1992, p. 444), and so forth.

To understand the meaning of "harmony without uniformity", we must first of all understand the meaning of "harmony" in Chinese culture, which is an ancient concept. The word and its related ideas appeared in early documents such as the *Book of Documents*, *Book of Songs*, and the *State Annals*. In Chinese philosophy, "harmony" is "the interaction and unity between different elements or forces, and as the possible condition for the occurrence of all things" (Yang 2001). This interpretation is based on the concept of Heaven.[2] If perceived from the concept of Humanity,[3] "harmony" is often perceived as a concept of value or an ethical principle of human interaction.

"Harmony", as an ethical principle of interpersonal interaction, presupposes the recognition of diversity. Confucius once made a distinction between "harmony" and "uniformity": "The superior man seeks harmony without uniformity, while the mean man seeks uniformity without harmony" (Confucius 2006b). "Uniformity" denotes the sameness without difference and is often built on the basis of a biased opinion, partiality, or interest, easily resulting in a clustering tendency. "Harmony", as opposed to "uniformity", means the recognition and tolerance of different opinions at the conceptual level, and refers to the establishment of harmonious social relations between different individuals and groups at the social structural level. Therefore, "harmony" has a dual meaning. When observed from a negative perspective, it requires the mutual understanding and communication between subjects to dissolve tension and restrain conflicts. If perceived positively, "harmony" denotes that different subjects must collaborate together with one heart and one mind. It can be seen that the so-called harmony without uniformity means harmony under the premise of acknowledging differences. Just as Mencius said, "Opportunities of time vouchsafed by Heaven are not equal to advantages of situation afforded by the Earth, and advantages of situation afforded by the Earth are not equal to the union arising from the accord of Men" (Mencius 2004). "The unity among people" is about the relationship between people who should respect and tolerate each other in order to achieve harmony and social cohesion. The resulting force will overcome the external

---

[2] The concept of heaven is a fundamental view regarding the origin of the world, debated around different understandings of heaven and the relationship between heaven and man.

[3] Humanity here refers to the human reason, ethical relations in society, respect for human rights, care for human life, and care about the moral concept of human nature.

natural elements such as favorable time and place. Here, the value of social integration is without doubt highly valued.

Second, in Chinese traditional culture loyalty and consideration are regarded as the basic way for people to coexist. If "harmony without uniformity" is the fundamental ethical principle of coexistence suggested by Confucianism, the basic way to realize this principle is the "Way of Loyalty and Consideration". Loyalty and consideration are considered a "way", in that they illustrate the basic concept of Confucianism regarding how to be and treat a man, which is also the basic way of seeking and practicing benevolence. The basic thinking logic of Confucianism is this: it is considered a "virtue" to "gain" from the "way". As such, the epitome of the Way of Heaven is the virtue of "life", while the epitome of the Way of Humanity is the virtue of "benevolence". Similarly the "Way of Loyalty and Consideration" refers to the way of human behavior, namely, the Way of Humanity.

In explaining "loyalty and consideration", Zhu Xi said, "To do one's part is to be loyal, and to be thoughtful of others is to be considerate"[4] (Sishu Zhangju Jizhu四书章句集注). The Way of Loyalty and Consideration as the Way of Humanity can be divided into two parts: the Way of Loyalty and the Way of Consideration. "Loyalty" mainly means a kind of attitude and spirit characterized by such virtues as a high level of responsibility, integrity, piety, and trustworthiness. What is consideration then? Confucius said, "This is being considerate! Do unto others what you would not have them do unto you" (Confucius 2006a). That is, we should put ourselves in others' shoes, and should not impose on others what we do not want ourselves.

Although both Loyalty and Consideration are ways to realize benevolence, in terms of their objectives, the way of loyalty is a requirement for oneself, while the Way of Consideration is a way of treating others. The former refers to one's awareness of benevolence, and to the spirit and attitude of "self-righteousness", "self-encouragement", and "self-realization" upon this awareness, namely, the attitude and spirit of extreme responsibility, extreme integrity, extreme piety, and extreme trustworthiness mentioned above. The latter deals with the relationship between oneself and others on the premise of "loyal" attitudes and spirits, that is, extending from the relationship between one and oneself to the relationship between

---

[4] Notes on the Chapters and Sentences from the Four Books. Sishu Zhangju Jizhu四书章句集注.

oneself and others. In this sense, "loyalty" is the preparation for the consciousness of benevolence, and the spirit, state, and attitude one has afterward, while "consideration" is the concrete enactment of benevolence. Therefore, loyalty and consideration are inseparable in moral life. If there is no "willing one's heart" (loyalty), there will be no "thinking in others' shoes" (consideration), or there will be no correct concept of thinking in others' shoes (such as notions based on evil thoughts). Conversely, without consideration for others, "willing one's heart" will always be a kind of consciousness or notion only, and seeking benevolence or acting with benevolence cannot be ultimately realized.

2.2 Repositioning Contemporary Chinese Cultural Identity: A Member of a "Community of Shared Future for Mankind"

Humankind has entered "a globalized society" in the twenty-first century (Giddons 2001). Globalization, a hallmark of our time, is the basis of today's open world and defines the fundamental direction of the twenty-first century. So the perpetual question of how can nations of the world get along in peaceful coexistence again arises. The Chinese government has been thinking about this issue since the 1990s and has put forward the concept of "a community with a shared future for mankind", originally proposed by Hu Jintao, former general secretary of the communist party of China (CPC), and now championed by Xi Jinping, the current general secretary. The Chinese government proposed the concept with the aim of establishing a new framework for international relations to promote and improve global governance (Ding and Cheng 2017). Some analysts say it is the first major amendment to China's foreign policy in more than 40 years, shifting from a state-centered approach to one that focuses on all mankind, with China as a member of a community with a shared future for mankind, understanding and positioning the development of China and humankind in the same framework.

Xi's vision of a community of a shared future for mankind revolves around the following five actions: (1) building a partnership based on mutual consultation and understanding; (2) creating a security pattern through joint contribution and shared benefits; (3) seeking prospects of development that is inclusive and mutually beneficial; (4) promoting exchanges among civilizations with a respect for differences; and (5) constructing an ecosystem with green development.

The concept of "a community of shared future for mankind" is an inheritance and an advancement of the spirit of traditional Chinese culture, further specifying our basic principle and position in cultural exchanges with the world. First, we should continue to carry forward the idea of "harmony and coexistence" in traditional Chinese culture with regard to cultural integration. Since the Qin and Han dynasties, China has generally adhered to the principle of interdependence and peaceful coexistence when handling relationships with ethnic groups within its borders or with neighboring countries. Today's world is increasingly becoming a community with a shared future, with countries sharing prosperity and common ground. We need to recognize that China and the rest of the world are all important members of this community. China needs to work actively with all parties to build this community and welcomes all countries in the world to "hitch a ride" on China's rapid development to promote the harmonious integration of the economy and culture of different countries, including China.

Second, we should continue to live in "harmony without uniformity". "The world is varied and colorful. Just as there cannot be only one color in the universe, there cannot be only one civilization, one social system, one development model, or one value in the world. … The diversity of nationalities, religions and civilizations should be fully respected" (Jiang 2006). As Xi has stressed:

> Each civilization is unique. There is not a matter of superiority, but only a matter of difference in haecceity, characteristics and nationality. Achievements of all civilization deserve respect and cherishment. Each civilization has its own value of existence, with its own strengths and weaknesses. Civilizations are enriched by exchanges and mutual learning, which is an important driving force for the progress of human civilization and the peaceful development of the world. (Xi 2014a)

We should respect the diversity of civilizations and, on this basis, emphasize their uniqueness, equality, tolerance, and mutual learning.

Third, we should continue to treat friends from afar (Confucian expression) with Chinese traditional "benevolence". The Chinese nation has pursued harmony and peace for centuries as an ancient society. They advocate amity, "associate with benevolent gentlemen [*sic* women], befriend good neighbors and promote concord among nations", creating a unique culture characterized by "harmonization" throughout its thousand-year civilization history and advocated harmony. Such a culture "contains the cosmological view of the Unity of Nature and Man, the international view of the concord among nations, the social view of harmony without uniformity, as well as the moral view of human heart and kindliness" (Xi 2014b). Confucius said, "Love everyone and become close with the kind-hearted"; "Isn't it a joy to have friends come from afar". Countries are different in size, not in superiority or inferiority. Civilizations are different in characteristics, not in being noble or lowly. To build a new global order of equity and justice, we must seek the new vision through extensive consultation and joint contribution. Similarly, the idea of a community with a shared future for mankind has made it clear that when it comes to cultural exchanges, one should be as inclusive as the vast ocean which admits hundreds of rivers. Different civilizations should communicate on an equal footing to make common progress, so that "the exchange of civilizations can become a driving force for the progress of human society and a link for maintaining world peace" (Xi 2017).

The position and principles of Chinese culture we advocate and adhere to today are consistent with the principles of cultural communication upheld in this book when partaking of the larger sister school project. For example, the collaborative nature of the Reciprocal Learning in Teacher Education and School Education Between Canada and China and its guiding concept of *reciprocal learning* are designed as positive responses to global conditions. The world is increasingly interdependent and relations between the West and the East are active and vital. Reciprocal learning is a concept designed to foster mutual adaptation and reciprocity in education as cultures come together. Immigrant countries like Canada have a history and future in which cultural and educational adaptation and reciprocity are inevitable (Connelly et al. 2008; Xu 2006, 2011; Xu and Connelly 2010; Xu et al. 2007).

2.3   A Century's East-West Dialogue About China's Education and Its Contemporary Appeal

Although the cultural positions of traditional Chinese culture, such as Harmony Without Uniformity, Cosmopolitan Harmony, and the Ways of Loyalty and Consideration, generally put China in the position of having a dialogue with the world on an equal footing, everything seems in flux when it comes to China's education. Except for some scattered discourse about traditional Confucianism, the voice of Chinese pedagogy in global academia is relatively weak. In its dialogue with other countries, the pedagogic discourse of modern China faces "difficulties in relation, in connection, in contribution and in recognition" (Li 2018). To comprehend this challenging situation, we first need to understand the historical situation and China's educational modernization.

Admittedly, the historical development of China's education since the end of the nineteenth century has revolved around two relations: "Sino-foreign relations" and "tradition and modern relations". Many scholars at home and abroad have made slightly different yet generally close divisions of this period of China's educational history (Ye 2004; Hou 2001; Wu 2011; Deng 2011; Hayhoe 2014). We have synthesized their views and will now present five stages of China's education from the perspective of landmark events.

The first stage is from the late Qing Dynasty to the May 4th Movement (1840–1919). China's educational modernization originated from the failure of the First Opium War between China and Britain in 1840. Some Chinese realized that agricultural culture could not triumph over industrial civilization. With the ambition of saving the country and striving for strength, Zuo Zongtang first set up a Shipbuilding School in Fuzhou in 1866, marking the starting point of China's educational modernization and opening up the road to modernization in China. In 1902, the Qing government promulgated the Imperial School Regulations, also known as the "Ren Yin School System" (壬寅学制), which became the first modern school system in China. With this as the starting point, China officially started its road to modernization following the mode of "introducing Western learning to the East". At this stage from 1840 to 1901, educational works by such authors as Spencer were mainly introduced or briefly translated. From 1901 to 1915, Japanese educational works were introduced into China which are said to be mainly about German educational thought (Hou 2001; Ye 2004). These measures triggered the controversy between Chinese reformists and traditionalists at that time, focusing on issues such as "Western cultural values" and "Chinese basic values", "Western utilitarianism" and "Confucian ethics", and "Christianity" and "Confucianism". A consensus was reached to adopt the strategy of addressing the controversies by selecting certain Western ideas and models while retaining the basic thoughts and values of Confucianism (Meiyao 2009; Wu 2011).

The second stage, from the May 4th Movement to the founding of the People's Republic of China (PRC) (1919–1949), was marked by a transition from learning from Japan and Europe to the United States. Several scholars are dedicated to pedagogical research in the Chinese educational circle. Tao Xingzhi (陶行知), Liang Shuming (梁漱溟), and Yan Yangchu (晏阳初) embarked on independent research on the reality and problems of Chinese education (Ye 2004). The mainstream influence on educational thought at that point was Dewey's pragmatism, together with other major Western educational trends and Marxist pedagogy. Under the influence of these thoughts, there appeared a variety of developments in China's education including school system establishment, citizenship education, universal education, rural education, and vocational education. More attention was drawn to the compilation of textbooks, teaching methodologies, intelligence tests, educational measurement, and psychological measurement in schools. In the aftermath of the Sino-Japanese War (1894–1895) and the Anti-Japanese War (1937–1945), the Chinese government needed people's loyalty to the country to assert itself as a nation. In order to resist the influence of Western democracy and equality, the national government retained the part of Confucianism aiming to cultivate people's loyalty and patriotism[5] (Ye 2004). Confucianism at this time was not completely eliminated, but of course went through a process of modernization. That is, Chinese intellectuals interpreted or reinterpreted traditional Confucianism according to Western or non-Confucian thought (Tan 2008).

The third stage is marked by the era of Mao Zedong (1949–1978), which occurred after the founding of New China. From the founding of the People's Republic of China to 1957, the pedagogical thoughts of the Soviet Union such as Kailov and Makalenko became the mainstream educational thought in mainland China. Admittedly, the core of Kailov's theory still resembles that of Herbart (Ye 2004) from Germany on which Dewey also drew. With the breakdown of Sino-Soviet relations in 1958 and the advent of the Cultural Revolution (1966–1976), Mao Zedong's theory assumed dominant status, with the educational function of schools becoming politicized. Meanwhile, criticism was directed at Soviet, European, or American education thought with Confucianism nearly being denied through "destroying the four dregs of society" (old ideas, old culture, old customs, old habits) (Central Committee of the Communist Party of China 1966). Hence, the Mao era "eliminated not

---

[5] This is different from the opinion of some contemporary Chinese scholars that the development of educational thought in the first half of the twentieth century in China was fractured. See Ye Lan (2004).

only the remnants of Western-style education and the early emulation of the Soviet educational model, but also eliminated any trace of Confucian education" (Yang and Frick 2009).

Then came the fourth stage: the period of reform and opening up (1980–1999). This period features China's educational recovery, prosperity, and the beginnings of independent consciousness (Ye 2004). In order to make up for the destructive influence caused by the Cultural Revolution as soon as possible, the modernization of education became a front-burner agenda item again. The first few years saw the introduction and compilation of Western educational theories as the mainstream, especially in 1983 when Deng Xiaoping put forward "Three Orientations" in education, namely, orientating toward modernization, the world and the future. At that point, countries like the United States, Britain, the Soviet Union, and Japan became the major sources of education theories in China's attempt to orient itself toward the world. The consciousness of an independent Chinese pedagogy began to emerge. Chinese educators began to realize that Chinese pedagogy needs to take a path of local development and could not always be the "Sinicized" version of Western pedagogy (Lei 1984; Zhou 1997; Qu 1998, 1999; Ye 2004). Chinese scholars carried out research of meta-pedagogy theoretically, on one hand, and combined theory and practice for local exploration, on the other hand. Meanwhile, Chinese traditional culture and the challenges of contemporary rationality were also included in the research framework.

This brings us to the current century and the fifth stage: the awakening of Chinese discourse in pedagogy of the new era (2000–present). Entering the new century, Chinese society commenced an overall transformation period oriented toward globalization, and China began to think about its position in the world. Although China continued to "import" various educational theories from the West, the legitimacy and applicability of Western theories began to be questioned in the Chinese educational circle because China has its own distinct cultural traditions and unique problems[6] (Hou 2001; Yi and Yang 2003; Ye 2004; Li 2004a, b; Jiang 2006;

---

[6] From 2001 to 2010, there were several papers on this topic. Hou Huaiyin. Basic Course of Chinese Pedagogy Development in the First Half of the Twentieth Century [J].] Journal of Shanxi University (Philosophy and Social Sciences Edition), 2001 (6): 1–6; Yi, Yang Changyong. Discussion on the Creation of Chinese Pedagogy School [J].] Educational Research, 2003 (4): 37–42; Ye Lan. A Review of the Century Question of Development of Chinese Pedagogy [J].] Educational Research, 2004 (7): 3–17; Li Hing Chau. Analysis on the Destiny of Chinese Pedagogy in the Context of Globalization [J].] Contemporary

Lu et al. 2007; Tian et al. 2010). In 2004, Ye Lan of East China Normal University (ECNU) argued the need to construct a school of Chinese pedagogical thought, and named the school "Life-Practice" Educology. For a while, it not only attracted the attention of Chinese educators but also the attention of international scholars. For example, in the book, *Portraits of Influential Chinese Educators*, by Ruth Hayhoe of the University of Toronto, Ye Lan was introduced as the youngest educator in contemporary China (Zhang 2008). In 2009, Shanghai's students earned first place in the PISA exams coordinated by the Organisation for Economic Co-operation and Development (OECD), which not only shocked the European and American education circles and aroused the world's attention but also established the confidence of Chinese educational scholars.

The issue of China's educational independence has increasingly become a focus. In 2011, Wu Zongjie of Zhejiang University published *Interpretation, Autonomy, and Transformation: Chinese Pedagogic Discourse in a Cross-Cultural Perspective* (Wu 2011), pointing out contemporary education should return to the traditional Confucian discourse system in order to break loose of the quagmire of Western technicism and instrumentalism. The modernization of Chinese education could then be restored to its original purpose. This article immediately triggered a heated discussion among internationally renowned Chinese scholars (Bai 2011; Cheng 2011; Cheng and Xu 2011; Liu 2011; Tan 2011; Deng 2011; Hayhoe 2014). In 2017, Xi Jinping championed the concept of Community of Shared Future for Mankind in the 19th CPC National Congress report, calling for a world knowledge production system different from the Western discourse system. "Chinese theory" and "Chinese experience" would coalesce the whole Chinese hunmanities and social science community, not be confined to the field of education. As a result, the Chinese government and universities have strengthened their efforts to globally disseminate their scholarship and committed themselves to

Educational Sciences, 2004a (18): 3–5; Li Zhengtao. Discussion on the Significance and Basic Path of the Creation of Chinese Pedagogy School [J].] Educational Research, 2004b (1): 6–8; Jing Guoping. On School Consciousness and Practical Direction of Chinese Pedagogy—From "Subject Standpoint" to "School Standpoint" [J].] Higher Education Studies, 2006 (1): 76–81; Lu Quyuan, Tian Hanzu, Tu Guanghui. On the Construction of Chinese Pedagogy—Also On the Lack of Chinese Pedagogy in the twentieth Century [J].] Journal of Educational Science, Hunan Normal University, 2007 (3): 11–15; Tian Hanzu, Lu Quyuan, Xie ZhiGuohua. On Chinese Pedagogy Towards the World [J] Journal of Educational Science, Hunan Normal University, 2010 (001): 34–37, 54.

introducing China's experience. Discussion papers, projects, and conferences have become "vibrant again" (Ding and Zhou 2006).

In general, the Chinese government and scholars who have walked the road of Westernization for more than a hundred years feel that it is time for China to make its own footprint and find its own voice in the world. Until now, their voice has been almost non-existent, so it is an important issue to be in search of themselves. In this regard, one proposition is to return to Chinese traditional culture to look for uniqueness (i.e., Wu 2011), or not simply to return, but to break through (Ye 2004; Ye et al. 2019); a further proposition is to plant Chinese educational practice to carry out local research and explore the Chinese way (Ye et al. 2019). International scholars think that the Chinese and Western educational thought are polar opposites because the road of educational modernization chosen by China and the West was not voluntary or disconnected. Modern education was chosen because of industrialized societies, and today, due to the arrival of information and intelligent society, we need to go beyond the drawbacks of industrial era education. Therefore, China and the West need to walk hand-in-hand to explore common problems and contribute to the richness and innovation of world education (Cheng 2011).

Indeed, the educational dialogue between China and the West captured by the reciprocal learning project is clear. Reciprocal learning involves interaction between two parties. Through interactions as partners, we would not only learn from each other and contribute to each other but also jointly explore problems, find solutions, synthesize successful experiences, and compound successful learning so as to create new cultural and educational possibilities for everyone involved.

2.4 The Two Contemporary Schools of Education Involved in This Project

In this section, we will explicate the academic pursuits and impact of two influential educational schools of thought in China and the United States in the transformation of modern society: one of which concerns the development and spread of the Dewey school of experiential philosophy in the United States and Canada and its subsequent development and inheritance of core thoughts of several generations after Dewey: Schwab, Schwab's students, Lee Shulman and Michael Connelly, Connelly's student Clandinin, Clandinin's and Connelly's student Cheryl Craig, and so forth. Another school is the life-practice pedagogy research team. Ye Lan, the head of the research group of East China Normal University in China, is the founder of the School of "Life-Practice" Educology. Yuhua Bu, one of the leaders of the research group, was a student of Ye Lan and a core member of the School of "Life-Practice" Educology. Although these two schools came into being in two different times and spaces, there are many similarities between them.

In terms of academic origin, the university researchers who presided over the study of sister schools on both sides of Canada and China belong to Dewey's school of empirical educational thought and Ye Lan's School of "Life-Practice" Educology respectively. As mentioned, Michael Connelly of the University of Toronto is a student of American educator Joseph Schwab, while Xu Shijing and Yishin Khoo are students of Connelly; so, their thoughts trace Dewey's empirical theory (Clandinin and Connelly 1992; Craig and Ross 2008). Ye Lan is the founder of the "Life-Practice" Educology as well as the head of the research group of East China Normal University. Yuhua Bu, head of another research group, is a student of Ye Lan as well as a core member of the school of Life-Practice Educology. The main ideas and pursuits of these two schools are respectively discussed below.

2.4.1 From Dewey and Schwab to Connelly and His Students: The Development of Empiricism Educational Theory

As is known, Dewey is the educational thinker who has the greatest influence on modern education in the world in the twentieth century. At the beginning of the twentieth century, standing on the development point of the time when the American society was transforming from an agricultural society to a modern society, he examined the shortcomings of transmission education and transformed the empirical theory, from which he began to discuss the modern educational thought almost systematically. Since then, his educational thoughts have influenced the whole world, and have been continuously interpreted and developed. Several educational scholars involved in this project have made important contributions to the inheritance and development of Dewey's educational thought. Starting from Dewey's view that "education is the endless process of continuous reorganization of experience", their breakthrough has had a great impact on contemporary curriculum reform, teacher education, and educational research methodology, as detailed below.

First, it is worth mentioning that the American curriculum theorist Joseph Schwab (1909–1988) is an important figure in the deepening Dewey's theory in the field of curriculum. He was the originator of *The Practical*, a program for educational improvements based on curriculum deliberations. Schwab's concern for education as a deliberative activity connects him to John Dewey (Craig and Ross 2008). His respect for the formulations and proper uses of theories connects him to the Aristotelian distinction between theoretical, practical, and productive activities. He thought that curriculum is more than a planned document or a program of study external to teachers. It is what teachers and students live as they interact with one another, although curriculum guides, textbooks, and other materials obviously play a part (Schwab 1969, 1973; Connelly and Clandinin 1992). Schwab thought that commonplaces are interrelated curricular components encompassing learners, teachers, content, and milieus. Scholars in curriculum studies should employ commonplaces to frame curriculum development, to develop a heuristic for understanding curriculum, and to create a structure of analysis for curriculum inquiry. Joseph Schwab delineated the curriculum commonplaces to guide the process of curriculum development. He explained that when people come together to revise curriculum, they need knowledge of these fundamental elements. Schwab's first commonplace, subject matter, means comprehension of content disciplines, their underlying systems of thought, and curriculum materials. His second commonplace, knowledge of learners, involves familiarity with students including children's developmental abilities, their unique qualities, and their probable futures as influenced by the environment of their families and communities (rather than how education might transform their possible destinies). Schwab referred to classroom, school environments, and all outward influences on them as the third commonplace, milieu; he called for recognition of the context of learning—social structures within schools, the influence of families, and the multitude of values and attitudes stemming from the community and culture surrounding the school. The fourth commonplace, teachers, includes educators' subject matter knowledge, their personalities—such as their flexibility or openness to new methods—and their biases or political stances. His thoughts have had a far-reaching impact in the fields of curriculum, teacher education, and educational research. Michael Connelly, the host of our project, is one of these far-reaching influences as are Connelly's students (Elbaz-Luwisch, Clandinin, Craig, Khoo, Xu).

As mentioned earlier, Michael Connelly was a student of Joseph Schwab. Dr. Connelly was a longtime Editor of *Curriculum Inquiry* and former Chair of Curriculum at Ontario Institute for Studies in Education of University of Toronto (OISE/UT). He studied with Joseph Schwab at the University of Chicago and has written on science education, curriculum studies, teacher education, multiculturalism, and narrative inquiry. Dr. Connelly has deep roots in American modern educational thought, especially since Dewey and Schwab had a great impact on him. He is a prolific and creative scholar. Many of his educational theories are very influential in the world. Among his major collaborative works are *The Functions of Curriculum Development* (1972), *Teachers as Curriculum Planners: Narratives of Experience* (1988), *Stories of Experience and Narrative Inquiry* (1990, which coined the term Narrative Inquiry), *The Sage Handbook of Curriculum and Instruction* (2008), *Narrative Inquiry for School-based Research* (2010), and the overview chapters on curriculum for the Elsevier International *Encyclopedia of Education* (2010) and *The Routledge Companion to Education* (2011). At present, Dr. Michael Connelly is Professor Emeritus at the Ontario Institute for Studies in Education of University of Toronto (OISE/UT). He co-directs the Social Sciences and Humanities Research Council of Canada (SSHRC) Partnership Project Grant Reciprocal learning in teacher education and school education between Canada and China with Dr. Shijing Xu of the University of Windsor. Through this project, they jointly constructed the concept of "reciprocal learning in cross-culture education" as the basic principle and method to study cross-cultural reciprocal learning.

Michael Connelly and Jean Clandinin advocate for Schwab's practical view and his curriculum theory. They have drawn on the commonplaces to understand and make sense of teachers' lived experiences in classrooms. Viewing curriculum as a fluid narrative arising from teachers' sense of self and minded practices, Michael Connelly and Jean Clandinin formulated the commonplaces as a heuristic to inspire teachers' self-reflection and articulation of their stances as curriculum makers (Clandinin and Connelly 1992). Unlike others, who placed the curriculum specialist as the expert in charge of curriculum planning, Connelly and Clandinin following in the footsteps of Schwab, viewed teachers as curriculum planners or makers and used the commonplaces as their analytic tools to develop their narratives, to understand historical trends of curriculum, and to gain insights into contemporary controversies (Connelly and Clandinin 1988, 1992). In particular, by attending to the commonplaces, curriculum workers uncover the logic or emphasis of curriculum deliberations. Their idea of teachers as curriculum makers is of great significance. This view is critical of the traditional role of teachers as curriculum implementers. In the traditional role relationship, teachers are knowledge transferrers and technicians. Policy makers mandate changes; teachers do what they are told. Policy makers treat teachers as functionaries who are totally reliant on state and national imperatives. In this technical rational view of the teacher, fidelity to others' directives reigns supreme (Craig 2008). But the image of teacher as curriculum maker views teachers as active agents, minded professionals, and makers of curriculum alongside students. Also, the teacher-as-curriculum-maker image works from the assumption that a classroom space exists within which teachers and students negotiate curriculum unhampered by, though not oblivious to, others' mandates and desires (Craig and Ross 2008). Teachers desire to use the discretionary spaces in their in-classroom places to make curriculum alongside students (Boote 2006). Accordingly, the teacher's responsibility is the organizer, planner, and arranger of the curriculum. They are no longer simply the transmitter of knowledge, but the agent of education. This echoes Schwab's view: "only as the teacher uses the classroom as the occasion and the means to reflect upon education as a whole (ends as well as means), as the laboratory in which to translate reflections into actions and thus to test reflections, actions, and outcomes, against many criteria is he [*sic*] a good … teacher" (Schwab 1954/1978). Moreover, Connelly and Clandinin have also proposed other important conceptualizations such as "professional knowledge landscape" (Clandinin and Connelly 1995), "narrative inquiry" (Connelly and Clandinin 1990), and "stories to live by" (Connelly and Clandinin 1999), which have had an extensive impact in the field of education.

Following Connelly's research tradition, his graduates (i.e., Jean Clandinin and Freema Elbaz-Luwitch) expanded and enriched this practice-oriented school of educational thought in two ways. Two former students involved in this project, one of whom is among his best students from China is Shijing Xu. Dr. Xu's research interests focus on narrative approaches to intergenerational, bilingual, and multicultural educational issues and school-family-community connections in cross-cultural curriculum studies and teacher education. Her current research focuses on the reciprocal learning between the West and the East in a "WE consciousness". She was the Principal Investigator (PI) of a project on circular migration (2008–2012) and Co-PI of the Canada-China sister school network project (2009–2013) funded by Social Sciences and Humanities Research Council of Canada (SSHRC). She is coordinating the Pre-service Teacher Education Reciprocal Learning Program between University of Windsor and Southwest University China, which is funded by University of Windsor Strategic Priority Fund.

In North America, Cheryl J. Craig is a leading scholar. She is Jean Clandinin's PhD student and Dr. Michael Connelly's former Post-Doctoral Fellow. Currently, she is Professor and the Houston Endowment Endowed Chair in Urban Education in the Department of Teaching, Learning and Culture in the College of Education and Human Development, Texas A&M University. Her empirical research is situated at the intersection where teaching and curriculum meet. Using the narrative inquiry research method, she conducts research with pre-service and in-service teachers within school contexts. She is a prolific scholar and has put forward many important educational concepts, such as teacher knowledge communities (Craig 1995a, b, 2005a, b) the best-loved self (Craig 2013), parallel stories (Craig 1999), story constellation (Craig 2007), serial interpretation (Craig 2018; Craig et al. 2018), and so on. She is Chair of the International Advisory Board for the Canada-China Reciprocal Learning Project and since 2016 has assisted East China Normal University's School of Life-Practice Educology.

Taken together, five generations of scholars, Dewey, Schwab, Connelly, Clandinin to Xu Shijing and Cheryl Craig, have constantly deepened and creatively developed Dewey's empiricism educational thought. They have put forward important ideas and concepts related to curriculum reform, teacher education, science teaching, educational research methodology, and cross-cultural education. The characteristics of their educational thoughts can be summarized as follows: They (1) consider the problems of education from the perspective of modern society, (2) acknowledge the uncertainty, openness, individuality, situational and complex diversity of practice, and respect these characteristics of practice in theory, (3) recognize the primary status of teachers, who possess personal practical knowledge that truly affects teachers' practice with children, (4) know that teachers' professional development is based on their own experiences and that through storying and restorying teachers become further developed professionally in their knowledge communities, and (5) recognize education researchers should change their traditional attitude toward education work alongside teachers and experience their professional development through adopting narrative inquiry as their research method.

2.4.2 *Ye Lan and Her Academic Team: School of "Life-Practice" Educology and "New Basic Education" Research*

As mentioned, the 100-odd-year history of China's educational modernization has taken place through the development of the relationship between China and foreign countries, and between ancient and modern. The educational thought of Japan, the United States, Germany, the former Soviet Union, and other countries have in turn affected the development of Chinese educational thought. In general, however, the mode of Chinese educational practice has not gone beyond the traditional mode of rote memory except for increasing disciplinary subject matter in the curriculum of study. At the end of the twentieth century, Chinese society is becoming more and more open and is in urgent need of novel educational ideas to lead the reform of educational practice. The school of "Life-Practice" Educology has taken shape against this background.

Born in 1941, Ye Lan came from a family of primary school teachers with her father being an art teacher at primary school. Since her childhood, she has been full of appreciation for her father's status as a teacher. After graduating from high school, she entered the Department of Education of East China Normal University with the intention to be a good teacher. After graduating from university, she stayed in school with excellent grades and spent her first two years teaching at a primary school affiliated with East China Normal University, where she was the head-teacher and Chinese teacher for one class. However, her two years of frontline teaching experience did not give her more professional self-confidence, but rather she felt that "no matter how well she learned pedagogy, she could not use it in practice". However, when "she had a real life experience of being a primary school teacher, [she] developed a sense of the complexity of the relationship between educational theory and practice" (Ye 2002). From this life experience, she began to critically examine why Chinese educational theory is "useless" in the face of practice when she returned to East China Normal University. She found that (Ye 2002):

> What is most lacking in our educational theory is the consciousness of the "human" and the study of the "human" ... Pedagogy only studies how to teach students the knowledge of the external world, but does not how to develop the inner strength of students. I think this is the more important half that pedagogy must make up. I am determined to work towards adding that half. (p. 4)

Thereafter, as her understanding of theoretical issues in education became more and more clear, she resolved to explore the path of theory to practice, with the intention of "letting theory generate practice power and enrich theory with practice!" (Ye 2002).

With this ambition in mind, in 1990, she initiated the first theory-practice project, "Basic Education and Students' Self-Education Capacity Development", and began her first research on the direct integration of theory construction and educational practice innovation at the Waigaoqiao Free Trade Zone Experimental Primary School, Pudong, Shanghai. The study, which took three years, opened her eyes to "the enormous potential and possibilities that exist in children" and led to many of her first steps (Ye 2002), which she described as:

> The first step to plunge into the torrent of China's basic education reform with in-depth practical research; the first step to open the way for practical exploration and enrich theoretical research with practical exploration; the first step to achieve a healthy interaction between theory and practical research in education research on my part as a research individual.

When Ye Lan's first explorations of combining theory and practice in education began to bear fruit in the early 1990s, her personal confidence began to grow and a new era of social development in China began to unfold at the same time. Sensing keenly that a new era was calling her, Ye Lan said (Ye 2002):

> Since 1993, our ancient nation has accelerated its pace on the road to reform and opening up. The times are increasingly calling for new people. The growth of new people and the great renaissance of the people are directly related to the reform of basic education. At this time, I, as an educator, was driven by a sense of historical mission as a member of the nation. … China's educational reform can only be undertaken by Chinese educators, and it is only through the research and practice of reform that Chinese educational theory can be born, grow and mature. If we do not commit ourselves now, it is not the times that have failed us, but we have failed the times.

Ye Lan's value lies in the fact that she is a person who believes in the rule of "words do, deeds do". Once she realizes what is most valuable and meaningful, she will act decisively. In 1994, she launched a five-year research project named "New Basic Education" (NBE) and "Exploratory Research", which directly combined theory and practice, with the first experimental school being the Waigaoqiao Free Trade Zone Experimental School. NBE's first five years of school reform research began in the areas of classroom teaching and classroom management, with the aim of recommending open classrooms and classes, giving students more autonomy in their learning and breaking the teaching delivery model. For this reason, almost every week, Ye Lan, her colleagues, and her students came to this school to listen to and evaluate lessons for five years. Gradually, there has been a significant change in the way teachers taught and practiced teaching in this school. In the last year, the NBE research results of Waigaoqiao Primary School held an on-site meeting, inviting the leaders of the Shanghai Municipal Education Commission, some district and county education bureau directors, and well-known local educators to the meeting. The quality of the teachers' teaching and the level of development of the students were highly rated during this on-site meeting. This was the first five-year research phase of NBE, which was called "exploratory research".

The results of the first five years of research were quickly disseminated. The director of the Minzhu District Education Bureau in Shanghai was so eager to change test-taking education that he invited Professor Ye Lan to conduct her second five-year research in Minzhu District. Thus, in 1999, NBE planned to conduct a larger-scale study in Minzhu District, Shanghai, called "Developmental Research". The Minzhu District Education Bureau has since provided strong support for NBE research. First, it established the New Basic Education Institute, which allows local education researchers to participate in NBE research projects. Second, three junior high schools and six primary schools participated in the NBE study, among which Minzhu Primary School (highlighted in this book) is one of them. Third, a nine-year school was specifically renamed the "New Basic Education Experimental School", with the intention of becoming a model school in the region. In addition, the Minzhu Bureau of Education has provided material and financial support to NBE. At the same time, Changzhou No. 2 experimental primary school is also eager to join the NBE, becoming the first NBE school outside Shanghai. The ECNU team working on the NBE research is small, with only four other colleagues besides Ye Lan, two of whom had already left for other important projects. In addition, most of the researchers involved (5–6) were Ye Lan's PhD students. The ECNU research team is divided into four teams: Chinese, mathematics, language (English study), and class teams, each team consisting of one to two people was responsible for conducting the NBE study with the corresponding subject teachers in nine schools in Minzhu District and one school in Changzhou City. Mentoring usually happens on Tuesdays, when each research group works together in one school to carry out research, and other schools will have two to three teachers participate in the discussion in the school of on-site research, and the school of on-site research will rotate every week. Every month, ECNU researchers hold a wrap-up meeting to share their research progress and build consensus. In this way, the project lasted for five years. By the fifth year, some changes had taken place in the ten schools, but they were not ideal. For example, ECNU researchers, while theoretically able to argue for an ideal educational model, were not very clear about the pathway from theory to practice. So, after the second five years were over, Ye Lan and the leadership at the Minzhu Bureau of Education felt that the study, while difficult, was valuable and needed a second five-year follow-up study.

From 2004 to 2009, NBE continued to conduct reform research in nine schools in Minzhu District and the Changzhou No. 2 experimental primary school, in the third phase of a five-year study called the "Transformational Study". Ye Lan realized that the previous school reform was unsatisfactory, mainly because it was only partially carried out (classroom teaching, classroom management). She knew it was because the school was not reformed as a whole, such as the organizational structure of the school, the system, the leadership philosophy and way of that principals deeply constrained enthusiasm for teacher reform. Therefore, she argued that if school reform in contemporary China was to be truly successful, it must focus on holistic reform and must recognize that contemporary school reform in China is a transformation of modern industrialized efficiency-oriented schools and the pursuit of modern schooling must be based on the development of students. Thus, she called the third phase of NBE research a "holistic transformational reform". In other words, in addition to teachers being the main agents of reform, the principal is also an active agent of reform, and is the first person responsible for school reform. Hence, there was a need for them to change the leadership concept themselves based on school culture, schools' organizational structure, school system construction, and other aspects of reform. Obviously, the key to this orientation is that the principal is the person who takes the lead in the whole school reform. Once they become actively involved in school reform, the enthusiasm of teachers increases significantly. At this stage, the NBE advises principals to develop an overall five-year plan for school development and reform. Then, the NBE team listens to the principal's term plan at the beginning of each semester and helps to analyze problems and challenges at the end of the term. The principal then has a clearer understanding of the development of the school, and the development goals and strategies of the school become even more targeted every semester. In 2009, the quality of classroom teaching and the development of teachers in ten schools achieved remarkable results. In 2009, NBE held a nationwide on-site seminar for all ten schools, inviting education scholars, heads of the Ministry of Education and the Shanghai Education Commission, as well as principals and teachers, to assess the development status of NBE schools, which was rigorously evaluated and widely publicized in the media.

Ye Lan believed that the ten experimental schools, despite the effectiveness of their reform, were accompanied by the ECNU team along the way, and their ability to develop on their own needs to be further examined. Only if these experimental schools are able to develop on their own, after leaving the ECNU research team, will the reform be truly successful. Therefore, the ECNU team agreed with the Minzhu Education Bureau to give the experimental schools three more years to see the results of the independent development of these experimental schools, so that the NBE concept can be firmly rooted in the daily practice of the schools. Thus, the period 2009–2012 was the fourth phase of the NBE study called "Grounded Research". At this stage, the ECNU research team simply convenes a workshop at the end of each semester in which the ten experimental schools were invited to share their developments and new experiences. Three years of grounded research shows that ten experimental schools are basically able to institutionalize the NBE concept in daily life, and during this period, the ten experimental schools produced many "famous teachers" and "famous principals", which basically proves the success of NBE. NBE has called these successful schools "cooperative schools".

In 2012, the Minzhu Education Bureau and the NBE team agreed that the NBE research should be disseminated and the NBE reform schools should be used as "seed schools" to reach the region. As a result, NBE started to establish 6 school ecological communities in Minzhu District, Shanghai, consisting of 1 NBE cooperative school and 10 or 12 member schools. NBE cooperative school promotes the common development of member schools. Among them, Minzhu Primary School described in this book also became a lead school in the cooperative schools and school ecological communities. By 2015, the number of NBE schools in Minzhu

District had expanded to more than 70, covering almost all primary and secondary schools in the district, with many more outstanding schools emerging. As a result, the nine-year compulsory education reform in Minzhu District of Shanghai has been basically completed and the quality of education and teaching has greatly improved. At the same time, Changzhou has expanded from one experimental school to two and then to the five districts of the city as a whole. The fifth stage is the development of "School Ecological Communities".

Since 2015, the NBE's influence has been growing, and its research scope has been extended to 14 regions in China, including Beijing, Tianjin, Guangzhou, Shanghai, Jiangsu, Zhejiang, Yunnan, Henan, Shandong, Guangdong, Guangxi, and Sichuan, with more than 100 experimental schools and nearly 10,000 teachers participating in this reform experiment (see Fig. 2.1). The sixth phase from 2015 to the present is called the "National Regional Advancement" research phase. During this period, the first district to enter the reform, such as Shanghai and Changzhou, and other NBE districts held annual national symbiosis conferences to observe and learn from each other, forming a national symbiosis of NBE schools. Minzhu Primary School, like all NBE cooperative schools, not only interacts regularly with other schools in the district but also participates in national network of NBE school experience sharing sessions, and its influence is growing.

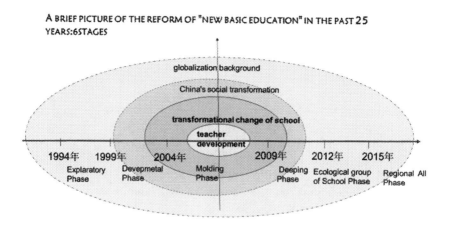

Fig. 2.1 NBE's influence in China

Together, Ye Lan and her students founded the school of "Life-Practice" Educology (2004) which coheres around the educational belief that "human life is the cornerstone of education while life is the starting point of pedagogical thinking" (Ye 2004; Bu and Liu 2017).

2.5 Conclusion

In sum, the nature of society and the background of the times produced two pedagogical schools: one in the East (China), another in the West (Canada and the United States). Both were confronted with similar issues in their transitions from a traditional to a modern society. Because of the differences in traditional culture, the basis of practice, and researchers' way of academic thinking, they have similar answers to common questions. That is, they both emphasize the openness and complexity of practice, and give educators (principals and teachers) and children more autonomy. But their differences are also multifaceted. First, the academic tradition of the United States and Canada focuses on curriculum, teachers, or teaching, not on the school as a unit of reform, while the Chinese school first considers the school as an organic whole, and then explores the factors of curriculum, teachers, teaching, and students as components of an organic whole. Second, the American and Canadian academic traditions insist that theoretical researchers are neutral in the face of practice, while the Chinese school insists on the mutual transformation and generation of theory and practice, and that theoretical researchers should be deeply involved in educational practice to form a symbiotic relationship with practice. Third, with regard to the way of thinking, although both advocate entering into practice and research practice, the American-Canadian school starts from the empirical theory, which is the way of exploring the epistemological orientation (an exception is narrative inquiry which has an ontological nature). The Chinese school, starting from life theory, is also an ontological way of inquiry. The above-mentioned differences may result from differences in cultural traditions. In other chapters in this book, we will further present educational differences between the two cultural traditions through inquiring into the state of intercultural reciprocal learning in the sister schools.

Lastly, the novel coronavirus pneumonia (COVID-19) is rampant around the world as we write this volume. China and the world are experiencing a common fate. This virus makes us realize that human destiny is tightly bound together. Before the pandemic, many great people have realized that human destiny is closely linked and win-win cooperation is very important. The great American poet, Walt Whitman, noted that the (human) race is never separated: "every atom belonging to me as good belongs to you". Martin Luther King similarly declared that we are "caught in an inescapable network of mutuality, tied in a single garment of destiny". Confucius also was acutely aware of this interdependency. In fact, he opened the *Analects* by addressing foreigners as "kindred spirits" ("And is it not delightful to have men [*sic*] of kindred spirit come to one from afar?" [有朋自远方来, 不亦乐乎?]).[7]

When different cultures meet, differences will first color our vision. Confucius' advice on the attitude toward differences is "harmony in diversity, beauty and sharing". It is precisely this attitude and principle that guided our participation in the sister school research project between China and Canada.

REFERENCES

Bai, T. (2011). Against Democratic Education. *Journal of Curriculum Studies, 43*(5), 615–622.

Boote, D. N. (2006). Teachers' Professional Discretion and the Curricula. In *Teachers and Teaching: Theory and Practice*. Abingdon: Taylor & Francis Group.

Bu, Y., & Liu, A. (2017). Lun 'Yushengmingzijue' de Duochong Neihan 论 '育生命自觉' 的多重内涵 (The Multiple Connotation of 'Cultivating Life Consciousness'). *Journal of Educational Studies, 13*(1), 10–15.

Central Committee of the Communist Party of China. (1966, August 8). Decision of the Central Committee of the Communist Party of China on the Cultural Revolution of the Proletariat.

Cheng, K. M. (2011). Pedagogy: East and West, Then and Now. *Journal of Curriculum Studies, 43*(5), 591–599.

Cheng, L., & Xu, L. (2011). The Complexity of Chinese Pedagogic Discourse. *Journal of Curriculum Studies, 43*(5), 606–614.

Clandinin, D. J., & Connelly, F. M. (1992). Teacher as Curriculum Maker. In P. Jackson (Ed.), *Handbook of Curriculum* (pp. 363–461). New York, NY: Macmillan.

Clandinin, D. J., & Connelly, F. M. (1995). *Teachers' professional knowledge landscapes.* New York Teachers' College Press.

Confucius. (2006a). Weilinggong 卫灵公 (Weilinggong). In *Lunyu 论语 (Analects)*. Beijing: Chinese Bookstore.

---

[7] Passage for NBE website authored by Cheryl Craig.

Confucius. (2006b). Zi Lu. In Y. Zhang (Ed.), *Analects*. Beijing: Chinese Bookstore.

Connelly, F. M., & Clandinin, D. J. (1988). *Teacher as Curriculum Planners: Narratives of Experience*. New York: Teacher College.

Connelly, F. M., & Clandinin, D. J. (1990). Stories of experience and narrative inquiry. *Educational Researcher, 19*, 2–14.

Connelly, F. M., & Clandinin, D. J. (1992). *Narrative Inquiry. Prepared for International Encyclopedia of Education*. Oxford: Pergamon.

Connelly, F. M., & Clandinin, D. J. (1999). *Shaping a professional identity: Stories of educational practice*. New York: Teachers College Press.

Connelly, F. M., Xu, S., Eisner, E. W., & Jackson, P. W. (2008). *The Landscape of Curriculum and Instruction: Diversity and Continuity*. SAGE Publications.

Craig, C. J. (1995a). Knowledge communities: A way of making sense of how beginning teachers come to know. *Curriculum Inquiry, 25*(2), 151–175.

Craig, C. J. (1995b). Coming to know in the professional knowledge landscape: Benita's first year of teaching. In D. J. Clandinin & F. M. Connelly (Eds.) *Teachers' professional knowledge landscapes* (pp. 79-87). + New York: Teachers College Press.

Craig, C. (1999). Parallel stories: A way of contextualizing teacher stories. *Teaching and Teacher Education, 15*(4), 397–411.

Craig, C. (2005a). The epistemic role of novel metaphors in teachers' knowledge constructions of school reform. *Teachers and Teaching, 11*, 195–208. https://doi.org/10.1080/13450600500083972.

Craig, C. (2005b). From stories of staying to stories of leaving: AUS beginning teacher's experience. *Journal of Curriculum Studies, 46*(1), 81–115.

Craig, C. (2007). Story constellations: A narrative approach to situating teachers' knowledge of school reform in context. *Teaching and Teacher Education, 23*(2), 173–188.

Craig, C. J. (2008). Joseph Schwab, Self-Study of Teaching and Teacher Education Practices Proponent? A Personal Perspective. *Teaching and Teacher Education, 24*(8), 1993–2001.

Craig, C. J., & Ross, V. (2008). Cultivating Teachers as Curriculum Makers. In F. M. Connelly (Ed.), *Sage Handbook of Curriculum and Instruction*. Thousand Oaks, CA: Sage.

Craig, C. J., You, J., & Oh, S. (2013). Collaborative curriculum making in the physical education vein: a narrative inquiry of space, activity and relationship. *Journal of Curriculum Studies, 45*, 169–197.

Craig, C. (2018). *Teacher induction: A curriculum of life? In D. McDonald (Ed.). Secondary teacher induction in urban America*. Charlotte, NC: Information Age Publishing.

Craig, et al. (2018). The narrative nature of embodied knowledge: A cross-study analysis of teaching, learning and living. *Teaching and Teacher Education, 71,* 329–340. Impact Factor: 2.473.

Deng, Z. (2011). Confucianism, Modernization and Chinese Pedagogy: An Introduction. *Journal of Curriculum Studies, 43*(5), 561–568.

Ding, J., & Cheng, H. (2017). China's Proposition to Build a Community of Shared Future for Mankind and the Middle East Governance. *Asian Journal of Middle Eastern and Islamic Studies, 11*(4), 1–14.

Ding, G., & Zhou, Y. (2006). Quanqiuhua Shiye yu Zhongguo Jiaoyu Yanjiu 全球化视野与中国教育研究 (Global Vision and Chinese Education Research). *Chinese Education: Research and Reviews, 10*(1), 1–37.

Fei, X. (2013). *Xiangtu Zhongguo 乡土中国 (Rural China)*. Shanghai: Shanghai People's Press.

Giddons, A. (2001). Shikong de Shijie: Quanqiuhua Ruhe Chongsu Women de Shenghuo 失控的世界: 全球化如何重塑我们的生活 (Run Away World: How Globalization Is Reshaping Our Lives) (H. Zhou, Trans.). Nanchang: Jiangxi People Press.

Guo Qingfan (Qing Dynasty). (1961). Zhunagzi Jishi莊子集釋 (Zhuangzi Collected Explanations); Collated by Wang Xiaoyu—Beijing: Zhonghua Book Company, p. 712.

Hao, F. (1993). Zhongguo Lunli de Gainian Xitong yu Wenhua Yuanli 中国伦理的概念系统与文化原理 (The Conceptual System and Cultural Principles of Chinese Ethics). *Journal of Fudan University (Social Science Edition)*, (3), 56.

Hayhoe, R. (2014). Hopes for Confucian Pedagogy in China? *Journal of Curriculum Studies, 46*(3), 313–319.

He Ning. (1998). Huianaizi Jishi淮南子集釋 (Huainanzi Collected Explanations), Beijing: Zhonghua Book Company. Reprinted in May 2011, p. 244.

Hou, H. (2001). Ershi Shiji Shangbanye Jiaoyuxue zai Zhongguo Yinjin de Huigu yu Fansi 20世纪上半叶教育学在中国引进的回顾与反思 (Retrospect and Reflection of the Introduction of Pedagogy in China in the First Half of the 20th Century). *Education Research, 12,* 64–69.

Jiang, Z. (2006). *Jiang Zemin Wenxuan 江泽民文选 (Selected Works of Jiang Zemin)*. Beijing: People Press.

Lei, Y. (1984). Shilun Woguo Jiaoyuxue de Fazhan 试论我国教育学的发展 (On the Development of Pedagogy in China). *Journal of East China Normal University (Educational Science Edition)*, (2), 39–47.

Liang, Y. (2004). Li Xiangfeng. Guanzi Jiaozhu管子校注 (Guanzi Annotation). Compiled by—Beijing: Zhonghua Book Company, p. 945.

Liang, S. (2005). *Zhongguo Wenhua Yaoyi 中国文化要义 (The Essence of Chinese Culture)*. Shanghai: Shanghai Century Publishing Group.

Liu, Y. (2011). Pedagogic Discourse and Transformation: A Selective Tradition. *Journal of Curriculum Studies, 43*(5), 599–606.

Li, X. (2004a). Quanqiuhua Beijing Xia Zhongguo Jiaiyuxue Mingyun zhi Fenxi 全球化背景下中国教育学命运之分析 (An Analysis of the Fate of Chinese Pedagogy in the Context of Globalization). *Contemporary Educational Science*, (18), 3–5.

Li, Z. (2004b). Lun Zhongguo Jiaoyuxue Xuepai Chuangsheng de Yiyi jiqi Jiben Lujing 论中国教育学学派创生的意义及其基本路径 (On the Significance and Basic Path of Chinese Pedagogy School). *Education Research* (1), 6–8.

Li, Z. (2018). Lishi Xiangsheng: Shifou Keneng, Ruhe Keneng? 理实相生:是否可能,如何可能? (Coexistence with Reality: Is It Possible, How is It Possible?). *School Administration, (1)*, 8–10.

Lu, et al. (2007). Lun Zhongguo Jiaoyuxue de Goujia—JianPing 20 Shiji Zhongguo Jiaoyuxue de Queshi 论中国教育学的构建———兼评 20 世纪中国教育学的缺失 (On the Construction of Chinese Pedagogy—with a Comment on the Deficiency of Chinese Pedagogy in the 20th Century). *Journal of Educational Science of Hunan Normal University*, (3), 11–15.

Meiyao, W. U. (2009). The transformation of the educational semantic within a changing society: a study of the westernization of modern chinese education. *Journal of Historical Sociology*, 22(4), 528–552.

Mencius. (2004). Gong Sun Chou II. In C. Wang (Ed.), *Mencius*. Taiyuan: Shanxi Ancient Books Publishing House.

Qu, B. (1998). Zhongguo Jiaoyuxue 中国教育学 (Chinese Education). *Education Research, 12*, 3–12.

Qu, B. (1999). Zhongguo Jiaoyuxue 中国教育学 (Chinese Education). *Education Research, 1*, 8–16.

Schwab, J. J. (1954/1978). Eros and Education: A Discussion of One Aspect of Discussion. In I. Westbury & N. Wilkof (Eds.), *Science, Curriculum and Liberal Education: Selected Essays*. Chicago, IL: University of Chicago Press.

Schwab, J. J. (1969). The Practical: A Language for Curriculum. *School Review, 78*(1), 1–23.

Schwab, J. J. (1973). The Practical 3: Translation into Curriculum. *School Review, 79*, 501–522.

Su Yu. (1992). *Chongqiu Fanlu Yizheng* 春秋繁露義證 (*Chunqiu Fanlu Yizheng*); Collated by Zhongzhe—Beijing: Zhonghua Book Company. Reprinted in February 2011, p. 444.

Tan, S. H. (2008). Modernising Confucianism and New Confucianism. In K. Louie (Ed.), *The Cambridge Companion to Modern Chinese Culture* (pp. 135–154). Cambridge, UK: Cambridge University Press.

Tan, S. H. (2011). Why Study Chinese Classics and How to Go About It. *Journal of Curriculum Studies, 43*(5), 623–630.

Tian et al. (2010). lun Zhongguo Jiaoyuxue Zouxiang Shijie 论中国教育学走向世界 (On the development of Chinese Pedagogy to the World). *Journal of Educational Science of Human Normal University*, (1), 34–37, 54.

Wang Xianqian (Qing Dynasty). (1988). *Xunai Jijie 荀子集解 (Xunzi Collected Explanations)*. Collated by Shen Xiaohuan & Wang Xingxian. Beijing: Zhonghua Book Company, p. 309.

Wu, Z. (2011). Interpretation, Autonomy, and Transformation: Chinese Pedagogic Discourse in a Cross-Cultural Perspective. *Journal of Curriculum Studies, 43*(5), 569–590.

Xi. (2014a). Zai Lianheguo Jiaokewen Zuzhi Zongbu de Yanjiang 在联合国教科文组织总部的演讲 (March 28). Speech at UNESCO Headquarters. People's Daily, p. 3.

Xi. (2014b). Zai Zhongguo Guoji Youhao Dahui ji Zhongguo Renmin Duiwai Youhao Xiehui Chengli 60 Zhounian Jinian Huodong shang de Jianghua 在中国国际友好大会暨中国人 民对外友好协会成立 60 周年纪念活动上的讲话 (May 15). Speech at the China International Friendship Conference and the 60th Anniversary of the Chinese People's Association for Friendship with Foreign Countries. People's Daily.

Xi. (2017). Juesheng Quanmian Jiancheng Xiaokang Shehui, Duoqu Shidai Zhongguo Tese Shehuizhuyi Weida Shengli: Zai Zhongguo Gongchandang Di Shijiuci Quanguo Daibiao Dahui shang de Baogao 决胜全面建成小康社会 夺取时代中国特色社会主义伟大胜利—在中国共产党第十九次全国代表大会上的报告 (2017, October 28). Decisive Victory, Building a Well-Off Society in An All-Round Way, and Winning the Great Victory of Socialism with Chinese Characteristics in the Times—Report at the 19th National Congress of the Communist Party. *People's Daily*.

Xi, J. (2017, October 18). Win the Battle and Build a Well-off Society in an All-round Way and Win the Great Victory of Socialism with Chinese Characteristics in the New Era–Report at the Nineteenth National Congress of the Communist Party of China.

Xu, S. (2006). *In Search of Home on Landscapes in Transition: Narratives of Newcomer Families' Cross-Cultural Schooling Experience*. Toronto: University of Toronto.

Xu, S. (2011). Bridging the East and West dichotomy: Harmonizing Eastern learning with Western knowledge. In J. Ryan (Ed.), *Understanding China's Education Reform: Creating Cross-Cultural Knowledge, Pedagogies and Dialogue* (pp. 224–242). London: Routledge.

Xu, S., & Connelly, F. M. (2010). Narrative Inquiry for School-Based Research. *Narrative Inquiry, 20*, 349–370. https://doi.org/10.1075/ni.20.2.06xu.

Xu, et al. (2007). Immigrants Students' Experience of Schooling: A Narrative Inquiry Theoretical Framework. *Journal of Curriculum Studies, 39*(4), 399–422.

Yang, G. (2001). Zuowei Zhexue Fanchou de 'He': 'He' de Zhexue Chanshi 作为哲学范畴的 '和'—'和' 的哲学阐释 (A Philosophical Interpretation of 'And' as A Philosophical Category). *History of Chinese Philosophy*, (2), 24.

Yang, J., & Frick, W. (2009). Will the Leadership of Chinese Education Follow the Footsteps of American Education: A Brief Historical and Socio-political Analysis. *Journal of Thought, 44*(3&4), 23–48.

Ye, L. (2002). Chongjian Ketang Jiaoxue Guocheng Guan: "Xinjichu Jiaoyu" Ketang Jiaoxue Gaige De Lilun Yu Shijian Tanjiu Zhi Er 重建课堂教学过程观—"新基础教育"课堂教学改革的理论与实践探究之二 (Reconstruct the view of classroom teaching process: The second research on theory and practice of classroom teaching reform of "New Basic Education"). *Educational Research, 10*, 24–30.

Ye, L. (2004). Zhongguo Jiaoyuxue Fazhan Shiji Wenti de Shenshi 中国教育学发展世纪问题的审视 (Examination of the Century Problems of Chinese Pedagogy Development). *Education Research, 7*, 5–19.

Ye, L., Luo, W., & Pang, Q. (2019). Zhongguo Wenhua Chuantong Yu Jiaoyuxue Zhongguo Huayu Tixi De Jianshe 中国文化传统与教育学中国话语体系的建设—叶澜教授专访 (Chinese Cultural Tradition and the Construction of Chinese Discourse System in Educology: An Interview with Professor Ye Lan). *Journal of Soochow University* (Educational Science Edition) (3), https://doi.org/10.19563/j.cnki.sdjk.2019.03.007.

Yi, L., & Yang, C. (2003). Lun Zhongguo Jiaoyuxue Xuepai de Chuangsheng 论中国教育学学派的创生 (On the Creation of Chinese Pedagogy School). *Educational Research*, (4), 37–42

Zhang, T. (2008). Portraits of Influential Chinese Educators by Ruth Hayho. *International Review of Education, 54*(2), 267–268.

Zhou, Z. (1997). Lun 'Zhongguo Jiaoyuxue Xianxiang' 论 '中国教育学现象' (On 'Chinese Pedagogy Phenomenon'). *Journal of Inner Mongolia Normal University (Philosophy and Social Sciences Edition)*, (4), 1–5.

CHAPTER 3

Dewey Meets Confucius

Shan Qi

3.1 INTRODUCTION

It is a good time to discuss the education of China and America. On the one hand, the process of globalization has closely linked countries around the world, and the trend of globalization in the field of education has become more apparent. Among them, China and the United States have had a 100-year history of collision in educational exchanges, and there have been two major educational and cultural exchanges in this century. One was the cultural impact and education reform brought on by John Dewey's coming to China between 1919 and 1921. The other was the Sino-American educational collision from the beginning of the twenty-first century to the present. The second was the launch by Professor Connelly, the third-generation inheritor of the Dewey School, and Professor Ye Lan, the founder of China's "Life-Practice" Educology, of a decade-long exploration of cross-cultural mutual learning in the field of basic education. They established the Shanghai-Toronto Sister School model and used field-based, non-pre set, long-term field observation and

---

S. Qi (✉)
Department of Education, Taiyuan Normal University, Jinzhong, Shanxi, China

© The Author(s), under exclusive license to Springer Nature
Switzerland AG 2021
Y. Bu (ed.), *Narrative Inquiry into Reciprocal Learning Between
Canada-China Sister Schools*, Intercultural Reciprocal Learning in
Chinese and Western Education,
https://doi.org/10.1007/978-3-030-61085-2_3

narrative to found "a vision of bridging the East and West dichotomy by harmonizing Eastern learning with Western knowledge". It is precisely because of the Partnership Grant Project (PGP) that the Shanghai-Toronto sister school could be built, and the two educologies of China and America could be exchanged and collide in a profound and full-scale manner. As a result, in-depth interaction and cooperation between China and America have been realized.

So before we present the Shanghai-Toronto Sister School model, it is necessary for us to briefly explain the spiritual connotation of Chinese and American culture and the two educologies from a historical, cultural and comparative perspective. Using this approach, we can explore the deep background and reasons why the Shanghai-Toronto Sister School model was developed.

The main questions addressed in this chapter are as follows:

1. Why did Dewey come to China to lecture? (What was Dewey's main assessment of Chinese education when he came to China? What influence did these suggestions have on later education theory and practice in China? In contemporary China, how do we understand Dewey's significance to China's education reform?)
2. Why did Connelly collaborate with China? (What did Connelly see and hear when he came to China? Why did he develop an interest in the study of intercultural reciprocal learning between China and Canada?)
3. What are the similarities and differences between Dewey's and Connelly's dialogues on Chinese education? How do we interpret the significance and value of cross-cultural communication from the respective cultures and eras?

3.2   Dewey's First Encounter with Chinese Education at the Beginning of the Twentieth Century

On the afternoon of April 30, 1919, the renowned American philosopher and educator John Dewey arrived in China to give lectures at the invitation of Chinese scholars Shi Hu, Xingzhi Tao and Menglin Jiang, who took advantage of Dewey's lecturing in Japan at the time. Dewey originally planned to give a speech or two while staying in China for a couple of days and becoming acquainted with Chinese culture. However, it turned out that he spent a total of two years, two months and twelve days in China, delivering more than 200 speeches in Beijing, Hebei, Shanxi, Shandong, Jiangsu, Shanghai, Jiangxi, Hubei, Hunan, Zhejiang, Fujian and Guangdong provinces (Kang 2014; Zhang 2001; Waks 2019), benefiting hundreds of thousands of scholars, students and citizens, forming a nationwide carnival of educational ideas, which had an extensive and far-reaching social impact. This widespread dissemination of Dewey's educational ideas had a sweeping social and academic impact. This was when China was fighting the tyranny of feudalism and traditional culture and abandoning classical Chinese writing. Dewey's popularity in China symbolized the tendency and determination of China to learn from the West and to take a Western path. From the perspective of an educationalist, he diagnosed the educational situation in China at that time, pointed out the future direction of Chinese education, and influenced the research and development of Chinese educational theory and practice (Chen 2006; Zhixin 2019; Ying Wang 2007; Zhang 2019; Waks 2019). Bertrand Russell called John Dewey the "Confucius of the West".

3.2.1 Dewey to China: A Basic Judgment on Chinese Education

As an educational philosopher, Dewey was influenced by the May Fourth Movement and its spirit when he came to China. In his opinion, the May Fourth Movement was accidental, emotional and negative. He felt that such student movements could enhance people's awareness and consciousness, and lead them to realize that "education bears social responsibility and plays a social role" (pp. 125–126), eventually transforming China (Kang 2014). This was an important period of national transformation for China. The biggest problem lay not in the ruling establishment, but in the enlightenment of the people (Mao 2008; Xu 2012). This required orientations toward science, technology and democracy, much of which can be acquired through education. Therefore, he devoted himself to spreading his ideas on education in his speeches to more people to help China save itself as a nation. Q. Kang observed: "The only remedy [was] to open the door to instill the splendid Western civilization, so that the new input of [a] true civilization can resist the previous harm and danger of the past and form a new class of talents" (Kang 2014, p. 37).

In his speech, Dewey spoke a great deal about his understanding of Chinese traditional education, such as Chinese students focusing more on memorization than reasoning, more on understanding what happened in the past rather than thinking about the future. Most of what teachers transmitted to students was Confucian classics and ideas, without paying attention to the development of human creativity, renewal and critical ability, separating intellectual training from moral cultivation and separating learning from doing. Chinese education also did not attach much importance to the understanding of children's instincts. Moreover, people emphasized the concept of "knowledge is not difficult, but practice is". Furthermore, the theories in Chinese self-cultivation books were too abstract to arouse students' desire for learning (Kang 2014). All of the above factors, Dewey believed, were closely related to the exam-oriented education in China, because exams encourage competition and students' passive development, while depriving students of their self-esteem. Still Dewey maintained a non-Eurocentric view. He did not believe that China's social and education reform should imitate the Western way, but that the future of Chinese society and education would be generated gradually from within. For example, Dewey believed that the real problem in China at that time was that of democracy, but he understood that China's democracy must come from its own cultural roots, not from foreign influence (Ying Wang 2007). Of course, Dewey was not optimistic about whether China could produce gradual changes from within, because he thought that China had a large population and emphasized group harmony, which would make it very easy to develop Chinese people's herd mentality. Therefore, the Chinese sense of autonomy is always weak, and it is not easy to emerge from the group. As Dewey said in *What Holds China Back?*:

> There is no doubt that many of the psychological characteristics of the Chinese people are the product of an unusually high and prolonged population density. Psychologists have discovered, or perhaps invented, a kind of 'mass psychology' to explain the conformity of people who behave like a mob at a lynching ground". They have not asked about the psychological impact of maintaining close contact with a large number of people and continuing to live in the crowd. (Dewey 1920, p. 373)

In Dewey's view, if China wanted to embark on the road of science and democracy, it should use external means such as policy and education to guarantee transformation on the basis of its original cultural roots. After observing the state of grassroots organizations in rural China, for example, he believed that it was easy to turn the emperor's policy of protecting the people into a democratic one based on the fact that China had no tradition of individualism in ancient times. Education can follow the path of universal education, that is, "to spread scientific knowledge in a living way so that most people can enjoy the benefits of science in the future" (Kang 2014, p. 84), so as to cultivate the ability of citizens to have equal opportunities in the future (Shen 2001; Yuan 2001). On the whole, there are two paths for China to follow. One of them is to develop a few people who have specialized scientific knowledge while the public knows nothing about science; the other is to arrange for everything 50 years later (Kang 2014). The second path was taken by Europe and the United States 100 years ago, and China, he advised, should take that path as soon as possible. In Dewey's view, this path would use education to achieve democratic and equal social transformation.

3.2.2   China to Dewey: The Reaction of China to Dewey in the Modern Age

Dewey left China on July 21, 1921. In the following 100 years, Dewey's educational thoughts have gone through periods of acceptance and periods of rejection in China's social reform. This section focuses on the discussion of China's influence on Dewey during his visit from two different dimensions. The first dimension briefly describes the general situation and stage of the spread of Dewey's educational thought in China chronologically. The second dimension focuses on landmark events and characters in order to depict the influence of Dewey's educational thought on Chinese academic circles and educational practices.

3.2.2.1   The Dissemination Stage of Dewey's Educational Thought in China

Dewey's departure from China did not mean the fading of the democratic and scientific spirit that he represented. To a greater extent, it meant that the public and the academic community were given more time to digest, understand and practice the connotations of Dewey's educational spirit. The spread of Dewey's educational thought in China can be roughly divided into three stages.

The first stage (1921–1949) was the peak period. During Dewey's visit to China and in the following two decades, a "Dewey rush" was set off in China's education circle. Dewey directly promoted the "new education reform movement" in the Republic of China and founded the *New Education* journal. Dewey's five lectures and major works were published, and his famous conceptualizations such as "education as life", "school as society" and "education is a constant reorganizing or reconstruction of experience" became popular. The most authoritative educational publications, *Education Journal, China Education Sector* and *New Education* have published Dewey's and his colleagues' papers on education (Wu 2001; Yuan 2001; Zhang 2019). Dewey's students Jiang Menglin, Tao Xingzhi, Hu Shi, Guo Bingwen and Chen Heqin, among others, all became the principals and heads of education departments of famous colleges and universities at that time. Based on the local educational tradition of China, they integrated Dewey's ideas, and consciously or unconsciously left a "Dewey mark" on theoretical explorations and educational practices (Chen 2006; Zhixin 2019; Zhang 1996). In addition, it was under the influence of Deweyan thought that the Ministry of Education specially convened the National School System Conference in 1922, which resulted in the establishment of the "Renxu School System", marking a milestone in China's modern education (Wu 2001; Zhang 1996, 2019).

The second stage (1949–1978) was the period of criticism and silence. After the founding of the People's Republic of China, China's educational theory and practice followed in the footsteps of the Soviet Union for a long time, and Dewey's "education without purpose" and "child-centered" and "interest-based" ideas were rejected and criticized (Waks 2019; Zhixin 2019). Cao Fu, Li Bingde and Chen Heqin disapproved of Dewey's liberalism and capitalist position, and Dewey's pedagogy was deemed to be that of capitalism, which supported the capitalist system and was ideologically opposed to socialism.

The third stage (1978–present) is the period of re-examination. After the implementation of the reform and opening policy in China, the academic and educational circles began to re-examine and reflect on Western academic thought, and Dewey's pragmatism and educational philosophy were carefully evaluated. Representatives such as Zhao Xianglin, Xia Zhilian, and Fu Tongxian believed that the study and evaluation of Dewey's educational thought should be based on an open, frank and realistic attitude (Zhixin 2019), without ignoring its significant contribution or exaggerating its theoretical shortcomings. Dewey's educational thought has gradually recovered its status and reputation in China, and *Democracy and Education* has been included in the required reading list in normal colleges and universities, and numerous studies on Dewey's educational thought have also emerged (Wu 2001; Zhang 1996). Some universities have also held special academic forums and commemorative activities for Dewey (Ding 2019; Ding and Zhou 2019; Zhixin 2019; Association 2019), and Dewey indirectly influenced the curriculum reform of Shanghai's basic education in 1988 and the New curriculum reform of basic education in 2001 (Zhang 2019).

Since the beginning of the twenty-first century, Chinese education has entered a stage of deepening reform. The core tasks of all Chinese educational scholars are about how to make good use of Western academic ideas, to carry forward the advantages of Chinese traditional education, and to cultivate "new people" with an international vision, reflective thinking, critical thinking and innovative thinking with roots in China's local educational practice. Dewey's ideas of "interest orientation", "being children-centered", "reflective thinking" and "educational democracy" have become important theoretical constructs of education reform in China today, and are also important resources for China to move toward "Oriental Enlightenment" and "Oriental Educational Democracy".

3.2.2.2 *The Specific Responses from the Theoretical and Practical Circles of Chinese Pedagogy*

Dewey's influence on Chinese education has been profound and lasting, and this is not only reflected in the respect evident in academic circles and educational practice circles during his stay in China. It is also apparent in follow-up studies on Dewey's theory and the series of reforms conducted in the field of practice after Dewey's departure from China.

A. *Chinese Researchers' Reactions*

During Dewey's stay in China, he gave many speeches, the five most important being on the following topics: social philosophy and political philosophy, philosophy of education, schools of thought, three modern philosophers, and a brief introduction to ethics. The five speeches spread widely, and people ranging from the Chief of the Ministry of Education to local primary and secondary school teachers have attained a smattering of his ideas. In fact, before Dewey came to China, Cai Yuanpei, Huang Yanpei, Hu Shi and Tao Xingzhi had already circulated his thoughts in many places, best represented by Hu Shi's "Experimentalism". In this paper, Hu Shi not only discusses the origin of "pragmatism", but also explains in detail the relationship between experimentalism and scientific development, which led to the publication *Scientific Experimental Attitude* (Shen 2001). In addition, he illuminated the influence of experimentalism on contemporary philosophy: the emergence of historical attitude. He summarized experimentalism as "the application of scientific methods in philosophy" (Shen 2001, p. 310). Tao Xingzhi, as a student of Dewey, also introduced Dewey's educational thought. He believed that the development of Western science and pedagogy depended on experiment. He observed: "In the past two hundred years, what progress in the educational circle has not been the result of experiments?" and that "Dewey's philosophy of integrated education is also experimental" (Yuan 2001, p. 173). He also noted that Dewey's educational thought can be summarized as "using populism as educational purpose, experimentalism as teaching method" (Yuan 2001, p. 173). In this way, he criticized the old education as relying on work of nature, following old methods, being capricious, following other countries' example, and trying occasionally, which led to little progress. He held that only by removing the old education and giving priority to experimentation can progress be made (Zhang 2001).

Prior to Dewey's visit to China there had been unprecedented research on Dewey's thought in the educational theoretical circles, represented by Jiang Menglin, Tao Xingzhi, Liu Jingshu and Cai Yuanpei, who had translated, explained and summarized Dewey's educational thought, explaining his profound theories in simple terms. Jiang Menglin introduced Dewey's ethics of thought and moral education (which is caused by ethics). He believed that what Dewey referred to as moral "is one, not two, and cannot be divided into two, which is only a matter of sequence of procedures. Mind is the beginning; the result is the end. Mind is psychological, the result is social. The psychological is the method, the society is the substance" (Shen 2001, p. 318). He believed that moral education in schools should promote three things well, social knowledge, social ability, social interest, so as to develop children with ability, judgment and emotional character (Shen 2001). Cai Yuanpei compared Dewey's ideas with Confucius' philosophy and educational thought, and considered that Confucius' concepts of "teaching all without class" and "teaching students according to their aptitude" were consistent with Dewey's civilian educational thoughts, while Confucius also attached equal importance to both experience and thought, and also agreed with the significance of experiment. In these ways, it is possible to realize the integration of Eastern and Western civilizations (Shen 2001).

After Dewey's departure from China, the "Dewey rush" did not subside. Over several years, Zhonghua Book Company and the Commercial Press translated and published a large number of Dewey's works on education in their original language, such as *The School And Society, Dewey's Philosophy of Education, Democracy and Education* and *Schools of Tomorrow*. Moreover, Dewey's educational theory also entered the normal universities and the Education Departments of comprehensive universities, in addition to becoming textbooks and reference books.

With the reform and opening up in 1978, the Chinese educational theory circle also rediscovered the research on Dewey's educational thought, shifting from questioning and criticizing Dewey's educational thoughts to promoting them objectively and positively. The academic circle is no longer obsessed with judging Dewey by his political standpoint, but pays more attention to the positive factors in Dewey's educational thoughts, such as educational purpose, the five-step thinking method, learning by doing, experience education, democracy as a way of life, curriculum centering on children's interest, and teaching to children's interests and motivation. In addition, Dewey's thoughts are also "in line with China's current ideological publicity and development needs, such as a harmonious society, quality-oriented education, emphasis on hands-on work, and moral education" (Zhixin 2019, p. 11). This not only provides a more open and inclusive platform for the study of Dewey's thought, but also makes possible the integration of Eastern and Western educational thought.

It has been 100 years since Dewey came to China in May 1919, to which the Education community from home and abroad has shown strong concern and attached attention. Related research outcomes include monographs (Zhang and Liu 2019), special symposiums held by Peking University, Capital Normal University, the China Education Improvement Association and other academic institutions (Global Center of Columbia University; China Education Improvement Association), and special columns in periodicals (*Journal of East China Normal University, Education Academic Monthly*) that discuss Dewey's influence on Chinese education for a decade. Given that Dewey is still currently discussed in China, there is no doubt that he has had a profound influence on the Chinese education circle.

B. *Chinese Practitioners' Reactions*

Before Dewey came to China, most of his philosophy and pedagogical thought was introduced and discussed in academic circles and only a small number of principals in primary and middle schools made some changes in teaching methods. For example, the Design Teaching Method and the Dalton Plan were founded under the guidance of Dewey's educational thought, and can be roughly regarded as based on the influence of Dewey's educational thought on China's practice circle. The Design Teaching Method was promoted by the primary school attached to Nanjing Normal School. The school's principal, Yu Ziyi, made a great contribution by instituting it in practice and it then became popular in primary schools all over the country. The Dalton Plan also followed the basic spirit of Dewey's educational theory, emphasizing that education is the reorganization and transformation of experience. This teaching method was taken up by the Ministry of Public Schools of China, and educators such as Shu Xincheng contributed to the promotion of the Dalton Plan throughout the whole country. However, these two teaching methods were gradually abolished due to issues related to social environment, teachers, equipment and funding.

After Dewey came to China, his thoughts immediately affected educational decision-making and the practice circle. The influence of Dewey's thought on educational decision-making was embodied in the reform of a new school system in 1922. Some studies state that Dewey's educational theory was the soul of the reform, and affected its key links, namely the fifth conference in 1919 and the seventh conference in 1921 that influenced the standard and content of the new school system. The new school system adopts the American 6-3-3 system, reflecting the core spirit of Dewey's educational thought, such as adapting to the needs of social evolution, exerting the spirit of citizenship education, seeking the development of personality, focusing on life education, and making education easy to popularize (Yuan 2001).

The practice of Dewey's educational thought was mainly promoted and implemented by his students in China. As a student of Dewey, Guo Bingwen took the lead in promoting the curriculum reform movement at Nanjing Teachers' College. He adopted the subject selection system there and vigorously opened summer schools, thus communicating the links between universities, middle schools and primary schools, and also communicating those between universities and society. Jiang Menglin assisted Cai Yuanpei in carrying out the reform of professor governance and student autonomy at Peking University, valuing science education, experimentation and student practice, and attaching importance to the construction of educational disciplines, all of which reflected Dewey's educational thought. Chen Heqin initiated the organization of "Chinese Children's Education Society", put forward the idea of "living education", and promoted the spread of Dewey's educational thought in the field of early childhood education. Other important figures include Tao Xingzhi, Zheng Xiaocang and Zhang Boling.

In his five speeches, Dewey promoted his citizenship education ideology and emphasized that the establishment of a free and equal society requires the education of the general public to improve people's ability to develop and innovate, and to cultivate citizens with independent character and strong personality. Under his influence, in October 1919, Beijing Normal University set up the "Civilian Education Association". In the same month, the journal of "Civilian Education" was published. The China Education Improvement Society was founded in 1921. In June 1923, Tao Xingzhi and Yan Yangchu set up the Civil Education Promotion Association in Nanjing, the aim of which is "to eliminate illiteracy and to be a new citizen". Its noblest objective was to prepare people with the basic knowledge of a democratic country to shoulder the responsibilities of a republic. The objective of The General Association of Civilian Education embodies the basic spirit of Dewey's civilian educational thought, and its establishment strongly promoted the popularization of education. Founded by Tao Xingzhi, Xiaozhuang School, Shanghai Engineering Group and experiments in Ding County of Hebei Province made outstanding contributions to the promotion of civilian education. Tao believed that the task of democratic education "is to teach people to strive for democracy on the one hand, and to teach people to develop democracy on the other" (Tao 2008). The educational practice in Xiaozhuang School contributed to Tao Xingzhi's theory of life education: life is education, society is school, and teaching and doing are integrated (Qi 2019). From his theory of life education, the effects of Dewey's educational thought can be clearly seen.

After the reform and opening up in China, Dewey's educational theory was repositioned and evaluated, and related education reform was restarted. In 1988, Shanghai took the lead in response to a national call to overcome the exam-oriented education problems to meet the needs of quality education. The government established a reform policy with quality-oriented education as the core and personality development as the objective. This gave rise to a quality-oriented education model with balanced development of students, and society and disciplines, and the construction of a three-part curriculum composed of compulsory courses, optional courses and activity courses which facilitate each other (Zhang 2019). Although the reform was implemented against the background of quality-oriented education, Dewey's education and curriculum philosophy are embodied in both the educational model and the curriculum structure.

The "New Basic Education" reform that began in 1994 also shows the influence of Dewey's educational thought. "New Basic Education" (NBE) is carried out by Professor Ye Lan and her team against the social background of China's transformation from a traditional society to a modern one. The core of the reform centers around concepts such as "children's position" (儿童立场), attaching importance to children's existing experiences, interests and motivation in classroom teaching, and values the integration of resources such as subject knowledge and children's experience, so as to realize the two-way interaction and knowledge generation between teachers and children (Ye 2014; Bu and Liu 2017). These core views are highly consistent with Dewey's emphasis on children's experience, and education as the restructuring and transformation of experience.

It has been over a decade since Dewey came to China. What he saw and thought during his stay in China has become history, and the "Dewey rush" he brought has become a shining pearl in the history of China's education. Suppose, 100 years later, that Dewey came to China again to inspect Chinese education. What would he see and what would he think of? What has and hasn't changed compared with 100 years ago? These questions are exactly what we want to the answer. Of course, Dewey will never come to China again, but one of his scholarly descendants did. That person was Professor Michael Connelly, who we will discuss next.

3.3 Connelly Coming to China: Another Meeting with China's Education at the Beginning of the Twenty-First Century

Professor Connelly's interest in Chinese education has several origins. First, his cooperation with Chinese Colleges of Education contributed to his initial impression of Chinese education. Second, his enrolled Chinese students subsequently dispelled his fear of Chinese education. Third, his own reading deepened his understanding of Chinese education and also aroused his interest in Chinese education. Fourth, the development of the PGP project strengthened his understanding of Chinese education and knowledge of Chinese culture.

3.3.1 Connelly to China: Basic Judgement About Chinese Education

Michael Connelly is a third-generation Deweyan-influenced scholar and a prominent professor at the University of Toronto, one who advocates for educational narrative inquiry. Upon the invitation of Ruth Hayhoe, then Dean of the Hong Kong Institute of Education, Connelly presided over a doctoral program in the early 1980s for the instructors from the Hong Kong Institute of Education who studied at University of Toronto's Ontario Institute for Studies in Education. At that time, Connelly read many books on politics, economics and education about Hong Kong, China, in order to make clear the basic structure and educational implementation of education there. Over the next few years, he recruited some Chinese students, and took notice of China's Cultural Revolution and the Tiananmen Square Incident: "This reading led me to question, rethink and ultimately to force myself to become less of a moralizing Westerner and to become more genially interested in the unfolding China landscape" (Connelly 2010, p. 352). But that concern and enthusiasm faded as news stories passed. However, in 2006, Xu Shijing's doctoral thesis rekindled his enthusiasm for cross-cultural research between China and the West, and "culture" became his greatest concern. These experiences form his intricate network of relationships with narrative inquiry, Hong Kong, Chinese students and Chinese people. After 2006, Professor Connelly read *The Democracy of the Dead: Dewey, Confucius, and the Hope for Democracy in China*, which was based on Dewey and Confucius and pondered China and the West from a cultural narrative perspective. Inspired by the book, he wrote a letter to Professor Ye Lan, who was far away in Shanghai, expressing his concern about Chinese education. Ye quickly replied and invited him to visit the New Basic Education schools in China.

3.3.1.1 Connelly's Narrative Inquiry Encounters with Ye Lan's New Basic Education

In 2007, Professor Connelly and Professor Xu Shijing of the University of Windsor came to visit Professor Ye Lan, founder of "New Basic Education" (hereinafter referred to as NBE) of East China Normal University in

Shanghai. Professor Connelly was full of curiosity and appreciated the school life of Minzhu Primary School and the educational and teaching activities with Chinese characteristics. He was surprised that Chinese classroom teaching was not stagnant, which was quite contrary to what he expected. He found that Chinese classes were still large, with more than 40 students, but that the classrooms were orderly and lively. At the same time, he also saw the rich and colorful school life, pictures reflecting the children's daily life everywhere and dynamic class activities. What surprised him most, however, was that such a large-scale school could mobilize groups of children so effectively that when the bell rang during recess the children would line up in neat lines to do exercises or eye massage. In his view, "the school was exciting, open, and innovative, and we realized we had much to learn about primary education from the Chinese schools" (Xu and Connelly 2017, p. 139). In 2008, Professor Connelly invited Professor Ye Lan and the principals of the six experimental schools in Shanghai engaged in "New Basic Education" to Toronto for educational visits. The two sides established a friendly foundation of communication and were full of interest in each other's educational culture. At that stage, Professor Connelly mainly entered Chinese educational circles as an academic researcher involved in academic exchange.

The following year, Shanghai took part in the Programme for International Student Assessment (PISA) exams sponsored by the OECD and ranked first in the fields of reading and mathematics. For the first time the Chinese basic education reform was known by the world, attracting many education experts who were interested in studying basic education reform in China. It also triggered Professor Connelly's continuous attention to the system of education in Shanghai China. He believed that global education is necessary in the context of post-modern society, and cross-cultural comparative studies can help to explore and form the potential future of positive comparative education. Xu and Connelly asserted: "We believe we need to reach beyond the study of similarities and differences and explore life-filled school practices of people in different cultures coming together and learning from one another" (Xu and Connelly 2017, p. 136).

After this, Connelly and Xu came up with the idea of promoting education reform and exchange between China and Canada through sister school cooperation. From 2009 to 2016, eight sister schools were established in China and Canada. In 2013, with funding from the Canadian Research Council for the Humanities and Social Sciences, the

"Canada-China Reciprocal Learning in Teacher Education and School Education Partnership Grant Project" (Xu and Connelly 2013–2020) was jointly launched by the University of Windsor, University of Toronto, East China Normal University, Northeast Normal University, Southwest University and Beijing Foreign Studies University. The collaboration was "an attempt to reach beyond 'knowledge for the sake of knowledge' to the idea of 'knowledge for the sake of the social good'" (Xu and Connelly 2017, p. 143). East China Normal University, led by professors Ye Lan and Yuhua Bu, worked with Professor Connelly's team in Toronto to conduct cross-cultural research carried out in the form of reciprocal learning at sister schools, with an eye to exploring how sister schools in China and Canada can discover possible paths of cross-cultural communication "without leaving their hometown".

The two sides did not know each other well at first. Professor Connelly is known for his advocacy of educational narrative inquiry, a method that many Chinese scholars understood around 2008 as telling stories about education. Professor Ye Lan was confused, asking questions such as "Can telling so many stories help change school education?" and "What's the difference between telling one story and telling a hundred?" In addition, concerning the project's theme and mode of cooperation, Professor Ye Lan wanted to be clear from the start about the research goal, content and corresponding methods. However, Professor Connelly believed that this was an open cooperation project and the goals and content could not be determined from the start, as the future is full of unknowns and uncertainties. Instead, the goals, content and corresponding methods would be gradually formed in the process of the collaboration. The starting point of this encounter and cooperation was characterized by openness, and dialogue and communication were seen as the main forms of reciprocal learning and cooperation.

3.3.1.2 The Thoughts of Connelly on the Sister Schools' Cross-Cultural Mutual Learning

With the deepening of the reciprocal learning cooperation and frequent exchanges, narrative inquiry, as advocated by Professor Connelly, gradually became a very important research methodology and method in Chinese educational circles. Professor Ye Lan's NBE reform has also entered into the extension period from the achievement period and is now moving from China to the world. In May 2018, Professor Connelly was again invited to Shanghai, and once again he visited the NBE schools there. Compared with 10 years earlier, he thought China had changed a lot. The schools were more beautiful and bigger, and the schools and students were equipped with technology. However, the changes in the classroom were small. The class size in China is still large, and classroom management remained very strict, which is reflective of the country's national conditions and cultural traditions. We all live in a comfort zone of the reform, and it is hard to get out of it.

Connelly believes that the success of cross-cultural reciprocal relations depends first on a tolerant and open mind, so even when dealing with criticism, opposition, disapproval and so on we should look at the problem from a narrative perspective. He points out that Chinese education needs to work hard on its own narrative perspective, such as the decentralization of education, and the cultivation of students' initiative and creativity (Huang 2014). He agrees that China is not easily colonized or assimilated by the West, because its institutional and cultural roots are very deep. "It is precisely because of the deep roots of Chinese history and culture that total Westernization will not take place in China, and China will always maintain its independence" (Huang 2014, p. 57).

Because of this consideration, the two sides of cross-cultural reciprocity agreed that such long and continuous cross-cultural communication must be rooted in cultural and value resonance: Canada is deeply influenced by the concept of Dewey's democracy, and Chinese Confucian culture has exerted an influence until today. Dewey's concept of democracy resonates with the two basic values of Chinese Confucianism: one is to achieve a win-win situation in diversity; the other is to tolerate the "big community" (Ames 2018; Grange 1996, 2004; O'Dwyer 2015; Radcliffe 1989; Sim 2009). In addition, Dewey and Confucianism have similar concepts of practical knowledge, are similar in the classification of knowledge, that is, theory, practice and production, and both emphasize thinking and action (Waks 2019; Tan 2015). Experience, personal knowledge and practical knowledge have become the cultural basis for China and Canada to effect cooperation in education. Supported by this project (Craig et al. 2015; KHOO 2017), through frequent, continuous and in-depth sister school exchanges and interactions, a local-style cross-cultural sister school exchange model has finally been realized which is rooted in the educational practice of China and Canada and benefits the children of the general public (Bu et al. 2019).

3.3.2 China to Connelly: The Reaction of Chinese Education to Connelly

Professor Connelly, the founder and representative figure of narrative inquiry, was known by some researchers before his arrival in China. Professor Ding Gang of East China Normal University translated Connelly's masterpiece *Narrative Inquiry* in 2003 and published it in the fourth issue of *Global Education*, in which is presented a detailed introduction, the basis of knowledge and practice, and the value, significance and research process of narrative inquiry (Ding 2003). It emphasizes that while narrative inquiry is guided by the narrator's account, it is because "narrative researchers focus on the representativeness, causality and immediacy of experience to ensure the infectivity, authenticity, adequacy and rationality of the research text, thus ensuring the credibility and extensibility of its research methods" (Ding 2003). This notion has triggered a small-scale discussion in academia, but has not attracted enough attention there. In the following years, empirical research, especially quantitative research, has become an important growth point and hot spot of educational research. As a method of qualitative research, narrative inquiry is also a questioned method because of its authenticity, scientific nature and objectivity. This continued until 2014 (see Fig. 3.1).

3.3.2.1 The Understanding by Chinese Scholars of Connelly's Narrative Inquiry

According to most Chinese educators, individual practical knowledge is historical, cultural and contextual, and is a kind of personal philosophy in action (Xu and Connelly 2009; Kang 2016). It is

> a term designed to capture the idea of experience in a way that allows us to talk about teachers as knowledgeable and knowing persons. Personal practical knowledge is in the teacher's past experience, in the teacher's present mind and body, and in the future plans and actions. Personal practical knowledge is found in the teacher's practice. It is, for any one teacher, a particular way of reconstructing the past and the intentions of the future to deal with the exigencies of a present situation. (Connelly et al. 1997, p. 666)

When this kind of personal experience and personal practice refers to the teacher, it becomes the teacher's personal practical knowledge, which occurs in the teacher's daily life, and the teacher often expresses his own opinion through "image". As a result, in the early stages of narrative

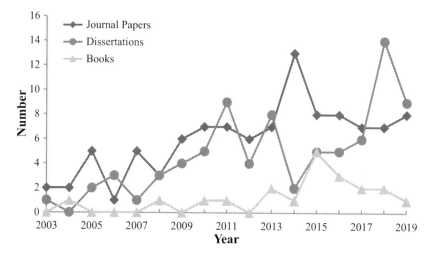

Fig. 3.1 Statistics on the number of educational journal papers, dissertations and books on the theme of "narrative inquiry" from 2003 to 2019. (The data in this table are from CNKI, Chao Xing and Wan Fang database, and the retrieval is carried out under the theme of "narrative inquiry")

inquiry research, scholars theoretically discussed the epistemological basis of narrative inquiry—the possibility and objectivity of individual practical knowledge.

After the discussion on the objectivity and authenticity of individual practical knowledge, the discussion on narrative exploration has shifted from the theory of knowledge to the narrative of education and the group of teachers. Through the narration of individual teachers' experience, the possibility of teachers' growth can be explored and discovered, which then becomes a cycle. Connelly believes that the acquisition of teachers' personal practical knowledge needs to be explored through narrative inquiry:

> The study of narrative, therefore, is the study of the ways humans experience the world. This general notion translates into the view that education is the construction and reconstruction of personal and social stories; teachers and learners are storytellers and characters in their own and other's stories … people by nature lead storied lives and tell stories of those lives, whereas narrative researchers describe such lives, collect and tell stories of them, and write narratives of experience.

"Narrative is a way of characterizing the phenomena of human experience and its study which is appropriate to many social science fields" (Connelly and Clandinin 1990, p. 2). Narrative inquiry is a means and a method for teachers to understand experience, and teachers gain understanding of the external world through continuous interaction between the narrative of experience and the external world; teachers acquire personal practical knowledge through narrative inquiry in the cycle of living, tellings, relivings and retellings to enrich their own story experience, and reflect on it, and finally present their own story experience (Xu and Connelly 2009; Ding 2003; Kang 2016).

3.3.2.2 The Future of Connelly's Narrative Inquiry in Chinese Academia

Professor Connelly's narrative inquiry has become a methodology from a method, and has caused a great disturbance in the field of educational research methods in contemporary China. At the beginning of the twenty-first century, few domestic scholars agreed with this method due to its lack of necessary evaluation criteria and reliability or validity. However, with the continuous popularization and advancement of empirical research methods in recent years, narrative inquiry as a qualitative research method has been gradually accepted, and there have been a number of doctoral papers based on narrative inquiry, which are mainly found in East China Normal University, Capital Normal University, Shandong Normal University and Guangxi Normal University, among others. Kang Xiaowei points out that narrative inquiry has changed people's judgment of the nature of knowledge in the past and regards knowledge as the existence contained in the human brain, body and practice, thus providing a new path for teachers' personal practical knowledge expression and knowledge acquisition (Kang 2016). At present, Chinese scholars' understanding of narrative inquiry is becoming more and more profound (Zhu and Chen 2008; Peng 2009). Narrative inquiry itself is also constantly supplemented and perfected. In sum, more and more Chinese scholars have begun to accept or have accepted narrative inquiry as a qualitative research method or methodology, and use it to explore pedagogical problems or phenomena.

3.4 Discussion and Conclusion

3.4.1 A Century of Chinese Education: What Has Changed and What Remains Unchanged

One hundred years ago, when surveying Chinese education, Dewey believed that Chinese education did not pay attention to the desires of children or the establishment of physical education courses, or the cultivation of independent, autonomous and democratic citizens, but attached importance to book knowledge, and the authority of teachers. Dewey's criticism of Chinese education was not unreasonable. Then, after the reform and opening up in 1978, Chinese education underwent tremendous and profound changes. After 100 years, if Dewey came to China today, what attitude would he hold toward the current social life and education in China?

3.4.1.1 What Has Changed?

A. China's Social Background Has Changed

One hundred years ago, when China was beset by internal troubles and foreign aggression, intellectuals were disappointed with the Bei Yang Government, shifting from studying devices to studying institutions and finally to studying ideas. Science and democracy became the symbol of this new cultural movement. The educational circle saw the shortcomings of the Japanese and German pedagogies, so it was eager to seek a new education reform method. Tao Xingzhi, Hu Shi and Jiang Menglin came back after studying in the United States, and exerted a certain cultural influence on China. Dewey's visit to China was a symbol of science and democracy (Waks 2019).

One hundred years later, China's policy of reform and opening up has made steady progress, and the overall transformation of society has entered a stage of deepening reform. An educational theory and practice rooted in the soil of China with a global view will be developed by China opening to the West and the world, showing the uniqueness and confidence of Chinese culture in comparison. Educational circles also welcome visitors from all over the world with an open and confident attitude to promote academic exchanges and symbiosis. As the creator of narrative inquiry, Professor Connelly's coming to China was warmly welcomed by those in academia and in the schools.

B. *The Attitude of Chinese Educational Academia Toward Western Educational Theories Has Changed*

The New Culture Movement set up the banner of "democracy" and "science", and Chinese intellectuals strongly desired and expected that these two banners could change conditions for the poor and weak in China. When Dewey came to China as a symbol of democracy and science, the social shock waves his visit triggered were inconceivable. Therefore, Dewey's whereabouts, investigations and even his speeches were of extraordinary significance. Dewey's speeches had a great impact on Chinese education at that time: he advocated for the acquisition of habits through social experience and the guidance of individuals in their actions. The intent was for people to meet their needs and achieve their goals with feelings and actions spontaneously generated by their thinking; his views on learning focused on doing and communicating (Waks 2019). This inspired Chinese scholars and set off vigorous educational change. Other influential educators included Cai Yuanpei, Chen Boling, Chen Heqin and primary and secondary school teachers who had knowledge about Dewey's educational ideas. Moreover, after Dewey came to China, the focus of study in China's education shifted from Japan to the United States as a whole (Hou 2008).

Today, although we are still learning and introducing Western educational theory, we are no longer as enthusiastic as Hu Shi and Chen Duxiu were 100 years ago. When Minzhu Primary School teachers first conducted face-to-face cooperative teaching with Bay Street School teachers in 2014, the teachers of Minzhu Primary School looked at the characteristics of both sides of education in a calm and confident manner, and seemed to see more similarities between them and hold a critical view regarding differences. Canadian teachers are general teachers teaching all subjects, and have all the time under their own control so that they are able to arrange time freely for students without a strict division of class hours, which is an important prerequisite for child-centered education. By way of comparison, China's education system is based on the division of teaching, with detailed curriculum arrangements and curriculum plans; every day teaching content is different, knowledge teaching being more systematic and detailed, and more efficient.

74 S. QI

C. *The Evaluation of China's Education Has Changed*

Dewey held a mixed view of both praise and blame concerning Chinese education. In his speeches he rarely spoke directly about Chinese education, but would use Chinese schools, Confucius and so forth to replace Chinese education when citing examples. We can infer his understanding of Chinese education to be as follows: Chinese education does not pay attention to the instinctive development of children, and "does not pay attention to sports" (Kang 2014, p. 18). Requiring children to be quiet means no activity is allowed. Further to this, Chinese textbooks are too abstract, buried in the books of ancient sages, and only talk about the present in terms of the past, "regarding history as a cycle, not as a process of progress" (Kang 2014, p. 33). The Chinese cannot adapt to the needs of society, and have created many useless experts. Nevertheless, Dewey agreed that there are some things that the West can learn from Chinese education, such as having children read aloud and recite in class in order to develop children's voices. He also agreed that Chinese education attaches importance to the concept of family and kinship, centers on the interests of family and clan, and has the spirit of unity and so on (Shen 2001; Yuan 2001).

For a long time, Western educators and philosophers have shown great interest in Chinese education, especially after Shanghai ranked first in the PISA test twice in a row. In the eyes of many Western researchers, excellent PISA scores indicate the great success of China's contemporary education and indicate that China's education reform is on the right path (Tan 2019; Jensen 2012; Niemann et al. 2017). Researchers believe that China's PISA results also show the bankruptcy and failure of "Market-based" education reform (Sahlberg 2013). Thus, to learn from the East and to learn from China prevail at the moment, and this is also one of the reasons for the success of RLP.

Connelly's assessment of Chinese education is scattered in progress reports on Sino-Canadian reciprocal learning programs in recent years, and in interviews during his visit in China. He argues that it is precisely because of the influence of Chinese students that he overcame his "fear" of China. When he first entered Minzhu Primary School in Shanghai, he was amazed by the vitality of the students and the harmonious campus culture. He was impressed by the learning efficiency and strict class management. After China achieved the world's highest PISA score in 2009, he began to believe that China's education reform was quite effective and worthy of learning by the West. After reading books on China, he believed that China's education reform had a better balance and coordination between Chinese and Western cultures, concepts and ideologies. He noted that "Lan Ye (2006) discusses Chinese cultural roots and strengths in education and sees the need for a balance between Chinese traditions and Western ideas" (Xu and Connelly 2009, p. 219). The reform is open-minded and rooted in the local culture.

3.4.1.2 What Has Remained Unchanged? What Has Continued?

A. The Attitude of Openness Has Not Changed

Since the British knocked on China's door through war, China has never been subjectively closed to the outside world. Over the past 180 years, many benevolent people have dedicated themselves to the revolution of anti-feudalism, anti-aggression, anti-imperialism and anti-capitalism in the motherland. "Behind will be beaten". Therefore, we must make progress and learn from the outside world. From the "artifact learning" of the Westernization Movement to the "institutional learning" of the Weixin Reform, and the "cultural learning" of the New Cultural Movement, 80 years of hard work tell us in China that only the enlightenment and emancipation of the people can truly achieve national independence and self-improvement. So the huge wave of Dewey's coming to China was not only because he was a world-renowned philosopher and educator, but also because he represented the "science" and "democracy" that people expected and needed at the time. Learning Dewey not only represents respect for the master, but also an open attitude toward the advancement of knowledge. The five well-known speeches delivered in those days were the proof.

In the twenty-first century, China is still open-minded and welcomes visitors from all over the world. Compatibility with multiple cultures is not only a diplomatic principle of China but also a spirit imprinted in the blood of the Chinese people. Hu Shi said that tolerance is more important than freedom. In the eyes of the Chinese, tolerance will lead to mutual respect, listening and diversity. Inclusion is reflected in the exchange of Chinese and foreign cultures. Because it is inclusive, it is open and willing to open up, showing us to the world and also respecting the cultural strategies and customs of other countries. We can see that China has been working hard to integrate into the world, from joining the WTO to participating in the PISA test, to introducing foreign educational theories, to establishing Confucius Institutes around the world, we are attempting to establish a reciprocal, respectful and equal open relationship of "you are in

76   S. QI

me, and I am in you". The establishment and development of the PGP project is also the result of the opening of both schools. Open curriculum philosophy, open classrooms, open teaching methods, open classroom organizational forms, open classroom evaluations and open campus culture could all show that this kind of opening up is not only the overall policy of the country, but also penetrates into the concept of every Chinese person and every educator.

B. *Adherence to the Excellent Traditional Chinese Culture Has Not Changed*

A hundred years ago, when the wave of Dewey's coming to China swept across all of East Asia, it aroused the Chinese people's enthusiasm for science and democracy. Some Chinese people expect to use Western political ideas and culture to transform Chinese society and Chinese people's thoughts, and thus the "new cultural movement" has emerged. They advocate vernacular writing and oppose feudal culture. However, they also did not discard the inheritance and praise of the excellent traditional Chinese culture. Chen Duxiu, Lu Xun, Hu Shi and Cai Yuanpei, the representatives of the New Cultural Movement, all exposed the ugliness of feudal culture and promoted the value of excellent traditional culture. Chen Duxiu states in *Advice to Youth* that the survival of the country lies in the spirit of youth, and in the youth who are "fresh and lively", "conscious" and who "struggle". "Consciousness", "struggle" and "saving people" (度人) are the core content of China's excellent traditional culture (Chen 1915, p. 1). Lu Xun continued to praise the Chinese for their hard work, thrift and simplicity while criticizing them for lacking knowledge and being indifferent (Lu 2008). Hu Shi continued to praise Western freedom while also tracing back to tolerance, self-control and introspection in Chinese culture (Hu 2014). Cai Yuanpei also advocated for democracy, equality and creativity, but he also believed that "since we recognize that the old civilization is also a civilization, it is not impossible to find in it a modern scientific spirit which does not conflict" (Shen 2001, p. 329). Therefore, he admits that Confucius' education is also a citizenship education, and his teaching methods are not limited to a single form.

In addition, there are also a group of scholars who use traditional Chinese culture as the foundation in this wave, and use Western thinking as a clue to interpret Chinese culture. The most representative of them are those that comprise "New Confucianism", such as Feng Youlan, Xiong

Shili, Liang Shuming, Mou Zongsan and Tang Junyi. They use "consciousness" (自觉) in traditional Chinese culture to explain "freedom" in the West, "Liangzhi" (良知) to explain "moral laws" and "rationality", and "presentation" (呈用) to explain "practice" (Qi 2019). In their view, all Western philosophical discourse can be explained through traditional Chinese discourse, and the study of Chinese traditional discourse on human morality and consciousness is much more thorough than the existing research in the West (Liang 1949, 2009). They are not ignorant of foreign culture and foreign philosophy, but they still feel that Chinese culture and philosophy are better and more accessible after studying foreign philosophy. To date, the Chinese still have not forgotten the Confucian spirit, and they retain the hard work and simplicity for which they have been known for thousands of years. Adherence to China's excellent traditional culture is not falling apart due to external forces. Instead, it has become more prominent and publicized in the torrent of the times.

As the following poem makes clear,

After going through all the hardships and dangers,
the return is still a teenager.

3.4.2 The Future of Reciprocal Learning Between China and Canada: Mutual Benefit and Symbiosis

A decade ago, Dewey's attitude toward Chinese education and the transformation of Chinese culture was not optimistic; he believed that "China is still a huge blank yet impenetrable wall" and that "the Chinese civilization is so thick and (self-centered) that there is no any show of foreign influence, even on the surface". "The unparalleled achievement of mankind in agriculture", he argued, explains much of the conservatism of the Chinese, who "learned to wait for the results of slow natural processes", and "because nature cannot be trampled on in their way of life", "it is easy to be passive and submissive with inaction". "[C]onservatism tends to make people stubbornly cling to the fixed habits of 'nature,' fearing and hating change" (MW 13:222–23). Admittedly, later generations, when studying the impact of Dewey in China, also believed that "the Orientals ... did not really grasp the significance of scientific development; they confused the results of science, that is, the development of technology, with science itself, and fail to cultivate a scientific attitude" (Clopton and Ou 1975, p. 238). Moreover, in traditional schools, the subject content "is

78   S. QI

still not assimilated and not really understood" (Waks 2019, p. 46). Then, is the conservatism of Chinese traditional culture unbreakable? Are we really unable to learn the spirit of science with an open mind?

The answer is perhaps no.

Education in contemporary China is integrated and inclusive, rooted in the soil of Chinese culture and oriented to the world. The school of "Life-Practice" pedagogy represented by Professor Ye Lan is a leader in the reform of basic education in China today. Ye Lan believes that an educational researcher should have the responsibility and mission to transform the world and discover the universal theory. She draws the value and significance of pedagogy from traditional Chinese philosophy, and holds that the unity of man and nature constitutes the basic spirit of Chinese education, and, taking life as an object, the unity of knowledge and action is the basic way to solve the problem of being an adult, establishing oneself and achieving success. The Chinese interpretation of the concept of education can be expressed as "cultivating consciousness of life by teaching about heaven, earth, and events" (Ye Lan 2018), which is also the highest educational purpose and objective of the school of "Life-Practice" Educology. Consciousness of life is a self-willed process of growing from being conscious to having self-consciousness and to being conscious of self-developmental goals after being born and living in the world, connoting the ability to exert individual initiative to control destiny, to realize the value of life as well as social value (Ye 2005, 2006, 2013, 2014; Ye and Li 2010/2011; Ye et al. 2019). Professor Ye Lan also attaches great importance to the absorption of Western educational thought. In her *Outlines of "Life-Practice" Educology: Recurrence and Breakthrough*, she comments on Western philosophers and educationalists from Bacon, Rousseau, Herbart and Dewey to Paul Lengrand and Moran. In her opinion, the reform of basic education in China must be rooted in Chinese traditional culture with an open mind, so as to develop the pedagogical theory and practice that can reveal the fragrance of Chinese soil (Ye 2014).

In educational practice, "New Basic Education" reform has gone through 25 years of ups and downs since 1994. It has been committed to changing the state of "text-only", "teacher-only" and "curricular-only" in China's education, aiming at cultivating self-motivated children. To "Give the class back to the students, let the class be full of growth", and to "give the classroom back to the students, let the classroom be full of vitality" are dual cries from the educational theoretical and practical circles. Today, we see students who learn spontaneously and autonomously in the classroom. In class activities, we can see the accumulation of students' daily experience and the cultivation of their individual character. We can also see that popular Western methods such as "micro-teaching", "MOOC teaching" and "project-based learning" are being imperceptibly integrated into China's educational and teaching activities.

After several education reforms, some schools in China have initially acquired the characteristics of modern schools: a school can develop and innovate independently without being driven by the government or the market. Teachers' teaching is open, allowing students to have time and space to study independently. Students are good at autonomous learning in the classroom, and so on. Dewey's expectation that "Chinese education needs to cultivate independent and lively children" has already begun to take shape.

Connelly partly agreed with Dewey's conservative views on traditional Chinese culture, but in the continuous cultural exchanges with China he has also seen the openness and inclusiveness of Chinese education, and the changes and results of Chinese education, which are gratifying. From the narrative point of view, he has also constantly stressed that education reform should go deep into the historical narrative of one's country and learn the local cultural tradition, which is the starting point of education reform, in which teachers are the core of the reform. They know and understand the ecological system and its history and can give full play to the advantages of being rooted in local cultural tradition. Therefore, respecting the cultural position of both sides is an important prerequisite for the sustainable development of reciprocal exchanges between China and Canada.

The purpose of cross-cultural communication is to learn and grow together. "Symbiosis" and "co-growth" have become core themes in the seven years of communication in the intercultural reciprocal learning program.

Professor Ye Lan asserts that:

> I have seen that the Chinese and Canadian teachers cooperate very well in the classroom. Why is their cooperation so good? The first is the language, they can communicate in English very well and smoothly; the second, they have two years of cooperation. From this reciprocity project, we found that first, especially young people must learn from each other. If we really want to do a good job in the China-Canada cooperation, our Chinese teachers must learn more English, and Canadian teachers must learn more or less Chinese. Language is the most important bridge of communication. The second is to cooperate continuously and in multiple ways.[1]

---

[1] This was one of Ye Lan's summary comments at the 2018 Reciprocal Learning Conference.

Professor Connelly believes that after six years of reciprocal exchanges, the original purpose of application has been achieved. "I have seen the efforts and work of Chinese schools, and also seen that sister schools have basically realized conscious communication, communication and learning, and the research assistants in colleges and universities have also faded out of communication support. I expect this cross-cultural communication and growth to continue.[2]

Michael Connelly added:

I have seen the rapid development of China's education. China has invested a lot in education reform and achieved remarkable results. However, no one can predict whether the results of China's education reform will last for a long time. It is expected to get some experience and reference to Canadian education reform in the wave of education reform in China. (Huang 2014, pp. 59–60)

Cross-cultural reciprocal learning is an equal dialogue between equal subjects and a subjective act of mutual respect. It has been proven that grassroots teachers have created a "new culture" in cross-cultural reciprocity, and have realized the state of "you being in me and me being in you" in educational concepts and methods. We believe that if today, Dewey were to meet Confucius, Confucius would probably say to him: "Along this century-old road, Chinese education has been marching toward the world, and the world is in us; but we also need to search for ourselves so as to become a part of the world". Because only when China contributes a universal educational concept to the world can it truly be "in the world".

References

Ames, R. T. (2018). China and A Transforming World Order: A Dialogue Between Confucianism and Dewey and Pragmatism. *Exploration and Free Views*, (2), 4–15.

Association, C. E. I. (2019). Zhongguo Jiaoyu yu Shehui Xiandaihua hai Xuyao Duwei ma? Duwei Laihua 100 Zhounian Jinian Huodong Dierci Xueshu Luntan 中国教育与社会现代化还需要杜威吗?—杜威来华100周年纪念活动第二次学术论坛 (Does Chinese Education and Social Modernization Still Need Dewey?—The Second Academic Forum on the 100th Anniversary of

---

[2] Professor Connelly's summary at the China-Canada International Conference on Reciprocal Learning in May 2018.

Dewey's Visit to China). https://www.sohu.com/a/303500247_108170?_f=index_chan25news_424. Retrieved March 25, 2019.

Bu, Y., & Liu, A. (2017). Lun 'Yushengmingzijue' de Duochong Neihan 论 '育生命自觉' 的多重内涵 (The Multiple Connotation of 'Cultivating Life Consciousness'). *Journal of Educational Studies, 13*(1), 10–15.

Bu, Y., Qi, S., Zhong, C., & Zhu, Y. (2019). Cong 'Li Tu' Dao 'Zai Di': Zhong Jia Zimei Xiao Kua Wenhua Huhui Xuexi de Shijian Tansuo 从 '离土' 到 '在地': 中加姊妹校跨文化互惠学习的实践探索 (From 'Grounding off' to 'Grounding On': The Practical Exploration on Cross-Cultural Reciprocal Learning in China-Canada Sister Schools). *Global Education, 48*(6), 62–73.

Chen, D. (1915). Jinggao Qingnian 敬告青年 (Told to the Young). *The Young Magazine, 1*(1), 1.

Chen, W. (2006). *Wusi Shiqi Duwei Laihua Jiangxue yu Zhongguo Zhishijie de Fanying* 五四时期杜威来华讲学与中国知识界的反应 (*Dewey's Lectures in China during the May 4th Movement and the Response of Chinese Intellectuals*). Shanghai: Fudan University.

Clopton, R. W., & Ou, T.-C. (1975). John Dewey, Lectures in China, 1919-1920. *Philosophy East and West, 25*(3), 365–369.

Connelly, F. M. (2010). An Ecosystem of Personal and Professional Reading, Writing, Researching and Professing. *International Journal of Leadership in Education, 13*(3), 349–356. https://doi.org/10.1080/13603121003739834.

Connelly, F. M., & Clandinin, D. J. (1990). Stories of Experience and Narrative Inquiry. [Article]. *Educational Researcher, 19*(5), 2–14. https://doi.org/10.3102/0013189X019005002.

Connelly, F. M., He, M. F., & Clandinin, D. J. (1997). Teachers' Personal Practical Knowledge on the Professional Knowledge Landscape. [Article]. *Teaching and Teacher Education, 13*(7), 665–674. https://doi.org/10.1016/S0742-051X(97)00014-0.

Craig, C. J., Zou, Y., & Poimbeauf, R. (2015). Journal Writing as a Way to Know Culture: Insights from a Travel Study Abroad Program. *Teachers and Teaching, 21*(4), 472–489.

Dewey, J. (1920). *What Holds China Back? The Middle Works of John Dewey Volume 14 1899–1924: Human Nature and Conduct 1922*. Carbondale: Southern Illinois University.

Ding, G. (2003). Narrative Inquire. *Global Education*, 6–10.

Ding, Y. (2019). Duwei Laihua 100 Zhounian Jinian Huodong zai Shoudu Shifan Daxue Juxing 杜威来华100周年纪念活动在首都师范大学举行 (Dewey's 100th Anniversary Event in China Held at Capital Normal University). *World Education Information*, (6), 1.

Ding, Y., & Zhou, X. (2019). Duwei Sixiang yiran shi Zhongguo Jiaoyu Xiandaihua de Zhongyao Ziyuan: Jinian Duwei Xiansheng Laihua 100 Zhounian Gaoduan Xueshu Huiyi Zaijing Juxing 杜威思想仍然是中国教育现代化的重要资源—纪

念杜威先生来华100周年高端学术会议在京举行 (Dewey's Thought Is Still an Important Resource for China's Education Modernization: A High-End Academic Conference to Commemorate Mr. Dewey's 100th Anniversary in China). [News]. *Journal of Hebei Normal University*, (3), 2.

Grange, J. (1996). The Disappearance of the Public Good: Confucius, Dewey, Rorty. *Philosophy East and West, 46*(3), 351–366.

Grange, J. (2004). *John Dewey, Confucius, and Global Philosophy*. Albany: State University of New York Press.

Hou, H. (2008). *Zhongguo Jiaoyuxue Fazhan Wenti Yanjiu: Yi 20 Shiji Shangbanye wei Zhongxin* 中国教育学发展问题研究:以20世纪上半叶为中心 *(Research on the Development of Chinese Pedagogy: Focusing on the First Half of the 20th Century)*. Taiyuan: Shanxi Education Press.

Hu, S. (2014). *Kuanrong Bi Ziyou Gengzhongyao* 宽容比自由更重要 *(Tolerance Is More Important Than Freedom)*. Beijing: China Business Federation Press.

Huang, J. (2014). Quanqiuhua Shiyexia Jiaoshi Jiaoyu de Xushi Tanjiu_Zhuanfang Jianada Maikeer Kangnali Jiaoshou 全球化视野下教师教育的叙事探究—专访加拿大迈克尔·康纳利教授 (Teacher Education in the Context of Globalization: A Narrative Perspective. An Interview with Dr. Michael Connelly, University of Toronto). *Journal of Teacher Education, 1*(1), 53–61.

Jensen, B. (2012). *Catching Up: Learning from the Best School Systems in East Asia*. Melbourne: Grattan Institute.

Kang, Q. (2014). *Duwei: Jiaoyu ji Shenghuo* 杜威:教育即生活 *Dewey: Education as Life*. Shanghai: Shanghai Cishu Press.

Kang, X. (2016). Lun Kangnali he Kelandining de Jiaoshi Geren Shijianxing Zhishi Sixiang 论康纳利和克兰迪宁的教师个人实践性知识思想 (Research on Teachers' Personal Practical Knowledge Thought of Connelly and Clandinin). *Studies in Foreign Education, 43*(5), 90–98.

KHOO, Y. (2017). Regenerating Narrative Inquiry for Teacher Growth on a Toronto-Shanghai Sister School Partnership Landscape. *Front. Educ. China, 12*(2), 180–199. https://doi.org/10.1007/s11516-017-0015-4.

Liang, S. (1949). *Zhongguo Wenhua Yaoyi* 中国文化要义 *(Highlights of Chinese Culture)*. Shanghai: Shanghai People's Publishing House.

Liang, S. (2009). *Dongxifang Wenhua Jiqi Zhexue* 东西方文化及其哲学 *(Eastern and Western Culture and Its Philosophy)*. Beijing: Business Press.

Lu, X. (2008). *Lun Zhongguoren de Guominxing* 论中国人的国民性 *(On Chinese Nationality)*. Wuchang: Changjiang Arts Press.

Mao, C. (2008). Duwei, Makesi yu Kongzi Guanyu Zhenli de Duihua 杜威、马克思与孔子关于真理的对话 (The Dialogue of Truth between Confucius, and Dewey and Marx). *Journal of Hangzhou Normal University (Social Sciences Edition), 30*(6), 42–47.

Niemann, D., Martens, K., & Teltemann, J. (2017). Pisa and Its Consequences: Shaping Education Policies through International Comparisons. *European Journal of Education, 52*(2), 175–183.

O'Dwyer, S. (2015). Epistemic Elitism, Paternalism, and Confucian Democracy. *Dao, 14*(1), 33–54. https://doi.org/10.1007/s11712-014-9415-9.

Peng, C. (2009). Jiaoyu Xushi Yanjiu zhong de 'Weixian' ji Yingran 'Lixing': Laizi Kangnali, Kelaididing he Kangli de Shijiao 教育叙事研究中的 '危险' 及应然 '理性'—米自康纳利、克莱丁宁和康莉的视角 (The 'Dangers' and Necessary 'Rationality' in Educational Narrative Inquiry: From the Perspectives of Clandinin, Connelly and Conle). *Journal of Educational Studies, 5*(3), 9–14.

Qi, S. (2019). *Ziyouzhiren Ruhe Yangcheng: Jiaoyu Sixiangshi de Shijiao* 自由之人如何养成—教育思想史的视角 *(How to Cultivate a Freeman: A History of Educational Thoughts)*. Shanghai: East China Normal University.

Radcliffe, R. J. (1989). Confucius and John Dewey. *Religious Education Association, 84*(2), 215–231.

Sahlberg, P. (2013). The PISA 2012 Scores Show the Failure of 'Market Based' Education Reform. Retrieved from https://pasisahlberg.com/the-pisa-2012-scores-show-the-failure-of-market-based-education-reform/.

Shen, Y. (2001). *Duwei Tan Zhongguo* 杜威谈中国 *(Dewey on China)*. Hangzhou Zhejiang Arts Press.

Sim, M. (2009). Dewey and Confucius: On Moral Education. *Journal of Chinese Philosophy, 36*, 85–105.

Tao, X. (2008). Tao Xingzhi Wenji 陶行知文集 (Collections of Tao Xingzhi's Works). Nanjing: Jiangsu Education Publishing House.

Tan, C. (2015). Beyond 'Either-Or' Thinking: John Dewey and Confucius on Subject Matter and the Learner. *Pedagogy, Culture & Society, 24*(1), 55–74. https://doi.org/10.1080/14681366.2015.1083046.

Tan, C. (2019). Pisa and Education Reform in Shanghai. *Critical Studies in Education, 60*(3), 391–406.

Waks, L. (2019). Duwei yu Kongzi de Duihua: 1919–2019 杜威与孔子的对话: 1919–2019 (John Dewey and Confucius in Dialogue: 1919–2019). *Journal of East China Normal University*, (2), 45–52.

Wang, Y. (2007). *Duwei Jiaoyuxuepai yu Zhongguo Jiaoyu* 杜威教育学派与中国教育 *(Dewey School Education and Chinese Education)*. Beijing: Beijing Institute of Technology Press.

Wu, J. (2001). Duwei de Jiaoyu Sixiang dui 20 Shiji Zhongguo Jiaoyu Gaige de Yingxiang 杜威的教育思想对20世纪中国教育改革的影响 (The Influence of Dewey's Education Thoughts to Chinese Education Reform in 20 Century). *Education Review*, (6), 58–60.

Xu, T. (2012). Duwei yu Kongzi de Jiaoyu Zhexue: Lishi Shiye yu Dangdai Yiyi 杜威与孔子的教育哲学:历史视野与当代意义 (The Educational Philosophy of John Dewey and Confucius: Historical Perspective and Contemporary Significance). *Education Science, 28*(4), 66–71.

Xu, S., & Connelly, F. M. (2009). Narrative Inquiry for Teacher Education and Development: Focus on English as a Foreign Language in China. *Teaching and Teacher Education, 25*(2), 219–227. https://doi.org/10.1016/j.tate.2008.10.006.

Xu, S., & Connelly, F. M. (2017). Reciprocal Learning between Canada and China in Teacher Education and School Education: Partnership Studies of Practice in Cultural Context. [Review]. *Frontiers of Education in China, 12*(2), 135–150. https://doi.org/10.1007/s11516-017-0013-6.

Xu, S., & Connelly, F. M. (2013-2020). Reciprocal learning in teacher education and school education between Canada and China. Unpublished research project proposal. Canada.

Ye, L. (2005). 21 Shiji Shehui Fazhan Yu ZHongguo Jichu Jiaoyu Gaige 21 世纪社会发展与中国基础教育改革 (The Development of Society and Chinese Basic Education Reform in 21st Century). *Journal of the Chinese Society of Education,* (1), 2–11.

Ye, L. (2006). *'Xinjichu Jiaoyu' Lun: Guanyu Dangdai Zhongguo Xuexiao Biange de Tanjiu Yu Renshi* 新基础教育'论—关于当代中国学校变革的探究与认识 (*'New Basic Education' Theory: Exploration and Understanding on Contemporary Chinese School Reform*). Beijing: Educational Science Publishing House.

Ye, L. (2013). 'Shengming-Shijian' Jiaoyu Xuepai: Zai Huigui Yu Tupo Zhong Shengcheng '生命·实践' 教育学派—在回归与突破中生成 (School of Life-Practice Pedagogy: Creation in Return and Breakthrough). *Journal of Educational Studies, 9,* 5.

Ye, L. (2014). *Huigui Tupo: 'Shengming-Shijiang' Jiaoyuxue Lungang* 回归突破: '生命·实践' 教育学论纲 (*Life-Practice Educology: A Contemporary Chinese Theory of Education*). Shanghai: East China Normal University Press.

Ye, L. (2018). Zhongguo Zhexue Chuantong zhong de Jiaoyu Jingshen yu Zhihui 中国哲学传统中的教育精神与智慧 (Educational Spirit and Wisdom in the Tradition of Chinese Philosophy). *Education Research, 39*(6), 4–7.

Ye, L., & Li, Z. (Eds.). (2010/2011). *'Xinjichu Jiaoyu' Yanjiushi* 新基础教育' 研究史 *The History of 'New Basic Education' Research*. Beijing: Educational Science Publishing House.

Ye, L., Luo, W., & Pang, Q. (2019). Zhongguo Wenhua Chuantong Yu Jiaoyuxue Zhongguo Huayu Tixi De Jianshe 中国文化传统与教育学中国话语体系的建设—叶澜教授专访 (Chinese Cultural Tradition and the Construction of Chinese Discourse System in Educology: An Interview with Professor Ye Lan). *Journal of Soochow University (Educational Science Edition),* (3). https://doi.org/10.19563/j.cnki.sdjk.2019.03.007.

Yuan, Q. (2001). *Duwei yu Zhongguo* 杜威与中国 *(Dewey and China)*. Beijing: People's Publishing House.

Zhang, L. (1996). Duwei Laihua dui Zhongguo Jiaoyu de Yingxiang 杜威来华对中国教育的影响 (The Influence of Dewey in China for Chinese Education). *Liaojing Higher Education Research*, (6), 97–102.

Zhang, B. (2001). *Duwei yu Zhongguo* 杜威与中国 *(Dewey and China)*. Shijiazhuang: Hebei People's Publishing House.

Zhang, H. (2019). Lun Duwei yu Zhongguo Jiaoyu Gaige 论杜威与中国教育改革 (On John Dewey and China's Educational Reform). *Journal of East China Normal University Educational Sciences*, (2), 18–28.

Zhang, B., & Liu, Y. (2019). *Duwei Jiaoyu Sixiang zai Zhongguo: Jinian Duwei Laihua 100 Zhounian* 杜威教育思想在中国:纪念杜威来华讲学100周年 *(Dewey's Educational Thoughts in China: Commemorating the 100th Anniversary of Dewey's Lecture in China)*. Beijing: Peking University Press.

Zhixin, J. S. (2019). Duwei yu Zhongguo Jiaoyu: Bijiao Fenxi yu Pipanxing Pinggu 杜威与中国教育:比较分析与批判性评估 (Dewey and Chinese Education: Comparative Analysis and Critical Evaluation). *Education Research Monthly*, (2), 3–18.

Zhu, G., & Chen, X. (2008). Jiaoyu Xushu Tanjiu yu Xianxiangxue Yanjiu zhi Bijiao_Yi Kangnali de Xushu Tanjiu he Fanmeinan de Xianxiangxue Yanjiu Weili 教育叙述探究与现象学研究之比较—以康纳利的叙述探究和范梅南的现象学研究为例 (A Comparison between Narrative Inquiry and Phenomenological Research in Education: Taking Michael Connelly's and Max Manen's Work as Examples). *Peking University Education Review*, 6(1), 70–78.

CHAPTER 4

Literature Review, Theoretical Framework and Research Method

Yuhua Bu

4.1 LITERATURE REVIEW

4.1.1 *Reciprocal Learning*

Japanese educationist, Professor Manabu Sato, first proposed the concept of reciprocal learning. According to Sato (Manabu 2004), people from diversified backgrounds in the twenty-first century need to respect each other's differences and coexist in the society. They seek to learn from each other by modestly listening to others while providing their own insights without reservation. From Sato's perspective, learning is a reciprocal process in which experience, knowledge and wisdom are shared between instructors and learners as well as between learners themselves. Therefore, in Manabu Sato's eyes, reciprocal learning is a basic concept and teaching method for building a "learning community", which is different from cooperative learning, because cooperation points more to the joint

Y. Bu (✉)
East China Normal University, Shanghai, China
e-mail: yhbo@dedu.ecnu.edu.cn

© The Author(s), under exclusive license to Springer Nature
Switzerland AG 2021
Y. Bu (ed.), *Narrative Inquiry into Reciprocal Learning Between Canada-China Sister Schools*, Intercultural Reciprocal Learning in Chinese and Western Education,
https://doi.org/10.1007/978-3-030-61085-2_4

87

completion of one task among multiple subjects, and does not necessarily require mutual learning and sharing of knowledge among them. Reciprocal learning has a deeper sense of dedication than cooperative learning in that it does not require everyone to accomplish the same task, but to share each other's knowledge and help each other achieve the goal together (A. Liu and Bu 2016). Therefore, harmonious coexistence is embodied in the original meaning of reciprocal learning.

As an academic concept in cross-cultural communication, reciprocal learning was proposed in 2012 by Dr. Shijing Xu of the University of Windsor and Professor Connelly of the University of Toronto in 2012. This concept was first put forward as a cross-cultural learning idea or goal. Researchers hoped to use reciprocal learning as a principle of value when studying teachers and schools from China and Canada in cross-cultural communication, respecting each other's cultural uniqueness with an open attitude, understanding each other, learning and developing together to achieve the goal of reciprocity. According to Connelly and Xu (2015, May), the idea of reciprocal learning in the context of the Canada-China Reciprocal Learning Grant Project involves two key elements: cross-cultural collaboration and learning for mutual benefit. They believe that reciprocal learning can be achieved between schools and teachers and, more generally speaking, between education in Canada and China when educators work together. Later, they found that the concept is a significant research methodology, which is to some extent a breakthrough in cross-cultural comparative research. They insist that learning between countries and cultures needs to go beyond simple comparison in terms of practices, values, culture, achievements and pedagogy and that reciprocal learning should be thought of and practiced as a type of two-way "learning in collaborative work situations" (Connelly and Xu 2015, May). Hence, the approach to reciprocal learning adds another dimension to the prevalent comparative education research that mainly deals with one-way knowledge transfer (Cowen 2006).

In general, it can be seen that "reciprocal learning", whether as an educational concept, an educational strategy or a research methodology, is reflected in the background of multicultural development in the contemporary world with respect to how people live in harmony, how they deal with differences and how symbiosis is achieved. In the context of economic and information globalization today, reciprocal learning is of more universal value and significance because it signifies people will get along with each other in the future. In this project, we learn how the two sister schools came together to overcome multiple difficulties in time and space, language, system and culture, using reciprocal learning as the basic communication principle to form a profound friendship.

4.1.2   Sister School

Concerning the history of sister schools, it is believed that when some developed countries expanded their influence around the world, schools between the native and colonial countries began to establish sisterships, although historical proof is not yet available. After the twentieth century, the establishment of sister schools was related to the emergence of "sister cities". For example, after the Second World War (1956), American President Dwight Eisenhower announced, at a White House meeting, the "people vs. people" program, which would encourage developed cities to help less-developed cities to effect rapid development. Originally, cities paired with each other in the form of sister cities enacted the "people vs. people" development program. Cities that established such relationship were commonly referred to as "sister cities". Sister Cities International (SCI) developed over the next few years to coordinate connections between American cities and 1400 communities from 92 foreign countries. Among other activities, SCI also encouraged and supported the participation of sister cities in their affiliated school programs. Thus, sister school came into being (Korich 1978). The activities of affiliated schools included projects such as the exchange of children's works of art, letters, photo exhibitions, music, drama, entertainment and handicrafts. Students were encouraged to experience the local customs of paired foreign schools. In 1972, Auckland California had a sister school partnership (Frank 1978) with Fukuoka, Japan. By 1977, 67 schools in Auckland and Fukuoka were involved in the program. As observed by staff and reported by parents, sister schools achieved many encouraging results. The American National Association of Secondary School Principals (NASSP) established an international inter-school exchange program with Britain and West Germany in 1972. Since then, about 100,000 teachers and students have participated in the international activities of the School Partnership, which has since expanded to Spain, Costa Rica, Italy, Australia, the United Kingdom, Japan, Mexico, Mexico and the Soviet Union. Some changes have been going on for ten years. NASSP developed guidelines for its communication projects and conducted on-the-job training to provide schools with exchange experiences. NASSP also matched schools according to preferred locations and offers insurance services. Later, the United States formed sister schools with the Soviet Union and other countries achieving positive results. Sister schools have proven themselves to be viable educational program that can have a huge long-term impact on participants (Pryor 1992).

From a broader perspective, the enthusiasm of some developed countries, such as the United States, to establish international sister schools with other countries in the world is naturally related to their foresight in anticipating that future intellectuals need to have some cross-cultural literacy to better participate in international affairs. In the 1990s, global education became increasingly important as countries around the world moved into a global market where cross-cultural communication was essential for economic, political and social survival. Students not only need to know the facts about other countries but also need to learn through experience how to communicate effectively with people in other countries and how to cooperate to achieve common goals. School pairing and partnership, commonly known as the "sister schools" program, have proven to be a highly motivating and deeply encouraging way to give young people, educators and others a global perspective. Courses can start with a simple letter exchange or an art project, but can be extended easily to a wide range of classroom projects, collaborative curriculum development and short-or-long-term communication between students and staff. While knowledge in many areas can be shared, building communication skills is the most important aspect of these sister school programs, through which administrators, teachers and student service staff have the opportunity to work with each other and with students, parents and other community members.

China started late in the construction of international sister school projects, which began in 1978 when China carried out its comprehensive reform and opening-up. In 1983, Deng Xiaoping put forward "Three Orientations" in education, namely orientating toward modernization, toward the world and toward the future. Taking this as a starting point, China has drawn open the curtain of internationalization of basic education in the new era. In 1993, China promulgated the Program for China's Educational Reform and Development, which clearly stated that it was necessary to further open up education, strengthen international exchanges and cooperation in education and boldly draw on the successful experience of other countries in the development and management of education. During this period, there were attempts to carry out cooperative education in the field of basic education in China. In June 1993, Guangzhou Huamei School, founded by overseas students returning home, became the first international cooperation school in China. "Beijing Sino-Canadian School" began preparation in 1994 and was officially established in 1997. It became the first Sino-foreign cooperative school approved by the Chinese government, followed by a number of other cooperative educational institutions. Since China joined the WTO in 2001, various forms of international schools and training courses have been booming one after another. According to incomplete statistics, the total number of international schools in China reached 661 in 2018, including 218 public international schools, 321 private international schools and 122 foreign international schools (Zhou 2008). In 2013, Xi Jinping put forward the "Belt and Road" initiative to promote international cooperation, further advancing international exchanges in China's basic education. In the process of internationalization, some sister schools or sister classes in schools have been established through exchanges between China and other countries, but there is not yet any international cooperation among universities to carry out research on sister schools in primary and secondary schools. Therefore, the current "cross-cultural reciprocal learning research project on sister schools" is pioneering for both China and Canada.

4.1.3   *Narrative Inquiry in China and in the World*

The concept of Narrative Inquiry first entered China around 2001. According to China National Knowledge Infrastructure (CNKI), the largest periodical library in China, the earliest article on this topic was written by Liu Lianghua (2002) who did not distinguish between "narrative research" and "narrative inquiry" at that time, but used "narrative" as a method to tell educational stories. Perhaps because of this confusion, many people still call it "narrative research" in Chinese mainland (Liu 2002). In 2003, Professors Connelly, Clandinin and Ding Gang jointly published a paper on "narrative inquiry", which precisely marked the entrance of the concept into the perspective of Chinese scholars for the first time (Connelly et al. 2003). After that, more and more articles or subjects in the Chinese mainland applied "narrative inquiry" or "narrative research" as a research method. Since 2004, F. Michael Connelly, D. Jean Clandinin and other works have been gradually translated into Chinese (2004, 2008, 2012).

After 2005, Professor Connelly, Clandinin and Cheryl Craig who is the representative figure in contemporary narrative inquiry, Cheryl Craig gradually became better known to Chinese educational scholars, and was constantly invited to China to attend conferences, make reports, write articles, receive interviews and so on (Wei and Chen 2016). Thus, the younger generation of Chinese scholars has become more familiar with narrative inquiry accepted as a research methodology and educational research method. In recent years, narrative inquiry has been included as a qualitative research method in "qualitative research methods" courses offered to pedagogical majors by some Chinese normal universities.

Since 2013, the China-Canada Reciprocal Learning Project has been working with East China Normal University, Southwest University and Northeast Normal University to carry out research collaboratively. For seven years, a large number of researchers have participated as volunteers. Their main research methods are narrative inquiry, and some students also use this as the research methodology for graduation theses (Yanting Liu 2016; Luxia 2020). These students have also used narrative inquiry in their future research.

In general, the last 20 years have seen the Chinese educational circles gradually understand narrative inquiry and apply it to educational research. Its influence on Chinese educational research is far-reaching. Admittedly, it is not enough for Chinese educators to merely understand it as a research method. It is closely related to the view of curriculum, teachers and knowledge held by Professors Connelly and Clandinin, and also to Dewey's empirical theory in origin, which has not yet been fully acknowledged by Chinese educational researchers. It is believed that with the deepening of educational exchanges between China and Canada, the theoretical essence of narrative inquiry will be recognized and even further developed by Chinese scholars.

Viewed globally, narrative inquiry has also received the attention and application of scholars from many countries worldwide. It is perhaps because narrative inquiry bases itself on the theory of experience, pays attention to the value of individual experience, respects relationship and so forth. Take the American Educational Research Association (AERA) conference held in the United States in April 2019 as an example. Scholars from around the world attached great importance to this academic conference, adding to it a strong international flavor. At the conference narrative inquiry was established as a prominent Special Interest Group (SIG) in which more than 500 scholars participated, and a thematic forum was held for five consecutive days, fully showing its high degree of influence and popularity.

4.2 Theoretical Framework and Methodology

Since we understand China and Canada from a cross-cultural perspective, the theoretical basis of this book is on the two schools of pedagogy from China and Canada that have influenced this project and also reflect the educational theories characteristic of their own cultural traditions. There are similarities and differences, which will be presented in form of dialogue in this book.

4.2.1 School of Life-Practice Educology

School of Life-Practice Educology is a pedagogical theory with Chinese cultural characteristics created by Ye Lan and her team since the 1990s. "Life-Practice" involves two interdependent concepts, expressing the mutually dependent relationship between life and practice. That is, life develops in practice and through practice. Practice, taking on different forms with the development of life, is the soil, path, condition and way for the realization of life. To this end, this school of educology systematically responds to a number of problems in education: (1) Education is "an enterprise of human life conducted throughout life, for life, on the basis of life, and facing up to life" (Ye 2015), and needs to be achieved through direct communication between people as it directly aims at impacting the physical and mental development of people. Only in educational activities can the special person-to-person relationship between teachers and students be established. (2) Teachers understand and grasp the cultural resources created, accumulated and provided by human life as a whole, and share them with students (Ye 2015). Therefore, to be an important creator of education and human spiritual life, every teacher should obtain inner dignity and joy through "creative work" (Ye 2000). (3) The teaching and learning activities of teachers and students are an organic whole which cannot be separated or bifurcated from each other, requiring the joint participation of teachers and students to exert interactive influence through dialogue, communication and cooperative activities, and to promote educational activities in a dynamically generated way (Ye 2002).

The school of "Life-Practice" Educology responded to and revived the traditional Chinese educational thought in multiple ways. In the ideas of

Classical Confucianism, the purpose of education and learning was "to let one's inborn virtue shine forth, to renew the people, and to rest in the highest good", as stated in the *Great Learning* (*Daxue*), showing a harmonious integration between the individual good and the benefit of society (Lee 2000). This goal first focuses on the individual's life state, from which the good of society can be achieved. In terms of the relationship between teaching and learning, Classical Confucians thought that teaching and learning is an interactive process, with teachers playing key roles as co-learners, cheerleaders, mentors and role models of individual integrity. Probably the most powerful example of the teacher in classical China is seen in the picture of Confucius that emerges from his dialogues with his disciples in *The Analects* (To quietly persevere in storing up what is learned, to continue studying without respite, to instruct others without growing weary—is not this me?" (7: 2)). The *Theory of Education* (*Xue Ji*) has a particularly profound explanation of all that is involved in becoming an effective teacher, as explained in the following depiction of "four successes" and "six failures" in teaching: The ways of higher education are as follows: To suppress what has not yet emerged is called *prevention*; to present what is opportune is called *timeliness*; not to transgress what is proper is called *conformity*; to observe each other and follow what is good is called *imitation*. These four things are accountable for the success of teaching. In the eighteenth century, this Confucian tradition was inherited and developed by the Academy tradition, for example, Zhu Xi regarded learning and practice as one integrated process, and he urged both teachers and students of the academy to integrate Confucian human relationships into daily life in the neighborhood, the local community and the wider society. Moreover, teaching and studying in academies was usually a life-long process, which involved close communications on a regular basis. The teacher-student relationship became one of tangible caring, sharing and responsibility to each other (Hayhoe and Li 2010). It can be said that the Chinese traditional educational thought itself contains rich thought of School of Life-Practice Educology. Therefore, using this school as the theoretical basis is also to understand ourselves from the Chinese traditional culture.

4.2.2 Narrative Inquiry

The establishment of narrative inquiry method is deeply influenced by Dewey's empiricism and Schwab's theory of practice. Dewey put forward the concept of "interactivity and continuity of experience" in 1938, and the past, present and future of individual life experience are closely related. Influenced by Dewey, Schwab first proposed the concept of "fluid inquiry", and narrative inquiry gradually emerged in this fluid form of inquiry. In order to achieve "deep inquiry", narrative inquiry advocates that front-line teachers truly participate in the research process. At the same time, narrative inquiry is to judge teachers from the perspective of teachers, rather than from the perspective of researchers. The method of narrative inquiry needs to explore the potential of teachers as curriculum developers and creators, rather than passively recognizing teachers as implementers of curriculum knowledge (Wei and Chen 2016; Craig 2005). These thoughts about educational philosophy and teachers are similar to "Life-Practice" Educology.

Narrative inquiry is a qualitative methodology that studies "the ways humans experience the world" (Connelly and Clandinin 1990). It is based on the premise that people understand or make sense of their lives through narrative (Bruner 1996). Connelly and Clandinin (1990) argue that "humans are storytelling organisms who, individually and socially, lead storied lives" (p. 2). In the development of narrative research, Xu and Connelly (2009) define narrative inquiry as "a way of thinking about life" (p. 221) that is not simply telling stories (Xu and Connelly 2009). In other words, narrative inquiry refers to understanding and inquiring into experiences through a "collaboration between researcher and the participants, over time, in the place or series of places, and in social interaction with milieus" (Clandinin and Connelly 2000). The purpose of narrative inquiry is not "what is life", but "how is life interpreted and reinterpreted, narrated and reinterpreted", which is what Freud called "psychic reality" (Wei and Chen 2016). Thus, narrative inquiry is defined not simply by storytelling, but by the critical reflection and analysis of stories that offer insights into the practical experience of people immersed in the social context of a given subject.

Narrative inquiry differs from "Life-Practice" Educology in research attitudes and methods. It may be, as Craig put it, "narrative inquiry does not facilitate changes. Teachers come together and influence each other to make a difference. Action research, however, with a clear goal in advance, has clear requirements in this regard and needs to facilitate changes in the participants, which may eventually lead to changes in school organization and situational environment. Narrative inquiry, on the other hand, points to the subtle changes in individuals or relationships, without any pre-set goals" (Wei and Chen 2016). "Life-Practice" Educology is closer to the positions of action research, but differ in its flexibility and open attitude toward the future, which is nevertheless close to narrative inquiry. It is from the perspective of a dialogue between the two theories that we are considering and interpreting the communication between sister schools. Nonetheless, although we are the main advocates of "Life-Practice" Educology in China, we adhere to the research standpoint of narrative inquiry to be consistent with the Sino-Canadian project on the whole.

4.3   Research Method

4.3.1   Researchers of the Sister School Project

The researchers who have participated in the Sister School Project (SSP) included members of the research group from the University of Toronto in Canada and the research group of East China Normal University in China. The composition of the bilateral membership is briefly stated below.

- *Toronto Researchers*

The lead researcher of the SSP program in Toronto is Professor Michael Connelly, who has conducted educational research for many years at Bay Street School, where he has maintained a very close relationship with the principal and teachers there. Connelly's role in the project is to guide the graduate students to understand the purpose of the project, instruct the graduate-student volunteers to write field notes, communicate with graduate students about the status of the project in progress whenever necessary, participate in important interactive activities of sister schools such as video meetings, write research reports and guide graduate students to write theses. Admittedly, as Professor Connelly is also one of the main persons in charge of the major project, he also has to participate in related events including the planning of the annual symposium, giving the thematic report and writing the annual review of the major project.

A group of graduate-student volunteers are directly involved in the daily work of the project. Most of them are Chinese students from the School of Education at the University of Toronto, including postgraduates and doctoral students, a few Canadian students and a couple of visiting scholars from China. These students understand Chinese language and culture, have a good command of English and desire to acquaint themselves with Canadian schooling. These qualities provide the necessary foundation for their smooth communication of information from both sides. In general, their tasks include writing field notes and sharing them with teachers at sister schools, translating in Chinese or English to facilitate communication between teachers from the two schools, helping teachers from the sister schools to take on tasks in everyday life, and conveying the wishes of both sister schools. Their job has effectively promoted the communication and interaction between sister schools.

Yishin Khoo, a PhD student, has played a principal role in the project from 2013 to 2020. She once said: "Based on my interest in conducting research in schools and with teachers, they suggested that I worked with a team of researchers from OISE and East China Normal University (ECNU) to support partnership building between a Toronto elementary school and a Shanghai elementary school" (Khoo 2017). Yishin Khoo, an important figure in this project, has a background of Chinese descent and can speak Chinese. She once lived in China for some time and understands and is interested in Chinese culture. Meanwhile, she also has learning experience in Canada. She not only is good at English language but also has a better understanding of Canadian culture. Such a background provides a solid basis for her participation in the project. Moreover, she has been steadily engaged in the project and paid many visits to Minzhu Primary School (MPS) in China for face-to-face interactive activities. Her friendship with both sister schools has greatly boosted their exchanges.

- *Shanghai Researchers*

There are also two types of researchers in Shanghai involved in the sister school project: professors and their graduate students. Professor Ye Lan and her student Professor Yuhua Bu, both from East China Normal University, are the principal figures involved in the project. Ye Lan is responsible for the overall progress of the sister schools, while Yuhua Bu is in charge of the direct advancement of the sister school project in everyday life. Her role, similar to that of Professor Connelly's, is to help postgraduate volunteers understand the project purposes, guide them to take field notes, and participate in the sister school exchanges of MPS. The volunteers involved are invariably Yuhua Bu's students, whose English level is relatively good. What they have done is basically similar to that of their Toronto counterparts, with whom peer exchanges have been maintained. For example, after Chinese volunteers send their field notes taken in

Chinese to Bay Street School, Canadian volunteers will translate the notes into English to facilitate the understanding of the Canadian teachers and vice versa. Postgraduate volunteers have played an indispensable and irreplaceable role in the whole project. From 2013 to 2020, about 20 postgraduates from East China Normal University have participated in the project to varying degrees.

4.3.2 Sister School Research Partners

4.3.2.1 Overall Participation of Teachers in Both Schools

There are significant cultural differences between the two schools in terms of the people involved in the project. Both schools have been interacting in the name of sister schools for ten years or so, during which BSS has changed four principals, who have nonetheless held a friendly attitude toward the sistership with MPS. But just because of the frequent changes in principals, the real continuation of the sister school exchanges owes itself to two teachers Ms. Barton (pseudonym) and Lily Hanny (pseudonym), who have a teacher-student relationship. Barton, being Hanny's teacher, was in her 40s when she first participated in the project. Hanny is a young teacher in her 20s. Through our continuous and friendly in-depth contact with these two teachers, we began to gain a deeper and more comprehensive understanding of Canadian teachers' daily routines. Therefore, it is necessary to provide a detailed introduction of these two teachers.

Unlike Bay Street School, the principal of MPS has not changed since the 1990s; nor has there been little change in its teaching staff, except for natural renewal of teachers because of retirement or new entry. Therefore, MPS has always been able to connect with BSS by the power of almost the whole school, such as the principal, research directors and teachers of various disciplines, who have also shown enthusiasm for participation. In comparison, there are only two teachers from the side of Bay Street School. During the entire seven years, the participants in both schools have been relatively stable, which are shown in Table 4.1.

As is shown by Table 4.1:

(1) Communication with BSS has basically been sustained by the continuous participation of two teachers with their urban school principal changing every two to three years. The individual force of these two teachers is very prominent. When it comes to communication, their school

4 LITERATURE REVIEW, THEORETICAL FRAMEWORK AND RESEARCH... 99

Table 4.1 Paired teachers of the two sister schools

Year	Bay Street School		MPS	
	Principal	Teachers	Principal	Teachers
2013–2014	Principal 1	Ann Barton and Lily Hanny	Ms. Dongmei	Director of research: Ms. Zhang Head teacher: Ms. LuMin Math teacher: Ms. Liu and Huang English teacher: Ms. Ding (5 teachers involved)
2015–2017	Principal 2	Ann Barton and Lily Hanny	Ms. Dongmei	Director of research: Ms. Zhang Head teacher: Ms. Zheng and Ding Math teacher: Ms. Liu Science teacher: Mr. ZhiGuo and Miss Liu English teacher: Ms. Ding (six teachers involved)
2018–2020	Principal 3	Ann Barton and Lily Hanny	Ms. Dongmei	Director of research: Ms. Zhang Head teacher: Ms. Dongmei Math teacher: Ms. Zheng Science teacher: Mr. ZhiGuo and Miss Liu English teacher: Ms. Ding (six teachers involved)

provides little institutional, organizational or funding support. MPS, on the other hand, has a project communication team comprising the principal, research director, head teacher and language and mathematics teachers. The organizational strength of the team is more prominent and funding or time is guaranteed by the institution. Facts show that Ms. Barton and Lily Hanny have to bear the cost of funding and time when the teachers of the two schools communicated with each other face to face, while MPS receives support from the school or local government.

(2) Ms. Barton and Lily Hanny are general teachers who teach all subjects, so they are able to communicate with the head teacher and teachers of math, language and science. There is a difference between a specialized teacher and a general teacher in this respect. These differences will be

further discussed in Chap. 5. The specific areas and pairing of teachers in the two schools are as follows:

The first pair of sister school teachers

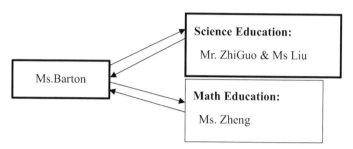

The second pair of sister school teachers

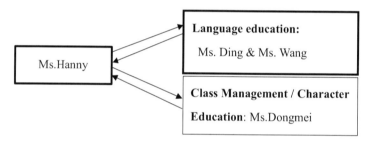

Additionally, the principals have also been in constant communication with each other, and they are involved in teacher management, curriculum, school culture, student management and so on. Also, the communication between each group means that there are many kinds of communication between the students in their classes.

4.3.2.2 An Overview of the Two Pairs of Sister School Teachers and Principals

A brief introduction will be provided for the teachers who have played prominent roles in the seven years of reciprocal learning at sister schools. They are main characters in forthcoming chapters of this book.

Ms. Ann Barton
Ms. Barton was one of the teachers who first received us when we visited BSS in 2008. She welcomed graduate students to her classroom to do

"narrative research with her" (Khoo 2018). Ms. Barton is an outstanding teacher, who teaches creatively, especially in mathematics and science. She loves children and has always been exploring the natural environment because of her deep love for her father who is an ecologist. She conducts studies with children in water lessons almost every year before and after the World Water Day, such as exploring water usage among Aborigines and looking for creative ways to protect the water environment alongside her students. She has received an award from the municipal environmental protection agency in Toronto. At the same time, she has also actively participated in ecology research with professors at the University of Toronto and has led teachers and children in Toronto to contribute to the protection of environmental resources.

Mr. ZhiGuo and Ms. Liu

The two teachers, who are both science teachers of MPS in Shanghai, have worked in partnership with Ms. Ann Barton. Mr. ZhiGuo is the mentor of Ms. Liu. Born in the 1960s, Mr. ZhiGuo graduated from a secondary normal school, but he works very hard and has a passion for research. In MPS a water culture education museum has been built as a research platform for the students of the whole school as well as students and residents from the neighborhood. ZhiGuo uses the museum as a base to offer lessons to the science society for the whole school and has greatly enriched children's scientific vision and research interest. His students' research projects have won frequent awards in Shanghai. At the same time, Mr. ZhiGuo has acted as an instructor of scientific teaching and research work for his own school as well as other science teachers from neighboring schools. Therefore, when Ms. Ann Barton first came to MPS, she formed a close partnership with Mr. ZhiGuo and became close friends like brother and sister.

Ms. Liu, a new teacher who has just graduated, is under Mr. ZhiGuo's guidance regarding her professional development. Therefore, she naturally joins in the cooperative partnership with Ms. Ann Barton. The young teacher has also studied hard and grown tremendously in the whole project.

Ms. Hanny

As a young teacher at Bay Street School, Hanny loves teaching and is creative. In Bay Street School, she is mainly responsible for the teaching of primary school students from grade 1 to grade 2. Being good at language teaching and character education, she is very much concerned with the growth of children. A Canadian of Greek origin, she has been greatly influenced by her mother since childhood, believing that all people should be equal, thus sticking to the position of educating cosmopolitan citizens. She fully acknowledges the cosmopolitan significance of the Sino-Canadian project and has made great contributions.

Ms. Ding

Being a teacher of English at MPS, she was the first with a bachelor's degree when joining the school in the 1990s. When she graduated from university, MPS had been involved in New Basic Education (NBE) research, and she became a backbone teacher in the NBE reform as well as a backbone teacher at MPS because of her high savvy and excellence in teaching. Again because of her proficiency in English, she naturally participated in the sister school project and has been the backbone teacher who has been involved in the project for the longest time. She and Ms. Hanny also formed a deep friendship through communication. They taught together face to face for many times and became good friends. In 2019, when the two teachers taught together for the third time, a consensus was easily reached in many aspects.

Ms. Dongmei

A teacher of Chinese at MPS, she is also a head teacher. She officially joined Sino-Canada reciprocal learning activities at Ms. Hanny's request in 2018. Ms. Hanny would like to know how a class is managed at MPS, hoped eagerly to communicate with a head teacher from China. After Ms. Dongmei's participation, the two also quickly became good friends and jointly carried out character education, benefiting greatly from each other.

Principal of MPS—Principal Ting

Principal Ting was born in the late 1960s in Shanghai. She graduated from secondary normal school. She was once a mathematics teacher. Because of her outstanding teaching achievements, she was attached great importance by the school. In 1998, she was the principal of MPS. At that time, she was only about 30 years old. In 1999, she led the school to participate in the NBE research and became one of the first ten experimental schools of NBE. At the beginning of her tenure as president, MPS was in a difficult period of reform, with weak teachers, dwindling student resources and slow improvement of school quality. But after joining the NBE, she led the whole school teachers to participate in the NBE and soon stood out in ten experimental schools.

President Ting has been working in MPS for more than 20 years since graduation. She is a friendly and enthusiastic person with an open mind and adheres to the principles of democracy, openness and innovation. Therefore, in the construction of sister schools in China and Canada, she realized that this is a good opportunity for to go to the world and understand the education of other countries in the world. She personally participated in the construction of sister schools in China and Canada and deeply understood the essence of the project, making her unique contribution to the construction of sister schools.

Principals of BSS

Since the sister schools started project learning in 2013, BSS has had a total of three principals. Almost every principal changes every two years. Nevertheless, all three principals strive to provide maximum assistance for reciprocal learning at sister schools. The first is Principal Paul. He is good at music, enthusiastic and cheerful. His impression of Chinese education is indoctrination. He thinks MPs school should learn more from BSS. Principal Lee is the second principal during the period. He is a Chinese descendant. He has a slight understanding of Chinese culture. He has the idea of democratic governance and treats every teacher and student equally, which leaves us with a deep impression. Ms. Green is the third principal. Her age is similar to that of Principal Ting. She is very good at mathematics education, likes to diagnose the development of teachers in the classroom and is loved by teachers and students of BSS.

The above teachers and principals will be mentioned in certain sections of this book. So much for the brief description of each of them.

4.4 DATA COLLECTION AND ANALYSIS METHOD

4.4.1 Data Sources

We have collected data for seven years till 2019 since the project was launched in 2013. Abundant research data have been collected, which can be roughly divided into three categories: (a) documentary data, (b) observation notes and (c) interview data. These multiple types of data helped the researchers to assure the validity of this study and enhance the transferability of findings (Burns and Bush 1994) as these documentary and observation data allowed for triangulation with interview data (Punch 2005).

Documentary Data

Literature materials, mainly collected during seven years' field study in schools and annual academic symposiums, are most abundant and diverse, including: (1) video, audio and written records of the project meetings; (2) video, audio and written records and reports during the video meetings; (3) audio and video recordings of face-to-face and on-site communication between sister schools; (4) teachers' teaching plans, teaching notes, teaching videos and students' classroom work; (5) pictures, charts and teaching tools in schools; letters and pictures of gifts exchanged by students; (6) graduate students' theses, conference papers and conference report PPTs; (7) written records of communication between teachers and students through modern media such as QQ or Wechat; (8) quarterly progress report to the major project.

Field Notes

Field notes at different stages of the project include those on daily classroom observations, school teacher's daily routines, student activities, face-to-face communication between Sino-Canadian sister schools, as well as other various field research notes made by postgraduate volunteers.

Interview Data

Interview data are also rich and varied, including random interviews in day-to-day field research and interviews conducted during or after an event (such as a face-to-face meeting or an annual symposium). The interviewees include principals, teachers, graduate assistants, university researchers, students and parents.

4.4.2 Research Tools

We used three data analysis tools to explain the experience of sister school teachers and students: broadening, burrowing, and storying/restorying (Connelly and Clandinin 1990). Broadening includes the background of Chinese and Canadian pedagogical thoughts, of educational policies, of traditions and cultures, of sister schools' own history, tradition, system and culture, as well as other factors that we think affect the ideas and behaviors of teachers and students in the two sister schools. For example, in the first chapter of this book, we put SSP in the background of cultural exchange between China and foreign countries and the background of Chinese education in Sino-Western relations, as well as the two academic thoughts of China and Canada, so as to make clear the significance and value of this project in this three-tier background. Chapter 3 is devoted to the relationship between Dewey and Chinese education. It is intended to present the origin of Chinese and North American educational thoughts from the perspective of Sino-American interaction. Moreover, it also presents the different states of East-West interaction, so that the SSP project can position its historical and cultural significance in a larger framework. In fact, in each chapter of this book, the theme of this chapter is placed and explored in the cultural, historical, institutional and other relevant background. Burrowing is reflected when we focus on the teacher's teaching events, student activities or images, and then put the focus on the interaction between the individual and his or her environment for an in-depth analysis. For example, in Chap. 8 of this book, we link MPS's attention to the construction of school culture with the background that China has advocated the development of school characteristics since the 1990s. This is a requirement of action put forward by China in the context of reform and opening-up, in order to stimulate the innovation consciousness of schools and encourage innovation capabilities, which embodies the spirit of the times in China, and is also related to the Chinese school image as an organic whole in need of a unique cultural temperament. Canada's Bay Street School, however, does not pay attention to the construction of a unique school culture. One reason is related to Canada's multicultural background, which emphasizes fairness between schools instead of advocating differences. The other reason is related to the Canadian holistic understanding of schools where individual teachers' classes comprise the basic unit and the school is composed of the mechanical combination of those classes. Such differences reflect different views on school. Storying/restorying refers to how we as researchers tell sister school development stories in texts to present changes and opportunities. This is reflected in Chaps. 5, 6 and 7 of this book.

4.5   ETHICAL CONSIDERATIONS

Our research objects include two schools in China and Canada. For their ethical considerations, we address the ethics in several ways: First, in the whole process of carrying out this project, our research intention was to inform sister schools. At the same time, our field notes are all used to inform them first and then pass on to each other. Second, identifying information was removed during transcription and pseudonyms were used, such as school name and person's name. Third, all participants in the project process are voluntary rather than forced. Fourth, all participants were free to withdraw their participation at any time without penalty.

REFERENCES

Bruner, J. (1996). *Culture and Education*. Cambridge: Harvard University Press.
Burns, A. C., & Bush, R. F. (1994). Introduction to Research Methods. Melbourne: Longman Cheshire.
Clandinin, D. J., & Connelly, F. M. (2000). *Narrative Inquiry: Experience and Story in Qualitative Research*. San Francisco, CA: Jossey-Bass.
Connelly, F. M., & Clandinin, D. J. (1990). Stories of Experience and Narrative Inquiry. *Educational Researcher, 19*, 2–14.
Connelly, F. M., & Xu, S. (2015, May). Reciprocal learning: Comparative models and the Partnership Project. Paper presented at the 2nd Annual Conference: Reciprocal Learning & Symbiotic Relationships in School Development, Shanghai, China.
Connelly, M., Clandinin, J., & Gang, D. (2003). Xushi Tanjiu 叙事探究 (Narrative Inquiry). *Global Education Perspectives, 32*, 6–10.
Cowen, R. (2006). Acting comparatively upon the educational world: Puzzles and possibilities. *Oxford Review of Education, 32*(5), 561–573. doi: 10.1080/03054980600976155.
Craig, C. (2005). The epistemic role of novel metaphors in teachers' knowledge constructions of school reform. *Teachers and Teaching: Theory and Practice, 11*(2), 195–208.

Frank, H. I. W. (1978). *The Sister Cities International School Affiliation Program: It Works and Seems to Have a Major Impact on the Students*. Paper presented at the Sister Cities International, Washington, DC, USA.

Hayhoe, R., & Li, J. (2010). The Idea of a Normal University in the 21st Century Front. *Frontiers of Education in China, 5*, 74–103.

Khoo, Y. (2017). Regenerating Narrative Inquiry for Teacher Growth on a Toronto-Shanghai Sister School Partnership Landscape. *Frontiers of Education in China, 12*(2), 180–199. https://doi.org/10.1007/s11516-017-0015-4.

Khoo, Y. (2018). *River Flowing and Fire Burning: A Narrative Inquiry into a Teacher's Experience of Learning to Educate for Citizenship—From the Local to the Global—Through a Shifting Canada-China Inter-school Reciprocal Professional Learning Landscape*. University Toronto.

Korich, M. (1978). *The Oakland Experience: A Case Study of a School Affiliation Program*. Paper presented at the Sister Cities International, Washington, DC

Lee, T. H. C. (2000). *Education in Traditional China: A History*. Leiden and Boston: Brill.

Liu, A., & Bu, Y. (2016). Reciprocal Learning Strategy in CALL Environment: A Case Study of EFL Teaching at X University in Shanghai. *Universal Journal of Educational Research, 4*, 1059–1070.

Liu, L. (2002). Lun Jiaoyu "Xushi Tanjiu".论教育"叙事研究" (On "Narrative Research" of Education). *Modern Educational Studies, 4*, 52–55.

Liu, Y. (2016). *Xuexiao Kuawenhua Huhui Xuexi Yanjiu* 学校跨文化互惠学习研究 *(Research on Cross-cultural Reciprocal Learning in Schools)*. Shanghai: East China Normal University.

Luxia. (2020). Narrative Inquiry of Teachers' Growth from the Perspective of Expansive Learning-----Research based on an Intercultural Reciprocal Learning Project between China and Canada. Master Thesis. East China Normal University. Shanghai, China.

Manabu, S. (2004). *Xuexi de Kuaile: Zou Xiang Duihua*学习的快乐—走向对话 *(Pleasure of Learning Toward Dialogic Practice)* (Q. Zhong, Trans.). Beijing: Education and Science Press.

Pryor, C. B. (1992). Building International Relations for Children through Sister Schools. *Phi Delta Kappan*.

Punch, K. (2005). *Introduction to Social Research–Quantitative & Qualitative Approaches*. London: Sage Publishing.

Wei, G., & Chen, X. (2016). Xushi Tanjiu Jiqi Zai Jiaoshizhishiyanjiu Zhong De Yunyong 叙事探究及其在教师知识研究中的运用—与美国休斯敦大学谢丽尔·克雷格教授对话 (Narrative Inquiry And Its Application in Teacher Knowledge Research—A Dialogue with Professor Cheryl Craig of The University of Houston). *Teacher Education Forum, 29*, 12–16.

Xu, S., & Connelly, F. M. (2009). Narrative Inquiry for Teacher Education and Development: Focus on English as a Foreign Language in China. *Teaching and Teacher Education*, 25(2), 219–227. https://doi.org/10.1016/j.tate.2008.10.006.

Ye, L. (2000). Zai Xuexiao Gaige Shijian zhong Zaojiu Xinxing Jiaoshi: <Mianxiang 21 Shiji Xinjichu Jiaoyu Tansuoxing Yanjiu> Tigong de Qishi yu Jingyan 在学校改革实践中造就新型教师—《面向21世纪新基础教育探索性研究》提供的启示与经验 (Fostering a New Type of Teachers in the Practice of Conducting Reforms in Schools). *Chinese Journal of Education, 4*, 58–62.

Ye, L. (2002). Chongjian Ketangjiaoyueguocheng Guan: "Xinjichujiaoyu" Ketang Jiaoxue Gaigeyanju de Lilun yu Shijian Tanjiu Zhi Er. 重建课堂教学过程观: "新基础教育"课堂教学改革研究的理论与实践探究之二. (Reconstructing the Concept of Classroom Teaching Process: A Theoretical and Practical Inquiry into the Reform of Classroom Teaching in "New Basic Education"). *Education Research, 5*, 24–30.

Ye, L. (2015). *Huigui Tupo: "Shengming-Shijiang" Jiaoyuxue Lungang* 回归突破: "生命·实践"教育学论纲 *(Life-Practice Educology: A Contemporary Chinese Theory of Education)*. Shanghai: East China Normal University Press.

Zhou, M. (2008). Jianchi Gaigekaifang, Tuidong Jichu Jiaoyu de Guoji Jiaoliu Yu Hezuo 坚持改革开放 推动基础教育的国际交流与合作 (Promoting International Exchanges and Cooperation in Basic Education through Reform and Opening Up). *World Education Information, 31*, 14–16 + 25.

CHAPTER 5

Society, History, and Interaction of Sister Schools

Yuhua Bu

In this chapter, we turn to the elaboration of cross-cultural reciprocal learning in sister schools. This chapter will address three topics: (1) the basic history and development status of the two sister schools; (2) the whole process of cross-cultural reciprocal learning in sister schools; (3) the basic methods and contents of cross-cultural reciprocal learning in sister schools.

5.1 An Overview of the Sister Schools

5.1.1 *History of Minzhu Primary School*

Minzhu Primary School (MPS), which was built in the first decade after the founding of Peoples Republic of China (PRC), has a history of more than 60 years. It mirrors the development history of many primary and

Y. Bu (✉)
East China Normal University, Shanghai, China
e-mail: yhbo@dedu.ecnu.edu.cn

© The Author(s), under exclusive license to Springer Nature Switzerland AG 2021
Y. Bu (ed.), *Narrative Inquiry into Reciprocal Learning Between Canada-China Sister Schools*, Intercultural Reciprocal Learning in Chinese and Western Education,
https://doi.org/10.1007/978-3-030-61085-2_5

109

secondary schools in China. From its establishment to the present, the development of the school can be generally defined by four stages.

Stage 1: A Private Primary School for Children of Civilian Families (1958–1966)

MPS was founded in Minzhu District, southwest of Shanghai, China, in 1958, which was a year of special historical meaning for China, marking the beginning of the Great Leap Forward. Because the Huangpu River flows from the north to the south across the district, Minzhu District is rich in water resources and natural resources and has a high yield of rice. It was also an important distribution center for the goods transported by the Yangtze River to and from Shanghai. Therefore, many small traders from the north and the south, longshoremen seeking a living, and local farmers working in the fields made up the majority of the residents. However, because of the wars before the founding of China, there were few local schools, and most of the children could not attend them. In 1958, new industrial bases were established and the Minzhu District became one of the important bases for industrial construction. Minzhu established factories for heavy machinery, electric machinery, steam turbine, and boilers and became Shanghai's mechanical and electrical industrial zone (Encyclopedia 2009) known for heavy casting and forging, large sets of generators set development, and heavy machine tool processing.[1] Correspondingly, a large number of industrial workers lived in the region and became important residents there. Hence, Minzhu District built primary and secondary schools, but there were still children of farmers or small traders who were not attending school. The local Chamber of Commerce and the village committee jointly funded the establishment of MPS. Not only was there a lack of funds, there were also a small number of students at the beginning (i.e. 136 students, 4 teachers, no principal). The school building was borrowed from the village committee with

---

[1] The "Great Leap Forward" refers to the nationwide movement of the CPC on the extreme "left" line from 1958 to 1960. It was launched on the basis of the third plenary session of the eighth CPC central committee and its subsequent erroneous criticism of the anti-aggression in 1956. In the great leap forward, such phenomena as high index, blind command, false reporting, pompous practice, and "communist ethos" prevailed. In industry, tens of millions of people across the country launched the "nationwide iron and steel smelting movement", which "took steel as the backbone" and led to the "great leap forward" in other industries, such as education, culture, public health, and other undertakings, bringing the great leap forward movement to a climax.

several broken houses, which was mocked as a "broken jar primary school" at that time. Of the four teachers, only one received short-term training, while the other teachers only knew some Chinese characters as they were housewives, not prepared teachers. Without a faculty, they assumed the role of teachers, taught themselves at night, and taught children to read during the day. They occasionally went to a nearby public school to consult formal teachers, or taught and learned from each other. Thus, MPS is originally a school set up for helping the local residents. After about three years, the number of local students and teachers increased, and more classrooms were needed. As a result, the school formally merged with another primary school, began to have formal classrooms, and finally had their first principal. The principal was very responsible and often called on teachers to learn together and improve their knowledge. The teachers were not highly prepared, so they often went to school on the weekend to prepare lessons together. Although life was hard, teachers felt that working together was rewarding. At the same time, the teachers and parents developed a friendly relationship. When some children were poor without food to eat at home, teachers would invite them to eat at their home and tutor them. Although the teachers' professional level was not high, they were serious and sincere and deeply loved by students and parents, and many parents were willing to send their children to this school. From the beginning, Minzhu Primary School (MPS's) image of community and unity was established; its harmonious tone set the stage for the years that would later come.

Stage 2: The Period of Naive Empiricism (1966–1978)

During the "Cultural Revolution", MPS was impacted, and sometimes normal teaching activities could not be carried out. Fortunately, however, this was a primary school, where students were under age and teachers were not harmed. The MPS principals and teachers were relatively simple and practical, always conscientious to teach and educate. Despite the absence of modern education concepts, local children were able to read and write after primary school, and some went on to secondary school.

Stage 3: Taking Moral Education as the Breakthrough Point to Build a Positive School Image (1978–1992)

China continued to carry out reform and opening-up policies. Deng Xiaoping and other state leaders recognized the importance of talents and advocated the modernization of education, which was met with a quick response from the Chinese people, and the era of valuing children's education began. In 1985, MPS was officially converted into a public school with an overall relocation to a workers' new village residential district. It had nearly 34 teachers and 500 students by this time, most of whom were children of workers' families. Perhaps because the school was an ordinary primary school, families of the new working class seemed to distrust it, and many of the nearby children who could have enrolled in it attended schools farther away. In other words, the reputation of MPS was not truly recognized by the local people even with new development opportunities. In 1989, the school recruited a principal by the name of Guo, who said,

> I would endure hardships to rise in great vigor. I must let the students who went away come back. My working ideology is: to improve school spirit and enhance the quality of teaching so as to promote the image of our school in the society and to win the trust of parents. This is my first goal, and also my minimum program of running this school. As for my highest goal, it is to make the school distinctive, which will be accomplished after the first goal is achieved. (Interview with Principal Guo, December 5, 2018)

Guo found that the teachers' educational level was low, most of whom did not go to high school, and only a few teachers graduated from secondary normal schools. It was almost impossible to improve teachers' professional quality in a short period of time. Therefore, she started from student practice, intending to cultivate students' behaviors by means of school-parent cooperation. Principal Guo continued to explain:

> While carrying out traditional values education, we focused on two tasks. Environmental education is a special carrier of traditional virtue education by promoting environmental education and carrying out "green education action". The practice of traditional virtues was extended to the field of environmental protection, which not only enhanced the depth of environmental education, but also extended the education of traditional virtues, promoting each other and complementing each other. Linked with traditional virtue education, it effectively enhanced students' awareness and sense of responsibility to protect the environment. (interview, 2018)

After three years of hard work, the teaching quality at MPS greatly improved, moral education got on track, and many local achievements were made. By the end of 1992, the school had won titles such as "Shanghai Primary School Code of Conduct Education Model School",

"National Advanced Unit of Family Education Guidance", Shanghai Environmental Education Advanced Collective", and so on. Driven by the moral education, the overall level of the school was also upgraded. It was appraised as an "Advanced Unit of Shanghai Primary School Education System" twice in a row, and "Advanced Unit of Education and Scientific Research in Shanghai General Education System". Therefore, the social reputation of MPS increased and did not lose students any longer. The school was now on an upward swing.

Stage 4: New Challenges (1993–1999)
Those in Minzhu District workers' community were mostly engaged in automobile manufacturing industry in the 1950s, so they were mainly children from workers' families. After China's reform and opening-up policy and market economy policy in the 1980s, the possibility of population mobility has increased. As a developed region, Shanghai has become one of the destinations of population inflow, and the community of MPS has become one of the areas attracting migrant population inflow with part of whose children from outside Shanghai have gradually been enrolled by the school. In the 1990s, the Chinese policy advocated quality-oriented education reform, requiring schools to break the mode of examination-oriented education. At the same time, Shanghai, as a developed region of Chinese economy and culture, became one of the first pilot areas to carry out basic education curriculum reform. Under this dual background, MPS is also challenged to join the ranks of reform team with quality-oriented education as the value orientation and curriculum reform as the main content. But how schools understand and implement the spirit of policy requirements is not an easy thing. MPS and many schools at that time were very confused and at a loss. In the 1990s, Professor Ye Lan of East China Normal University launched the "New Basic Education" research, whose focus is school reform. The research is consistent with the spirit of quality-oriented education and the new curriculum reform concept advocated by the Chinese government and has obtained breakthrough results in the first five years of research. MPS became a member of the "New Basic Education" reform project in 1999. After more than ten years of persistent reform and research, great progress has been made in the development of the school. The school is becoming more and more innovative with remarkable achievements in all aspects.

The goal of the school is to keep pace with the times, to innovate "to create a green school with harmonious development and people's satisfaction, to cultivate a healthy, active and happy new generation", and to develop a school culture of "harmony without uniformity, happiness without looseness, concordance with connection, joy with success". More than 80% of the teachers in MPS are Shanghai locals, and the staff structure is generally composed of three types of teachers. The first type involves teachers mostly born in the late 1960s and early 1970s, most of whom were admitted to secondary normal schools in the late 1980s and early 1990s, and became teachers after graduation. Most of them hold traditional educational views. When the tide of educational reform in China came in the 1990s, they were both reformers and reformees. When they joined the project in 2013, most were about 40 years old and had been school leaders, curriculum heads, or teacher trainers. The second type includes teachers who were born in the 1980s and 1990s. Most of them graduated from normal universities and received four-year teacher education degrees, have superior academic backgrounds, and appear to have more professional qualities. Also, they have more modern educational ideas. However, because of their lack of practical experience in education, they need to let the first type of teachers lead the way in the early stage of the work and glean specific practical experience in education and teaching from them. This is how these two types of teachers have both participated in the sister school project.

5.1.2 The Landscape of Bay Street School

Bay Street School is located on Denison Avenue in the heart of Toronto's Chinatown and on the south side of Kensington Market, in the former City of Toronto. It was built in 1877 and has undergone many structural, cultural, and social changes since then. Egerton Ryerson, the originator of Ontario's public education system, founded this school. Ryerson studied various education systems in the U.S., England, and Europe and combined the best of these to develop his own system in Ontario. Today, Ryerson Community School is a vibrant and diverse Kindergarten to Grade 8 school, both culturally and linguistically. It is the 1999 recipients of the Ruth Atkinson Hindmarsh Award for excellence in community-based programming. In 2008, it received the prestigious Anne Hope Award for its commitment to promoting social justice, human rights, and anti-racist education. The school celebrated its 125th Anniversary in 2002. The campus motto is "Bay Street School... Where you belong". The school can be understood more comprehensively via the following passage:

Urban community school. As an urban community school, Bay Street School implies some special social and cultural connotations. Historically, urban communities have been characterized as having high density, high diversity, high migrancy and transience, limited job opportunities and high unemployment, limited social services, assisted housing, and depleting wealth (Solomon 2007). Furthermore, 'urban' is often used as a euphemism for high concentrations of racialized and poor students, complete with challenges of truancy, lack of motivation, parents' lack of involvement, behavioral challenges, low academic performance, and so on (Milner 2012). It highlights learning needs and strengths related to the acquisition of new language and literacy skills, the development of cultural competencies, and critical thinking and literacies needed to explore factors giving rise to racism, ethnocentrism, classism, homophobia, sexism, and ableism, which are often more concentrated and visible in urban spaces (Solomon 2007). Indeed, immigration, multiracial, multicultural background, low and middle income of students' families, and so on are the basic cultural characteristics of this school, which presents the basic cultural characteristics of such public community schools in Canada as a whole. Therefore, in terms of the source structure of students, the similarity is that MPS is a school for the children of ordinary people, with the basic purpose of pursuing equality and quality. The difference is that the cultural background of the students in MPS is not as complex as that of Bay Street School, and there is no ethnic and cultural diversity in MPS.

Multicultural immigrant society. Toronto is the largest city in Canada with more than 2.5 million people and it is among the most diverse cities in the world with regard to language, culture, religion and faith, gender and sexual diversity, and many other social identities. Today, more than 50% of the city's population is born in another country, making it a large immigrant-receiving center that includes many non-status immigrant families and their children (Immigrants 2004). As Solomon et al. (2011) point out, "Canada has a multicultural policy that is legally embedded in the Canadian Charter of Rights and Freedoms, the Canadian Human Rights Act, the Employment Equity Act, the Official Languages Act, the Pay Equity Act, and the Multicultural Act (Solomon et al. 2011). And, as was stated earlier, the Ontario Ministry of Education (provincial-level) introduced the Equity and Inclusive Education Strategy in 2009 to support all students in educational contexts. Indeed, every time we visit the school, we can see signs or illustrations in the hallways, classrooms, canteens, and other places that advocate respect for differences and equal treatment of others. On the school's website, it says:

> Anti-Bullying campaigns are always running at our school. If you walk through our halls you will see work created by students on what is bullying, how to stop it, and how to stand up for yourself and your friends. Workshops are held regularly for students in many areas such as anti-homophobia, cyberbullying, racial bullying, sexual harassment, and much more. We promote an inclusive environment at Ryerson and bullying is not tolerated in any fashion. (School Board 2015)

Public school. As a public school, Bay Street School also has its special mission. Public education is highly valued by Canadian citizens because they have recognized the impact that a strong public education system has made to the Canadian way of life. Michael Den Tandt, a national political columnist for *Postmedia News*, wrote in 2012, "The acceptance, respect and 'openness to all' that are fundamental to public education has helped to shape Canada and influence the world" (Gooijer and Huber 2018). Similarly, as a public school, Bay Street School has always adhered to the principles of equality, respect for diversity, and improvement of quality.

The history of school reform in the last 40 years. By 2020, Bay Street School will be more than 140 years old. We cannot present its history of more than 140 years in such a short space, but we would like to compare it with Minzhu Primary School's development history of nearly 40 years in the same period.

From the 1970s to 2020, Toronto's education reform has gone through three stages: the "innovation implementation" era in the 1970s and 1980s, the effective schools movement in the 1980s and 1990s, and more recently the standards-based reform movement in the last 20 years (S. E. Anderson 2006).

In 1996, in the wake of the accountability era, the ensuing Conservative government introduced Bill 160, or the Education Quality Improvement Act, which:

> mandated the development of a standards-based provincial curriculum, with common content and performance standards for student learning outcomes defined by subject and grade level, K-12. Bill 160 also mandated the creation of a provincial accountability bureau, the Educational Quality and Accountability Office (EQAO), and authorized that Office to manage the development and implementation of provincially developed standardized

tests of student learning in reading, writing and mathematics at specific intervals (grades 3 and 6 in all subject areas, grade 9 mathematics, grade 10 literacy). The tests, aligned with the curriculum standards, are defined at four levels of performance. (S. Anderson and Rodway-Macri 2009)

With the incoming Liberal government in 2003, steps were taken to institutionalize the standards-based curriculum movement in Ontario, by defining acceptable performance measures, providing support to schools that did not meet these measures, and holding the government accountable for meeting these targets (Anderson and Rodway-Macri 2009).

The focus on equity was further supported by the introduction of Ontario's Equity and Inclusive Education Strategy in 2009. The purpose was "to provide a vision for an equitable and inclusive education system, focused on respecting diversity, promoting inclusive education, and identifying and eliminating discriminatory biases, systemic barriers, and power dynamics that limit students' learning, growth, and contribution to society. These barriers and biases, whether overt or subtle, intentional or unintentional, need to be identified and addressed" (Education 2009).

From the mid-2000s until 2013, the mandate of the Ministry of Education was to increase the achievement of students in literacy and numeracy, to close the gap between populations of students, and to increase public confidence in a publicly funded education system (Education 2008). Since 2014, Ontario's education goals have been slightly adjusted; instead of focusing solely on quality improvement, it has turned to achieve excellence, ensuring equality, promoting well-being of students, and enhancing public confidence (Education 2014).

One more point to note is the Toronto District School Board (TDSB) was established in 1998 as a result of the amalgamation of seven distinct school districts, each of which had a different history with regard to equity and diversity. In 2004, one of the key equity initiatives of the board was a program called Model Schools for Inner Cities (MSIC). The program was meant to address the needs of students from economically disadvantaged backgrounds. Recognizing that economic poverty is often linked with other kinds of social disadvantage that influences school achievement, the TDSB has identified four essential elements of model schools:

1   *Equity: achieving fairness and equity to ensure the lives and realities of our students are reflected and affirmed. The strategic focus is on closing opportunity gaps and removing barriers to support equitable outcomes for all students.*

2   **Community**: *equitable educational opportunities and adequate school resources to allow schools to become the heart of their communities.*

3   **Inclusiveness**: *an inclusive culture that respects, reflects, welcomes and encourages all students and families;*

4   **Expectations**: *high expectations to enable all students to reach their full potential as valuable and contributing members of society.* (Board 2006)

At first, 150 model schools were set up, each in a cluster with 20–30 schools. In this way, there needs to be a new organizational structure that goes beyond the school level. This body, at first, which included administrators, trustees (i.e. elected members of the school board), researchers, representatives of the provincial government, and one parent, was developed in 2004 with a mandate to identify effective models of inner-city education (Board 2006). Over the years, there have been changes to staffing in the MSIC program. It turned out that way. Between 2008 and 2014, each cluster was supported by a combination of a central superintendent of education, a central coordinating principal, a central lead teacher, and a program coordinator. In addition to the central program staff, each cluster included a combination of superintendent of education, three administrators who play a leadership role in guiding the direction of the program, one lead teacher responsible for supporting administrators in implementing the five essential components (although this position has been phased out), three community support workers who strengthen the home-school-community partnerships, two teaching and learning coaches to support training, professional learning, and capacity-building among the schools, and a learning classroom teacher in each of the 150 schools to build the teaching and learning capacity at the school level (Shah 2016). In 2016, the ten-year development review of the project reported that the project as a whole has achieved the expected goals and has a greater international influence. Bay Street School became a model school in the fourth phase.

5.1.3   Summary

In our opinion, the Model Schools for Inner Cities (MSIC) has had a great impact on each school, which also enables us to understand the differences between Bay Street School and our campus from a Chinese perspective. Here are four points:

5 SOCIETY, HISTORY, AND INTERACTION OF SISTER SCHOOLS 119

First, there is a new educational organization between the education bureau and the schools to coordinate the school clusters. This educational organization has new leaders who are the resource holders in each school cluster and determine the allocation of resources in each. This means that the power of the head of each school is greatly reduced. In fact, through our contact with Bay Street School, we also have learned that the principal has little power or even less power than the teacher. In terms of the relationship between the principal and the teacher, it is not at all like what is between the manager and the managed. The principal is basically a server or a coordinator. Even when there is a conflict between students, if it is handled by the principal, it is usually necessary to have someone from the school union present to avoid bias on the part of the principal. In the teachers' own words, principals are more like curriculum leaders, which impressed us deeply. We visited the principal in April 2019. There was a math syllabus on the desk and a math formula on the whiteboard on the wall. The principal told us in the interview that every week she goes to teacher's class to discuss the issues concerning mathematics teaching. We learned that she has been recently in the middle of a new curriculum plan. This is very different from the leadership role of BSS. The relationship between the principal and the teacher in BSS is very clear. Although the principal of BSS does not simply control and order teachers, they also respect and advocate for the autonomy of teachers, but when it comes to the overall work of the school, the relationship of leading and being led is always top-down.

Second, at Bay Street School, the teachers' professional development platform is not in the school, but is trained and evaluated by a school organization. So, the teacher holds a loose relationship with the School. Every school teacher is a relatively independent individual; professional cooperation between them is unlike the situation in BSS where teachers cooperate and are developed within the school. On this point, we can understand why Mr. Barton said:

> The teachers at your school are so happy that you can get together every week to share your experiences and solve difficult teaching problems together. But I feel very lonely in my own school. We all do our instruction behind closed doors, and we seldom communicate with each other. I want to participate in this program because I want to interact with you and be a part of you. (Interview, March 2016)

Third, the organizational background of Bay Street School is like being a member of a social network with the requirements for social development determined by the development concept of each school. Principals and teachers are independent educational practitioners, and they do not need to determine their own school characteristics and culture. This also explains why Bay Street School, despite 140 years of history, does not have its own unique cultural traditions. But when Principal Ting gave a report on school culture exchange, the head of the local education bureau, Bay Street School principals, teachers, and professors at the University of Toronto were surprised that a school would have its own ideas and cultural traditions. This will be further explained in Chap. 7.

Fourth, from the perspective of historical and cultural background, there are similarities and differences between the two schools in the past 40 years. Bay Street School is set up against the background of an immigration, multiculturalism, and differentiation of urban social strata; its basic education tasks include respect for differences, improvement of quality, and promotion of fairness. The basic path it followed were pursuing innovation in the 1960s and 1970s, developing school efficiency in the 1980s and 1990s, and seeking excellence and fairness today. By way of contrast, MPS was set up against the background of the transformation from a traditional society to a modern one, from agriculturalization to industrialization, urbanization, the intensification of population mobility, and the information society. Its basic mission of education is to eradicate the traditional way of knowledge transmission, improve teaching quality, promote teacher professional development, and perfect the school system and culture.

Against the backdrop of different practices and cultures, the two schools formed a sister school partnership. Next, we outline their path to cooperation.

5.2 The Process of Reciprocal Learning Between Sister Schools

We will briefly outline the communication process of the sister schools in the past seven years and the basic situation of the whole process. We have already briefly introduced the five-year communication process from 2013 to 2017 (Bu et al. 2019). Now, we will provide some more description.

5.2.1 Exploratory Phase (September 2013–September 2014)

The first exchange took place on October 11, 2013, with a video meeting bringing the partners together. This first video-meeting was attended by BSS's principal, one deputy principal, the teaching director, two to three teachers and several pupils, by Bay Street School's principal, deputy principal, teachers and five pupils, by Professor Yuhua Bu and her graduate students from East China Normal University, and by Professor Connelly and his graduate students from the University of Toronto. For the first time, we met and communicated with each other on points of interest that we believed could be learned from each other, including how to conduct an inquiry-based teaching model, how to manage child bullying in class, and how to cultivate students' explorations relating to environmental education. Possible ways of cooperation were also discussed, such as collective lesson preparation, recording teaching videos for exchange, cooperation on major festivals, and establishing resource-sharing websites. At the same time, we established sister classes and partner teachers, who agreed to a monthly one-hour video meeting.

Interestingly, despite the many agreements, everyone returned to their work and life after the meeting and seemed to forget the commitments made in the meeting. From October 2013 to May 2014, five video meetings between the two schools were conducted, the themes of which were scattered. They came up with a new theme each time, yet they lacked continuity. It was obvious that the stage of communication was more at the information-exchange level. The Sister Schools did not really learn from each other or do joint research at the practical level. They had no real topic that could help the teachers' day-to-day practice to be sustained, except for students giving gifts to each other around Christmas and Spring Festival.

At this stage, we adhered to the requirements of narrative inquiry and did not intervene in the reciprocal learning of the sister schools. However, our anxiety was deepening as we always felt that the reciprocal learning that the project hoped to achieve had not really occurred.

5.2.2 Breakthrough Phase (September 2014–December 2015)

In September 2014, Liu Yanting, a graduate student at East China Normal University, sent a section of BSS's math-class field notes on tangram to Canada. In October, Yishin Khoo told BSS that Ms. Ann Barton of the Bay Street School, who had already given her students a tangram lesson, was very interested in the teaching of tangram in BSS. When this message reached China, not only were we excited, Minzhu's principals and teachers were also surprised and excited. Cross-cultural learning between teachers finally took place. It can be said that Ms. Ann Barton was the critically important figure in the emergence of the sister schools. It was her initiative that truly marked the starting point of cross-cultural communication between teachers of the sister schools involved in this project.

From September to December 2014, Ms. Huang from Minzhu gave eight tangram lessons to the children in the lower age group. Liu Yanting and Li Lingyu, postgraduate volunteers from East China Normal University, recorded all the lessons in detail and sent them to Ms. Barton, who, in December of the same year, also carried out eight tangram-teaching activities for her class. Of course, instead of replicating Minzhu's classes directly, Ms. Barton creatively transformed them to adapt to her own teaching.

Beginning in January 2015, BSS introduced photos and information of children's activities during the Water Culture Festival and the school-based curriculum on water culture to Ms. Barton, who again became very interested. She and the children carried out a series of water conservation activities in February–April 2015, that were acknowledged by the Ontario Environmental Resources Bureau, which rewarded them with $5000. This development became known in Bay Street School and among local community residents. Parents and schools thought highly of it. Ms. Barton was also very happy. Among other things, she asked Mr. Min of BSS to provide them with various ways of writing "water" in Chinese and spent the 5000 Canadian dollars to have blue T-shirts custom-made with the word "water" in Chinese, as is shown in Fig. 5.1.

At the international conference held by the Canada-China Project in May 2015, the progress of reciprocal learning between the two schools was discussed by taking tangram learning and water culture learning as examples, which was positively acknowledged by the international review team of the project. This message naturally strengthened the initiative of the two schools in the Canada-China Reciprocal Learning Project in terms of intercultural reciprocal learning. Since then, Ms. Barton and Mr. ZhiGuo from Minzhu entered into a new stage of communication.

On the whole, reciprocal learning between sister schools in this stage occurred and had two distinguishing features. First, the learning took place partially. Second, the learning was presented asymmetrically. That is, the teaching experience of the Chinese school was more borrowed and

5 SOCIETY, HISTORY, AND INTERACTION OF SISTER SCHOOLS

Fig. 5.1 All kinds of artistic writing methods of Chinese "water" written by BSS students on World Water Day

learned by the Canadian side. However, the teachers from Shanghai seemed to have limited educational experience of Canada.

5.2.3 Development Phase (March 2016–October 2019)

If the second stage of sister school reciprocal learning is more about Chinese teachers exporting experience with their Canadian counterparts learning and transforming the Chinese experience, reciprocal learning is characterized by one-way output, instead of two-way communication. That is, the real cycle of reciprocity was not generated after the Canadian teachers transformed the experience of Chinese way of teaching if Chinese teachers did not consciously draw on or transform the Canadian experience. Fortunately, two-way reciprocity finally happened in March 2016, when the Bay Street School teachers paid a visit to Shanghai.

First Face-to-Face Communication: At BSS
Ms. Barton and Ms. Hanny, two teachers from Bay Street School, visited BSS from March 14 to 21, 2016. BSS gave them a warm welcome by not

only opening and presenting teaching and class life but also showing them other daily routines of the school: flag raising ceremony, morning exercises, exercises during the class break, and so on, as well as courses featuring school characteristics, such as the science classrooms and the water science and technology museum of the school. In addition, the principal, staff, students, and their parents also made and ate dumplings together with them. Their warm welcome to the guests from afar was especially illustrated by children's own paintings, music, and dance.

The exchange lasted five days during which time activities were rich and diverse. The teachers launched a comprehensive exchange in courses on Chinese, mathematics, English, scientific inquiry, music, nature, dance, as well as other class activities. Teachers of the two schools took cooperative teaching as the main mode of communication, basically presenting a class in each field. They observed each other's lessons and discussed and exchanged ideas immediately after each class. In this process, all the participants involved gained a lot, having a more intuitive, vivid, and profound understanding of each other's way of school life, style of teaching practice, and caring for students' growth. Later, they participated in the fourth annual symposium of the project held in Chongqing and delivered a group report together.

Second Face-to-Face Meeting: At Bay Street School
From May 28 to June 3, 2017, both BSS and Bay Street School were invited to attend the Canadian Education Annual Symposium and submitted a report. During this period, Bay Street School gave BSS principal and teachers the most enthusiastic reception which was attended by all the staff and students, parents, directors from the Toronto Education Bureau, and so on. The principal and teachers of BSS conducted a five-day inspection and study in all aspects in Ryerson. They participated in the Canadian Humanities and Social Sciences Academic Conference as well as the annual symposium of the Reciprocal Learning Project and made a group report together.

When the two teachers of Bay Street School paid a visit in March 2016, BSS learned more about each other only from the perspective of teaching philosophy and methods. This time, the principal and teachers of BSS had a comprehensive experience and understanding of the daily life of Bay Street School during the five-day return visit.

5.2.4 Continuous Symbiosis Phase (March 2018–Present)

With face-to-face contact and daily communication, the friendship between the two sister schools has deepened and entered a stage of continuous symbiosis.

The Third Face-to-Face Communication: In BSS

From May 12 to 17, 2018, Ms. Barton and Ms. Hanny visited BSS again. During this event, they faced a greater common task not only to communicate and make exchanges in education but also to hold a May 16 national on-site demonstration of "Intercultural Reciprocal Learning of Chinese-Canadian Sister Schools" attended by schools in Minzhu District as well as nearly 180 representatives from schools in 14 regions of the "New Basic Education" country-wide. They formed three cooperative teaching pairs: a class meeting jointly held by Ms. Hanny and Ms. Dongmei with the theme of character education; an English as a foreign language lesson taught together by Ms. Hanny and Ms. Ding; and a science inquiry lesson given by Ms. Barton and Ms. Liu. For the first time, they worked together to design, test, and then present the lessons to teachers across the country. The event was also attended by Professor Michael Connelly of the University of Toronto, Professor Ye Lan of East China Normal University, and Professor Cheryl Craig of the University of Texas A&M. At the meeting, we discussed the characteristics of their teaching class.

It was expected that they would complete the teaching in a harmonious way because of their mutual understanding for more than four years. Unfortunately, there was a conflict in the lesson preparation. For example, Ms. Barton thought that Ms. Liu and Mr. ZhiGuo always prepared too much content for students before class, fearing that the students would not be able to succeed in class. She does not understand why Chinese teachers do not allow students to be confused in class. "Isn't this a normal situation? Why are they not allowed to make mistakes? Why give them the answer in advance, so the inquiry is fake?" She repeated. The teacher at BSS simply explained, "This is what happens in China, and we must do this!" But what is it exactly? They do not really know.

Of course, this is not enough to prevent the two schools from continuing to communicate. Later, they made a team report together at the fifth annual symposium of the project held in Changchun, China.

The Fourth Face-to-Face Communication: At Bay Street School
In October 2019, the sixth annual academic symposium of the project was held in Windsor, Canada, marking the conclusion of the project. In order to participate in the symposium, the teachers of the two schools began to write papers together in July, gave group reports at the academic conference, and discussed how the friendship would last after the end of the project. Everyone expressed optimism. From October 4 to 7, Ms. Dongmei, principal of BSS, Ms. Ding, Ms. Dongmei, and members of the project team from East China Normal University visited Bay Street School again. Again, this visit was warmly welcomed by the Bay Street School. Also, Bay Street School was in the middle of a strike organized by the Toronto Teachers' Union, but the school overcame its difficulties to welcome its visitors as much as possible. In Bay Street School, we talked with the principal, teachers, and children in a usual way, just like visiting relatives. The teachers observed each other's classes, and Ms. Barton and Ms. Hanny showed us all the contents of their daily teaching in a completely open way, who at the same time had a cooperative teaching session with teachers from BSS. Afterwards, they worked together to make plans for future cooperation between the two schools.

Finally, the principals of the two schools, teachers, and the university professors and graduate volunteers held another meeting together. We agreed that even if the project was over, we had become one "family" and our friendship would last forever.

5.3 Basic Methods and Content of Cross-Cultural Reciprocal Learning Between Sister Schools

The interaction between the two sister schools takes place between multiple personnel (as is shown in Fig. 5.2): principals, teachers, and students. These people are sometimes present at the same time during face-to-face communication to achieve multidirectional communication. Due to language barriers and teachers' tight schedules, graduate students were organized by their respective professors of research groups from the University of Toronto and East China Normal University to act as volunteers to assist with the communication between the two sister schools. In other words, the participants in the sister schools' interaction are mainly teachers, who are assisted by graduate assistants who facilitate their communication.

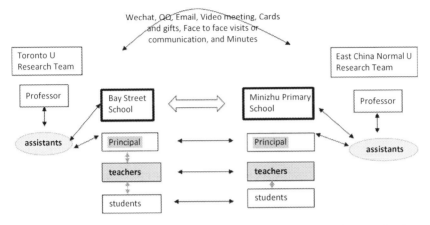

Fig. 5.2 Communication subjects and interactive relationship of sister schools

Graduate assistants mainly interact with teachers, and then communicate with principals, students, or university professors through teachers or graduate assistants.

5.3.1 Modes of Communication Between Sister Schools

The communication mode involves time, tools, and frequency of communication.

Mode 1: Skype Videoconferencing
In September 2013, the first communication between the two schools was via Skype videoconferencing. At that time, other convenient video media such as Zoom or Tencent Conference were not available. It was decided that a Skype videoconference was to be held at the beginning of each month during the semester, for the purpose of periodic summary and planning. The videoconferences were participated by a variety of subjects: principals, vice-principals, teachers, and sometimes students from both schools, as well as professors and graduate assistants from East China Normal University and the University of Toronto.

Due to the time difference of 12 hours between the two countries, in order to facilitate each other and show respect to the principle of equality, each exchange was arranged at either 7:00 p.m. in China (7:00 a.m. in

Canada) or 7:00 a.m. in China (or 7:00 p.m. in Canada). Being too early or too late would cause inconvenience such as teachers on one side might not be able to make it for their own lessons in time, or it would not be safe for teachers on the other side to be on the road home if it was too late. Therefore, the duration of communication is generally limited to about one hour. Sometimes, because the network signal was not good the meeting could be delayed by about ten minutes, and each time both sides would feel in a hurry, being able to exchange more important issues only. But video communication is still very important, as consensus could be reached more quickly, and everyone could see each other's faces and express and feel friendship through the video. Moreover, everyone could happily greet each other. The friendly atmosphere also contributes to the establishment of bilateral friendship.

Mode 2: QQ and WeChat Group Communication

This type of communication is also very important. We set up a QQ group and a WeChat group with the participation of all members and set up four to five groups according to differences in pairing of teachers or students. There are one to two graduate assistants or university professors in each group. The most frequently used means of daily communication is QQ and WeChat, both of which are convenient and low in cost. Over the first three years or so, more QQ groups were used, but as the frequency of WeChat use increased, most of the teachers in both schools turned to the latter. Over the last year, teachers also spontaneously set up WeChat groups for private communication as well.

Mode 3: Face-to-Face Interactive Communication

As mentioned earlier, sister schools have had the opportunity to visit each other once a year since 2016 for face-to-face communication. Each visit usually lasted about one week. This kind of communication is very important in deepening friendship and mutual understanding. Each time a sister school visits, the other school would plan ahead of time with well-arranged activities to welcome guests from afar. Take the visit of two teachers from Bay Street School to BSS from March 14 to 18, 2016 as an example. The schedule of the week was as follows:

5 SOCIETY, HISTORY, AND INTERACTION OF SISTER SCHOOLS

5.3.1.1 *March 14*

7:45 Principal, vice-principal, logistics director, and teaching director of BSS (MPS) picked up two teachers at the hotel in person

8:15 MPS held a welcoming ceremony at the school stadium for teachers and students, and the principal addressed the students, introducing the guests from afar

8:40 The principal, vice-principal, and related teachers showed the two teachers around Minzhu campus and gave an overview of the school

10:00 The two teachers attended one science class and one music class respectively

11:35 The two teachers and principal, vice-principal, and teachers had lunch together in the school canteen

13:00–16:30 Three teachers from MPS accompanied them to take part in World Water Day activities organized by WET with pupils from the Water Society of MPS

5.3.1.2 *March 15*

8:30–9:15 Met with the teachers of the research group, communicated with them, and gave them gifts. MPS introduced the one-week arrangement. The meeting involved 13 teachers from MPS and 7 graduate assistants.

9:25–10:00 Attended a science lesson given by Ms. Liu from MPS

10:15–10:50 Sister school teachers held a discussion exchanging ideas on Ms. Liu's lesson

11:00–11:35 Visited Mr. ZhiGuo's Science and Technology Studio and exchanged ideas with this head teacher about student management

13:00–16:30 Visited the surrounding communities of MPS to learn about local customs and culture

5.3.1.3 *March 16*

8:00–8:30 The two teachers took part in the morning exercises of MPS teachers and observed the students' morning exercises

8:40–11:35 Ms. Ding and Ms. Barton worked together to give two English lessons and held a discussion afterward

13:20–13:55 Ms. Barton attended Ms. Yanni's "Advanced Mathematics Class"

14:15–14:50 Ms. Barton attended Ms. Yanhong's math class on the teaching of "angles"

15:00–16:00 Ms. Barton exchanged views on mathematics teaching with all math teachers of MPS

5.3.1.4 *March 17*

8:40–9:15 Barton taught a nature lesson: "What is renewable energy?" (heterogeneous teaching on the same subject) observed by teachers from MPS

9:25–10:10 Mr. ZhiGuo taught a nature lesson: "What is renewable energy?" (heterogeneous teaching on the same subject) observed by Barton, Lily, and teachers from MPS

10:15–11:30 Teachers of the sister schools exchanged views on the two classes

13:00–13:35 Head teacher Zheng Xia's fourth-grade class meeting: "What to do when encountering contradictions?" (heterogeneous teaching on the same subject)

13:45–14:15 Ms. Barton and Ms. Hanny cooperated in a class meeting: "What to do when encountering contradictions?" (heterogeneous teaching on the same subject)

14:30–16:30 Ms. Barton, Ms. Hanny, and fourth-grade students, parents, and teachers of MPS made dumplings, ate dumplings, wrote calligraphy, exchanged gifts, and so forth.

5.3.1.5 *March 18*

8:45–9:45 Exchanged views with MPS principal, teaching director, teacher representatives on their four days of learning experience

10:00–11:20 Drew a "friendship map across the mountains and rivers" with Mr. ZhiGuo and the children from the Water Society and took pictures as a souvenir

13:00–16:00 Exchanged views with project members of East China Normal University and visited its campus

From their first face-to-face communications above, it can be seen that both sides had very rich content matter experiences and ways of communication. Through face-to-face communication, Ms. Barton and Ms.

Hanny almost experienced all the subject matter at BSS within one week, including morning exercises, classes, lunch, and their teaching and research culture. The teachers also had various forms of teaching communication, including heterogeneous classes, cooperative teaching, continuous teaching of two classes before and after class, discussion workshop after class, and joint lesson preparation before class. In this way, they could not only understand each other's ideas but also each other's educational and teaching characteristics in the process of cooperation and interaction. At the same time, various cultural experience activities further enhanced the friendship between the two sides.

Mode 4: Participate in the Annual Academic Symposium of the Grand Project
From 2014 to 2019, the Reciprocal Learning Project held an annual academic symposium every year. The two sister schools did not attend the symposium in the first two years, but for four consecutive years from 2016 to 2019, the sister school teachers jointly wrote conference papers, delivered group reports at the annual symposium, and participated in the internal meetings of the project team to summarize and address cooperation issues of the sister schools. For BSS principals and teachers, to participate in an academic symposium participated by university researchers and even speak there had not happened before. At first, BSS principals and teachers were very nervous, not knowing how to write papers or conference report. But after two years of experience, the teachers seemed very confident at the symposiums in 2018 and 2019. They communicated the theme of the conference report and worked together to complete conference papers. In the process, they also had more opportunities to learn from each other conceptually. Among the teachers in the sister schools, Ms. Barton is the one who stands out. Not only is she highly skilled in her teaching practice and often commended by Chinese teachers, she is also a teacher with great ability to do research. She has mastered a whole set of research methods like the university researchers. She is good at collecting data and writing research papers. Her analysis of certain issues is also very profound, making BSS teachers often feel a bit ashamed, yet very appreciative of their Canadian sister teacher in this grand project.

132 Y. BU

5.3.2 Contents of Communication Between Sister Schools

What we will present now is how people with different roles communicate differently. Here we specifically mean the principals, the teachers, and the students.

5.3.2.1 Communication Between Principals

During the seven years of the project, Bay Street School had three principals: the first from 2013 to 2015; the second from 2015 to 2017, and the third from 2018 to now. Due to frequent changes in principals, the communication between principals also was different. For example, during the two years from 2013 to 2014, the two principals of the sister schools had a warm communication, and the nature of their communication was relatively broad. As is shown in Table 5.1, the content of their conversations involved principal's responsibilities and evaluation, teacher evaluation, student development evaluation, the convening of parent meetings, the formulation of student behavior norms, the resolution of student bullying, and so on.

From 2015 to 2017, the second principal of Bay Street School was not particularly enthusiastic about the sister school project at first because he did not know much about it. However, he still supported the communication between the teachers of the two schools. During their visit to Bay Street School in May 2017, the principal and teachers of BSS were warmly received by the principal of Bay Street School, who introduced them to the school's curriculum, the school environment, the role and duties of the principal, and the manner in which the teacher was evaluated. Principal Ting was deeply moved and also gave Bay Street School a comprehensive introduction to her school's history, educational philosophy, school system, and school culture, which was highly appreciated by Bay Street School principals and teachers.

From 2018 to 2019, the principal of BSS and the third principal of Bay Street School first met each other at a video conference, and everyone pledged their friendship. When they met face-to-face in October 2019, the third principal also showed warmth and friendliness, exchanged the basic situation of school development, and looked forward to the future together.

5 SOCIETY, HISTORY, AND INTERACTION OF SISTER SCHOOLS 133

Table 5.1 Reciprocal learning between principals of sister schools (2013–2014)

Year	Content of reciprocal learning by school principals	
	Bay Street School	Minzhu Primary School
2013	• Inquiry-based teaching model	• How to determine the responsibilities of the vice-principal
	• Environmental science education	• How to hold the staff meeting
	• Bullying among children	• How to hold parent meetings
	• How to formulate methods and contents of student behavior norms	
2014	• The success criteria for students' performance evaluation	• The principal's weekly log, to understand the daily work of the principal
	• The principal's weekly log, to understand the daily work of the principal	• The work plan of teaching and evaluation based on curriculum standards in Shanghai
	• A sample of teacher research reports	• Comments on the implementation of the job evaluation of primary and middle school teachers in Shanghai
	• Student assessment samples	• Video of Principal Ting's participation in student activities
	• Assessment criteria for principals and vice-principals	
	• Ontario teacher evaluation mechanism	

The content of communication among teachers is characterized by different stages:

In the first year (2013), sister school teachers were mainly at the stage of getting to know each other and shared some basic information such as the school, curriculum, teacher responsibilities, teaching methods, student composition, and the like, intended to find common grounds in interest, as well as the most appropriate content and way of communication. Other exchanges around specific themes were not listed.

In the second year (2014), communication was mainly carried out through video, and daily communication was rare. Even when the graduate assistants provided videos or field notes about teaching, it did not seem to stimulate the willingness of both sides to learn from each other. In each meeting, participators determined some topics for the next meeting. The principal arranged teachers based on those meeting topics which resulted in too many participants with nothing to do. What is worse is that those teachers did not achieve their goals and then they dropped out gradually without satisfying their expectations. Frequent shifts on personnel make it very hard for us to promote collaboration. From Table 5.2, we see that Ms. Gu's and Ms. Barton's participation was a turning point of collaboration.

The classes of two teachers have been chosen to be sister class, thus a sustained relationship has been built. Since June 26, 2014, the two teachers' communication became the main stream of collaboration. They actively participated in the cooperation, and most themes were discussed between them.

In the third year (2015), communications between Bay Street School and Minzhu Primary School involved three pairs of teacher partners and three themes. First, there was Mathematics teaching with Ms. Gu/Ms. Huang and Ms. Barton. They carried out exchanges on math-art integrated lessons using tangrams. There were 56 letters communicated through email. The communication includes two key activities and achievements: (1) Ms. Gu in BSS shared the Chinese tangram lesson and curriculum with Ms. Barton in Bay Street School; (2) Ms. Barton's class had the tangram project. They shared their lesson notes with one another. Second, Mr. ZhiGuo and Ms. Barton had exchanges on the theme of Water Science. Their exchanges involved 41 letters communicated through email. On January 3, 2015, Ms. Gu's students sent Ms. Barton's students three videos: the first video was about Minzhu's science and technology camps; the second video was about Minzhu's water world; the third video was about Minzhu's water culture school-based curricula. Ms. Barton and her students were very excited after they saw these videos. Ms. Barton wanted to engage her students in building a water culture in Ryerson too. She also wanted to conduct further exchanges with Minzhu around water activities. Ms. Barton worked with her students for a period of two months to plan and execute a series of activities that promote water awareness at Ryerson. On May 12, 2005, both Ms. Barton and Mr. ZhiGuo agreed to get their students to design the character of water collaboratively. After

5 SOCIETY, HISTORY, AND INTERACTION OF SISTER SCHOOLS

Table 5.2 Themes of video conferences of sister schools in 2014

	February 14, 2014	*May 29, 2014*	*June 26, 2014*	*September 17, 2014*	*October 24, 2014*
BSS	1. Exchange of videos 2. Students: how to finance 3. Students how to confirm their studying level	A summary of exchanges between Principal Ting and Principal Tsuji on the following topics: 1. Principals' works and responsibilities 2. Students' performance appraisal exchanges 3. Teachers' works and learning	Conversation between Ms. Barton and Ms. Gu's: 1. Plan for summer vacation 2. Math learning 3. Hobby and sports 4. Conflict between classmates cultivation of team spirit 5. Preparation plan for graduation conversation among Ms. Barton, Ms. Gu, and Mr. Xia: a. teachers training b. teachers' teaching content c. students assessment	Discussion between Ms. Barton and Ms. Gu: 1. Assessing learning in Math 2. Seat-pockets in Ms. Barton's classroom 3. To what degree can teachers incorporate creativity and subject-integration in their classes 4. Potential collaboration activities between two teachers	1. Ms. Huang: tangram class 2. Ms. Barton: integrated lesson 3. Class collaboration will be discussed in the next meeting
MPS	1. Introduce new participators 2. Students' activities in winter vacation 3. The Lantern Festival activities between sister class 4. Collaborated forms of students 5. Performance-based assessment 6. Discussion: potential English lesson exchange 7. Schedule of principals of two sides				

Mr. ZhiGuo's students had designed the water characters according to Chinese calligraphy, Mr. ZhiGuo sent those pictures to Ms. Barton's students, hoping that Ms. Barton's students could add water-related pictures and words to the water characters made by students of BSS.

Third, language teaching communication. Ms. Lyli and Ms. Ding exchanged notes with each other about students' writing English poems called "I'm from…" The two sides found huge cultural differences in English poetry writing between the students of the two countries: students in Hanny's class were more likely to depict the life experience of "I" in the real world, while students in Ding's class were more likely to write virtual or metaphorical "I", such as "I" representing the country, society, bird, spaceship, or monster.

From the fourth to the seventh year (2015–2019), the two sister schools entered the stage of regular communication, which mainly occurred between two pairs of teachers. The first pair is Ms. Barton versus Mr. ZhiGuo and Ms. Liu, who mainly focused on some of the teaching themes for the Water Society, such as the impact of water on people's lives, the relationship between indigenous people and water, designing activities for the theme of World Water Day, water conservation, the design of innovative topics in water science and technology, and so forth. The second pair is Ms. Hanny versus Ms. Ding, who focus on language and culture teaching communication, such as the teaching of picture books and stories, the teaching of Chinese Dragon Boat Festival culture, and the teaching of writing. Of course, teachers also communicate about teachers' daily cooperative research when paying face-to-face visits. Sometimes Ms. Hanny also communicated with Ms. Dongmei about the character education of students as well as class management.

In a word, through communication on such contents, teachers became increasingly focused on topics, which have become more extensive and flexible. By 2019, the two sides had often carried out heterogeneous teaching on the same subject and common project research studies.

5.3.2.2 Communication Among Students

The content of communication between students is relatively limited mainly due to language barriers. Their communication mainly includes pictures and gifts of festive cultural activities and favorite daily life topics such as games they love to play, activities during the break, favorite sayings, and movies. Sometimes, they would exchange letters or homework. Meanwhile, the two schools selected some classes as sister classes and set up a pen pal for each participant allowing them to communicate autonomously. The most important thing is not the content of communication, but that the children of the two schools got to know each other that there are friends on the other side of the ocean, and their affections are felt for each other, of profound significance to the cultivation of children's awareness of cross-cultural communication at an early age!

5.4 Summary

It can be found that this pair of sister schools, one with a history of more than 200 years, one with a history of more than 60 years. They are in different social and cultural background, with different development history, bearing different educational missions given by society and the state, but they meet and communicate closely for more than ten years in the twenty-first century. What a magical fate! Although their whole communication process was not very smooth at the beginning, it seems that the difference itself is the biggest attraction. The principals, teachers, and students of sister schools have overcome many difficulties. The further they go, the deeper their friendship, the more they learn, and the deeper their mutual understanding! Then, they all feel that in the process of meeting each other, they not only have a clearer understanding of themselves and each other but also achieve the best of themselves. In the next few chapters, we will learn more about their detailed learning process and their growth and harvest!

References

Anderson, S. E. (2006). The School District's Role in Educational Change. *International Journal of Educational Reform, 15*(1), 13–37.

Anderson, S., & Rodway-Macri, J. (2009). District Administrator Perspectives on Student Learning in an Era of Standards and Accountability: A Collective Frame Analysis. *Canadian Journal of Education, 32*, 192–221.

Board, T. D. S. (2006). Model Schools for Inner Cities Brochure. Retrieved September 30, 2019, from www.tdsb.on.ca

Bu, Y., Qi, S., Zhong, C., & Zhu, Y. (2019). Cong 'Li Tu' Dao 'Zai Di': Zhong Jia Zimei Xiao Kua Wenhua Huhui Xuexi de Shijian Tansuo 从"离土"到"在地": 中加姊妹校跨文化互惠学习的实践探索 (From "Grounding off" to "Grounding on": The Practical Exploration on Cross-Cultural Reciprocal Learning in China-Canada Sister Schools). *Global Education, 48*(6), 62–73.

Education, O. M. o. (2008). Delivering Excellence for All Ontario Students. Retrieved June 22, 2019, from www.edu.gov.on.ca/eng/document/reports/excellence/ontedu.pdf

Education, O. M. o. (2009). Ontario's Equity and Inclusivity Education Strategy. Retrieved July 23, 2019, from https://www.edu.gov.on.ca/eng/policyfunding/equity.pdf

Education, O. M. o. (2014). Achieving Excellence: A Renewed Vision for Education in Ontario. Retrieved June 22, 2019, from http://www.edu.gov.on.ca/eng/about/renewedVision.pdf

Encyclopedia, C. (2009). Minzhu District *China Encyclopedia Database*. Shanghai: China Encyclopedia Database Press.

Gooijer, B. d., & Huber, L. (2018). The Importance of Public Education to Canadian Society. https://leaderpost.com/opinion/columnists/the-importance-of-public-education-to-canadian-society.

Immigrants, O. C. o. A. S. (2004). The Regularization of non-status immigrants in Canada 1960–2004: Past policies, current perspectives, active campaigns. Ontario: Ontario Council of Agencies Serving Immigrants.

Milner, R. (2012). But What is Urban Education? *Urban Education, 47,* 556–561.

School Board. (2015). Retrieved July 2019, from http://www.tdsb.on.ca/Community/Model Schools for Inner Cities/The Program.aspx

Shah, V. (2016). *Urban District Reform for Equity: The Case of the Model Schools for Inner Cities Program in the Toronto District School Board.* Toronto: University of Toronto.

Solomon, P. (2007). What is Urban Education? In W. Hare & J. Portelli (Eds.), *Key Questions for Educators* (pp. 120–123). Halifax, Nova Scotia: Edphil Books.

Solomon, P., Singer, J., Campbell, A., & Allen, A. (2011). *Brave New Teachers: Doing Social Justice Work in Neoliberal Times* (Key Questions for Educators). Toronto: Canadian Scholars' Press.

CHAPTER 6

Circles and Straight Lines: Teachers' Life Worlds

Yuanyuan Zhu

6.1 Introduction

In this chapter, we focus on the narratives of the teachers in sister schools in "Reciprocal Learning in Teacher Education and School Education Between Canada and China" Program (RLP). Their stories show different characteristics in teachers' teaching, lesson preparation and discussion between China and Canada. We try to explain the reasons for the differences from the perspective of education systems and cultures. To some extent, the reflection on these differences presents what the Chinese and Canadian teachers can learn from each other and the positive role of reciprocal learning in teacher development.

"Circles" and "straight lines" are metaphors. Initially, we used them to describe the differences in students' school life between China and Canada. During the visits to two schools, we found that in Canadian classrooms, students were free and relaxed, and they would choose their most

---

Y. Zhu (✉)
Department of Education, East China Normal University, Shanghai, China

© The Author(s), under exclusive license to Springer Nature
Switzerland AG 2021
Y. Bu (ed.), *Narrative Inquiry into Reciprocal Learning Between Canada-China Sister Schools*, Intercultural Reciprocal Learning in Chinese and Western Education,
https://doi.org/10.1007/978-3-030-61085-2_6

139

140   Y. ZHU

comfortable posture; they would sit with the teachers as the center. Chinese classrooms have stricter requirements for behavior. Teachers' podiums are in the front of classrooms with children's desks arranged in parallel, orderly lines. In China's primary school, "lines" are everywhere. Children line up for school, line up for morning exercises, line up for physical education, line up for lunch and so on. "Circle" and "lines" are our most intuitive feelings of students' school life in the two countries at the beginning of research. Furthermore, in this chapter, "circle" and "lines" are not only a description of the differences but also metaphors about teaching concepts and the methods of teachings used.

6.2   Conceptualizing the Background

6.2.1   Teachers and Teachers' Teaching in Different Contexts

6.2.1.1   Classroom Teaching Reform and Teachers' Development in Chinese Context

In China, challenges and educational reform brought about by globalization and rapid economic development have become the key concerns in education studies in the past 30 years. At the end of the twentieth century, more and more Chinese education scholars found that the traditional classroom teaching has been unable to meet the needs of cultivating "new people in new era". The goals of teaching need to shift from transferring knowledge to developing students' initiatives and their awareness and capacity (Ye 1994, 1997; Zhong 1999; Lu 1998; Sun et al. 1995). A high-quality classroom teaching is no longer just about how much knowledge students have mastered, but students' understanding and application of knowledge, as well as the development of abilities, such as questioning, criticism and creativity, which are basic competences to meet the challenges of modern society. Such classroom teaching usually has the characteristics of full participation and openness (Ye 1997, 2002, 2005; Bu 2016). In this context, schools all over China conducted classroom teaching reform through experimenting with different ways of providing official guidance, university-school cooperation and interschool cooperation. However, regardless of the form adopted, how to shift teachers' thinking and doings on teaching in classroom teaching reform was always considered as the core issues of the reform. Teachers' roles need to shift from "transferring knowledge to students" to "constructing knowledge with students", from "curriculum implementer" to "curriculum maker" or "knowledge constructor", which has become a basic consensus in the classroom teaching reform and teacher development research (Bu et al. 2019; Shi 1998; Ye 1998; Bai 2002; Ning and Liu 2000).

Since 1994, the "New Basic Education" (NBE) research program led by Professor Ye Lan has made 26 years of research in solving the above problems of classroom teaching reform and teacher development, and accumulated a set of practical and effective methods and strategies. Compared with other reform projects, NBE has several distinctive characteristics. (a) A reconstructive research approach promoting the overall transformation of entire schools (nine-year compulsory education) as its units of change. As Li explains, "NBE's aim is to alter people's perspectives on education, to include school leadership in the reform, to change teaching and to mend the theory-practice chasm" (Li 2019). (b) Lesson type research on communicating "theory" and "practice". Lesson type research is an overall structural analysis and understanding of teaching objectives, contents, process methods, evaluation methods and their relationships. It urges teachers to pay attention to and combine the structural characteristics and educational value of knowledge in literature, mathematics, language and other disciplines, and turn the "knowledge structure" into learning process and strategy for students. (c) Through the cooperative and symbiotic research model, teaching research activities and cultivating of "backbone teachers" (Bu and Han 2019), affecting the understanding and practicing on teaching of other teachers, thus driving the development of the whole teacher community.

Minzhu Primary School (MPS), a participating school in Shanghai-Toronto Sister School Network, is one of the lead schools in the NBE research project and the model school in its district. The school is open and innovative and has the common characteristics of NBE schools. Most of the school students come from working-class families, which is similar to Bay Street School (BSS, the sister school in Canada). How to better promote the development of children in urban, working-class families through school education, and how to enable children to adapt to the challenges of an increasingly open and interconnected world, the thinking of such issues laid the foundation for their cooperation.

6.2.1.2 Diversity and Cross-Cultural Learning in Teachers' Teaching in Canadian Context

Teacher development and school education in the context of globalization are also the key issues examined by Western education researchers.

Compared with the East, Western studies have studied more about how to build a globally oriented education system and cross-cultural reciprocal learning model in education (Cushner 2007; Merryfield 2000; Shijing Xu and Connelly 2017).

As is well recognized by public, Canada is a multicultural country, especially since the twenty-first century. With the influx of new immigrants from Asian countries, the Canadian school landscape has been altered significantly. The proportion of Asian students in Toronto Schools is increasing, especially with those who are Chinese. Changing migration patterns and demographics have had an important impact on education, which raises issues of diversity in education. Therefore, teachers need to help students acquire and enhance the twenty-first-century competencies including appropriate skills, knowledge, attitudes and perspectives in a globalized world that is more and more interdependently connected. This has gradually become the consensus of Canada education reform. The Ontario Ministry of Education claimed that teachers should "highlight the importance of inclusion" (Ontario Ministry of Education 2015, p. 17) and have "an appreciation for the diversity of people, perspectives, and the ability to envision and work toward a better and more sustainable future for all" (Education 2015, 2017). That is to say, in an increasingly diversified society, it is important to respect diversity and appreciate different cultures, rather than promoting one-sided integration and adaptation of newcomers and immigrants. Teachers need to possess a multicultural and cross-cultural view. They need to believe that newcomers and immigrants could bring values and ways of thinking that are educationally useful and important in the Canadian setting.

Bay Street School, an urban Toronto school cooperating with Minzhu Primary School in Shanghai-Toronto Sister School Network, has a large proportion of Asian immigrant students and 70% of its children born outside Canada speak either Mandarin or Cantonese (Shijing Xu 2011; Xu and Connelly 2017) in school. Cultural diversity and inclusiveness have been the key in teaching them. In order to better understand the Chinese children from the cultural context and "become both culturally responsive and globally minded teachers for the increasingly diverse society and the constantly changing international world" (Shijing Xu 2019) through international and intercultural reciprocal learning, Bay Street School joined the RLP.

6.2.2 *Reciprocal Learning Across Cultures in RLP*

Reciprocal learning is the core concept of the RLP. Instead of a competition, the conception of reciprocal learning is "built around the metaphor of a two-way bridge in which two-way learning occurs" (Connelly and Xu 2019) in RLP. This kind of two-way learning is based on the relationship of equality, understanding and respect of participants, and is expected to be mutually beneficial in knowledge, values and teaching methods. When reciprocal learning takes place in teachers of two countries, it symbolizes the communication between different historical-cultural narratives and different contexts of education, which may promote teachers to learn new ways of thinking and concept. As Xu and Connelly (2017) state, it is based on but goes beyond the model of comparative education, comparative achievement/values and comparative pedagogy (Xu and Connelly 2017). It is a collaborative partnership model among different cultural contexts of education.

In order to better promote the reciprocal learning among teachers in China and Canada, the Shanghai-Toronto project team established the sister school network, which provided the possibility of establishing a close relationship between MPS and BSS (Bu et al. 2019; Xu and Connelly 2017). Sister schools are reciprocal learning pathways for equal dialogue and collaborative research in basic education in China and Canada. The communications between sister schools are based on shared vision and the principle of autonomy and willingness. The goal is to promote cross-cultural reciprocal learning among teachers and to clarify their own cultural characteristics and cultural identity. That is to say, the result of cross-cultural reciprocal learning in sister schools is not "I become you" or "you become me", but "I become a better me, you become a better you, and we together become members of the new world" (Bu et al. 2019).

6.3   RESEARCH METHODOLOGY

Narrative inquiry was developed by Connelly and Clandinin (1990) when they studied the problem of "what teachers know", which later was termed "personal practical knowledge" by them (Connelly and Clandinin 1990). Personal practical knowledge was described as being "in a person's experience, in the person's present mind and body and in the person's future plans and actions", and was "constructed and reconstructed as we live out our stories and retell and relive them through the process of reflection"

(Clandinin and Connelly 1992). Narrative inquiry, as a research approach, is a way of elucidating teachers' personal practical knowledge in their own terms (Craig et al. 2012). Narrative inquiry studies human experiences through story and interprets personal experience in a meaningful way. Through the process of telling and retelling the stories teachers live, changes happen in individual's practices and socially change the educational landscape, which is an important embodiment of the image of "teacher as the curriculum maker" (Clandinin and Connelly 1992).

6.3.1 Data Collection

This chapter focuses on the language group of paired teachers in Shanghai-Toronto sister schools. Since the sister school relationship was established, teachers have communicated online through QQ, WeChat and email. Graduate assistants regularly (usually weekly or monthly) visit sister classes to observe cooperative research courses and make field notes. All records are translated and sent to teachers and researchers by graduate assistants from both sides. Since 2015, our author team has been involved in the RLP project, maintaining formal and informal contact with teachers in sister schools, and participated in three mutual visits of teachers in sister schools, collecting a large number of data, including interview transcription, field notes, audios of classroom teaching and activities. Our data also includes analysis of documents such as policy documents, participants' personal reflections and their research papers presented in conference or journal.

6.3.2 Data Analysis

The analysis of data involves the three interpretation tools of narrative inquiry: broadening, burrowing, storying and restorying (Connelly and Clandinin 1990). The first tool, broadening, situates the sister schools and teachers' teaching in historical and social-cultural context. The second tool, burrowing, explains teachers' experiences in micro-detail while concurrently paying attention to competing and conflicting points of view (Craig et al. 2013). Storying and restorying help us discover and understand all the changes happening in a period of time, whether obvious or not. Following the RLP research ethics protocol, the authors used fictionalization as a research tool (Clandinin et al. 2006; Craig et al. 2013). The name of the school and all of the participants have been replaced with pseudonyms in addition to other subtle changes.

6.3.3 Introducing the Teachers and the Researcher

There are three teachers in the language group of Shanghai-Toronto sister schools. They are Ms. Hanny from Bay Street School and Ms. Dongmei and Ms. Ding from Minzhu Primary School. Later, their stories and narrative experiences will appear. For now, we briefly introduce the three teachers and the researcher, one of the author team.

6.3.3.1 The Teachers

Lily Hanny is a comprehensive teacher at Bay Street School. She is young and has developed her own understanding and ways of teaching, especially where language and character education are concerned. Ms. Hanny's participation in the project is fueled by her students' need for growth experiences. Since there are many Chinese children in Ms. Hanny's class, she hopes to take this opportunity to improve her understanding of the students and their culture. In addition, her cooperation with two Chinese teachers is based on her professional interests. Ann Barton, who joined the program earlier, is familiar with her and has been actively encouraging her to join. She joined the RLP in 2014, but there was no mature cooperative relationship and communication model between the Chinese and Canadian teachers at that time. The situation changed when Ms. Ding joined the project.

Ms. Ding is an excellent English backbone teacher in Minzhu Primary School. She joined the NBE research project in 1999 and was among the first group of backbone teachers cultivated in Minzhu Primary School. At that time, she had just become a teacher and was not influenced by the traditional classroom teaching model. Therefore, she came to be a teacher with modern teaching ideas and often conducted public demonstration courses on behalf of school or district backbone teacher. Her classroom is lively, interesting and often highly praised by other teachers. Children in her classes are active and participate positively. In September 2015, Ms. Ding voluntarily participated in the RLP and become the paired language teacher with Ms. Hanny. Their classes became sister classes and began to focus on explorations concerning language teaching. Later, as teachers of sister classes, they carried out various activities such as pen pal letter writing, creation of alphabet books and dictionaries, exploration of cultural festivals, picture book exchange and lesson study. Their long-term cooperation made the two teachers very familiar with and appreciative of each other.

Ms. Dongmei is a very experienced Chinese teacher and has been a headteacher (also called Banzhuren, in Chinese, is responsible for the students' management and development of a class) for many years. In fact, she participated in RLP in 2008; at that time, the project was in the initial stage, but she still remained in basic communication, giving gifts and writing letters. Later, because her grade level changed, Ms. Dongmei left the project. In March 2016, when Ms. Hanny first visited Minzhu Primary School, she observed a Banhui lesson with the theme of "gratitude". Banhui lessons are irregular courses that assist with classroom management and student development in China. They are similar to class meetings and character education in Canada. Therefore, Ms. Hanny became interested in the Banhui lesson, a themed class meeting for moral education. When Canadian teachers visited Minzhu Primary School again in May 2018, the RLP teachers tried to co-teach a Banhui lesson. They taught the lesson, *Brave Duck, Brave Me*, for the first time. In the 2018–2019 semester, the two teachers started a series of lessons and research around "self-awareness" and produced rich results. Ms. Dongmei is a very reflective teacher. Both partners pay keen attention to vulnerable groups of students and seek their professional growth.

6.3.3.2 The Researcher

As a member of the NBE RL team, Yuanyuan Zhu had two roles. As an assistant, she participated in the project and promoted the communication between Chinese and Canadian teachers; as a researcher, she was living and telling her story as she observed and presented their stories. Therefore, let us begin with her experience of "meeting" and "entering" into the project in 2015 and how the teachers' "focus" shifted over the time.

When the project began, Yuanyuan Zhu just thought it was a reciprocal project between schools in different countries. It was not until March 2016 that she had the first close contact with this project and the teachers because of the visit of Canadian teachers from Bay Street School to Minzhu Primary School. Yuanyuan Zhu was surprised at the way Canadian teachers teach and how their ideas are different from those in China. Their way of teaching is not what Chinese teachers are "accustomed to", and they, in return, are also surprised by how efficiently Chinese teachers teach classes in such short frames of time. Both teachers and researchers focused on the "differences".

In May 2017, Yuanyuan Zhu attended the experience sharing meeting held by Minzhu Primary School after they visited Bay Street School in Canada. In the stories that the teachers and researchers shared, she found that they were balanced and confident. They appreciated the atmosphere and ideas they experienced in the Canadian school and how the classes there were different from those of China. The teachers thought about the reasons for the differences from a practical perspective. It seems a shift had occurred. They were no longer focusing only on differences but on the causes of the differences as well (i.e., structure of curriculum).

In March 2018, the Canadian teachers visited Minzhu Primary School again and co-taught with the Chinese teachers again. In the co-teaching activity of Ms. Hanny and Ms. Dongmei, Yuanyuan Zhu was surprised that the "differences" seemed less obvious, and the two achieved a kind of tacit understanding and integration of the East and the West. Then, she interviewed Ms. Dongmei and noticed that the local administrators became involved and influenced their lesson discussion and preparation. From Ms. Dongmei's narrative, she saw her growth, her interaction with Ms. Hanny, her subsequent confusion and the restraint from outside, which prompted me to shift my focus from the differences to a focus on teachers themselves as they engaged in reciprocal learning. After that, Yuanyuan Zhu wrote the project report with Dr. Bu, Cheng Zhong and Shan Qi. The report gave her a systematic understanding of the RLP. She learned how teachers, graduate assistants and university professors have been exploring and supporting each other step-by-step since the beginning of the project. She also began to focus on growth and on teachers' personal stories.

In October 2019, Dr. Bu and Yuanyuan Zhu attended the "East-West Reciprocal Learning International Conference" in Canada and visited Bay Street School. In the lesson preparation discussion of Ms. Hanny, Ms. Dongmei and Ms. Ding, she confirmed that they had developed implicit understandings and a mature reciprocal learning mode, even without an "expert" from the educational administration or university faculty. This state continues to this day. As graduate assistants and researchers gradually left the RLP, teachers began to communicate independently and creatively to promote their sister classes themes.

6.4 SHANGHAI-TORONTO SISTER SCHOOL TEACHERS STORIES

In this section, we mainly present three narratives of experience (Connelly and Clandinin 1990). The first story happened in March 2016, when teachers of Bay Street School visited Minzhu Primary School and co-taught with Chinese teachers. This story is about different approaches to teaching the same theme and involved Ms. Hanny and Ms. Ding. They illuminate different teaching styles between China and Canada. The second story took place in May 2018, when teachers of Bay Street School visited Minzhu Primary School once again and participated in the on-site meeting of Minzhu Primary School. This story revolves around Ms. Hanny and Ms. Dongmei in the lesson preparation. The third story took place in October 2019, when teachers of Minzhu Primary School visited Bay Street School. It is also a story about lesson preparation. The protagonists of the story are still Ms. Hanny, Ms. Dongmei and Ms. Ding. Although the background is similar, the third story takes a different direction from the second story.

6.4.1 Heterogeneous Lesson: "The Tree's Shadow"

The theme of the Heterogeneous Lesson (heterogeneous forms for the same subject) is "The Tree's Shadow". This is the third unit of the first module of fourth-grade Oxford English book. Ms. Ding is in charge of the first lesson, while Ms. Hanny is in charge of the second lesson.

Part 1: Ms. Ding's Teaching Process
The students sat quietly in their seats waiting for the class. In order not to disturb them, the teachers, the assistants and the principal all sat at the back of the classroom. But I noticed that Ms. Xia, the headteacher (*Ban Zhu Ren*, 班主任), was sitting right in front of the classroom, next to the door. Ms. Ding was wearing a pink sweater and a black skirt today, which made her look beautiful and sunny. With a smile, she asked the students, "Are you happy today?", "Are you ready?" The students all answered "Yes!" Ms. Ding clapped her hands and said, "OK, class begin". She beckoned the students to "say hello to our teachers". The students turned around and waved, "Hello teachers, welcome to Minzhu".

The class began. Ms. Ding first presented a riddle using a PowerPoint slide and asked the students to guess the riddle. Then a boy raised his hand

and said, "This is a shadow". Ms. Ding led the students to read the word "shadow" and use their hands to indicate the rise and fall of intonation. Then she asked a row of students to demonstrate the word. Then Ms. Ding played a hand shadow video where there were shadows of various small animals. Ms. Ding asked the students, "I see the people shadow, how about you?" The students answered: "I can see the rabbit shadow", "I can see the deer shadow"... Ms. Ding concluded: "So we can see many shadows in the movie. Today we will talk about shadows".

Then Ms. Ding showed a picture of the shadow of a tree. She told the students that the shadow of a tree changes a lot during a day. "Let us think about the difference between the shadow in the morning, noon and evening", she said. Ms. Ding then invited the students to listen to a recording carefully, and then queried: "Where is the tree's shadow in the morning, at noon and in the evening?" While listening to the recording, she turned around and wrote three time-phrases on the blackboard: "in the morning, at noon, in the evening".

After listening to the recording, Ding pointed to the PowerPoint slide (a picture of tree shadow is shown above): "Who can have a try? Where is the tree's shadow in the morning?" One student answers: "It's on the lawn". Ms. Ding then slowed down her speech: "lawn [lɔː n]. How do we spell the "lawn"? Who can have a try?" One student replied: "L-A-W-N, lawn". Ms. Ding smiled and praised the student and wrote "on the lawn" after "in the morning". Ding pointed to "aw" to pronounce /ɔː/ and asked the students to read the phrase "on the lawn". Then, she led the students to answer the location of the tree shadow at noon and night, which is "on the bench" and "on the path". When reading "bench", students often read "beach" by mistake. Ms. Ding did not directly point out the students' mistakes, but she would show a questioning expression when the students read the mistakes. It seems that she asked the students to confirm the pronunciation again, and then focused on leading the students to read the pronunciation of "en".

After that, another PowerPoint slide presented the complete three sentences that represent the change of tree shadow at different times:

Lawn, lawn, on the lawn.
In the morning, the tree's shadow is on the lawn.
Bench, bench, on the bench.
At noon, the tree's shadow is on the bench.
Path, path, on the path.
In the evening, the tree's shadow is on the path.

Ding asked students to cover their mouth with their hands and read the sentences softly, and then clapped their hands and read aloud in the music.

Next, by listening to the recording and observing the pictures, Ms. Ding asked the students to describe the changes of the tree shadows in different time, and expressed it with "long", "short", "grow long" and "grow short". She asked the students to think about why the tree shadow change? Some students answered. Ms. Ding presented the answer with PowerPoint and asked the students to read it three times.

Finally, Ms. Ding presented three pictures and asked the students to judge whether it was morning, noon or evening based on the shadow. After the discussion, the students gave the answers. From the results of the answers, the students were able to fully express the phrases taught by Ms. Ding. Ms. Ding then demonstrated how to do hand-shadow games, and the class ended.

Part 2: Ms. Hanny's Teaching Process

Moving on to the next lesson, Ms. Hanny claps her hands rhythmically. Her clapping successfully attracts the children's attention. Although Ms. Hanny did not say a word, the children seem to understand that their teacher reminds them to prepare for class.

Match and Retell the Words Learnt Last Class

Ms. Hanny takes out a stack of prepared cards. There are two kinds of cards. One has a picture; the other is an English word. Each picture card has a word card corresponding to it, such as the picture of grass corresponds to the word "lawn". Hanny gave the cards to individual students and asked them to look for matching students to sit together, according to the cards they received.

The card game disrupts the original seats students were sitting in (in China, because there are more students in each class, each student has his own fixed seat and partner, and generally there is a seat adjustment every semester). By matching words, each student's location and partner changed. However, not all of the students can accept this kind of "breaking the rule". One student refused to sit with the student who matched the word. Because she did not like him, she thought he was usually annoying and did not want to cooperate with him. She went to Ms. Hanny, hoping that Ms. Hanny could help her find another partner, but she was rejected. Ms. Hanny told her to follow the rules of the game and not to blame her partner at will. In the end, the girl reluctantly accepted to sit down. Later I observed that the collaboration between the two in class was not as "bad" as the girl had imagined.

At the end of the match, Ms. Hanny asked the children, "What are the words learnt today?" the students said the words of "lawn, bench, hill, path" written on the card one after another. Ms. Hanny wrote the words on the blackboard. She asked, "Why are these words important?" Using four words written on the whiteboard, Ms. Hanny retold what students learned in previous class: "*When the sun goes up, the tree's shadow is on the lawn. When the sun is on the top of the hill, the shadow is on the bench. When the sun goes down, the shadow is on the path*". Ms. Hanny asked the students to imagine the scene in their mind. The students' imaginations went wild with thought. They had been pulled back to the content of the previous lesson.

The Shadow Experiment: "First…"
Then, Hanny led the children through experiments to experience the changes of the tree's shadow. With Ms. Ding's help, Ms. Hanny gave all the students the materials and tools they needed for the experiment and asked students to draw a tree and a hill on the paper. She stressed that "so your first step is to make a hill and a tree" to make sure the children understand; she asked, "Can someone tell me what the first step is?" Some children answered: "make a hill and a tree". The children took out their pens and paper, and began to draw hills and trees conscientiously. The quick students even took out scissors to cut the mountains and trees. Ms. Hanny was walking around the classroom, checking the children's progress. She did not rush to the next step, patiently waited for each child to draw the trees and mountains, and encouraged and praised the children's paintings.

After ten minutes, Ms. Hanny came to the front of the class and clapped her hands again. The children quieted down and put down the work at hand. Ms. Hanny pointed to the "First" written on the paper and guided the students to say the first step of the experiment they had just done in English. The children said, "First, draw a tree and hill", and Ms. Hanny wrote the sentence completely on the big white paper.

Continue the Shadow Experiment: "Next…", "Then…"
Ms. Hanny went on to write "Next" and told the student that this was the word describing the next step. Then she asked what the second step was? She did a "cut" action, the children said: "Cut the tree and hill", and Ms. Hanny wrote the sentence on the white paper. Ms. Hanny gave the

children plenty of time to make sure they cut the mountains and trees. During the experiment, the students were very excited. The teachers who watched the class were also involved.

Seeing that all the children were done, Ms. Hanny continued to guide the children to describe the experiment's steps. She first reviewed the "first" and "next" used before, and then said, "The third word we use is 'then'", while saying "Then" on the white paper. Everyone followed Ms. Hanny to read the three keywords, and then read the two sentences on the white paper: "First, draw a tree and hill" "Next cut the tree and hill".

Ms. Hanny then asked, "Does anyone know what we are going to do next?" seeing the students feel overwhelmed, Ms. Hanny looked around the classroom, came to a boy, pointed to the "hill" that had been pasted on his desk, and said, "You are doing it right now". Then she knocked down the "hill" and stood it up again. Some children quickly responded and said, "Stick!" Ms. Hanny wrote on the white paper: "Then, stick the tree and hill on your desk".

Continue the Shadow Experiment: "Finally…"
Ms. Hanny pointed to the three keywords on the white paper and said, "There are four words. The fourth word is…" Some children have already pre-emptively said "Last!" Ms. Hanny said: "Oh!" But she wrote "Finally" on blackboard. This led everyone to read "finally". Ms. Hanny wrote the fourth step on white paper. She wrote and said, "You can use 'last' as well!" Some children found Ms. Hanny writing "Finall" on paper. Ms. Hanny quickly corrected it, while shrugging and saying, "I make mistakes!"

In order to guide the children to the fourth step, she reminded the students, "We have our torches, what do we do with our torches?" At the same time, she raised her right hand, like a flashlight in her hand. She motioned a child to demonstrate with a flashlight, and then wrote on the white paper: "Finally, shine your torch on the hill and tree".

Then she turned off the classroom lights and asked the students to turn on the flashlights. The light of the flashlight shone on the mountains and trees from different angles to imitate the sunlight at different times of the day. Ms. Hanny reminded the students to observe the length of shadows at different times.

Five minutes later, Ms. Hanny asked her classmates to talk about what they had seen in the experiment. "What did you see?" she wrote on the white paper. A girl stood up and uttered a complete paragraph. Her fluent spoken English garnered a lot of admiration. Finally, Ms. Hanny wrote on the white paper: "*In the morning, the shadow is long. In the afternoon, the shadow grows short. In the evening, the shadow is long*". After writing these, Ms. Hanny summarized the lesson, hoping that children would not only learn how to describe the shadow, but also learn how to describe the experimental steps. With the children's warm applause, Ms. Hanny's class was over.

6.4.2   Lesson Preparation and Discussion: "Brave Duck, Brave Me"

At the on-site meeting of Minzhu Primary School, Ms. Dongmei and Ms. Hanny planned to carry out a Banhui lesson based on the picture book story, "the duck on a bike". All students in the sister classes have read this picture book, but the children in the two classes are concerned about different characters. Students in Ms. Dongmei's class paid more attention to the bravery of the duck in the story, while students in Ms. Hanny's class saw the persistence of the duck in the story. This is very interesting for the two teachers, which is why they want to continue the topic.

This Banhui lesson is taught by Ms. Hanny and Ms. Dongmei, but there are not just two teachers who participate in the lesson preparation and discussion. According to the recording, video and field notes, I found that there were six people who participated in the lesson preparation, including Ms. Hanny, Ms. Dongmei, Ms. Chao (grade leader, in charge of teaching affairs in a certain grade), Ms. Chen (a young teacher) and two graduate assistants. Here is the map where everyone was seated (see Fig. 6.1).

Another "invisible" teacher was Ms. Qin, who is the teaching and research staff in the district where Minzhu Primary School is located and mainly responsible for teacher training and teaching researches in the district. Although she was not involved in the discussion, she was mentioned by other Chinese teachers all the time, and her ideas seemed to dominate in discussion. Let us now focus on some interesting scenes from these two discussions.

Scene 1 "That's not the key point!"
"That's not the key point" is the sentence Ms. Chao often utters. Ms. Chao is the grade leader of Chinese courses in Minzhu Primary School. Due to her responsibility and attention to Banhui lesson, she participated

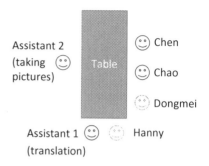

Fig. 6.1 Seat map of the lesson discussion

in the lesson preparation and discussion with Ms. Hanny and Ms. Dongmei.

But Ms. Chao is not a silent observer or companion. During the discussion, she has been controlling the direction of the discussion and constantly stressing that the two teachers should pay attention to the length of this lesson and their specific work.

The discussion recording:

Ms. Dongmei:	"I also have a book 'Xiang Fei' (want to fly). I won't take it this class. It's about a rabbit who wants to fly very much. It also tried for a long time, but didn't succeed. If it's not suitable for you, you also have to learn to give up and adjust."
Ms. Hanny:	"Have the students heard these two books?"
Ms. Dongmei:	"No, we'll just mention it after class."
Ms. Hanny:	"Do you have the English names of these two books?"
Ms. Dongmei:	"No."

Ms. Hanny began to look for the books with the iPad…

Ms. Chao:	"These two books are <u>not the point</u>, <u>not the point</u>. Today's discussion, one goal is to make two teachers familiar with the steps, the other is to hope that Ms. Hanny thinks about what her part could do. There are only 35 minutes in a class, 40 minutes at most."

Ms. Hanny:	"I thought it would take longer." (She is still looking for the two books mentioned earlier.)
Graduate Assistant (GA):	"Ms. Dongmei, do you know the English of those two books?" (She wants to help Ms. Hanny find the books.)
Ms. Chao:	"This is <u>not the point</u>. It's the content after this class. Because every time we carry out the Banhui lesson, there will be pre-extended and follow-up class (that is, Banhui lesson is a series of courses). It doesn't matter. The focus of this class is 'Duck on a bike'."
GA:	"OK, I see."

This kind of dialogue is very common during the lesson preparation and discussion. The graduate assistant later told me that she felt Ms. Chao's behavior affected the communication between the two teachers and sometimes seemed impolite. But neither Ms. Dongmei nor another young teacher expressed any dissent. In May 2018, I interviewed Ms. Dongmei and asked her if she felt that Ms. Chao's behavior had affected her. Ms. Dongmei denied it had any effect. She thought Ms. Chao was just too "worried" about her (perhaps Ms. Dongmei wanted to express that Ms. Chao was very concerned about her and the lesson), because she had just joined the project, and it was the first time for her to co-teach with Ms. Hanny. However, she also felt that Ms. Chao did not give Ms. Hanny more opportunities to express herself, which made Ms. Dongmei feel dissatisfied. Actually, Ms. Dongmei told me it was not Ms. Chao, but Ms. Qin that affected her lesson preparation most, especially about "which story is better" in the class.

Scene 2 "Which story is better?"
The steps of Banhui lesson designed by Ms. Hanny and Ms. Dongmei unfurled in the following way. First, the students discussed their feelings about "The Duck on a Bike", with most students focusing on the "courage" of ducks. Then, the teachers will lead the children in playing games to understand the importance of "persistence". Finally, through another story created by the students, let the students know that sometimes they may also not succeed but they just need to be courageous and show their perseverance. In the first two steps, Ms. Hanny and Ms. Dongmei quickly

reached an agreement. But in the final step, teachers differed on the question of "which story is better".

Dongmei preferred the story of "Rabbit Swimming" created by students, but this story was opposed by Ms. Qin, who did not participate in discussion but conveyed her opinions to Dongmei. Ms. Qin's opinions are as follows: (1) if the story of "Duck on a Bike" is to be extended, the animal should still be the duck and (2) that rabbits can swim is not realistic and can't be achieved through courage. Ms. Qin suggested choosing the story of "Duck Running".

"Duck Running" tells the story of a duck who wants to become a good runner and run over cows, horses and dogs by his own efforts. Ms. Dongmei hopes that students can think about the ending by themselves that ducks may succeed or fail, and think about whether they can always succeed with courage and perseverance. But Ms. Dongmei was not satisfied with this story.

The discussion recording:

Ms. Hanny:	*"Well, we want our students to know that ducks don't always win, so we can prepare an ending and show them something different. If the students think the duck won, then we can say, 'I had a different ending, a happy ending, the duck didn't win, but the duck found herself running faster than before, so even though it wasn't the fastest. It can't make progress if it doesn't try."*
Ms. Dongmei:	*"That's what I thought when I designed it, but students..."*
Ms. Chen:	*"They can't think of it. Students can't think of it by themselves."*
Ms. Dongmei:	*"It's just that the students can't say it. Can the teacher help the students to say it out loud? If a student says, 'I don't think a duck can win no matter how hard he tries,' can I ask, do you think the duck is sad or happy?"*
Ms. Chen:	*"What Ms. Hanny means is that you can make progress if you work hard."*
Ms. Hanny:	*"Well, if you ask a student, 'do you think the duck is happy or sad?', and then you can ask the student, 'what do you think of the duck's effort?' Because if students are only asked if the duck is happy, they may not realize the importance of working hard."*
Ms. Dongmei:	*"So, I think the story is not better..."*

6 CIRCLES AND STRAIGHT LINES: TEACHERS' LIFE WORLDS   157

Then teachers in MPS began to discuss Ms. Qin's suggestions:

Ms. Chen: *"If you have to be realistic, duck cycling itself is not realistic."*
Ms. Dongmei: *"Yes, why can't the rabbit swim?"*
Ms. Chen: *"That's right!"*
Ms. Dongmei: *"Duck race seems more reasonable, Ms. Qin said..."* *(Dongmei smiles and scratches his head.)*

Hanny also thinks that duck running does not require much courage and is not very good. She prefers the story of "Rabbit Swimming" provided by Ms. Dongmei. "Rabbit Swimming" tells the story of a rabbit who wants to swim after seeing the duck learn to ride. But after she practiced, she still failed.

GA: *"What do you think of the rabbit story?"*
Ms. Hanny: *"I think it's a good story. It's a story of courage. It's a story of persistence. It doesn't have to be duck."*
Ms. Dongmei (laughing):   *"Yeah, I'm also subject to... the teacher who instructs us, some of their ideas are... (smile), I was hoping to use the story of the rabbit, because there are two rabbits swim story, but one success, one failure, I was going to use these two, but the teacher (Qin) told me not to do so, first, time is not enough, second, the children may only focus on how the rabbit trains, so she said, you should use the duck's story."*

Finally, this problem was solved after another teacher (Ms. Lu) arrived. Ms. Lu is the gold medal teacher in Shanghai and has a high position in Minzhu Primary School. She thought that Ms. Dongmei can follow her own ideas, and not worry too much about how to guide students. It can be decided according to the students' answers. With her encouragement, Ms. Dongmei finally chose the story of Rabbit Swimming. Afterwards, the researcher asked Dongmei, if she didn't have Lu's support, would she still insist on the story of Rabbit Swimming? Ms. Dongmei told us she might. In addition, she also expressed a sense of confusion, because she felt that Ms. Qin and Ms. Lu were both expert teachers of Banhui lessons, but their suggestions were contradictory. One focused on the process of class,

158   Y. ZHU

the other paid attention to the live feedback of students. She admitted that although she had been a headteacher for many years, her understanding of how to teach and organize Banhui lesson was not so deep. So, she couldn't tell whose advice was more valuable.

6.4.3   Lesson Preparation and Discussion: "My School"

This story happened in October 2019 when teachers from Minzhu Primary School visited Bay Street School. Ms. Ding, Ms. Dongmei and Ms. Hanny planned to teach a class together under the theme of "My School". On the one hand, this theme would be consistent with Ms. Ding's language lesson plan. "My School" was a required subject class in the curriculum outline. On the other hand, Ms. Hanny and Ms. Dongmei have taught Banhui lessons related to character education for the last school year. They have already carried out the courses on "self", hoping to further expand the relationship between "self" and "others", and "My School" met their needs.

Scene 1: "Great, we think the same!"
Compared with the lesson preparation in China in 2017, no one outside the project participated in this lesson preparation and discussion. Only the three teachers and two graduate assistants in charge of translation and recordings participated in the discussion in the library of Bay Street School. Because they were familiar with each other and no one else was present, the three teachers were in a natural and relaxed state.

During the discussion, we found that Ms. Dongmei was more willing to express herself this time. At first, because of the language barrier (Dongmei's English is less proficient), Ms. Dongmei has been quietly listening to Ms. Hanny and Ms. Ding discuss the choice of the theme. As the discussion deepened, Ms. Dongmei began to express her own ideas in Chinese. Interestingly, after translation, we found that Ms. Dongmei's and Ms. Hanny's ideas coincided with each other.

The discussion recording:

Dongmei:	*"Can it be, that is, my class or ..." (Dongmei expressed her thoughts in Chinese, but the other two teachers did not notice)*

Hanny (writing key words while speaking):	*"We have done... Self-confidence, like that? So, do we want to, do we want to add something new? Do we want to start getting them to look at their community and how they can impact the school or the community? um...?" Helen indicated the graduate assistant to translate.*
GA:	*"I just saw Ms. Dongmei wanted to say something." (in Chinese)*
Dongmei:	*"I just said, haven't we already done something about self? Can it just become my..." (in Chinese)*
Ding:	*"My family?" (in Chinese)*
Dongmei:	*"My family, or my class, to put students in a class or a group." (in Chinese)*
GA:	*"She just talked about the same thing, just you said the community, she said the class or school"*
Ms. Hanny (excited):	*"Yeah, that's what I want you to translate! So, what did she say? I said community, she said school? Ok, so we will be looking at My School...this is my school...who am I in the school, and how do I impact?"*
GA:	*"Who am I in school? What responsibilities may I have?" (translate in Chinese)*

Dongmei nodded and said "right, right" in Chinese, which seemed to fit her idea very well.

160   Y. ZHU

This happened from time-to-time in the discussion. For example, when discussing what open questions teachers could ask and can be extended, Ms. Dongmei told us in Chinese, "We can ask students that where they think is beautiful in school? Why is it beautiful?" She believed that this is an emotional expression, which would help students to think about how and what they can do to make the school more beautiful. Ms. Hanny's idea was similar to Ms. Dongmei's. She designed the questions as "where do you like the school best?", "which place do you dislike the most and why?" and "what do you think you can do to improve it". It can be seen that they are both concerned about the roles and responsibilities of students in the school.

The coincidence of Hanny and Dongmei's ideas meant that their teaching concepts and methods were becoming more and more consistent. That is, they are not only teachers in two schools but also partners in a cooperative and reciprocal group in which they share the common identity and teaching concepts. It was this kind of identity that made them connect with the ongoing Banhui lessons of sister classes when choosing the theme, and actively combined this discussion with the previous Banhui lessons.

Scene 2: "That's their style. Don't care too much about the details"
After the series of courses was determined, Ms. Hanny, Ms. Dongmei and Ms. Ding selected the storybook that can be used in the class tomorrow, and then determine the main tasks of each teacher, and the discussion and preparation for class was over. Ms. Hanny rushed to print the worksheets to be used in class tomorrow, leaving Dongmei and Ding to continue to communicate. The researcher (Yuanyuan Zhu) asked if Ms. Dongmei and Ms. Ding need to confirm the details. "That's their style", Ding told the researcher. "Don't care too much about the details. It's all right to play according to the students' reflections tomorrow". The researcher was curious about their understanding of "their style", so they went on talking about it.

Zhu:	"It seems that their curriculum design has only a main line, not as detailed as ours".
Ms. Dongmei:	"Yes, so their classes are very flexible. She thinks about several sections, what to do in the first step, what to do in the second step, and there won't be too many details, so you will see that their classes are very open, but sometimes they

	are also very trivial. Of course, with fewer students, it's okay."
Ms. Ding:	*"They will spend a lot of time for students to discuss and express. That's what we did in our last co-teaching class. Half of the time is for children to find information and ask questions themselves."*
Ms. Dongmei:	*"It's also very good, but we have many students, we can't control the time."*
Zhu:	*"I'm curious how they can control the course time."*
Ms. Ding:	*"They don't care a lot. It can be a little longer or a little shorter. Anyway, she is the only teacher (of the class). From morning to night, she can go on the same content if she needs. We envy this very much."*

It seemed that in the years of cooperation with Ms. Hanny, Ms. Ding had been used to and mastered this way of teaching. Ms. Dongmei, who had been very concerned about the specific steps, seemed relaxed this time, but she still sorted out the overall thinking of the next day's course seriously. In the next day's co-teaching, the cooperation of the three teachers was very tacit, and they had completed their ideas discussed in lesson preparation. Ms. Dongmei, in particular, was spontaneous and lively and motivated students' mood and attention, which pleasantly surprised us.

From the conversation with Ms. Dongmei and Ms. Ding, we can also know that after years of reciprocal communication, they are very familiar with the Canadian classes and their way of teaching. They are sensitive to discover "their style" and analyze the advantages and disadvantages objectively. They will analyze the reasons for the differences from factors such as teacher roles, curriculum structure and number of students. This kind of rational and objective evaluation is not uncommon among teachers in RLP. This kind of comment is based on the understanding of the current state of the school life in both countries.

Although Ms. Hanny didn't care much about the details of the next day's class, she spent a lot of time thinking about what follow-up classes can be taken in sister classes around the theme of "My School". In just 30 minutes, she had designed a series of lessons to cooperatively use with Ms. Dongmei and Ms. Ding respectively. The lessons of study were connected with each other and gradually deepened students' understanding of their roles in school. For instance, Ms. Hanny used three open questions to link up the series of Banhui lessons. First, let students discuss "favorite and least favorite places in the school and why". Second, inspire students to think about "my role as a student in the school" through picture books or stories. Third, let students think about "where the school can improve and what I can do", so as to change their roles, and help students to establish a real reform plan that can be implemented. When Canadian teachers first visited Minzhu Primary School, they were impressed by the strong connections between the lessons. In the course design of 'My School', we have seen this correlation as well.

6.5 Findings

Through the stories of the Chinese and Canadian teachers of the sister schools, we can see the differences in their life. In general, teachers' life in Chinese school is marked by segmentation, and teachers' life in Canadian school is expressed as a comprehensive integration. As mentioned earlier, we use "circle" and "straight line" as a metaphor to compare this difference. The metaphor, "circle", represents a kind of integration, openness and diversity, while the "straight line" shows the segmentation, goal-oriented and systematism.

6.5.1 Curriculum Structure

The biggest difference in the structure of the school curriculum is that Canada uses integrated learning while China employs subject area specialization, which leads to the curriculum of the two like "melting-pot" and "chessboard" respectively, and embodies the forms of "circles" and "straight lines" vividly. These two types of curriculum structure directly lead to the differences in curriculum design, daily arrangement and teacher division of work between Chinese and Canadian schools.

In the curriculum design, Canada's curriculum is comprehensive, focusing on interdisciplinary integration, without absolute boundaries, while Chinese curriculum is a sub-discipline course, which pays more attention to the acquisition of knowledge in various disciplines. The courses in different disciplines vary widely and can be described as "difference in profession makes one feel worlds apart" (隔行如隔山). In the first story of this chapter, Ms. Hanny and Ms. Ding's heterogeneous lessons are a good example of the differences in curriculum design between the two countries. In the lesson of "the tree's shadow", Ms. Hanny let

6 CIRCLES AND STRAIGHT LINES: TEACHERS' LIFE WORLDS   163

students learn and output language through experiment, and well integrated scientific inquiry into language course. To better achieve the goal of second language class, Ms. Ding was committed to making students master the spelling and pronunciation of words, and strived to make students learn and articulate language knowledge as much as possible in a short time. The two teachers' teaching focuses are different, and no comparison is made here. In fact, this really reflects the influence of the curriculum structure on teaching and curriculum design.

As for the division of work, Chinese teachers (6–8) of various disciplines are jointly responsible for one class and each teacher communicates with students in his subject area. In Canada, a particular teacher is responsible for a class of students and all of their subject matter learning in the elementary grades. As far as the teaching schedule is concerned, Chinese classes are divided into sections due to the design of the curriculum while the schedule of Canadian students is more flexible. This division of work and teaching arrangement allows Canadian teachers to have full autonomy in both class management and curriculum design. This may help us understand the anxiety and extreme concern of Ms. Chao, the grade leader in the second story, about the timing and specific details of the Banhui lesson. This specific division of teaching and established curriculum led Chinese teachers to form the habit of focusing on time and specific details. They are always thinking about how to complete the teaching task effectively.

Strict time division and disciplinary boundaries make the daily life of Chinese schools a "chessboard", and the "chess"-like teachers conduct discipline teaching step by step along straight lines. Unlike China's detailed curriculum requirements based on grades and disciplines, the Canadian syllabus only provides direction and advice. Therefore, Canadian teachers are free to design courses with more autonomy and flexibility. Based on actual needs, they can plan more comprehensive, structured lessons. This is also a main point that impresses Chinese teachers regarding Canadian school life through RLP.

6.5.2   Teachers' Teaching

"Circles" and "straight lines" are also reflected in teachers' different understanding and methods of teaching. Chinese teachers pay more attention to the realization of the ultimate goal ("straight to the goal"), and often adopt the most direct and concise methods to achieve the teaching

164   Y. ZHU

Table 6.1   Comparison of heterogeneous lessons by Hanny and Ding

Teacher	Hanny	Ding
Goal of Teaching	Development of cognition and thinking;	Acquisition and application of knowledge;
Teaching Focus	To let students understand the relationship between light and shadow through experiment and express the steps of experiment in an orderly and complete way.	To let students master the new words and phrases and use new words and phrases to make complete sentences and discourse expression.
Tools and Materials of Teaching	Lots of paper-writings; Specific experiment.	Pictures and videos; A few blackboard-writings.
Interaction in Teaching	Focusing on two kinds of interactions: teacher-student interaction and student-student interaction;	Focusing on kinds of interactions: teacher-student interaction and student-student interaction;
	More time for student-student interaction	More time for teacher-student interaction
	Constructive oriented	Directing oriented

goal. Canadian teachers emphasize "many ways of achieving the goal". Although the goal is similar, the methodology is more diverse and open. In our eyes, the Canadian way of teaching is like the river with flexible forms, while the Chinese way is like the railway tracks with solid foundation.

Taking the first story in this chapter as an example, we can analyze the heterogeneous lessons of Ms. Hanny and Ms. Ding from the viewpoints of course objectives, tasks, media and teaching interactions (Table 6.1).

Influenced by the notion that "education in order to accomplish its ends both for the individual learner and for society must be based upon experience" (John Dewey 1997), Ms. Hanny attaches great importance to students' hands-on experiments. From Ms. Hanny's teaching, what can be found is that the growth of intelligence through teaching can not only stay at the level of imparting knowledge, but knowledge into intelligence must have "experience" in it. The "experience" is a kind of experience that takes life as the premise and directly integrates objects into one's life consciousness. This "experience" is reflected not only in the hands-on experiments but also in the "anchor charts" (Hanny's paper writings) and "success charts" made in classes. "Anchor charts" and "success charts" are completed by the teacher and the children together. Such "anchor charts" and "success charts" will be kept in the class for students to read and recall their learning experience at any time. Ms. Ding's lessons have achieved her teaching goals very well. Her teaching has an obvious structured form, and it is promoted step by step through the link of "raising opening questions—recycling students' resources—refining blackboard writing", so that students can understand the relationship between the length of shadow and the height of the sun.

Through comparison, we can summarize the different characteristics of the two classes. Ms. Ding's class reflected the characteristics of large capacity, high density, and emphasis on understanding and application, while Ms. Hanny's class focused on "student-centered inquiry" teaching, giving students more time for independent inquiry, with the characteristics of strong practicality and process experiences. In addition, in the story about "My School", there is an interesting phenomenon: in designing the course, Ms. Dongmei is more concerned with character education, while Ms. Ding is more concerned with language education. I suspect that this is related to their subject teacher identity in China. Ms. Dongmei is a Chinese teacher and a headteacher. Moral education is one of her main tasks. Ms. Ding is an English teacher, so she pays more attention to how to learn and use language better. China's sub-disciplinary system has its existing value. "Any comprehensive curriculum must be premised on the existence of disciplines, and on the development of the intrinsic value of each discipline" (Ye 2019). They often mainly consider how to teach the knowledge of this lesson, sometimes think about the relationship between lessons, but seldom about the relationship between the discipline they teach and other disciplines.

In general, classroom teaching in Canada is like a river, freer and more inclusive in form, while classroom teaching in China is like a railway track, though the direction is clear, the openness and relevance of the disciplines are weak. River-like teaching can accommodate differences. The individuals growing up in the river are more diverse and freer. Track-like teaching emphasizes order and homogeneity. Trains and passengers running on tracks can reach the "destination" at a higher speed.

6.5.3   Teachers in Community

The two stories in this chapter about lesson preparation, one in China and one in Canada, vividly explain the daily work and teaching research of teachers in the two countries. In the preparation and discussion for the Banhui lesson, we saw that not only Ms. Dongmei and Ms. Hanny but also the grade leader and another young teacher of Minzhu Primary School actively participated in the discussion. Hanny thinks this is unlikely to happen in Canada. Canadian teachers are used to "fighting alone"; they are afraid of giving suggestions to other teachers' teaching, because it represents a challenge to the professional competence of another teacher. But this situation is very common in China. Chinese lesson preparation activities are usually conducted by a lesson preparation group or teaching research group (usually a teacher community with the same or similar subjects in the school). Such group includes the grade leader, experienced teachers and new teachers. It is considered an important way for teacher professional development in China (He 2005; Chen 2007; Li 2006; Wang and Li 2014). In addition to the lesson preparation and teaching research groups, there are also mentoring pairs, university-government-school partnership and other forms.

In this context, of course, Chinese teachers are more susceptible to influence by the person in authority. For example, in the first narrative story of this chapter, Ms. Chao, as the grade leader, Ms. Qin, as a regional teaching and research staff, and Ms. Lu, who has been praised as outstanding headteacher, are all authoritative representatives. In the multi-agent teaching and research activities, the "voice" of teachers with insufficient experience or authority status will be drowned out, even Ms. Dongmei, the actual teacher of Banhui lesson, is no exception. Before discussing with Ms. Hanny, the Banhui lesson plan drafted by Ms. Dongmei was guided by a number of authoritative teachers. In fact, Ms. Dongmei was puzzled by some suggestions from the experts. "In fact, it is different from what I think of as Banhui lesson". Ms. Dongmei told me in the interview after the Banhui lesson, "But I don't know whether I think is right, you know, they are more experienced". When Ms. Dongmei's understanding is different from that of the authoritative teacher, she has no confidence in her own ideas. But when I asked Ms. Dongmei whether her ideas had changed after the co-teaching, Ms. Dongmei was suddenly excited, "I found that my thoughts are consistent with Professor Ye, I should be right". Professor Ye is the founder of NBE and is a famous pedagogic scholar in China. It can be seen that Ms. Dongmei's understanding of teaching comes not from her self-confidence and professional competence, but from the affirmation of experts. However, it is great that, after a year of self-directed reciprocal communication with Ms. Hanny, Ms. Dongmei gradually has her own ideas and judgments on Banhui lessons. From the lesson discussion and co-teaching with Ms. Hanny in 2019, we can see that Ms. Dongmei no longer relied on the affirmation of the outside world, but clearly knew what she should teach and how to teach.

In Canada, teachers are more confident in their profession, and even principals cannot question their teaching. But Canadian teachers at sister schools also say they sometimes feel "alone". In Canada, primary school principals are only in charge of administration. In China, primary school principals not only are school administrators but also have the responsibility of providing professional development platform for school teachers. In addition, teachers and research staff in the region, such as Ms. Qin, are also important person in the professional development of teachers. They are responsible for the training, teaching research and other matters related to teacher development in the whole region. Therefore, in China, teachers live in various teacher communities. While in Canada, teachers usually cooperate in the form of team teaching and co-teaching, rather than various forms of teacher communities with clear organizers and leaders like China. After joining the sister school program, Canadian teachers in RLP feel that they have found like-minded research partners, which promotes their professional growth and reflection.

The different teacher professional development contexts in two countries cause us reflect on a series of issues in the current situation of teacher development, such as the support and needs of teachers' professional development, the significance and limitation of teacher community in teachers' professional life, the role of different subjects in multi-subject teaching and research activities, the role that principals should play in teachers' growth and so forth. And we also need to think further about the impact of reciprocal learning on teacher development in different cultures.

6.6 Conclusion and Discussion

In this chapter, the view of the teachers' life in different cultural backgrounds is shown through three stories of the teachers in RLP. As we could see, there are significant differences between China and Canada in terms of curriculum structure, teacher teaching and development. The existence of such differences has its historical and realistic rationality.

From the cultural perspective, Canada is an immigrant country. Its multicultural background cultivates openness and inclusiveness of individuals to differences, and urges individuals to think about the specific meaning of their role as "global citizenship". Although China is a multiethnic country, since the integration of ethnic groups in Tang dynasty, all ethnic groups have basically followed a set of unified values and ethical norms, among which Confucianism is the most respected. Confucianism emphasizes the autonomy of individual and also emphasizes the organic connection between individuals. Individuals must be within the family, society and state, and cannot exist in isolation (Gao 2001; Liu 2002). This kind of ideology makes it difficult for China to treat individuals completely apart from the group, and it is indeed insufficient to accommodate individual differences.

From the perspective of national conditions, because of the population, the class size in China is much larger than that in Canada. When faced with a class with an average of more than 30 students (like Ms. Ding's and Ms. Dongmei's classes) and another class with only a dozen or so students (like Ms. Hanny's class), perhaps we can understand why the curriculum, teacher teaching and daily schedule are so different between China and Canada. The huge population also brings competition and pressure, which infiltrate the contemporary education (Gao 2016). Parents expect their children to acquire real survival skills through education, so that they can gain a favorable advantage in survival competition after leaving the school. The embodiment of this expectation in Chinese classroom is the knowledge and goal orientation. Similarly, taking the students' seats mentioned above as an example, the free sitting posture and seat choice of Canadian students reflect an inclusive attitude toward differences. In the Chinese classroom, teachers must consider the height of children and whether most students can clearly see the blackboard. Seemingly opposite are the results, but they can all be explained in terms of equality. But Canadian teachers think that better solutions should be considered. Class size is an influencing factor, but it is not a determining one. They once put forward some suggestions, "If we are in a large class, we can divide the students into different groups, and then each group will do different activities, and then take another turn. This kind of teaching method can also be used in large class model", which were seriously considered by teachers in Minzhu Primary School. Actually, "fairness in large size class" is an important issue often examined in Chinese education studies. Teaching in large size class cannot be simply identified as the conflict between group development and individual development. Large group teaching also has its irreplaceable value, such as promoting students to learn from each other, contributing to the development of students' social quality and so on. In fact, the suggestions of group cooperation provided by Canadian teachers have already become a common way in Chinese classroom teaching. But why do Chinese teachers still think that large class restricts their teaching? The fundamental reason is that Chinese teachers and education researchers began to think about how to enable all students to participate in classroom learning "fairly and with quality". Recognizing the differences between students and using the educational resources brought by these differences are considered as effective solutions to this problem (Bu 2016). But how to implement it in teaching still needs further exploration.

But even if there are realistic reasons, it does not mean that we can accept without reflecting on the existence of this difference. In fact, Chinese education officials and scholars have realized the main problem of the Chinese education system that the structure is too clear and not comprehensive. For example, the "Basic Education Reform Guidelines" (2001) put forward that we should "change the current situation of curriculum structure with too much emphasis on subject standard, too many subjects and lack of integration", "set up a comprehensive curriculum…, reflect the balance, comprehensiveness and selectivity of curriculum structure". The second curriculum reform plan of primary and secondary schools in Shanghai proposed the new curriculum structure composed of basic courses, expansion courses and research courses ("Curriculum Plan for Primary and Secondary Schools in Shanghai" 2002). Basic course is a compulsory course for students, which is composed of various subjects corresponding to each area of study in primary school. An extended course is an open course designed to stimulate students' personality and potential. The purpose of research courses is to promote students' independent inquiry spirit and ability through thematic and comprehensive research. Although the basic courses are still based on the sub-disciplinary system in Shanghai, the extended courses and research courses, as well as the use of comprehensive activities and thematic teaching methods, to some extent, make up for the shortcomings of the existing curriculum structure. Recently, the "Opinions of the State Council on Deepening the Reform of Education and Teaching and Improving the Quality of Compulsory Education in an All-round Way" (2019) put forward some operational suggestions: that is, "exploring the comprehensive teaching of courses based on disciplines and carrying out research-oriented, project-based and cooperative learning". Such methods represent a new attempt in China's elementary education curriculum reform, which aims to improve the disadvantages of "straight lines" and draw on the advantages of "circles".

Affected by this trend and inspired by the Canadian teachers' teaching, teachers at Minzhu Primary School also made some new changes to the curriculum in the new school year. They combined the Inquiry Curriculum with other subjects in the way of project-based learning in which the class time was extended by 70 minutes for giving children full time to explore and providing more autonomy to teachers. From those we can see the efforts made by teachers at Minzhu Primary School in order to change the disadvantages brought about by the current curriculum structure. Changes also happened to the teachers in Canada; as mentioned earlier, Ms. Hanny paid more attention to the relationship between classes and renewed her understanding of character education inspired by her cooperation with Dongmei. The reciprocal learning program prompted the three teachers to reflect on and better recognize their teacher identities, which brought out changes in teachers' teaching and made our teachers become more confident and inclusive curriculum makers.

References

Bai, Y. (2002). Jiaoshi de ziwogengxin: Beijing, jizhi yu jianyi 教师的自我更新: 背景, 机制与建议 (Teachers' Self-renewal: Background, Mechanism and Suggestions). *Journal of East China Normal University (Education Science Edition), 4*, 28–38.

Bu, Y. (2016). Woguo ketang jiaoxue gaige de xianshi jichu, kunju yu tupo lujing 我国课堂教学改革的现实基础, 困局与突破路径 (Realistic Basis, Dilemma and Breakthrough Path of Classroom Teaching Reform in China). *Education Research, 37*, 110–118.

Bu, Y., & Han, X. (2019). Promoting the Development of Backbone Teachers through University-School Collaborative Research: The Case of New Basic Education (NBE) Reform in China. *Teachers & Teaching Theory & Practice, 25*, 200–219.

Bu, Y., Qi, S., Zhong, C., & Zhu, Y. (2019). Cong 'Li Tu' Dao 'Zai Di': Zhong Jia Zimei Xiao Kua Wenhua Huhui Xuexi de Shijian Tansuo 从"离土"到"在地": 中加姊妹校跨文化互惠学习的实践探索 (From "Grounding off" to "Grounding on": The Practical Exploration on Cross-cultural Reciprocal Learning in China-Canada Sister Schools). *Global Education, 48*(6), 62–73.

Chen, J. (2007). Cong jiaoyanzu zouxiang hezuoxing jiaoyan zuzhi: cong jiaoshi zhuanye gongtongti dedaode jiejian 从教研组走向合作型教研组织: 从教师专业共同体得到的借鉴 (From Teaching and Research Group to Cooperative Teaching and Research Organization: From the Professional Community of Teachers). *Liaoning Education Research, 2*, 32–35.

Clandinin, D. J., & Connelly, F. M. (1992). Teacher as Curriculum Maker. In P. Jackson (Ed.), *Handbook of Curriculum* (pp. 363–461). New York, NY: Macmillan.

Clandinin, D. J., Huber, J., Huber, M., Murphy, S., Murray Orr, A., Pearce, M., et al. (2006). *Composing Diverse Identities: Narrative Inquiries into the Interwoven Lives of Children and Teachers*. New York, NY: Routledge.

Connelly, F. M., & Clandinin, D. J. (1990). Stories of Experience and Narrative Inquiry. *Educational Researcher, 19*(5), 2–14. https://doi.org/10.2307/1176100.

Connelly, M. F., & Xu, S. (2019). Reciprocal Learning in the Partnership Project: From Knowing to Doing in Comparative Research Model. *Teachers and Teaching, 11*, 627–646.

Craig, C., You, J., & Oh, S. (2012). Why School-Based Narrative Inquiry in Physical Education Research? An International Perspective. *Asia Pacific Journal of Education, 32*, 271–284.

Craig, C. J., You, J., & Oh, S. (2013). Collaborative Curriculum Making in the Physical Education Vein: A Narrative Inquiry of Space, Activity and Relationship. *Journal of Curriculum Studies, 45*, 169–197.

Cushner, K. (2007). The Role of Experience in the Making of Internationally-Minded Teachers. *Teacher Education Quarterly, 34*, 27–39.

Dewey, J. (1997). *Experience and Education*. Free Press.

Gao, D. (2016). Jingzheng de dexing jiqizai jiaoyu zhongde kuozhang 竞争的德性及其在教育中的扩张 (The Virtue of Competition and Its Expansion in Education). *Journal of East China Normal University (Education Science Edition), 34*, 14–23 + 110.

Gao, R. (2001). "Qun ji zhi bian" yu jindai zhongguo de jiazhiguan biange "群己之辩"与近代中国的价值观变革 (The Debate between "the Group and the Individual" and the Transform of Values in Modern China). *History of Chinese Philosophy, 4*, 73–78.

He, F. (2005). Goujian xiezuoshi wenhua cujin jiaoshi zhuanye fazhan 构建协作式文化促进教师专业发展 (Building a Collaborative Culture and Promoting the Professional Development of Teachers). *Journal of Northwest Adult Education, 1*, 41–43.

Li, Z. (2006). Shenme shi "jiaoyanzu wenhua"? jiaoyanzu wenhua xilie zhiyi 什么是 "教研组文化"?教研组文化系列之一 (What is the "Teaching and Research Group Culture"?—One of the "Teaching and Research Group Culture" Series). *Shanghai Education and Research, 7*, 4–5.

Li, Z. (2019). Collaborative Research Approaches between Universities and Schools: The Case of New Basic Education (NBE) in China. *Educational Studies*, 1–19.

Liu, X. (2002). Cong Quntiyuanze Dao Zhengtizhuyi: Zhongguo Chuantong Jiazhitixi Zhongde Qunjiguan Tanxi. 从群体原则到整体主义: 中国传统价值体系中的群己观探析 (From the Principle of Group to Holism: An Analysis of the Group and Individual in Chinese Traditional Value System). *Literary History and Philosophy*, 4, 112–119.

Lu, J. (1998). Tiaozhan Zhishi Jingji: Jiaoyu Yao Peiyang Chaungxin Rencai 挑战知识经济: 教育要培养创新人才 (Challenging Knowledge Economy: Education Should Cultivate Innovative Talents). *Shanghai higher education research*, 12, 32–34.

Merryfield, M. M. (2000). Why Aren't Teachers Being Prepared to Teach for Diversity, Equity, and Global Interconnectedness? A Study of Lived Experiences in the Making of Multicultural and Global Educators. *Teaching and Teacher Education*, 16, 429–443.

Ning, H., & Liu, X. (2000). Jiaoshi Chengwei Yanjiuzhe: Jiaoshi Zhuanyehua De Yige Zhongyao Qushi 教师成为研究者: 教师专业化的一个重要趋势 (Teachers become Researchers: An Important Trend of Teacher Professional Development). *Education Research*, 7, 39–41.

Ontario Ministry of Education. (2015). *Towards Defining 21st Century Competencies for Ontario: 21st Century Competences*. Toronto: Queen's Printer for Ontario.

Ontario Ministry of Education. (2017). *Framework of Global Competencies*. Toronto, ON: Author. Retrieved from http://edugains.ca/resources21CL/21stCenturyLearning/FrameworkofGlobalCompetencies_AODA.pdf.

Shi, Z. (1998). Dangdai Zhishi De Zhuangkuang Yu Jiaoshi Juese De Zhuanhuan 当代知识的状况与教师角色的转换 (The State of Contemporary Knowledge and the Shift of Teachers' Roles). *Higher Normal Education Research*, 6, 53–58.

Sun, X., Cheng, X., Chu, H., Huang, W., Tian, H., & Chen, J. (1995). Ren de Zhutixing Neihan Yu Ren de Zhutixing Jiaoyu 人的主体性内涵与人的主体性教育 (Connotation of Human Subjectivity and Human Subjectivity Education). *Educational Researcher*, 10, 34–39.

Wang, T., & Li, M. (2014). Jiaoshi Gongtongti De Tedian Ji Yiyi Tanxi 教师共同体的特点及意义探析 (Analysis of the Characteristics and Significance of Teacher Community). *Educational Theory and Practice*, 34, 25–27.

Xu, S. (2011). Bridging the East and West Dichotomy: Harmonizing Eastern Learning with Western Knowledge. In J. Ryan (Ed.), *Understanding China's Education Reform: Creating Cross-cultural Knowledge, Pedagogies and Dialogue* (pp. 224–242). London: Routledge.

Xu, S. (2019). Reciprocal Learning in Teacher Education between Canada and China. *Teachers & Teaching*, 25(2), 1–27.

Xu, S., & Connelly, M. F. (2017). Special Issue Introduction. Reciprocal Learning between Canada and China in Teacher Education and School Education: Partnership Studies of Practice in Cultural Context. *Frontiers of Education in China, 12*(2), 135–150.

Ye, L. (1994). Shidai Jingshen yu Xinjiaoyu Lixiang de Jiangou: Guanyu Woguo Jichu Jiaoyu de Kuashidai Sikao 时代精神与新教育理想的构建—关于我国基础教育改革的跨世纪思考 (The Spirit of the Times and the Construction of New Education Ideals). *Education Research* (10), 4–9.

Ye, L. (1997). Rang Ketang Huanfa Chu Shengming Huoli: Lun Zhongxiaoxue Jiaoxuegaige De Shenhua 让课堂换发出生命活力: 论中小学教学改革的深化 (Let the Classroom Glow with Vitality—On the Deepening of Teaching Reform in Primary and Secondary Schools). *Education Research, 9*, 3–8.

Ye, L. (1998). Xinshiji Jiaoshi Zhuanye Suyang Xintan 新世纪教师专业素养新探 (Initial Exploration of Teachers' Professional Knowledge in the New Century). *Educational Research and Experiment, 1*, 41–46 + 72.

Ye, L. (2002). Chongjian Ketang Jiaoxue Guocheng Guan: "Xinjichu Jiaoyu" Ketang Jiaoxue Gaige De Lilun Yu Shijian Tanjiu Zhi Er 重建课堂教学过程观—"新基础教育"课堂教学改革的理论与实践探究之二 (Reconstruct the View of Classroom Teaching Process: The Second Research on Theory and Practice of Classroom Teaching Reform of "New Basic Education"). *Educational Research, 10*, 24–30.

Ye, L. (2005). Shenme Shi Yijie Haoke? 什么是一节好课? (What Kind of Class is a Good One). *Fujian Forum (Social Science Education Edition), 11*, 4–6.

Ye, L. (2019). "Xin Jichu Jiaoyu" Neishnegli Jiedu "新基础教育"内生力的深度解读 (An In-depth Reading of the Endogenous Power of the "New Basic Education"). In *Biange zhong Shengcheng: Yelan Jiaoyu Baogaoji* 变革中生成: 叶澜教育报告集 *(Generated through Change: Ye Lan Education Report Collection)* (pp. 234–247). Beijing China Renmin University Press.

Zhong, Q. (1999). Suzhi Jiaoyu Yu Kecheng Jiaoxue Gaige 素质教育与课程教学改革 (Quality Education and Curriculum Reform). *Education Research, 5*, 46–49.

CHAPTER 7

Interaction Between Teachers and Students

Yangjie Li

7.1 Introduction

Since the 1990s, with the coming of China's social transformation, students' subjectivity has been highlighted. Accordingly, the key issue of teacher-student relationship needs to be reconsidered. On the one hand, Chinese society is becoming more and more pluralistic and open. "Focusing on choice" has become an important marker of this era, and students play the role of active "chooser" rather than passive "receiver", which unavoidably affects the teacher-student relationship (Ye 1994). Given the rapid development of mass media and "we media", students can independently obtain knowledge and information selectively and challenge the authority of teachers (Wu 2003). On the other hand, with the rise of the market economy, people's ideas and behaviors have tended to be individualized and diversified, which also permeates the school education, and students' individualization also put forward new requirements for teacher-student relationships (Xu 2000). It is worth mentioning that there are some problems in the teacher-student relationships in China,

---

Y. Li (✉)
Department of Education, East China Normal University, Shanghai, China

© The Author(s), under exclusive license to Springer Nature Switzerland AG 2021
Y. Bu (ed.), *Narrative Inquiry into Reciprocal Learning Between Canada-China Sister Schools*, Intercultural Reciprocal Learning in Chinese and Western Education,
https://doi.org/10.1007/978-3-030-61085-2_7

such as alienation and conflict (Li 2012), which has prompted this research to focus on these matters of great importance.

The influence of "New Basic Education" (NBE) research in China has been increasing since the 1990s. It realizes school transformation as a stage of basic education, with the ultimate goal being to change the way of life in schools for teachers and students (Wang and Ye 2003). In particular, NBE pays attention to the teacher-student relationship in the period of social transformation. Specifically, the core values of NBE research are based on people's active and healthy development. Hence, basic education pertains to concrete individual life growth and lets children yearn for life. The goal of classroom teaching is to promote all-round development of students and stimulate the vitality of teachers and students (Ye 1997). On this basis, NBE emphasizes the teacher-student relationship in the process of teaching, that is, the relationship between creative subjects, which can be realized in the dynamic generation of teaching process (Ye 2002).

As mentioned, Minzhu Primary School (MPS) is a base school of NBE. The school has a unique understanding of the teacher-student relationship and the development of students in the new period, which coincides with the ideal of NBE. To be specific, the school takes "cultivating people with vigor and sustainable development" as the educational goal. What's more, MPS adheres to the principle of "returning the class to students and return the initiative of creation to teachers and students", and advances and implements it from four aspects: Environmental culture education, curriculum culture education, management culture education, and class culture education. In addition, we can see the similar phenomenon in the school's teacher evaluation. "Loving students and democratic teaching style" are also included in the evaluation index.

Based on the review of existing researches of teacher-student relationship, this chapter takes Engeström's cultural-historical activity theory and Ye Lan's compound subject theory as the theoretical basis. Besides, this chapter explores the teacher-student interaction of a Chinese teacher and a Canadian teacher in the process of cross-cultural reciprocity by using the method of narrative inquiry, and tries to analyze differences between the Chinese teacher and the Canadian teacher in the teacher-student relationship and explores influence factors for the differences. This chapter also questions whether the Chinese teacher changed the way of teacher-student interaction through the reciprocal learning project, and the factors that affected reciprocal effect are discussed as well.

7.2 Literature Review

This chapter focuses on the teacher-student relationship, an important issue in the field of education, which had not been paid enough attention in the past. Some researchers attributed this to decisions made by the educational administration department, which, specifically, used to regard the teacher-student relationship as a "soft role" affecting students' learning. They also believed that the teacher-student relationship is a factor that could not be easily controlled, while a focus on decision-making could have controllable factors related to students' academic achievement (Bernstein-Yamashiro 2004). However, in recent years, students' problems in social cognition and emotion have made researchers deeply reflect on school education. Many researchers believe that the teacher-student relationship is an important cause of the above problems and teacher-student relationship has garnered researchers' attention (Tao and Li 2016; Bernstein-Yamashiro 2004).

Researchers had three different stances on this issue. The first stance held that the teacher-student relationship should be a power-sharing relationship which has a positive impact on students' academic achievements, rather than a controlling relationship between one side and the other (Dobransky and Frymier 2004). The second stance advocated learner-centered teacher-student relationship, which can promote students' academic development (Cornelius-White 2007). The third view held that the degree of control given by teachers in teacher-student relationship is closely related to the appropriate communicative behaviors enacted by teachers and students in the cultural context (Xie 2010). In other words, the analysis of teacher-student relationship should reflect specific cultural contexts.

However, in reality, teacher-student relationships in China are different from all of the stances presented. Teachers exert more control in teacher-student interaction, which is far removed from students' expectations, and can only be called control-oriented teacher-student relationship. Specifically, Chinese teachers not only hindered students from making positive contributions in the process of teaching (Xie 2010), they also spent too much time managing students' problematic behaviors (Shen et al. 2009). This, of course, leads us back to Chinese teachers' strong control of teacher-student interactions. In addition, there are many differences between the ideal teacher behavior from the perspective of students and the actual teacher behavior. This is also reflected in many aspects of the teacher-student relationship (Wei et al. 2015). In the view of some scholars, such relationships are due to the biased value of education, namely, the absolute authority of teachers, and the rationalization of education management (Wu 2002). These factors are ultimately inseparable from the Chinese culture. In fact, in the context of China, teachers can empower students by recognizing their rights and responsibilities in learning and sharing their rights with students (Wong 2015). One researcher even directly suggested that Chinese teachers should relax their control over students and cultivate a more open classroom culture (Xie 2010).

From the perspective of researchers, most Chinese and Western scholars do not agree that teachers need to use additional control methods in their communication with students (Li and Xiao 2006). However, in actual school life, the West and China present a different scenario in their teacher-student relationships, which can be summarized as control-oriented teacher-student relationship where China is concerned and freedom-oriented teacher-student relationship where countries like Canada are concerned (Yan Wu 2012). It should be emphasized that "control" and "freedom" are both relative terms.

As early as the end of the twentieth century, Chinese researchers realized that culture is an important factor affecting the nature of teacher-student relationship (Weng 1997). With the integration of diverse cultures in a globalized world, school culture exhibits tensions between control and freedom, which is also reflected in teacher-student relationship (Wang 2015). In some recent studies, researchers have attempted to explain the differences between teacher-student relationship in different countries from a cross-cultural perspective (Zheng and Wu 2013). However, most of the existing studies only examine the teacher-student relationship in different cultures from the perspective of presenting the status quo, and barely show the changing process of teacher-student relationship in cross-cultural reciprocity. Also, some studies have explored teacher professional development in cross-cultural reciprocity from a dynamic perspective, but no researchers have explored the teacher-student relationship in cross-cultural reciprocity (Xu and Connelly 2009). In this chapter, we will discuss the relationship between teachers and students in cross-cultural interaction within the context of the Canada-China Reciprocal Learning Project.

7.3 Theoretical Basis and Research Methods

7.3.1 Theoretical Basis

7.3.1.1 Cultural-Historical Activity Theory

The cultural-historical activity theory originated from the theory of activities put forward by Vygotsky and Leontyev in the early twentieth century and was expanded on by Engeström in the late twentieth century (Engeström 2015). It is widely used in many fields such as education and management. This theory holds a materialistic position, believing that knowledge emerges in specific cultural and historical environments.

In addition, the theory holds that all psychological phenomena of human beings are manifested through activities, which are regarded as a complete model with multiple components and subsystems. Among them, elements in each activity system interact with each other, and the activity system can also interact and negotiate with each other, which makes the theory more inclusive and expansive.

The most important point of the theory is that the change of the object makes the subject learn under the rules and division of labor of the practice community through the mediating role of social culture, so as to realize the dynamic knowledge construction (Wells 2002). This is of great value for revealing the internal learning mechanism of individuals and groups.

This theory provides an important starting point for analyzing the way of teacher-student interaction in the context of classroom teaching and the like. For example, what rules, tools, and division of labor are used in the teacher-student interaction? In addition, the theory can also be used to explain the differences in teacher-student relations between the two countries, for example, the differences may be due to teachers' personal experiences and cultural backgrounds.

7.3.1.2 Compound Subject Theory

Ye Lan's (2006) compound subject theory holds that both teachers and students are the agents and subjects of educational activities, and their common object is educational content. In addition, in educational activities, teachers' activities and students' activities are closely related and influence each other, so teachers and students are also known as the compound subjects of educational activities. Ye thinks there are two kinds of activities in education: teaching activities and learning activities. In the former, teachers are the agents of the activities, while students are the objects teachers understand and teach, and are the important conditions for teachers to carry out the activities. In the latter, students are the subjects of learning, and teachers become one of the necessary conditions and objects which the students learn from (Ye 2006).

Therefore, the compound subject theory reflects the actual teacher-student relationship in educational activities in a more comprehensive way, which is different from the previous view that only teachers or students are the subjects. Because compound subject theory providing multiple angles and levels for the analysis of teacher-student relationship, this chapter uses this theory to analyze the teacher-student relationship in specific interaction processes.

7.3.2 Research Method

This article mainly uses the narrative inquiry to analyze the teacher-student interaction in cross-cultural reciprocity. Narrative inquiry is a way of thinking about life (Connelly and Clandinin 1990), which is widely used in the fields of education, anthropology, linguistics, philosophy, and the like. Narrative inquiry is not only a concept of understanding phenomena but also a method of exploring the phenomena (Xu and Connelly 2009).

Based on Dewey's theory of experience as the intersection of personal and social dimensions over time and Schwab's practical, a language for curriculum, we can regard the living space as three-dimensional, defined by a temporal continuum (past-present-future), a personal-social continuum, and a situated place (Xu and Connelly 2009). Among them, a temporal continuous means that everything should be regarded as a process in time, in other words, any phenomenon is from the past and points toward the future. A personal-social continuum means that when narrative inquirers think about people living in three-dimensional space, they should consider not only people in the personal dimension but also people in a social dimension, which is especially fitting for the Chinese culture where a person is represented by two characters leaning in to one another. In addition, the phenomenon will change with place and time. What needs to be added is the teachers' personal characteristics, social characteristics, and places interacting with each other and changing with time (Xu and Connelly 2009).

Furthermore, there are four main tools of narrative inquiry (Craig 2012). The first is broadening, which focuses on the change history of the school where the research study is located and the corresponding national policy being implemented. The second is burrowing, that is, exploring research participants' thinking and life situation through their experiences. The third is storying and re-storying, that is, telling and retelling the story to discover opportunities for transformation. The fourth is fictionalization, which mainly refers to subtly shifting details to further protect those participating in the research project.

Therefore, in this study, we entered the school site and collected relevant data through observation, in-depth interviews, and the like. Data collection not only focused on the dynamic development and location characteristics of the phenomenon but also focused on the history of the school where the teachers are located and relevant policies to the study. It is also necessary to collect the past stories of the campus and the stories of colleagues. The more background details I can seam together, the richer the lived storied we will be able to tell and re-tell and live and re-live.

7.3.3 Research Participant

The research participants in this chapter are Ms. Liu from MPS and Ms. Barton from Bay Street School (BSS), as well as some students from both schools. Ms. Barton joined the reciprocal project in 2014, while Ms. Liu joined the project in 2015.

Ms. Liu is a female teacher born in 1990. She graduated with a master's degree in organic chemistry from East China Normal University (ECNU) in 2015. She entered MPS in September of the same year and taught the subject of nature. Since she was a new teacher, Mr. ZhiGuo, leader of the science curriculum, became her mentor. In September 2017, Ms. Liu became the new leader. Also, it is important to note that she once won the first teaching prize in the National Youth Innovation Competition. Since joining the China-Canada project in 2015, Ms. Liu has become an important member of the project.

Ms. Liu's cross-cultural counterpart is Ms. Barton from BSS in Canada. She is also a research participant in this chapter. Ms. Barton completed her undergraduate degree in science at Concordia University in Montreal, Quebec. She devoted herself to research in water striders during the undergraduate period, and the aquatic thread of her research continued with her graduate research at University of Toronto. Then she transferred to the Ontario Institute for Studies in Education, University of Toronto (OISE/UT), to become a teacher. Within weeks of graduating, she received her first teaching contract with the Toronto District School Board (TDSB) working in BSS. She has been working at the same school for 19 years. At the beginning, she mainly taught mathematics, science, and technology. She has taught all subjects except French for the past several years. Ms. Barton values opportunities to engage in collaborative research and believes that these opportunities can promote her professional development. This is why she actively chose to participate in the China-Canada Project.

Since this chapter mainly explores the teacher-student interaction in cross-cultural reciprocity from the perspective of the Chinese teacher, we mainly pay attention to the important reciprocal activities that Ms. Liu engaged in through observation and in-depth interviews. The data about teacher-student interaction arises from five lessons and three video conferences, which clearly show the key reciprocal activities and the changes of Ms. Liu. In addition, the interview with Ms. Liu is also included. It focuses on Ms. Liu's cognition and her attribution of the differences in teacher-student interaction between the two countries in key reciprocal activities.

The key reciprocal activities mentioned include individual teaching, cooperative teaching, and video conferences. Among them, individual teachers observe others' teaching and reflect on the teaching independently. Cooperative teaching gives the teachers sufficient space to interact. Video conferences play an important role in cultivating students' communication skills and experiencing cultural differences. Taken together, the three activities are all important parts of the reciprocal project. This has had a major influence on Ms. Liu; it also reflects the differences between China and Canada where teacher-student interactions are concerned.

7.3.4   Research Process

As a member of the research team, the researcher participated in the reciprocal project as a research assistant in 2017. Since Ms. Liu joined the project, the researcher has begun to track the reciprocal activities and teaching activities of Ms. Liu and Ms. Barton until the end of 2019. During the period from 2017 to March 2019, the researcher mainly collected data related to teacher-student interactions based on observing and writing field notes through three important activities: individual teaching, cooperative teaching, and video conference. The detailed research data before the researcher entered the research project was obtained from the project team. The following is the general process for our project team, and the three activities explored.

The first activity involved individual teaching. In January of 2016, the sister schools in China and Canada held a video conference. During the conference, the two partners drew up the related activities for the Canadian teachers' visit to China in March, including applying heterogeneous teaching methods for the same subject, observing teaching, school-based teaching, and research activities. In mid-March of 2016, Ms. Barton visited MPS and the two teachers observed each other's classroom teaching. While following up the two lessons given by the two teachers, we also observed a lesson that Ms. Liu taught in November 2016, which was used to show the changes after Ms. Liu observed the classroom teaching of Ms. Barton.

The second activity is cooperative teaching. In May 2018, Ms. Liu taught together with Ms. Barton for the first time, which had a great impact on Ms. Liu. In order to find out whether Ms. Liu changed after the incident, the researcher observed a lesson with Ms. Liu in November 2018 as well.

The third activity was a video conference. At the video conference of China-Canada teachers in February 2017, the following teachers were present: Ms. Liu, Mr. ZhiGuo who was Ms. Liu's mentor, and Ms. Barton. They reached an agreement on the interaction through video between students of both schools. The first students' video conference that Ms. Liu participated in after joining the school was held in March 2017. To find out if Ms. Liu changed after her observation of a Canadian lesson, I watched the students' video conference in March 2019.

In April 2019, the researcher mainly explored Ms. Liu's thoughts and attitudes toward teacher-student interaction in reciprocity through in-depth interview and conducted in-depth analysis combined with theoretical basis and personal experience (see Table 7.1).

The most important activity in the project that made me focus on the teacher-student interaction was a video conference between students of both sides. When watching the video conference, the researcher found an interesting phenomenon that Chinese teachers were more involved in students' interaction, and less Chinese students actively asked Canadian students in the free question session. However, Canadian students performed actively in the video conference, and their teachers gave them more space when they communicated with students. This contrast prompted me to

184   Y. LI

Table 7.1   Important activities covered in this chapter

Date	Activity	Data collection method
March 15, 2016	Ann Barton observed Ms. Liu's classroom teaching	Observe and write field notes
March 17, 2016	Ms. Liu observed Ann Barton's classroom teaching	Observe and write field notes
November 3, 2016	Ms. Liu's classroom teaching after observing Ann Barton's class	Observe and write field notes
May 16, 2018	Ms. Liu and Ann Barton's cooperative teaching	Observe and write field notes
October 19, 2018	Ms. Liu's classroom teaching after the cooperative teaching	Observe and write field notes
March 21, 2017	The first students' video conference	Observe and write field notes
March 22, 2019	The second students' video conference	Observe and write field notes
April 22, 2019	Ms. Liu reviewed the important activities	In-depth interview

focus on the teacher-student interaction in cross-cultural reciprocal learning.

7.4   Findings

7.4.1   *Teacher-Student Interaction in Classroom Teaching Between Two Sister Schools*

7.4.1.1   *Individual Teaching for the First Time of Face-to-Face Reciprocal Learning*

1. Teacher-Student Interaction in Ms. Liu's Classroom Teaching

On March 15, 2016, Ms. Liu gave a science lesson about the Food Chain to the fourth-grade students in MPS. Ms. Barton sat in the back of the classroom and observed the lesson. Let us turn our attention to the particular lesson.

In the first stage of classroom teaching, Ms. Liu enabled her students to discover the food chain in nature. At the beginning, she showed a dynamic picture of little rabbits, guiding students to say what they know about little rabbits as much as possible. Under the guidance of the teacher, students gave many answers, such as "rabbits like to eat carrots" and "rabbits like to stay in the grass". After Ms. Liu wrote students' answers on the black-board, they embarked on the theme of this lesson. The following is a snippet of the teacher-student dialogue at this stage:

Liu:	*Think about it. We know what it likes to eat, and we know where to find it, right? What would it be afraid of?*
Student 1:	*It is afraid of foxes.*
Liu:	*How about the foxes?*
Student 1:	*Foxes will eat it.*
Liu:	*Foxes will eat it, will they? Anything else?*
Student 2:	*They are afraid of people.*
Liu:	*Why?*
Student 2:	*If they see people, they'll run away.*
Liu:	*So they are afraid of people, are they? Sit down, please. Is there anything else to add?*
Student 3:	*They are afraid of eagles.*
Liu:	*What will eagles do with them?*
Student 4:	*Sometimes eagles hurt rabbits.*
Liu:	*Oh, so, please take a seat.*

From the dialogue in the early stage of the class, we find that Ms. Liu mainly started out with common sense, taking rabbits as a case to guide students to probe into the biological chain in nature. Most of the questions raised by Ms. Liu were questions related to facts. At this time, the teacher is the questioner, while the student is the respondent. The teacher-student relationship is the relationship between the questioner and the responder.

In the second part of the class, Ms. Liu introduced the topic to the food chain. The following is a snippet of the teacher-student dialogue in the middle of the class:

Liu:	*We know that rabbits like to eat carrots and stay in the grass. They are afraid of fierce animals such as foxes and eagles. Right? I would like to let you focus on carrots, rabbits and foxes. What is the relationship between them? Who wants to say something? Xu Kaiwen, please.*
Student:	*There is a food chain here.*

Liu:	Oh, there is a food chain here. What is the food chain?
Student:	The big one eats the small one, the bigger one eats the big one.
Liu:	Let's take these three types of organisms as an example. Can you tell us about the food relationship between them?
Student:	Little rabbits want to eat carrots, but foxes want to eat little rabbits.
Liu:	Is that so? Do others agree?
Students (collective chorus):	Agree.

From this fragment, we can see that Ms. Liu is the questioner, the enlightener, and the evaluator at this time. She affirmed the students' answers and gave more examples. The students are the thinkers, the responders, and the monitored in her enlightening, thinking about the meaning of the biological chain. Teachers and students played multiple roles in close interaction.

In the third part of the classroom teaching, Ms. Liu further guided the students to understand the abstract connotation of the food chain and hoped students to analyze more food chains based on the connotation of core concepts they had learned. The following is the dialogue between teachers and students in class:

Liu:	Is there anyone who can sum up the food chain in simple words? Anybody? (Only one or two hands went up) Think about how we discover the food chain. What is the connection between the three kinds of creature? Can anyone talk about it? No? (Ms. Liu finds that Xu Kaiwen raise his hand) Ok, Xu Kaiwen?.
Student:	Everything has its vanquisher.
Liu:	Oh, everything has its vanquisher.
Student:	Anyway, it has its own natural enemies, um...
Liu:	It has its own natural enemies, right? Please sit down. When there is such a food chain between living things, we call it the food chain. What is the connection between the three kinds of creature? Food, right? So now that you know what a food chain is, I'm going to test you. (Show the picture) Please take a closer look. What food chains are included in this picture? Ok?

In this session, Ms. Liu is the first questioner to inspire the students to summarize, and then she gives the exact answer, and becomes the provider of knowledge; students are naturally inspired.

The whole class shows that the teacher's role is the controller and the students' roles are as the responders. Therefore, there is no way to know what the students' questions are or whether they have other ideas or thoughts.

2. Teacher-Student Interaction in Ms. Barton's Classroom Teaching

On March 17, 2016, Ms. Barton also gave a lesson on the theme of "renewable energy and non-renewable energy" to the students of MPS. Ms. Liu observed the class. Next, let us turn our attention to Ms. Barton's classroom and see how the Canadian teacher interacts with students.

Ms. Barton wanted to focus on renewable and non-renewable energy by experiment. Before the class began, Ms. Barton prepared the lab materials for the class and put them in a basket at each table. After the children arrived at the classroom, they were very excited to see so many things in the basket. They could not wait to have a look at them carefully. At this time, Ms. Barton began to say hello to the children and began to discuss the topic of the lesson. Here is the dialogue between the teacher and students at the beginning of this lesson:

Ms. Barton:	*Today I've brought you an activity about energy. Some props of the game have been put in the basket, but I hope you don't touch them first. There are two small blue paper bags in each basket. The reason why I chose blue paper bags was that blue represents the shared earth and the earth is blue. There are many beads in this paper bag. These beads represent the energy of the earth. I want you to tell me which are the energy we use in our daily life? Can you give me an example?*
Student 1:	*Gasoline for cars. Thank you.*
Student 2:	*Electricity at home.*
Student 3:	*Gas for cooking.*
Ms. Barton:	*Okay. That's the one. I see a lot of children who haven't raised their hands. Those children who haven't raised their hands, raise your hands bravely! Just now, some of you talked about the energy used by cars, and the energy used at home. Are there any other examples of daily energy use? The answers you just gave me were where energy came from. I want to know how*

you use it. Can you give me an example? Now I see four students put their hands up, and I hope ten students put your hands up.

Here, Ms. Barton creates the teaching environment and motivates students' active learning. She was a questioner, and the students were thinkers and respondents. She is similar to Ms. Liu in this respect.

Then Ms. Barton began to introduce the experiment to students:

Ms. Barton: *In our daily life, we use energy without thinking. When we do this little game, we just put our hands in and grab a handful of energy. When we do this, we also grab these beads without thinking, OK? There are 100 beads in this bag. Every time we take the bead from the bag, it means that we use energy every year. Every year we use 10 beads. When we take beads, we don't need to look at them. You can see that there are many gray beads, but also a green bead. Then we write down the number of gray and green beads. The green beads should be put back into the paper bag, and the gray beads should be put back into the basket. The next year, I repeat the steps I just made…. I'll give you five minutes. Here are beads representing 10 years. When you run out of energy, you'll be 22 years old. Start!*

In this experiment, each experimental material chosen by Ms. Barton had a certain symbolic meaning. Through this open experiment, she tried to make students fully feel and understand the connotation of renewable energy and non-renewable energy in simulated situations. Then the children began to conduct the experiment in groups, and the scene began to be lively. In the meanwhile, Ms. Barton observed different groups and she did not instruct the children directly. After five minutes of group work, Ms. Barton clapped her hands to keep quiet and began to ask questions:

Ms. Barton: *Now tell me, what did you observe when you played this game?*
Student 1: *The further you go, the greener beads you have.*
Student 2: *Sometimes we take out gray beads and we don't have green beads.*
Student 3: *There are fewer gray beads as time goes on.*
Student 4: *Sometimes we take out the same beads.*

7 INTERACTION BETWEEN TEACHERS AND STUDENTS   189

Ms. Barton: *When I was designing the game, I chose two colors of beads. In this game, there are gray beads and green beads. I use these two colors specially; do you know why? I'll give you time to think about it. There are no wrong answers in my class, so you can say whatever you want. (The children started a heated discussion, and at this time, Ms. Barton was gradually counting the number of children who raised their hands.) When I was just playing this game, I don't want you to have the same idea as me, so you can give me any idea.*

Student 5: *One is renewable and the other is non-renewable.*

Student 6: *One is the energy that is useful to nature and the other is the energy that is harmful to nature.*

Ms. Barton: *Thank you!*

Student 7: *The green one represents the energy with flowers and plants, and the gray one represents the energy without flowers and plants.*

Ms. Barton: *Any other ideas?*

In this dialogue, the teacher is not only the provider of learning materials but also the guide who helps students to discover scientific laws and reasons. This is mainly reflected in the types of questions she asks: What do you find? Can you explain why? At this time, students naturally became the discoverers of laws and the inferences of scientific reasoning. Obviously, Ms. Liu's questions were "What do you know?" and "What else do you know?" Her queries point to the problem of students' memory that students are expected to store and recollect knowledge. Therefore, the relationship between teachers and students in the teaching of the two teachers is quite different.

3. *Ms. Liu's Reflection on Ms. Barton's Classroom Teaching*

After the classroom teaching, the Chinese teacher and the Canadian teacher had a brief exchange. When talking about her teaching method, Ms. Barton stressed that "the class will be constructed according to students' interests and current news", which was guided by the larger goals which Ms. Barton set, although the Ontario government would give them some sub-goals as well.

Ms. Liu found that there were great differences between China and Canada in the teacher-student interaction after listening to the classroom teaching and her short interaction with Ms. Barton. The difference was mainly manifested in teaching strategies as she discussed below:

Liu: *Because we (Chinese teachers) are used to starting research from theory and separating from practice [theory-practice split], but they (Canadians) start the study from the situation around themselves [an ontological, dialectical, or problem-solving approach]. We tend to do it in another way. We tend to learn the theory first and then think about whether we can apply the theory to practice. The difference surprised me a lot.*

Obviously, Ms. Liu was able to pinpoint the differences between teacher-student interaction and classroom learning. Of course, her findings were mainly based on the overall process of classroom teaching, but the differences in the types of teachers' questions, potential rules for teacher-student interaction, and the way students respond were not mentioned. Also, she did not mention the essential differences in the teacher-student relationship between the two countries. Based on the differences above, Ms. Liu mainly attributed the reasons to the education received by teachers:

Liu: *Growing up is really like this, we tend to read books first, what is taught in the book, then our teacher will ask what you think you can apply to life. Their teaching is to solve a problem with a specific aim.*

From Ms. Liu's comment, we can infer several things. First, Ms. Liu realized that teachers' educational experience had a great influence on teacher-student interaction, which was essentially an external attribution, and this factor could be corrected through self-adjustment in her view. For example, Ms. Liu actively learned and absorbed knowledge through cross-cultural reciprocal learning projects, and reflected and questioned some experience. Second, she thought that the differences in teacher-student interaction were related to the more pragmatic culture. In her impression, teacher-student interaction in teaching pointed to specific goals. Finally, Ms. Liu's attribution essentially reflected her teacher-student interaction when she was a student, which was likely to be pragmatic and deductive.

The Changes of Ms. Liu's Classroom Teaching After the First Reciprocal Learning Exchange

So, did Ms. Liu change the way of student-teacher interactions after this key influence? Let us start our analysis with the nature class taught by Ms. Liu on November 3, 2016. In this class, Ms. Liu's teaching goal was that students should understand the relationship between rivers and human beings. This lesson had more experiments than her previous lessons. At the beginning, Ms. Liu introduced the theme of this lesson using some experimental equipment, which made students interested in the topic of this lesson:

Liu: *Well, I just observed the sand table you build. And I found that every group put some trees and animals beside the river, didn't you? Who can explain it to me? (Nobody raises hand) Yu Kaitian, what's your opinion?*

Student: *Because plants and animals can't live without water.*

Liu: *That's right! Sit down please. So, let's think over the relationship between rivers and human beings since rivers give plants and animals life. Now, I would like you to watch the picture carefully, and try to work out the features of cities' geographical position along the Yangtze River and Yellow River. Here are the pictures.*

In the above dialogue, we can find that this lesson started from the experimental device, and the intermediary for teacher-student interaction changed, such as the use of sandboxes and pictures. Intuitive presentation could arouse students' interest in teaching goals. In addition, in the dialogue between the teacher and students, we can see that the type of question asked by Ms. Liu was no longer a factual question, but an inquiry type question. She hoped that students could make subjective interpretations. However, the students were not able to adapt to the new question type, and passively responded. After the students answered, Ms. Liu expressed a positive attitude, which was also different from the past.

In addition, in the follow-up teaching, Ms. Liu collected students' views on the development and utilization of rivers through the form of a "public opinion survey", divided students into two groups according to the results of the survey, and triggered students' thinking and discussion through the form of debate:

Liu: *Here, have you thought about a question, human develop the river, whether it is true to the benefit of our human development? I've seen someone shaking his head, and someone is nodding. Well, I want to do a public opinion survey first, those who hold that the development and utilization of rivers is conducive to human development, please raise your hand. (After a while) OK, put your hands down. I find that the number of students with both views is equal. You are divided into two groups. Then how about this, today we have a debate on the scene about whether developing the rivers or not is more conducive to human development. Those who held that the development and utilization of rivers is more conducive to human development is one group. Others will go in the opposite group.*

On the one hand, we can find that Ms. Liu changed the rules of teacher-student interaction, that is, there were no correct answers and she hoped that students could speak out their own views and explain them. On the other hand, Ms. Liu changed the intermediary of teacher-student interaction, which increased the interest of activities. Readers will recall the public opinion survey and the debate that followed, which allowed students to inspire each other's learning.

Taken together, Ms. Liu's strategies changed dramatically by encouraging students to think, by conducting the experiment, by organizing debate and by introducing the specific problems of daily life. Compared with the last time, the inductive logic was adopted this time and achieved her teaching purpose as well. More uncertainty was included in teacher-student interaction, and the degree of freedom of teacher-student interaction was improved. In other words, Ms. Liu gradually realized that students were the participants in learning activities and she was only the facilitator of their learning activities—not the determiner of what students should learn.

7.4.1.2 Cooperative Teaching for the Second Time of Face-to-Face Reciprocal Learning

1. Ms. Liu and Ms. Barton's Cooperative Teaching

In March 2018, Ms. Liu and Ms. Barton reached an agreement with cooperative lesson preparation and teaching and agreed on the teaching content. The two teachers met in MPS in May 2018. On May 14, 2018, the first day of preparing lessons together, Ms. Liu and Ms. Barton made relatively detailed plans on teaching and activity design, and engaged in a made preliminary discussion about teaching objectives, students' learning situation, and so on. On the second day of preparing lessons together, the teachers further cooperatively planned, this time filling in teaching details and specific division of labor. In this discussion, Ms. Barton emphasized that the teachers should pay more attention to the difficulties encountered by students and allow them to fully think and experience, rather than over-controlling the teaching process:

> Ms. Barton: We hope that we can choose groups that have problems and chal-lenges during the cooperation process, and we can encourage students. I will ask students "What you are doing now?", "Where have you gone?", "Have you encountered any difficulties and challenges?", and "What kind of help do you need?".... When we ask students to show on the stage, we will not say that there is a problem with the design of this group, we should say that this group encountered challenges in measurement and let other groups think what solutions can be used. Students will then propose solutions, Ms. Liu can write down these sugges-tions. Next, we asked the groups presenting to choose the sugges-tion that they think is most helpful to them and explain why. As we go through these steps, we also want other students to think about which suggestion is most useful for the group presenting. I hope students can discuss multiple possibilities.

Ms. Barton's suggestion gave teacher-student interactions a new pos-sibility for the division of labor: that is, to allow students experiencing difficulties to display and choose solutions. Meanwhile, other students become responsible for providing a variety of solutions for the students, and the teachers provide guidance for students' interaction.

On May 16, 2018, the two teachers officially launched a cooperative teaching lesson. Before class, Ms. Liu worried about the lack of time, espe-cially when students encountered difficulties and could not complete the lesson. Ms. Barton persuaded Ms. Liu not to pay too much attention to the results, but to let students experience the process. Ms. Liu felt relieved after taking the advice of Ms. Barton.

After the formal class began, Ms. Barton greeted everyone and said that she heard about the expiratory system and inspiratory system before she came. She wanted to have a breathing competition with everyone. Ms. Barton asked one student to represent MPS, Ms. Barton would represent BSS and other students would act as judges. Ms. Barton asked if anyone would like to take part in the competition on stage, many students raised their hands. Then Ms. Barton introduced the rules and said that everyone could only breathe once. In the first round of the official competition, the student did not succeed, while Ms. Barton played better obviously. Ms.

Barton asked everyone who won, and students responded in unison that it was Ms. Barton. Then Ms. Barton asked students for their criteria for judgment. She constantly fueled everyone's enthusiasm and encouraged them to raise their hands and to express their opinions. Given time for thinking, some students expressed that the standard was height. Immediately after the start of the second round, Ms. Barton won the competition again. She asked everyone if the game was fair, a part of students answered that it was unfair. At this point, she admitted that the rules were better for her. She then continued to make everyone think about who won the competition and the criterion of judgment by group discussion. She emphasized the time schedule and ended the group discussion on time. Students had a lively discussion in the process and gave multiple answers.

Ms. Barton guided the students to focus on core topics through competition. She not only made students think about who won the competition but also let students reflect on the evaluation criteria in the game. She also had an open attitude to students' answers. Although a time limit was set, students were given sufficient time to think and discuss freely.

During the students' discussion, Ms. Liu and Ms. Barton observed children's performances in different groups. At the same time, Mr. ZhiGuo who was the mentor of Ms. Liu sat next to the leaders of Minzhu District School Board (MDSB) and Principal Ting, listening to their comments and observing Ms. Liu's actions. Then Mr. ZhiGuo came on the stage to communicate with Ms. Barton and Ms. Liu, and began to observe students' performances in each group by himself. This triggered the discussion between Ms. Barton and Ms. Liu and affected their subsequent behavior.

From the above description, we can see that the teaching process in Chinese classrooms is affected by various influences, such as Ms. Liu's mentor and education administrators, which indirectly determined the degree of freedom in teacher-student interaction.

In the co-teaching situation, an "unexpected situation" happened. One group of students did not complete the design. Ms. Liu did not want to choose this group in the exhibition part. However, Ms. Barton expressed a totally different view:

Ms. Barton: *Why not invite them to communicate? This is a good case. The well-done groups have done it, and the uncompleted groups are worth discussing. If these students think about "what problems they have encountered" and "why they should change", instead of thinking about stopping and running out of time, it shows that they have the spirit and attitude of exploration and innovation, and that they want to pursue completion.*

At the suggestion of Ms. Barton, Ms. Liu still chose the better group to report first. However, she also invited the unfinished group to report later and encouraged other students to ask questions so as to promote the reflection of all students.

The two teachers had diverse views, which reflected the differences in their focus. Ms. Barton paid more attention to the teaching process and the active involvement of more students in the activities, while Ms. Liu paid more attention to the teaching results and possibly the audience members observing her.

2. Ms. Liu's Reflection on the Cooperative Teaching

After the cooperative teaching, Ms. Liu reflected on the "unexpected situation":

Liu: *My main focus is how to let students learn more in limited time, while Ms. Barton's focus is how to let students think more. I also want to learn more about how to promote students' thinking from Ms. Barton in the future.*

Ms. Liu was aware of the basic differences in the teacher-student interaction between the two countries and expressed a willingness to learn from Ms. Barton. At the end of lesson, the two teachers had a private exchange, and Ms. Liu still expressed regret about the results, while Ms. Barton's feedback had a profound impact on Ms. Liu:

Liu: *It's a pity that the group didn't do well just now. If the group had more guidance, it may have been able to do well. Maybe others will think our class is not so perfect. After all, there is a group that has not done their task.*

Barton: *Students enjoy the process, learn something in the process, you also find something and gain something in the process. That's enough. Why should you care about what others think?*

Ms. Liu, as a beginning teacher, cared too much about the results. She worried about how the group's not doing well might be perceived by audience members. On the other hand, Ms. Barton, an experienced teacher, believed that the teacher-student interaction in teaching does not need to pay attention to others' ideas or demands for results. The most important thing is that teachers and students develop in the teacher-student interaction. This reflected their contrasting understanding of teacher-student relationship in teaching.

After many conversations with Ms. Barton before, during, and after class, Ms. Liu gradually accepted the idea of letting students experience the teaching process. She attributed the difference between China and Canada in this way:

Liu: *If students don't do well, it means that the class is not particularly good. The general direction of our evaluation is still like this. So when you see Ms. Barton in class, she is very relaxed, and she just needs to finish what she wants to do in her mind.*

Ms. Liu's implication here is that Ms. Barton is not subject to the same external constraints as she is. Based on her felt restraints, Ms. Liu hoped to adjust her teaching strategies in the follow-up lesson and adhere closely to the teaching objectives. If there was an unanticipated surprise in the teaching process, Ms. Liu would continue teaching and work with the contingencies to complete the teaching objectives and then help the other students to promote their thinking so they too could have a more profound experience. Could Ms. Liu handle the relationship between the realization of teaching objectives and promoting students' thinking after this critical activity? Let us analyze the STEM lesson taught by Ms. Liu on October 19, 2018.

3. The Changes of Ms. Liu's Classroom Teaching After the Cooperative Teaching

At the beginning of the lesson, Ms. Liu asked everyone to observe differences between the three leaves posted on the blackboard. Students said that the leaves differed in terms of color, size, and chlorophyll content. Immediately afterwards, Ms. Liu asked her class of students to identify differences in the chlorophyll content of the three leaves and what caused the differences, and some students thought nutrition and age might be the reason. Then Ms. Liu informed students that the difference in chlorophyll content among the three leaves was mainly caused by the difference in light. In the subsequent experiment, Ms. Liu asked the students to extract chlorophyll, let students verify and consider whether chlorophyll content caused leaves' color to be changed. She also introduced the specific steps of the experiment and stipulated the experiment time limits. Then, students began to discuss and experiment in small groups.

In this lesson, Ms. Liu let students explore the core issues independently through experiments, and then let the students work in groups to give students sufficient autonomy. As a teacher, she was mainly responsible for introducing the rules and providing students with some suggestions.

However, an unexpected situation arose again. Ms. Liu asked the students if they had any ideas. The students did not have a good, shared plan. One person came up with a plan, which others accepted. Ms. Liu suggested that students could cooperate with a division of labor. Then everyone in the group did the lesson's different parts spontaneously.

In this instance, Ms. Liu tried to help students think independently and learn to cooperate through guidance under the premise of ensuring teaching objectives and controlling teaching time. This time, she did not rush to interrupt the discussion of the students or let the completed students report on the stage, but gave students time to allow more students to participate in the group cooperation, so that students could think more effectively through the division of labor. It is clear that Ms. Liu learned from Ms. Barton from the previous situation. She relaxed the control she had over the teaching-learning process and regarded all students as participants in the educational activities.

However, due to the large number of students in the class, Ms. Liu could not pay attention to every student. In the group settings, sometimes a few students were unable to participate and/or the group members were unable to communicate effectively.

7.4.2 Teacher-Student Interactions in Two Video Conferences Between Two Sister Schools

7.4.2.1 The First Student Video Conference

In the first student video conference held on March 21, 2017, the science team of MPS introduced their performance, students of water club from MPS, and students from BSS exchanged photos of rivers. In the whole activity, the following aspects attracted my attention.

First, in terms of preparation before the key activity, the activities of taking pictures of rivers had begun since the winter holiday in MPS. At the end of the holiday, all students in MPS handed in their works. After the first stage of selection, shortlisted students participated in activities similar to an interview by explaining their work. After a second time of selection, students who were good at spoken English were finally selected to participate in the first student video conference. But this situation did not really happen in BSS. Although Ms. Liu encouraged all students to submit their works, the teachers screened students according to the quality of their works and language proficiency, which prevented some students from participating in the reciprocal activities. In essence, Ms. Liu held the dominant power in teacher-student interaction.

Second, according to the on-site arrangement of the video activity of the day, the seat distribution of MPS was similar to previous classroom teaching. Although Ms. Liu did not interact with students because she was responsible for taking photos of the video conference and regulation of the equipment, Mr. ZhiGuo, who was Ms. Liu's mentor, sat at the right rear of students to guide Chinese students' interactions with the Canadian students. The seat distribution of BSS was different from that of MPS. BSS formed a half circle with students' sitting on one side and Ms. Barton sat on the other side. In this regard, we can interpret this phenomenon in this way. Whether the teachers are in the back or the teachers are in the front, the two ways of seating reflect the teacher-student relationship. These relations can be described as superior and subordinate with the teachers and students being unequal participants. As for the circle seating, it reflects relationships among equals, with everyone having the choice to speak up.

Third, in terms of interaction, MPS students walked to the front of the classroom and showed the photos of rivers they took during the winter vacation. Teachers and students of BSS asked questions to students of MPS from time-to-time; they showed interest in their partners' photos. Similarly, two BSS students showed the rivers they painted and the poems about rivers, which were appreciated by the Chinese students. Mr. ZhiGuo who was Ms. Liu's mentor directly instructed the Chinese students on how to interact with Canadian students, which was very different from the Canadian teacher who indirectly guided students by personally asking questions. I believe that Ms. Barton's indirect guidance may have been a more productive way to stimulate the enthusiasm of students' active questioning, while Mr. ZhiGuo's direct guidance may have made students more passive receivers rather than active participants in the learning activities.

In short, the three highlighted examples fully reflect the differences in the ways that the teachers from both countries handled the first video interaction. This was the first time that Ms. Liu was involved in students' interaction in an exchange such as this.

7.4.2.2 Ms. Liu's Reflection After the First Student Video Conference

In the interview, Ms. Liu mainly mentioned the difference between the two sides in terms of students, and I did not mention the difference in the degree of teacher intervention in students' interaction either:

Liu: *I think the two countries' children also have differences, as our side was ready to draft and practice again and again in advance, when the teacher said who wanted to speak, students would stand up and prepare themselves, feeling like they made a speech unilaterally, and hadn't thought about other questions in order to interact with them. We had not thought about interacting in depth. The Canadian students probably figured out what they would talk about today, and then they talked it interactively. They wanted to treat us as friends or classmates.*

Ms. Liu basically grasped the differences in the behaviors of the students of the two countries, but apparently was not thinking about the differences in the behaviors of the teachers in the two countries and the differences in teacher-student interaction.

When talking about the reasons for the differences, Ms. Liu attributed the reasons to the family education and school education that students had received before:

Liu: *Because of the education they have received since childhood, our children are a little passive and teachers need to guide them and tell them what and how to do.*

Ms. Liu hoped to adjust students' enthusiasm in interaction through actions, so she mainly planned the following:

Liu: *So I told the students before that you should treat them as classmates or friends. It is useless if they have not really practiced. So, if I have a class now, I will arrange it deliberately. For example, we will make posters and introductions in this class. What could we do? Several*

> *members of a group would work together. Next, let students of other groups ask questions, and evaluate the advantages and disadvantages, thus forcing them to interact and think deeply. When students mention the advantages and disadvantages, the children who are on the stage should also respond and think. If we continue to practice this mode, when we hold a video conference again, we will feel that there is no difficulty... It is just interaction and students will be used to this mode.*

Here, Ms. Liu aimed to attend to the current situation. She thought of short-term changes, but did not seem to keep the long-term perspective in mind. Also, the intervention focused on teachers, while still carrying out exercises and screening students in advance.

Based on the above cognition of Ms. Liu, did she adjust behaviors in the following activities? How did she adjust? Next, I will use a video conference in March 2019 as an example to analyze how the Chinese teacher intervened in students' interaction, which is also based on field notes.

7.4.2.3 The Second Student Video Conference

On March 22, 2019, Mr. ZhiGuo, Ms. Liu, Ms. Barton, and the students from China and Canada conducted the second student video conference. The conference mainly focused on the exhibition works of Chinese students and Canadian students, and students of both sides expressed their own design intentions.

During the student presentations, the Chinese teachers and the Canadian teacher assumed different positions. In the video conference, the Chinese teachers pointed out the correct posture of holding the indicator board, encouraged students to respond politely and to ask questions of the Canadian students. They asked the Canadian students if they had any confusion about the Chinese students' presentations, and guided the Chinese students' voice levels, positions and order, and so on. However, the Canadian teacher stood at the back of the classroom and did not enter into the students' discussion. Correspondingly, the Chinese students still only introduced their work and rarely asked questions of the Canadian students. Only through the guidance and encouragement of the Chinese teachers, a small number of students asked questions of the Canadian students.

We can see that the Chinese teachers intervened in the interaction between students of the two countries by informing students through words or answering for students, while the Canadian teacher still did not interfere too much. The Chinese teachers did not change their interactive behavior with the students in students' video conferences, and students still did not make the learning activities their own. Obviously, Ms. Liu, after the last video conference, had named differences between students of the two schools. So why did she not change? Which factors hindered Ms. Liu? How should we understand these phenomena? These problems require more deep thought.

7.5 DISCUSSION

We begin by summarizing the activities and the interaction between teachers and students in Table 7.2.

7.5.1 Comparison of the Characteristics of Teacher-Student Interactions in China and Canada

As mentioned, previous studies have shown the differences between China and the West in teacher-student relationship. The core characteristics of China and the West can be summarized as a fixed mindset approach and a growth mindset approach, which can be seen in an American Chinese student called Shi Tan (Craig et al. 2017).

First, we see that the Chinese teacher used deductive logic more in teaching communication, which held the end in view and ignored the thinking characteristics of students along the way. Comparatively, the Canadian teacher mainly used inductive logic, which unfolded from concrete to abstract. It was student-centered and scaffolded their growth. Although the Chinese teacher guided students to discover the food chain in nature, for example, she asked some students who had prior knowledge of the food chain to answer, and then let students apply the concept to other cases. This made other students unfamiliar with this concept to abstract concepts directly. The feedback from students was not as positive as it might have been. In contrast, the Canadian teacher used experiments to stimulate students' desire to participate in discussions. She used experimental equipment and she had an open attitude toward students' answers and valued the participation of more students. In other words, the Canadian teacher started with a more concrete and experimental approach and paid more attention to students' thought process disregarding the so-called standard answer, so that students could think about the core issues

202   Y. LI

Table 7.2 Teacher-student interaction in important reciprocal learning activities between two sister schools

Date	Activities	Specific performance	Teacher-student relationship
March 15, 2016	Ann Barton observed Ms. Liu's original classroom teaching	Ms. Liu followed deductive logic and rejected uncertainty	Teachers are questioners and students are responders
March 17, 2016	Ms. Liu observed Ann Barton's original classroom teaching	Ann Barton followed inductive logic and accepted the uncertainty in teacher-student interaction with an open attitude	Teachers are guides, students are discoverers and explorers
November 3, 2016	Ms. Liu's classroom teaching after observing Ann Barton's classroom teaching	Ms. Liu continued her way of teaching in inductive logic, and there was more uncertainty in teacher-student interaction than before	Teachers give students more space to think and more space to explore independently
May 16, 2018	Ms. Liu and Ann Barton's cooperative teaching	Ann Barton focused on allowing students to experience the process, while Ms. Liu hoped to achieve the teaching results through controlling process	Ann Barton regarded the teachers and students as composite subjects of educational activities, while Ms. Liu regarded only the teachers as the subjects of educational activities
October 19, 2018	Ms. Liu's classroom teaching after the cooperative teaching	Although still concerned about the achievement of teaching objectives, Ms. Liu gave students enough time and let students experience the teaching process	Teachers become diagnosticians and listeners, and students become explorers and discoverers
March 21, 2017	The first students' video conference	The Chinese teachers selected students ahead of time, sat at the back of students and guided them directly, while the Canadian teachers did not interfere too much	Chinese teachers are evaluators, screeners, and controllers, and students are passive participants, and the status of the teachers and students in Canada were relatively equal

(continued)

Table 7.2 (continued)

Date	Activities	Specific performance	Teacher-student relationship
March 22, 2019	The second students' video conference	The Chinese teachers still intervened in the interaction between students of the two countries by informing students through words and substituting for students, while the Canadian teacher still did not interfere too much	The status of the teachers and students in China and Canada was basically the same as before

themselves. The less-experienced Chinese teacher did not seem to realize that she was only the facilitator of learning activities, a person who creates suitable conditions for students' learning. In this scenario, students are front and center in the learning activity work, of which the Canadian teacher was clearly aware.

Second, in the key activity "cooperative teaching", the Chinese teacher wanted to control the teaching process. Her concern was fixed on achieving the teaching goal. She wished the students to gain more knowledge and to avoid "the unexpected". However, the Canadian teacher tended to let students experience the process. Specifically, before class, the Chinese teacher was worried that some groups of students would not be able to complete the experiments in time, while the Canadian teacher thought that they should not focus too much on the results, but on letting students experience the process. In lesson preparation and teaching, the Chinese teacher did not want to let unfinished group present their results, but the Canadian teacher proposed that the unfinished group should display their results, allowing other students to think about such questions as "What problems did they encounter?" and "How should they change?" In addition, the Chinese teacher's teaching behavior was influenced by many subjects, including her mentor and educational administrators. Ms. Barton regarded the teachers and students as epicenters to the educational activities, whereas Ms. Liu only regarded the teachers as central to the task at hand.

Finally, in the key activity "video conference of students", the Chinese teacher and her mentor perhaps intervened too much in students' interaction both at the preparation stage and at the video interaction stage, while the Canadian teacher gave students more space. Specifically, the Chinese teacher screened students several times based on their performance during presentations before the start of the video conference. On the day of the video conference, the Chinese teacher's mentor sat in the right rear of the Chinese students, in order to provide timely guidance on how to interact with the Canadian students. In contrast, the Canadian teacher did not screen students before the video conference began. On the day of the video conference, she sat on the other side of the Canadian students and asked Chinese students questions together with Canadian students. In a word, she guided the Canadian students indirectly. It can be seen that the status of the Chinese teachers and Chinese students were not equal, and the status of the teachers and students in Canada were more equal, but not absolutely equal due to their assigned roles.

7.5.2 The Factors Influencing the Differences of Teacher-Student Interaction in Two Countries

7.5.2.1 Chinese Traditional Concepts on Teacher-Student Relationship

Studies have shown that the differences between China and other countries in teacher-student interaction are mainly due to cultural values, which precipitate in the long historical process and make teacher-student interaction relatively stable (Zheng and Wu 2013). Cultural values are embedded in the Chinese traditional concepts on teacher-student relationship. Chinese traditional concepts on teacher-student relationship can be divided into the following categories (C. Huang and Si 2013), which have profound impact on contemporary teacher-student interactions.

The first category can be seen as "respecting teachers and prioritizing education". The original intention of "respecting the teachers and prioritizing the education" is to build an atmosphere emphasizing education in the society. Under the influence of the hierarchical patriarchal system, this good original intent was alienated in later generations and gradually changed into "obeying authority". In this concept of teacher-student relationships, teachers are the authority of knowledge, students are objects to be taught, and the content of education is the guarantee of the existence and continuity of human society.

The second category could be described as "father-son relationship", that is, teachers and students are like father and son, as the Chinese proverb goes: "A teacher for one day is like a father for life". This conception of teacher-student relationship not only emphasizes teachers' respectful position but also emphasizes the emotional connection between teachers and students. In other words, teachers have authority in the teaching process, on the other hand, teachers care about students, and teachers' teaching methods are no longer hard indoctrination.

The third category could be described as "homocentric relationship". This concept of teacher-student relationship holds that teachers and students are equal in personality and stimulate each other in the interaction. Teachers are no longer one-way promoters of students' growth, but partners who experience cultural explorations alongside students. Teachers and students achieve common development in this process.

It should be noted that among the three concepts of teacher-student relationship, the first concept and the second concept have more current influence on the teacher-student relationship and teacher-student interaction in Chinese education field (Huang and Si 2013; Yuejun Wu 2010). The first two concepts regard teachers as the authority in teacher-student interaction, and they are not aware of teachers' self-development in teacher-student interaction. This is also reflected in the teacher-student interaction in the above reciprocal activities. Before the shift in her thinking, Ms. Liu did not realize that she was not the sole director of the learning activities and that she should provide proper support for her students who were co-participants alongside her. She regarded students as passive recipients of knowledge and regarded herself as the knowledge authority.

7.5.2.2 Chinese Traditional Concepts on Teaching

Chinese traditional culture contains collectivism values, which emphasizes the cooperation and social responsibility. Similarly, in the Chinese traditional concepts on teaching, students are regarded as "abstract people" rather than "specific individuals". This suggests that students lack distinct personality characteristics, and students' development is regarded as the result of a combination of genetic factors, environmental factors, and other factors that cannot be controlled by themselves (Ye 2003). On this basis, the knowledge in the traditional concept on teaching has the characteristics of subjectivity, and teaching is regarded as a one-way process of transferring knowledge to students. Chinese traditional concepts of teaching overemphasize the authority of teachers and ignore subjective initiative and individual differences of students. This may cause students to lack independence, to not be autonomous intellectually, and to think in a less-strong way (Zhang 2001).

In this chapter, the interaction between Ms. Liu and students was influenced by the traditional concepts on teaching. Being part of traditional culture, Ms. Liu did not pay attention to the individual differences of students nor pay attention to promoting students' in-depth thinking through various forms. In other words, Ms. Liu taught from the cultural position in which she had been inducted. It was not until she observed Ms. Barton did other worlds and other ways of doing things open up for her.

Teacher-student interaction in contemporary China needs to break loose of the shackles of traditional concepts and cultivating students' higher-order thinking is an important place to start. Cultivating students' higher-order thinking would ease the transition from teacher control to student-centered learning, from focusing on knowledge transfer to focusing on the learning process, and from closed questions to open questions (Wang 2001).

7.5.2.3 Evaluation of Teachers by Administrative Department for Education

The different teacher-student interactions of the two teachers from MPS and BSS are also related to the evaluation of teachers by the administrative department for education, which influences the behaviors of the teachers in a subtle way.

In the assessment of MPS by the Education Supervision Office of Minzhu District People's Government (The Minhang District People's Government 2017), we can find that the indicators directly related to teachers mainly include "teacher management", "teacher's moral quality", "educational practice", and "curriculum and teaching management". There is no explicit mention of teacher-student interaction in any of these indicators. It should be noted that the measurement of these indicators is mainly based on the collection of easily accessible and comparable data. However, the dynamic and complex teacher-student interaction is not included in the relevant indicators. However, in the evaluation of BSS's teachers by the Ministry of Education, Ontario (Ontario Ministry of Education 2010), it explicitly includes the dimension of "commitment to pupils and pupil learning": Teachers are dedicated in their efforts to teach and support pupil learning and achievement; teachers provide an environment for learning that encourages pupils to be problem solvers, decision-makers, lifelong learners, and contributing members of a changing society.

Under the influence of the above-mentioned China teacher evaluation, Ms. Liu paid more attention to the one-way teaching of knowledge, which was relatively easy to measure. However, she did not focus on the stimulation of students' thinking and adapting to students' thinking characteristics and the like because she was not being evaluated on those criteria, which are relatively difficult to measure. Ms. Barton was also influenced by teacher evaluation. She promoted students' in-depth thinking by not interfering with the interaction between students from two countries, promoting mutual motivation between students and following students' thinking characteristics. Students really became co-participants in the learning activities and Ms. Barton became a co-facilitator of the meaning that students took away from them.

7.6   Conclusion

In conclusion, the factors that affect cross-cultural reciprocal learning have been explored. Previous studies have shown that the effectiveness of cross-cultural reciprocal learning was mainly affected by attitudes and strategies of reciprocal participants (Bu et al. 2019).

From the analysis in Table 7.3, Ms. Liu was very active in trying to find differences and had the desire to productively learn. She changed her thinking and shifted her mindset in practice, which has had important impact on promoting the development of reciprocal activities.

However, she had different degrees of problems in finding differences, attributions, and follow-up actions. In terms of "differences found", the problem was mainly in the key activity of video conference. Although the Chinese teacher felt that the teachers in the two countries had different degrees of intervention in students' interaction, she mainly focused on the differences in students' performance between the two countries, which reflected that the Chinese teacher was not aware of teachers' roles and led to a subsequent attribution and action. Also, the Chinese teacher traced causes to the education received in the past as well as the form of evaluation. Most of the above reasons were external and uncontrollable. In the follow-up actions, there were mainly three types of problems for Chinese teachers. First, the Chinese teacher let students practice directly for short-term goals, but seldom thought about measures from a longer-term perspective; second, the Chinese teacher did not try different plans many

208 Y. LI

Table 7.3 Impact of reciprocal activities on Ms. Liu in teacher-student interaction

Specific link	Key activity		
	Classroom teaching		Video conference
	Individual teaching	Cooperative teaching	
Differences	Whether the teachers neglected the thinking characteristics of students	Whether the teachers excessively control the teaching process	Whether the teachers gave students sufficient interactive space (the Chinese teacher mainly mentioned differences between students)
Attitude	We should learn from Canada and make adjustments	We should learn from Canada and make adjustments	We should learn from Canada and make adjustments
Attribution	Education received by the Chinese teacher	Impact of assessment	Previous family and school education received by students
Action	The Chinese teacher made adjustments through self-regulation, such as the use of experiments, debates, and other forms in classroom teaching	On the basis of persistence in teaching goals, a backup plan was formulated to actively help students cope with unexpected situations	The Chinese teacher encouraged students to share and express on stage in daily classroom teaching, while other students ask them questions
Effect	It stimulated students' interest in learning	Some students got her indirect guidance, but some students were not noticed	Students were still not active enough

times, but only made single adjustment; third, the Chinese teacher seldom thought deeply about the preconditions for learning from other countries, such as cultural context, class size, and other factors.

In other words, with the rise of the market economy and the change of media, people's thoughts and behaviors tend to be more and more personalized and diversified. Students tend to be personal and they are motivated. We find that Ms. Liu's interaction with students adapted to the above changes of students' characteristics in the classroom teaching situation. In other words, she could find the differences of teacher-student interaction in the two countries, while taking into account the thinking characteristics of students, promoting students' independent thinking, and truly returning the classroom to students and making the classroom full of vitality, which is what NBE emphasizes. However, in the context of the video conference, the differences of teacher-student interaction in the two countries were not yet identifiable to her, possibly because she was a beginning teacher. She focused on the differences in students' performance between the two countries instead. Following how she had been prepared, Ms. Liu intervened in students' interaction in the video conference and did not yet see the need to return the classroom to students.

REFERENCES

Bernstein-Yamashiro, B. (2004). Learning Relationships: Teacher-Student Connections, Learning, and Identity in High School. *New Directions for Youth Development*, (103), 55–70. https://doi.org/10.1002/yd.91.

Bu, Y., Qi, S., Zhong, C., & Zhu, Y. (2019). Cong "Litu" Dao "Zaidi": Zhongjia Zimeixiao Kuawenhua Huhui Xuexi De Shijian Tansuo 从"离土"到"在地": 中加姊妹校跨文化互惠学习的实践探索 (From "Off the Soil" to "On the Ground": A Practical Exploration of Intercultural Reciprocal Learning in Sister Schools of China and Canada). *Global Education* (6), 62–73.

Connelly, F. M., & Clandinin, D. J. (1990). Stories of Experience and Narrative Inquiry. *Educational Researcher, 19*(5), 2–14. https://doi.org/10.3102/0013189X019005002.

Cornelius-White, J. (2007). Learner-Centered Teacher-Student Relationships are Effective: A Meta-analysis. *Review of Educational Research, 77*(1), 113–143. https://doi.org/10.3102/003465430298563.

Craig, C. (2012). Tensions in Teacher Development and Community: Variations on a Recurring School Reform Theme. *Teachers College Record, 114*(2), 1–28. https://doi.org/10.1002/JAAL.00054.

Craig, C., Zou, Y., & Curtis, G. (2017). The Developing Knowledge and Identity of an Asian-American Teacher: The Influence of a China Study Abroad Experience. *Learning, Culture and Social Interaction, 17*, 1–20. https://doi.org/10.1016/j.lcsi.2017.09.002.

Dobransky, N. D., & Frymier, A. B. (2004). Developing Teacher-Student Relationships Through Out of Class Communication. *Communication Quarterly, 52*(3), 211–223. https://doi.org/10.1080/01463370409370193.

Engeström, Y. (2015). *Learning by Expanding: An Activity-Theoretical Approach to Developmental Research.* New York: Cambridge University Press.

Huang, C., & Si, X. (2013). Chuantong Wenhua Yu Neiyin Guannian Xia De Shisheng Guanxi Yanjiu 传统文化与内隐观念下的师生关系研究 (A Study of the Teacher-Student Relationship under the Traditional Culture and the Implicit Concept). *Education Science, 29*(1), 46–50.

Li, C. (2012). Shisheng Guanxi De Gujin Zhi Bian 师生关系的古今之变 (The Evolution of the Relationship between Teachers and Students). *Educational Research* (8), 113–119.

Li, D., & Xiao, Z. (2006). 20 Shiji Xifang Shisheng Guanxi Guan: Huisu, Fansi Yu Chong gou 20世纪西方师生关系观: 回溯、反思与重构 (Western Teacher-Student Relationship in the 20th Century: Retrospection, Reflection and Reconstruction). *Studies in Foreign Education, 33*(11), 7–12.

Ontario Ministry of Education, O. M. o. E. (2010). Teacher Performance Appraisal: Technical Requirements Manual.

Shen, J. L., Zhang, N., Zhang, C. Y., Caldarella, P., Richardson, M. J., & Shatzer, R. H. (2009). Chinese Elementary School Teachers' Perceptions of Students' Classroom Behaviour Problems. *Educational Psychology, 29*(2), 187–201. https://doi.org/10.1080/01443410802654909.

Tao, L., & Li, Z. (2016). Guowai Shisheng Guanxi Yanjiu Jinzhan Tanxi 国外师生关系研究进展探析 (Research Progress of Teacher-Student Relationship in Foreign Countries). *International and Comparative Education* (3), 61–68.

The Minzhu District People's Government, M. D. P. s. G. (2017). Minzhu Xiaoxue Banxue Jixiao Dudao Pinggu Zipingbiao 阅竹小学办学绩效督导评估自评表 (Self-assessment Form of Performance Supervision and Evaluation of Minzhu Primary School).

Wang, J., & Ye, L. (2003). "Xinjichu Jiaoyu" De Neihan Yu Zhuiqiu: Ye Lan Jiaoshou Fangtan Lu "新基础教育"的内涵与追求—叶澜教授访谈录 (The Connotation and Pursuit of "New Basic Education": An Interview with Professor Ye Lan). *Exploring Education Development* (3), 7–11.

Wang, S. (2001). Guowai Gaojie Siwei Jiqi Jiaoxue Fangshi 国外高阶思维及其教学方式 (Foreign Higher-order Thinking and Its Teaching Methods). *Shanghai Research on Education* (9), 31–34.

Wang, Z. (2015). *Ziyou Yu Zhixu: Xuexiao Zhidu Wenhua Jianshe Jiazhi Quxiang Yanjiu* 自由与秩序—学校制度文化建设价值取向研究 *(Freedom and Order: A Study on the Value Orientation of School System Culture Construction)*. Central China Normal University, Wuhan.

Wei, M., Zhou, Y., Barber, C., & Den Brok, P. (2015). Chinese Students' Perceptions of Teacher–Student Interpersonal Behavior and Implications. *System, 55*, 134–144. https://doi.org/10.1016/j.system.2015.09.007.

Wells, G. (2002). The Role of Dialogue in Activity Theory. *Mind, Culture and Activity, 9*(1), 43–66. https://doi.org/10.1207/S15327884MCA0901_04.

Weng, X. (1997). *Dangdai Woguo Zhongxiaoxue Shisheng Guanxi De Wenhua Tantao* 当代我国中小学师生关系的文化探讨 *(Cultural Discussion on the Relationship between Teachers and Students in Primary and Secondary Schools in Contemporary China)*. East China Normal University, Shanghai.

Wong, M.-Y. (2015). A Qualitative Examination of Teacher-Student Power-Sharing in Chinese Classrooms: A Study in Hong Kong. *Frontier Education in China*, 10(2), 251–273. https://doi.org/10.3868/s110-004-015-0017-2.

Wu, K. (2003). Xuesheng Jinjin Shi "Shoujiaoyuzhe" Ma? Jiantan Shisheng Guanxi Guan De Zhuanhuan 学生仅仅是"受教育者"吗?—兼谈师生关系观的转换 (Are Students Merely "Educated"? Also on the Transformation of the Relationship between Teachers and Students). *Educational Research* (4), 43–47.

Wu, Q. (2002). Xiandai Jiaoyu Jiaowang De Queshi, Zuge Yu Chongjian 现代教育交往的缺失、阻隔与重建 (The Absence, Barrier and Reconstruction of Modern Educational Interaction). *Educational Research* (9), 14–19.

Wu, Y. (2010). Chuantong Shisheng Guanxi De Toushi Jiqi Xiandai Zhuanxing 传统师生关系的透视及其现代转型 (Perspective of Traditional Teacher-Student Relationship and Its Modern Transformation). *Modern Education Management* (1), 73–75.

Wu, Y. (2012). Wei Zhiyi Er Jiao: Zhong Mei Ketang Jiaoxue De Bijiao Jiqi Sikao 为质疑而教—中美课堂教学的比较及其思考 (Teaching for Questioning: A Comparison and Reflection of Classroom Teaching in China and America). *Primary & Secondary Schooling Abroad* (5), 57–61, 23.

Xie, X. (2010). Why are Students Quiet? Looking at the Chinese Context and Beyond. *English Language Teaching Journal*, 64(1), 10–20. https://doi.org/10.1093/elt/ccp060.

Xu, J. (2000). Minzhu-PingDeng-Duihua: 21 Shiji Shisheng Guanxi De Lixing Gouxiang 民主, 平等, 对话: 21世纪师生关系的理性构想 (Democracy, Equality and Dialogue: A Rational Conception of Teacher-Student Relations in the 21st Century). *Theory and Practice of Education* (12), 12–17.

Xu, S. J., & Connelly, F. M. (2009). Narrative Inquiry for Teacher Education and Development: Focus on English as a Foreign Language in China. *Teaching & Teacher Education*, (25), 219–227. https://doi.org/10.1016/j.tate.2008.10.006.

Ye, L. (1994). Shidai Jingshen Yu Xinjiaoyu LiXiang De Goujian: Guanyu Woguo Jichu Jiaoyu Gaige De Kuashiji Sikao 时代精神与新教育理想的构建—关于我国基础教育改革的跨世纪思考 (The Spirit of the Times and the Construction of the Ideal of New Education: A Cross-century Reflection on the Reform of Basic Education in China). *Educational Research* (10), 3–8.

Ye, L. (1997). Rang Ketang Huangfachu Shengming Huoli 让课堂焕发出生命活力—论中小学教学改革的深化 (Rejuvenate the Class Teaching: Deepen Primary and Secondary School Teaching Reform). *Educational Research* (9), 3–8.

Ye, L. (2002). Chongjian Ketang Jiaoxue Guocheng Guan: "Xinjichu Jiaoyu" Ketang Jiaoxue Gaige De Lilun Yu Shijian Tanjiu Zhi Er 重建课堂教学过程观—"新基础教育"课堂教学改革的理论与实践探究之二 (Reconstruct the View of Classroom Teaching Process: The Second Research on Theory and Practice of Classroom Teaching Reform of "New Basic Education"). *Educational Research* (10), 24–30, 50.

Ye, L. (2003). Jiaoyu Chuangxin Huhuan "Juti Geren" Yishi 教育创新呼唤"具体个人"意识 (Educational Innovation Calls for "Specific Individual" Consciousness). *Social Sciences in China* (1), 91–93.

Ye, L. (2006). Jiaoyu Gai Lun 教育概论 (Introduction to Education). Beijing: People's Education Press.

Zhang, J. (2001). Cong Chuantong Jiaoxueguan Dao Jiangouxing Jiaoxueguan: Jianlun Xiandai Jiaoyu Jishu De Shiming 从传统教学观到建构性教学观—兼论现代教育技术的使命 (From Traditional Teaching Concepts to Constructive Teaching Concepts: Also on the Msion of Modern Educational Technology). *Theory and Practice of Education* (9), 32–36.

Zheng, X., & Wu, D. (2013). Biaoyan Yu Duihua: Kuawenhua Chuanbo Shiye Xia De Shisheng Hudong Yanjiu: Yi Nanjing Daxue Guoji Jiaohuansheng Wei Li 表演与对话：跨文化传播视野下的师生互动研究—以南京大学国际交换生为例 (Performance and Dialogue: A Study of Teacher-Student Interaction from the Perspective of Cross-cultural Interaction: A Case Study of International Exchange Students in Nanjing University). *China University Teaching* (7), 92–96.

CHAPTER 8

Leadership and Power

Cheng Zhong

Funded by the Canada-China Social Sciences and Humanities Research Council of Canada (SSHRC) Partnership Grant Project (2013–2020), this research draws on data gathered about our sister schools—Bay Street School in Toronto (BSS), and Minzhu Primary School (MPS) in Shanghai, which are "quite representative of Shanghai and Ontario schools" (X. Huang 2017). Since 2017, the sister schools have been carrying on principal-level reciprocal learning on teacher leadership and school culture. The focus of this study is elucidating and comparing Canadian and Chinese principals' role identity, situations, and relationship networks in engaging teachers. This chapter is divided into six sections. Section 1 begins with an introduction to the HE (和) LE (乐) school culture at MPS. MPS is the initiator of Principal-level communication on teacher leadership. The stories of reciprocal learning center on school culture. Along with ongoing conversations and stories, the topic of reciprocal learning evolves from "culture of the school" into the "culture as principal teacher leadership". Through story narrated, lived, and told/retold, the research background is

C. Zhong (✉)
Department of Educational Administration and Policy, Chinese University of Hong Kong, Hong Kong, China

© The Author(s), under exclusive license to Springer Nature Switzerland AG 2021
Y. Bu (ed.), *Narrative Inquiry into Reciprocal Learning Between Canada-China Sister Schools*, Intercultural Reciprocal Learning in Chinese and Western Education,
https://doi.org/10.1007/978-3-030-61085-2_8

213

unpacked, and the research questions emerge. In Sect. 8.2, I establish an theoretical framework based on literature review of "Life-Practice" Educology (LPE) and Ontario Leadership Framework (OLF). In Sect. 8.3, I introduce the narrative inquiry research method, the researchers, research participants, and the narrative inquiry process. In Sect. 8.4, I illustrate principals' teacher leadership images such as big sister/parent, teacher master, lead learner, and co-learner are presented and interpreted through interweaving parallel stories (C. J. Craig 1999). In Sect. 8.5, I analyze the traditional Chinese family culture, principal appointment system culture, and the theoretical exchange between LPE and OLF embodied and embedded principals' teacher leadership images. In Sect. 8.6, I suggest the future reciprocal learning on moral leadership. The three-year reciprocal learning provides substantial evidence that though sister school roots in different cultures, they share commonplaces on experience (F. Michael Connelly and D. Jean Clandinin 1990; Crites 1971; J Dewey 1938).

8.1 BACKGROUND

8.1.1 The Trajectory of HE LE Culture in Minzhu Primary School

The stories of HE LE culture in MPS are situated in a historical context, which consist of the social transition narrative of China (1956–) and the school change narrative of MPS. Besides, new stories of experience (D. J. Clandinin and Connelly 2000) count, such as the encounter with BSS and the following reciprocal learning on principals' leadership. As seen, we live in consecutive and nested stories (Okri 1997). Thus, it is important to examine the historical elements of school culture in MPS as it provides temporality, sociality, and place (D. J. Clandinin and Connelly 2000) for us to think over and comprehend what HE LE culture is, what the relationship between HE LE culture and Chinese culture is, and what influence it has on Principal Ting's knowledge of school leadership.

Originally established in 1958, MPS was run to answer the Chinese government's call for "Walking on two legs, running school both by government and society" (The State Council of PRC 1958). Born with a political task, schools like MPS served to release the contradiction between insufficient educational supply and people's increasing demand. What is worth mentioning is that the year of 1958 was simultaneously the last year of "Socialist Transformation" (1953–1956) and the first year of

"Second Five-Year Plan" (1958–1962), which is known as the Great Leap. It was the era when "Party-led" was a fundamental and strict demand for all activities. Especially after the great success made by the "First Five-Year Plan", the government had the unprecedented public appeal and authoritarian power over the whole country. Mobilised by the government, the entire nation was enthusiastically engaged in constructing a New China with a poor financial base. The passion also reflected in MPS: Although MPS was located in a dilapidated alley with only four classrooms and four teachers (three of them did not accept any professional training), the teachers were willing to "learn new things for their students with heart and soul". In this context, MPS headteacher and teachers concluded their school spirit as Struggling (奋斗) culture, which not only reflects the spirit of the time but also unleashed the prototype of HE LE culture.

In 1985, after three relocations, MPS finally settled at its current address, which was a newly built residential area for senior technicians. The technicians were from industries like Shanghai Electrical Machinery, which presented then advanced level of Chinese industry. In the same year, MPS transformed into public schools. For MPS, the change of school type and prospective student body demanded a high quality of education. In the 1980s, there was a growing realization that if the central government delegated more power and constructed a looser environment, the creativity and agency of regional education would be stimulated and national education would develop more systematically (Lu Liu 2013). Therefore, the Ministry of Education enacted *The CPC Central Committee Decision on the Reform of Educational System* (The Ministry of Education 1985) and partly assigned the central government's power to local government and local education bureaus. In this context, principals were authorized to administer their schools while adhering to local and national policies.

In the last two decades of the twentieth century, Principal Guo managed MPS and lifted MPS's educational quality to a high status (1989–2000). Principal Guo, according to others, was a "tough woman" who was "strict, dictatorial, and had clear school development objectives". A teacher, Chun, who worked at MPS in 1974 had the following to say:

> As you may know, if you (school) want to have good educational quality, you need resources. If you want to get resources, you need to be famous. If you want to be famous, you need good educational quality. Do you see? In this chain, the weak school has no chance to receive support. In the 1990s, the new curriculum reform was launched, but we did not have the chance to be an experimental school. No one was reconciled to that situation, and we needed a tough leader.

Teacher Xia, who served at MPS from 1989 onward, added:

> Principal Guo was the director of Moral Education in the District Ministry of Education before she served as principal at MPS. She had a good command of launching Chinese traditional morality education and Chinese Young Pioneer education....When she came, MPS was a weak school but was at a turning point where a better environment was concerned, and she saw this. She invented the slogan 'developing the outstanding quality of education with normal condition'....She led us to take moral education as a key school characteristic and made great efforts to help MPS take a place in districts.

During her tenure, Principal Guo led MPS to be a famous school known for moral education and environmental education. The school culture was redefined as an Achievement-chasing (图强) culture with a mission to "develop high education quality with a normal condition". In the transition from a Struggling culture (1958–1984) to Achievement-chasing culture (1985–2001), what never changed was the philosophical base of school culture. It is called *Fire* (火) that "*We are like Fire (火), flames then comes into silence*" (Ye and Li 2010/2011). The metaphor "fire" was initially proposed by Professor Lan Ye in 2005 and perfectly reflects the philosophical base—the passion—of MPS culture from 1959 to 2000. Defined in ancient Greek philosophy and in traditional Chinese five-element theory, *fire* means permanent *change* (Heraclitus) and *fire* asks for continuously moving forward (Blofeld and Calthorpe 1965). The fire culture highlighted competing with others. It encouraged teachers to strive for the promotion of the school's educational quality, school's fame, to attract, or in other words, to be acknowledged by the government, society, and parents. In this background, Principal Guo's tough leadership ignited teachers' enthusiasm and assembled a power block that boosted MPS's development.

However, problems arose. First, teachers' educational creativity and career positivity were repressed. Teacher Chun, for example, shared that "we (teachers) were not allowed to have our own ideas; we had to obey her rules...If not, we could not get promoted". Second, everyone (school leaders, teachers) were obsessed with competing with other schools. Teacher Yan, for example, offered: "Our activities were like a stray bunch of pearls scattered on the ground and nothing was left after it all....We did not have a continuous goal in those years of effort".

These two problems were resolved when Principal Ting was appointed to the position in 2000.

Teacher Dong, who retired from MPS in 2008, explained the principal change in more detail:

> We were all afraid of her (Principal Guo). It was almost impossible to be praised by her. Young teachers often cried because of her harsh attitude....Principal Ting is different, she is democratic in her demeanor and is kind. Under her leadership, all teachers in the school are like a family....Principal, middle-level managers, and those with no administrative position are all united with each other tightly.

Teacher Quan who now is the deputy principal in MPS expressed a similar opinion:

> The past principal...was not as easygoing as Principal Ting. However, no one can deny the past principal's contribution to MPS.

Viewed through Mary Douglas's grid-group cultural theory (Douglas 1996), we can see from MPS teachers' narration that Principal Guo's leadership style was "high grid" and "high group", which means the principal has supreme power that everyone conformed to. By way of contrast, Principal Ting's style is "low grid" and "high group" where the "conscience of the community [is] reformist in objective and holistic in [its] modes of reasoning". Besides the personal characteristics, Why did Principal Ting choose a different grid to work with her colleagues? Here we seek input from the group of teachers who experienced "the turn of centuries".[1] On the one hand, older teachers are "tired of military leadership". On the other hand, Chinese teacher education from the 1990s onward promoted Normal School preparation, which most of MPS's teachers received. According to the 2009-MPS annual report, 80% of teachers at MPS were young teachers.[2] They are more professional by virtue of their normal school preparation and are comfortable with humanistic and democratic initiatives.

With the change of the school leadership style, Principal Ting attempted to develop a new school culture to guide her teachers and students. In

---

[1] Principal Guo served at MPS from 1989 to 2000; Principal Ting has led MPS since 2001. The transition of principals mirrored the turn of centuries.

[2] In China, "young teacher" indicates teachers whose age range is below 35 years.

218 C. ZHONG

2002, supported by the Bureau of Education of Minzhu District, Principal Ting was given the chance to participate in the First "New Basic Education" Principal Workshop. Through taking part in the workshop, Principal Ting "strongly felt that the 'New Basic Education' is a career worth aspiring after and insisting on". As she wrote in response to the workshop she attended, "It is the school spirit that I earnestly seek" (Principal Ting's workshop notes, 2002). With the help of the New Basic Education research team, MPS's school culture transferred from a fire culture to "Integrating fire and water through harmonizing reason and emotion. Principal Ting confirmed in her own words:

> In 2005, Professor Lan Ye helped us to refine our school culture as HE LE culture. Four years later, Professor Lan Ye refined the philosophical base of the HE LE culture as "Integrating Water (水) and Fire (火), harmonizing emotion and reason".

8.1.2   HE LE Culture Met Bay Street School

The stories that follow are about the moments that the HE LE Culture met Bay Street School. The stories focus on how reciprocal learning between the sister schools changed from "a culture of school" to "a culture of principal leadership".

8.1.2.1 Fire and Water from Shanghai: Exchange on School Culture

The first story took place in BSS in 2017. The year 2017 is special for sister schools because BSS welcomed their new principal, Principal Yung, the first Asian principal of BSS. It was also the second time for MPS teachers and Principal Ting visited Canada (the first visit was in 2008). During the visit, Principal Ting delivered a presentation *Developing Well-being at School: HE LE Culture at MPS* at the welcome reception. Principal Yung, teachers in BSS, officers of Bay Street Education Board, researchers from University of Toronto, University of Windsor, and East China Normal Universities attended the meeting.

In the presentation, Principal Ting introduced and interpreted MPS's school culture in this way:

> HE LE culture was not built in one day; it instead was refined through the continuous weaving of practice and theory....HE means harmony in diversity. It emphasizes that teachers' and students' personalities should be

respected, and everyone is encouraged to achieve their own progress. Additionally, HE means harmony in relationships. It pays close attention to reciprocity among teachers and students, but also among functional departments...no one lives in solitude....LE means happiness that highlights teachers and students working and studying in a free and positive atmosphere...HE LE culture is rooted in and influenced by school management, teacher development, student development, curriculum development, school environment development, school-community relationship development and so on. (Field note, 2017/5/30)

Principal Ting's address aroused a high interest in "school culture", which is Chinese lexicon for which there is no equivalent in Canadian education discourse, most particularly in the part relating to Chinese philosophy.

After the address, Principal Yung and teachers in the sister class expressed interest in HE LE Culture. They regarded it as the philosophical basis of school management and teaching in MPS. School culture then became the theme of reciprocal learning in next semester. Besides introducing the developing history, main content, and operation mechanism of HE LE Culture in MPS, the research team from East China Normal University (ECNU) also tried to excavate the school culture of BSS. It was recognized that "there exists a school culture in BSS, but it is invisible because there is no defined term like culture, slogans, or any written profiles to delineate and interpret its certain school character" (field note, 2017/6/26).

In this context, the sister school's exchange on school culture ran into a dilemma because there is no way to conceptualize the school culture of BSS. Every Chinese school builds their own school culture through texts, plans, and programs, and presents its school culture with the name of the school, the environment, and so on, most of which are visible. Therefore, guided by the definition of school culture in Chinese discourse, we met trouble to understand and explore Canadian school culture. Thus, there was a need to build a new understanding of "school culture".

8.1.2.2 From "Culture of School" to "Culture as Principal Leadership"
When communication about school culture was stuck because of the Canadian school barely using the term, the sister school principals moved their focus onto school leadership, which was in the context that Principal

220   C. ZHONG

Darlene who has rich experience in school leadership research began to serve in BSS in 2018.

In a principal online meeting, Principal Darlene and Principal Ting both shared their opinions on leadership. Principal Ting talked about her idea from the perspective of school culture:

> School culture is not a thing that is worked out by the Principal or some leaders, and it is not developed in the principal's office. There is no school culture without the participation of all teachers and students. School culture will never be carried out without the understanding and practices of all teachers and students. We should let everyone to be an "I" instead of "me" in school culture building and let numerous "I" practices together be a "we". Only when people in the same school co-practice and co-experience the creative production of school life can the characteristics of a school culture be brought out. The principal-oriented school culture lacks "we" and "our independent thinking".

In this address, Principal Ting clearly expounded her idea that the co-practice of all members in school is the source of school culture. School culture is a thing that is not written but co-practiced and lived.

Principal Ting continued,

> As the first person responsible for running the school, the principal should be the main designer and decider in school culture building. The principal should build awareness on developing a school with culture and make school culture be the spiritual values of teachers and students.

As Principal Ting transferred her discourse from a discussion of "school culture" to "culture-as-principal leadership practice", she and Principal Darlene successfully found a new bonding point to further reciprocal learning between the sister schools. Though not proposed from a practical perspective, the transformation of understanding did happen and opened new prospects for both schools to exchange knowledge and experiences.

From 2018 to 2019, Principal Ting and Principal Darlene communicated with each other on the topic of school leadership continuously. In this chapter, we will unpack the images of Shanghai-Toronto sister school principals' views of teacher leadership to inquire into who leads and how to lead the schools in Shanghai and Toronto through exploring questions such as these below:

1. What are the sister school principals' images while leading their teachers?
2. What is the culture base of China and Canada principals' views of teacher leadership?
3. What can sister school principals learn from each other?

8.2 RESEARCH METHOD

8.2.1 *Narrative Inquiry*

With a long intellectual history in education research, narrative inquiry, as a methodology that inherit pragmatism and empirical philosophy legacy from Dewey and Schwab, was first defined by F. Michael Connelly and Clandinin in 1990 (J. Dewey 1938; J. J. Schwab 1954/1978; F. Michael Connelly and D. Jean Clandinin 1990; Polkinghorne 1995; Lyons 2007; Shijing Xu and Connelly 2010). As Connelly and Clandinin (1990, p. 2) pointed out, "The main claim for the use of narrative in educational research is that humans are storytelling organisms who, individually and socially, lead storied lives. The study of narrative, therefore, is the study of the ways humans experience the world. This general notion translated into the view that education is the construction and reconstruction of personal and social stories; teachers and learners are storytellers and characters in their own and other's stories". Experiencing the experience and thinking narratively are two core tenets of narrative inquiry (D. J. Clandinin and Connelly 2000; Shijing Xu and Connelly 2010). Temporal, personal/social, and place dimensions are the three-dimensional narrative space (D. J. Clandinin and Connelly 2000), which are applied to thinking of practical school settings as life spaces (F. M. Connelly and Clandinin 2006). Considering there are many different approaches to narrative inquiry in social science research (D. J. Clandinin and Rosiek 2007), Craig's research, along with Xu and Connelly's framework, focus on school-based narrative inquiry to tell, retell, live, and relive the stories in order to unpack the teacher and principals' experiences, and draw them into the research process (C. J. Craig 1999; Shijing Xu and Connelly 2010; C. J. Craig et al. 2015).

The research tools of broadening, burrowing, storying, and restorying fictionalization are applied (D. J. Clandinin and Connelly 2000; C. J. Craig 2012) in this work. Various approaches are used in these four related but non-linear steps. Burrowing is used to examine research participants' thinking and life situations through their experiences. Field observations focus groups and interview will be utilized. Broadening situates stories told by participants in a wider social and life context. Storying and restorying allow us to know more about our participants through deeper unfolding their experiences (life stories) and linking them together in a complete storyline. Fictionalization protects the participants, creates distance between researchers and experiences, as well as enriches inquiry spaces (Caine et al. 2016).

Therefore, in this research, I deeply participated in the research participants (principals)' school lives through engaging in field research and observation. People connected to the main research participants will also be mentioned.

8.2.2 Introducing the Researcher and Research Process

In 2016, with the support of Dr. Yuhua Bu, Cheng Zhong began his first research study focusing on how principals cooperated with each other to enact school-based education reform. The research involved six principals who shared their experience stories (F. M. Connelly and Clandinin 2006) with Cheng Zhong in different "New Basic Education" schools in Shanghai, one of which was Minzhu Primary School. After that, Cheng Zhong became a research assistant for the partnership project *Reciprocal Learning in Teacher Education and School Education and School Education Between Canada and China*, which was funded by the Social Sciences and Humanities Research Council of Canada (SSHRC, 2013–2020).

As a research assistant, Cheng Zhong followed the exchanges between Minzhu Primary School and Bay Street School for nearly three years. While conducting research with the sister school principals and teachers in 2017, he discovered that Canadian basic education schools like BSS did not have so-called school culture like that in Chinese schools like MPS. After returning to China, MPS held a symposium to share their principal and teachers' visits to BSS. The research team led by Dr. Yuhua Bu was also invited. In the symposium, Cheng Zhong delivered a research report, which discussed the unwritten school culture in BSS. Though firmly believing that BSS had a school culture, Cheng Zhong had not found access to it other than merely describing it.

In 2018, Principal Darlene assumed the position at BSS. As a principal with rich experiences in school leadership research, Principal Darlene wanted to know more about the school culture of MPS and Principal

Ting's experiences as the "New Basic Education" school leader in their first online meeting held at the end of 2017 (Minute_20171012). Since then, exchanges about topics such as school management, teacher development, and student assessment have been stressed in sister school principals' endeavors.

While sister school principals were launching their mutual exchange, Cheng Zhong, supported by Dr. Yuhua Bu and the project, participated in all the workshops concerning narrative inquiry from September 2016 to May 2019. For example, Dr. Michael Connelly (professor at the University of Toronto) and Dr. Shijing Xu (professor at Windsor University) held the narrative inquiry online workshop Doing Fieldwork from a Narrative Inquiry Perspective: Experience and Lessons Learning Together in October 2018. Research assistants from four mainland China normal universities participated. In this workshop, Cheng Zhong learned narrative inquiry from aspects of methodology and method practice and wrote a workshop minute. Besides these online workshops, Cheng Zhong escorted Dr. Cheryl Craig and Dr. Connelly each time they came to East China Normal University. While Dr. Craig and Dr. Connelly were hosting the narrative workshop or doing fieldwork in MPS, Cheng Zhong was the interpreter. In this way, Cheng Zhong accumulated relatively rich knowledge and experience in using narrative inquiry in research investigations.

As the focus of inquiry shifted from school culture to school leadership, Cheng Zhong began to use narrative inquiry to collect data. Cheng Zhong experienced and recorded the whole progress of Principal Darlene and Principal Ting's exchange, and collected data through observation, interview, audio recording, video excerpts, field notes, minutes, and photos.

8.3   Literature Review

8.3.1   Image, Metaphor, and Experience

It has been examined that metaphor, which permeates daily life (Lakoff 1993), has the power to "invite people to understand one thing in terms of another" (Steen 2008) and to disclose human conceptual system (Lakoff and Johnson 1980). A successful metaphor always emerges from story teller's schema of ideas (Lakoff 1990). There is no doubt that a successful narrative inquiry research has a good command of exploring metaphor through principal and teachers' living stories.

Narrative inquiry preliminarily built its theoretical system on John Dewey's experience philosophy, which pointed out the link between education and experience (J. Dewey 1938) and Schwab's deep participants in school teaching, which privileged teacher agency (J. J. Schwab 1954/1978, 1969). These two root sources support the narrative inquirer's intent to understand and interpret principals' and teachers' school life experiences through unpacking teachers' personal practical knowledge (D. J. Clandinin 1986) via methodological eclecticism (J. J. Schwab 1969). It is commonly recognized that principal and teachers' knowledge are expressed in their narratives of experience (F. Michael Connelly and D. Jean Clandinin 1990). What is more, principal and teachers are used to presenting their experiences through metaphors which directly point to experiential images (F. M. Connelly and Clandinin 1988). As seen, in narrative inquiry, images, metaphors, and experience constitute a conceptual system for presenting, interpreting, and understanding principal and teachers' lives in school affairs. So, what is the relationship between image, metaphor, and experience?

For an understanding of researchers' self and research participants, Connelly and Clandinin (1990) regarded people's narratives which embedded their life experience as metaphor in education research. The metaphors are used to understand teaching-learning relationships. Such as the very first is Clandinin and Connelly's research (1992) that proposed the curriculum maker found a methodological way to unpack teachers' agency and teachers' personal practical knowledge. Through the *curriculum maker* image, teachers' personal experiences on teaching, student communicating, personal development, and so on are interpreted and understood. As seen, the *image* is a visualized portfolio of principals' and teachers' *experiences*. And the *image* is an epistemological anchor that provides stable access to teachers' *experiences*. Standing from the perspective of teachers, Craig (2005) found it was easy for educators to turn to metaphors to present and communicate their experiences. As she examined in a later work (2018) that affirmed the value of metaphors in presenting teachers' embedded, embodied knowledge of experience. For example, in "butterfly under a pin", one of the most cited works of Craig (2012), she examines an experienced teacher's *curriculum implementer* image (C. J. Craig and Ross 2008) and the dynamic of it, burrowing into teacher Laura Curtis's dilemma in curriculum reform. The *image* "butterfly under a pin" captures Laura's situation and helps readers to feel and understand the exact experiences. In the meantime, the *image* "butterfly under a pin" is a metaphor that is rooted in principal and teachers' own experience landscape. The *metaphor* "butterfly under a pin" vividly indicates "the events that led up to the imposed transition and demonstrate how the press for accountability in U.S. schools appeared to supersede in importance other ethical and professional considerations" (C. J. Craig 2012). In "the dragon in school backyards", another Craig's representative narrative inquiry work (2004), the interwoven *image* and *metaphor* of "the dragon in school backyards" reveals how the state-mandated accountability testing shaped and reshaped Eagle High School's development and how the principal and teachers feel, understand and implement the reform.

Through the research studies already mentioned, we can draw the relation network between image, metaphor, and experience as in Fig. 8.1.

As seen, *experience* is visualized through *image* and the *image* offers a theoretical anchor to understand the *experience*. Most of the time, *image* is co-made by research participants and researchers while refining the experiences in observation and interview. Being different from the *image*, *metaphor* is always proposed by research participants and it is borrowed by researchers to interpret participants' lived experiences through unpacking, telling, living, and reliving. Therefore, we regard image and metaphor as two sides of the experience presentation and representation. They provide access for us to characterize our experiences. The paper, co-authored by Craig, Zou, and Poimbeauf (2015), provides a good exemplar for using the *experience*, *metaphor*, and *image* to understand principalships in China. Principal Xu's (Xu Xiaozhang 校长) images/metaphors as a lead teacher, an agent of harmonious learning community, and a teacher-maker are presented in Principal Xu's narratives and reflect her lived experiences through storying, restorying, and interpretations.

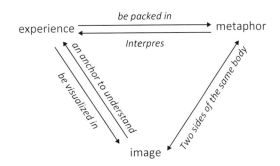

Fig. 8.1 The relation network between image, metaphor, and experience

8.3.2 Encounter of Teacher Leadership Images in Life-Practice Educology and the Ontario Leadership Framework

The exchange between MPS and BSS essentially is a dialectic dialogue between Life-Practice Educology (LPE) and the Ontario leadership framework (OLF). The professional support behind the sister schools is East China Normal University "Life-Practice" Educology research team and the Ontario Ministry of Education respectively. The principals' actions are influenced by these academic and governmental powers. Therefore, it is important to figure out the similarities and differences in principal leadership at LPE and the OLF. Both will help us comprehend how reciprocal learning happens between sister schools.

The historical background is that China is in a key period of social transition and national rejuvenation within the context of fierce global transformation (Ye 2005, 2009b, 2014). Thus, *school reform* is the constant focus of LPE since it gave birth to "New Basic Education" (NBE) school reform practices from the 1990s on. From the perspective of LPE, school reform should never be a treat-the-head-when-the-head-aches issue but a systematic project involving the transformation of school values orientation, elements in the school system (including physical aspects such as school building, teaching equipment, campus environment, and quality of teachers and administrators), management system and operational mechanisms (Ye and Li 2010/2011; Ye 2014). Among all of these, the school management system reform is the leading part (Zunmin Wu and Li 2007).

Situated in the context of the national principal responsibility system, LPE sees the principal as the prime person responsible for school reform. While speaking of what kind of schools can participate in the NBE school reform project, Professor Lan Ye said, "We are not picky about schools but we are picky about principals...whether the principal has a strong willingness to change and improve his/her school is the pass line to NBE" (X. Zhang and Ye 2015). As can be seen, both the national education reform policy and the LPE count on principals' leadership to improve the quality of schooling. More specifically, the national policy is the source of the LPE principal image because it determines the principal's legal status and power in school. LPE provides a suite of theory portfolios to guide principals on the standpoint of Educology. Here, a key difference needs to be pinpointed. In terms of the national principal responsibility system, the principal is an administrator (Z. Huang 2009, 2010). The image, *principal as administrator*, reflects general management theory that has constituted the base of science of educational management in China in the past twentieth century (Feng 2002). But with respect to LPE, school management firstly is an educational affair and the principal's administration work should be educational. The LPE insists on the standpoint of education and puts school management reform in the span of Educology, to consider management issues from the perspective of school education development requirements.

However, it is incomplete to say that LPE school leadership theory is proposed in the vision of school reform and innovative school management theory creation. As professor Lan Ye said, "the ultimate aim of the reform is 'being a *Man* (人) through *Working* (事)' and vice versa (成事成人)" (Ye 2009a, 2009b; Ye et al. 2019). The intent is not to cultivate a group of education model operators or manipulators. What we want to achieve is not just to change *Working*, but also the change the *Man* [*sic*] (X. Zhang and Ye 2015), which includes students, teachers, and principals (including males and females).

Therefore, LPE re-describes the ideal principal image in the vision of "'being a *Man* (人) through *Working* (事)' and vice versa". The new proposed images not just are about the principals' professional qualities in managing school affairs but also refer to the principals' *life* (生命) development. Drawing lessons from the LPE literature, the image first can mean as *Principal as lead learner*. There are three types of learning: theory learning, education scene learning, and learning in one's own practice. Principals are urged to recognize their existing knowledge and experiences, their ongoing education site, and their own school leadership practice. The principal is described as a *reflective learner* who should be able to apply theories into practice and build up theories through practice. The principal should learn how to evaluate discipline teaching and provide professional suggestions (Z. Li 2013). The principal should also be a *supportive pedagogic expert*. Furthermore, the principal should learn to program a school's mid-long-term development. Only when a principal becomes a *chief designer* can the principal know the development path for his/her own school and can truly lead the school. In the meantime, the principal is expected to be the school manager with proactive, dynamic, and systematic thinking. The principal is also expected to be a *life conscious person*. Drawing lessons from Confucian philosophy, Professor Lan Ye expounded a *life conscious person* as the aim of education, as she pointed out,

The so-called "life consciousness" refers to the individual's awareness of the existing status of their own life. They have clear development goals, established ideal moral standards, and strive for their dreams..."Life consciousness" is a process for a person to understand himself. Since birth, people develop consciousness and self-consciousness, and later they develop consciousness of their own development in life and establish goals in life. They take the initiative to control their own life, fulfill their life and realize their social value. This is a long process throughout one's life, which distinguishes man from animals by inherent stipulation of consciousness. It is also the highest level that man's subjective consciousness can reach. (Ye 2014)

Besides, LPE also pays attention to the principal role in the school district. Through the practice of NBE, LPE has developed the school ecological community theory (Bu et al. 2016; T. Wang 2016; Q. Yang 2016; Bu and Zhong 2017; Yeting Wang 2017) which focuses on the mutual learning among basic education schools in the same school district. And Principal Ting is the leading principal in *the MPS School Ecological Community* which consists of 12 primary schools in the district. The leading principal is described as an *altruistic contributor* (Bu et al. 2016).

In conclusion, standing on the vision of "'being a Man (人) through Working (事)' and vice versa" in a changing world, "Life-Practice" Educology expects a principal to be (1) a leading reflective learner, (2) a supportive pedagogic expert, (3) a chief designer (with proactive, dynamic, systematic thinking), (4) a life conscious person, and (5) an altruistic contributor in the school district. None of these qualities is sufficient on its own. They are a holistic entity. These images are presented, represented, and practiced through principals' school leadership.

Being different from "Life-Practice" Educology, the Ontario Leadership Framework built its ideal principal image in the context of meeting the province's core education priorities focusing on student achievement and well-being (Vitaska 2008; Leithwood and Louis 2012). Principal's leadership is assumed to be the guarantee to achieve the province standard (Hallinger and Heck 1996) because it is the driving force to implement school improvement initiatives (Leithwood et al. 2008), and the "second only to classroom teaching as an influence on pupil learning" (Leithwood et al. 2008). Principal leadership is viewed as "the peak of a pivotal school leadership role" (Rintoul and Bishop 2019), and in terms of its function, principalship is as well called "the promise of school leadership". However, what is commonly acknowledged by Canadian scholars is that there is no direct relationship between principal leadership and students' achievement and well-being, which is verified by Hallinger and Heck's most cited article (1996). In this case, why does principal leadership still play such a remarkable position in student achievement improvement? The answer is that the principal can benefit their students by working with their teachers (Witziers et al. 2003; Hallinger 2011; Lambersky 2016). In this case, we can temporarily understand the principal image as a *teacher leader*. However, it is still obscure because as a teacher leader, what does the principal do? How can the principal lead teacher? What kind of principal's leadership practice is it?

Dancing to the baton of the province's core education priorities (Rintoul and Bishop 2019), the work of Ontario principals has become more complex and multi-faceted in the last two decades. Policy places much more stress on the principal to ensure student outcomes. Being transformational has become a prior standard for successful principal and effective school (Leithwood and Jantzi 2005; Elmore 2006; Leithwood and Azah 2014). Guided by so-called transformational leadership theory, principals' responsibilities and works were not only expanded but also transferred from supervising teachers to motivating and empowering teachers to reach promoting students (Wallace 2001; Pollock and Hauseman 2015; Pollock 2016). We can get more detailed hints about the Ontario principal leadership image from the *Ontario Leadership Strategy 2013*, whose center is the Ontario Leadership Framework that describes a set of core leadership competencies and practices for principals and other school leaders. Besides, the Ontario MoE published the special issue *Ideas into Action* (www.edu.gov.on.ca/eng/policyfunding/leadership/IdeasIntoAction.html) and held the Ontario Leadership Congress (OLC) to support training principal and system leaders. As shown beneath, we collect the topics respectively from the *Ideas into Action* and the OLC to conclude the ideal principal image in OLF (see Table 8.1).

Aligning with OLS, the Ministry of Education, Ontario, adopts five Core Leadership Capacities (CLCs) as principal leadership practice, which is described as "*setting goal, aligning resources with priorities, promoting collaborative learning cultures, using data, and engaging in courageous conversations*" (http://www.edu.gov.on.ca/eng/policyfunding/leadership/IdeasIntoAction.html). These capacities are respectively expounded in 2012 and 2014. Setting goals refers to the principal as the *school vision developer*, aligning resources refers to the principal as *a good-for-student knowledge learner and sharer*, promoting collaborative learning

Table 8.1 The *Idea into Action* and the OLC

Years/topics	Ideas into Action	OLC
2009–2010	/	School leaders need integrative thinking (www.edu.gov.on.ca/eng/policyfunding/leadership/martin.html)
2010–2011	/	Mobilizing leaders' knowledge to improve instruction (City et al. 2009)
2011–2012	/	Mobilizing leaders' knowledge to foster student engagement in learning (www.edu.gov.on.ca/eng/policyfunding/leadership/2011willms.html.)
2012–2013	Five core capacities of effective leaders: engaging in courageous conversations, using data, aligning resources with priorities	*Building knowledge about leadership practices and personal leadership resources that contribute to positive and improved student achievement and well-being*
2013–2014	/	*Leadership as the exercise of influence, specifically with regard to leadership practices that bring about improvements in mathematics outcomes for students*
2014–2015	Setting goals: the power of purpose Exploring the "social" Personal leadership Resources: relationship-building and manage emotional responses	System-level leadership
2015–2016	Exploring the "psychological" personal leadership resources: optimism, self-efficacy, resilience, proactivity	Developing the transformational leadership
2016–2017	/	/
2017–2018	Exploring the "cognitive" personal leadership resources: problem solving, role-specific knowledge, systems thinking	/

cultures refers to the principal as *a school-community-district collaboration relationship builder*, using data refers to the principal as *a research school improvement plan designer*, engaging in courageous conversations refers to the principal as *a trust principal-teacher relationship builder*. Moreover, all of which refer to develop principal's "expertise in the field of curriculum, instruction, and assessment in the company of their colleagues" (Marzano et al. 2005). From 2015 to 2018, according to Personal Leadership Resources (PLRs) (Leithwood 2012), Ontario Education Ministry expected the principals to develop their social resources, psychological resources, and cognitive resources, which respectively refer to the principal as a *relationship builder, ambiguity and risk solver*, and *systems thinker*.

As seen, there are overlaps between *Ideas into Action* and OLC on the principal leadership image. Therefore, we need to further "focused code" and "theory code" (Charmaz 2009, 2014) into analytical categories that not only fit the data but also have the power to interpret the principal leadership image. The theory codes, or in other words, the ideal principal leadership image in *OLF*, are as follows: the principal is expected to be (1) school vision developer (with system thinking), (2) trust (interpersonal and interinstitutional) relationship builder, and (3) a supportive pedagogic expert.

For clearly comparing the principal leadership image, we hereby put the images in "Life-Practice" Educology and OLF together as in Table 8.2.

Remounting to existed leadership research framework (Hoy and G 1987; Yukl 2002), it's easy to find that there are three key components: leader, follower, and situation. Almost all the leadership theories are based on this basic framework to explore and interpret the single component, or the relationship between two of them, or the interrelationship among all the three, with principal-centered perspective. Thus, we revise the table with the framework (Table 8.3).

As seen, both LPE and OLF highlight the principal's thinking ability in leading school development. The principal is required to be a systems thinker. With regard to the relationship with teachers, both LPE and OLF stress the principal's pedagogic leadership image. The key difference is that LPE pays more attention to the principal's leading role in the school symbiotic learning community (学校共生体). The relationship between principals and teachers in LPE is the profession-centered relationship. On the other hand, OLF appreciates interpersonal trust and relationship building for principals better motivate and gather teachers together toward

Table 8.2 The images in "Life-Practice" Educology and OLF

LPE	OLF
A chief designer (with proactive, dynamic, and systematic thinking) 　(1)　A leading reflective learner 　(2)　A supportive pedagogic expert 　(3)　An altruistic contributor in school district (4) A life conscious person	School vision developer (with system thinking) 　(1)　A supportive pedagogic expert 　(2)　A Trust interpersonal and relationship builder (3) A Trust interinstitutional relationship builder

Table 8.3 The framework of LPE and OLF

Aspects	LPE	OLF
In school development leading In relationship with teachers	A chief designer (with proactive, dynamic, and systematic thinking) 　(1)　A leading reflective learner 　(2)　A supportive pedagogic expert	School vision developer (with system thinking) 　(1)　A supportive pedagogic expert 　(2)　A Trust interpersonal and relationship builder
In relationship with other institutions Leader's own development	(3) An altruistic contributor in school district (4) A life conscious person	(3) A trust interinstitutional relationship builder /

the same goal. Compared to the highlight of contribution in LPE, OLF obviously puts more stress on the cooperation based on trust. With respect to the principal's own development, LPE not only emphasizes the principal's professional development but also highlights the principal's *life* development, which is of distinct Chinese life philosophy characteristic.

8.4　Story Constellations of Principals and Their Teacher Leadership Images

While restorying the stories told by principals and teachers, Clandinin and Connelly (1996) suggested several narratives, such as teacher stories, stories of school, and school stories. In this chapter, we draw lessons from C. J. Craig (2007) in order to make the narratives into story constellations, relating the principal's stories and stories of principal to each other like the "nets of boxes" (Crites 1971, 1975)—a stories matrix. According to Clandinin and Connelly (1996), stories of principal are stories respectively given (1) by LPE and OLF to shape their principals and (2) by teachers in school about their impressions and ideas on their principal. Principal stories are told by the principals. In this part, we interweave the story constellations of the stories of principal-principal stories to present and interpret the images of sister school principals.

8.4.1 Images of Principal Ting

8.4.1.1 Image as a Big Sister (Parent)
When asked the question "What do you think of Principal Ting?" teachers at MPS non-hesitantly replied: "Principal Ting is a big sister (parent)". The older teachers respond with "sister", while the younger ones choose the word "parent". These answers are fully indicative of China's filial piety culture. Let us now look at the responses more in depth.

Seated in front of me is Ms. Hua, who transferred to MPS in 2004. Snuggled in her feathered boa, she recollected her memories of her teaching life in MPS. After Ms. Hua's daughter was born, she searched for a campus with better educational quality. She chose MPS to be her daughter's primary school and she transferred to MPS as well. As an experienced teacher, she had received enough awards and titles in another district through ten years of hard work. However, she still met challenges in MPS. She recalled:

> I used to teach grade 1 and grade 2 in FX [other school district]. I had no experience in teaching grade 3 and upper-grade students. Besides, the requirements for teaching quality here (MPS) is much higher here than that in the school I worked in the past.

Ms. Hua described herself as a steady person who needs more time than others to prepare for new circumstances. She further explained:

> As you may know, the former principal was very strict. If you tell her that you don't have the confidence or are not prepared enough to teach an upper grade, she may ask you to leave. Luckily, when I came to MPS, Principal Ting assumed the position. She gave me enough time to prepare and adapt.

With the more lenient mindset of Principal Ting, Ms. Hua "successfully adapted into the new circumstance steadily". In her eyes, Principal Ting is like a big sister who is always on your side and encourages you. She added,

> Though I came to MPS to find a better education for my daughter, I also want to improve my teaching and education. Principal Ting and other school leaders are quite different (from the school I worked in). Each teacher's office is equipped with one school leader, included the principal.

Ms. Hua said that four school leaders visited her office last year. They were Vice Principal Q, Principal Ting, the Chinese teaching leader, and the moral education leader. Ms. Hua said that she discovered that the leaders had rich experiences in teaching, curriculum design, student management, and designing and launching project-based projects, and so forth. "I learned a lot from them", she said, "and what surprised me is that they were keeping learning new things". Ms. Hua showed her certificate of counselor and added,

> I wanted to get this certificate for a long time. But I always delayed my plan. Inspired by the leaders, I spent three months and learned four thick books to get it! Principal Ting showed her full support and even paid the application fee. Though it's an affordable sum for me, it's never about money, is it? It's about the feeling. You feel you are supported and cared.

Regarding Principal Ting's encouraging and supporting teachers like a sister (parent), Ms. Yan, the younger academic sister of Principal Ting, insisted that she got a say in it. Ms. Yan and Principal Ting both graduated from Shanghai No. 1 Normal School (now the Shanghai Normal University). She has been working in MPS since 1989 and experienced both the Principal Guo period (1989–2001) and the Principal Ting period (2001–present). Now she is the middle-level administrator in MPS taking the position as the director of moral education. Comparing Principal Guo and Principal Ting, Ms. Yan made the following observations:

> Principal Guo runs the school as her own company. We are her employees. She is energetic and creative. However, no one can bear life only with criticism...though Principal Ting is Principal Guo's apprentice, she inherited Principal Guo's ambition and creativeness but abandoned the harshness.

In Ms. Yan's eyes, Principal Ting is a typical Shanghai lady who is charming, attractive, and clever. "She has the magic to drive you forward", as Ms. Yan said, "she will ask for your help instead of demanding you to do something. She will consider your feelings and make you feel at ease".

However, being an amiable sister is never an easy thing. Accompanying Principal Ting for more than 30 years, Ms. Yan indicated that MPS has become more famous day after day. It changed from a poor educational quality school that had no resources and chances from the Minzhu District School Board (MDSB) to a "Window School" that represents the highest education quality of Shanghai education. Principal Ting must conduct all the affairs required by the MDSB. Currently, everyone in the school is busy with classroom visits and implementing education reform projects in addition to daily teaching.

"Though teachers in MPS are united, complaints always exist", Ms. Yan said with tears. She continued: "Imagine you devote so much time and energy to complete a task but fail to get a high-class award. A principal is like the filling of a **sandwich**, stressed by teachers' complaints, and upper administration's blame. This is especially the case with teachers who are not willing to complete or even revolt against doing the assigned tasks."

The dilemma of the principal that Ms. Yan outlined can be verified in a new teacher's narratives. Mr. Yi, who has worked at MPS for two years, emphasizes that as a post-1990s teacher, he is not willing to do things in which he has no interest. He admires the teachers who take teaching jobs to explore the unknown world together with students. But that fact disappoints him a bit, as he explained,

> In school, people highlight responsibility. Students' responsibility is studying. Teachers' responsibility is teaching. What is worse, responsibility can be everywhere if the person with power want you to do something.

Mr. Yi works on several curriculum initiatives at MPS, such as serving as a host and heading up the robot program, the water science exploration, and so on. When being asked whether these curriculums are his responsibilities, he laughed. Our conversation unfolded this way:

> Zhong: I hear that you teach many curriculums here.
> Mr. Yi: Yes, I do.
> Zhong: Are they your responsibilities?

Mr. Yi: Nope. I don't think they are responsibilities. They are what I like. They are the explorations. I want to explore these with my students instead of taking _____ responsibilities together with them.

Zhong: Then what responsibilities do you take at present?

Mr. Yi: Well, like an international math curriculum. I was appointed (by the principal) to do it. But, you know, I have no interest in it. I just kept foot-dragging and showed the leaders that I am not capable to do it. Then I was freed from it.

Zhong: Were you in trouble then?

Mr. Yi: Nope.

The other new coming teacher, Ms. Fei offered another side of Mr. Yi's story:

Fei: He is versatile and he can do many things. But he only does those he is interested in...He doesn't like that (international math curriculum). But I like it (laugh). Thus, I take over it.

Zhong: Is Mr. Yi in trouble for behaving not that good in the international math curriculum?

Fei: No. It will never happen (points out her finger and draws a circle around the ceiling). Here we have freedom. You can choose what you like to do even if you are appointed to other issues at the very beginning. The Principal and other leaders will give you maximum freedom.

When asked of her impression of Principal Ting, Ms. Fei said with a smile,

Umm, saying like this is a bit awkward, but, you know...she's just like a parent for us, umm, for me...She has the power to demand things of us. However, she never does that. She asks our thought and willingness. It is even better than some real parents (laughing).

As evident in Mr. Yi's and Ms. Fei's narratives, teachers at MPS have different personalities, hobbies, and abilities. There is no program introduced by school leadership that can be acknowledged and liked by all teachers. However, just as Ms. Fei and another teacher indicate, Principal Ting offers "humanitarian care", and she "respects our personalities and choices". Teachers in MPS are allowed and supported to have "personal development".

Considering the close relationship between Ms. Yan and Principal Ting, Ms. Yan is quicker than other teachers to stand in Principal Ting's shoes. If Ms. Hua's narratives show us an amiable big sister image of Principal Ting who always stands by her teachers, then Ms. Yan and Mr. Yi's narratives unpack the unknown side of the big sister who bears a huge load of pressure from teachers with different personalities and upper admiration officers. What does this mean? Through the stories about the principal above, the image of Principal Ting as a big sister (parent) is enriched. The image as a sister (parent) mainly refers to two aspects. First, the term of sister (parent) refers to an elder generation, which is equal to a natural higher power in Chinese culture. They always face the most burdens while holding the responsibilities and necessary high power to sustain and improve the family. In this aspect, we can not only identify Principal Ting's static image of power and responsibilities but also tell Principal Ting's dynamic image lives in practice in her complex work with her teachers and upper administration. Second, the sister (parent) is a close relationship marked by love and affability. We recognize Principal Ting leads and works with her teachers with the support of funds, opportunities, platforms, and psychology.

8.4.1.2 Image as a Teacher Master

Almost all the basic education school principals in China spend more than ten years being a teacher before they assume the position of principal. Such was the case with Principal Ting. She had been a math teacher from 1988 to 2001 in MPS. After she took over MPS from Principal Guo, Principal Ting no longer taught students.

Mr. Quan and Ms. Gu are Principal Ting's teacher apprentices. Mr. Quan assumed the position of Assistant Principal since 2015 and then he was appointed as the Vice Principal in 2017. Ms. Gu now is the director of the math teaching research group. Both talked about their experiences as Principal Ting's teacher apprentice.

> Mr. Quan: I went to MPS in 1996 when Principal Ting was a math teacher and Assistant Principal. She was appointed as my teacher master. As you know, in 1996, MPS is led by Principal Guo...Do you know what I mean? (laugh) Principal Ting needed to teach math and to assist Principal Guo at the same time. Imagine (looks up at the ceiling). Double harshness...but she still taught me with her heart and soul no matter how busy she was...I could feel it.

238   C. ZHONG

According to Mr. Quan, Principal Ting read and revised every teaching plan for him, and visited every class in the first year. When Mr. Quan completed one lesson, Principal Ting would help him to reflect on the lesson and revise it once more. In China, the master teacher usually supervises his/her apprentice for about one to three years. The length depends on whether the apprentice teacher can pass the new teacher assessment. From Mr. Quan's narratives, we can see that Principal Ting was a devoted and selfless master teacher. Ms. Gu's story expands Principal Ting's image as the teacher master.

> Zhong: Who impresses you the most in the school?
> Ms. Gu: It's Principal Ting. She is my master teacher....I came to MPS in 2000. She (Principal Ting) was very busy as the Assistant Principal...I didn't get much time with her but she always opens her class for me to listen and observe...maybe you don't believe it, but she is a good math teacher. I can still remember the rhythm of her class teaching and the instructions into deep thinking.
> Zhong: Does she visit your class?
> Ms. Gu: Yes, but not very often. We usually meet at the public class, especially after she became the principal. She has sharp eyes and acute observations to find the shortcomings and advantages of your teaching design and practice. She can diagnose the flow of class teaching acutely. It is rare for a principal.

J.Sun (2009), in his Ph.D. thesis, interviewd 44 principals who were selected to participate in national principal training project host by East China Normal University. The analysis indicated that Chinese principals' teaching leadership is lower than other leadership dimensions. It shows a separation between the principal's administration leadership and teaching leadership. However, in teachers' eyes, teaching leadership is much more important. In a journal, one teacher wrote, "I don't think that titles like professor, principal, director is equal to your teaching ability. I will, or we, the frontline teachers only admit people with the real stuff". At MPS, Principal Ting's teaching leadership won her respect of her teachers.

However, being the principal means you should not only be individual teachers' master. Principal Ting wrote in the *MPS School System Reform Collection (2005–2012),*

> A principal is not the one who sets various obstacles for promoting cultivating a few excellent teachers, but the one who builds space and platform to help every teacher reach excellence.

Led by Principal Ting, MPS launched its school system reform nearly seven years back. It gradually changed from copying the theory books, Education Bureau portfolios, and relative research papers to building a living system. The system tool kits of MPS pertain to different disciplines, personalities, education background, and teaching experiences. As seen, Principal Ting as a teacher master is not just for those teachers who are her apprentices, but also for the frontline teachers. She applies her leadership to design and launch systems to improve all the MPS teachers. In short, Principal Ting as a teacher master is every teacher's master. The teacher master is not only capable in specific discipline teaching, curriculum design, education research, and project design and launch but also capable of building a humanistic, effective, and flexible school environment featuring a grand space for teachers to develop freely.

8.4.2 Images of Principal Darlene as the Lead Learner and Co-learner

Since the first day Principal Darlene met Principal Ting, she continuously addressed her experiences as a math teacher. She thinks highly of this working experience. In the following communication, Principal Darlene introduced that she and her colleagues' focus in 2019 are improving the students' academic achievements and performances, especially in math.

Principal Darlene's narratives leave the first impression that she considers herself as a math teacher leader. However, we find that the math project is just one of the Principal Darlene's working highlights. Other projects like reading and special education were being launched at the same time. Then why does she address her lived experiences as a math teacher? Principal Darlene further said, to enact a new initiative, the biggest challenge for the principal is to "break through teachers' beliefs that administrators no longer understand the realities of the classroom". She cited the words used in her paper that if the researcher who advocates a new teaching strategy fails to show their deep and all-round understanding of reality then the reform will be regarded as a utopia and be kept at a distance. Principal Darlene further added, "As an experienced school leader, changing teachers' beliefs (that the leader knows little about) is more challenging…teachers will judge from your performance to see if you have the capability".

As can be seen, addressing math teaching is a strategy for Principal Darlene to show her expertise and "reach out to teachers' understanding". In Principal Darlene's narratives, she refers to her experiences being a principal in four different schools. She found that "building relationships and developing people is the pillar that is most important". Then, how does she build a relationship with teachers? Principal Darlene explained, "A leader must understand the initiative and has to show herself to be the lead learner at all times in the school…It is also important to build relationships and capacity with staff by developing distributed leadership…the focus is co-learning".

In the aforementioned excerpt, Principal Darlene mainly referred to two strategies: being the lead learner and a co-learner. Being a lead learner requires the principal to understand new strategies, new policies, new initiatives, and so on and then share them with the teaching staff. Being a co-learner compels the principal to distribute leadership and to mobilize all staff in the school to "generate more opportunities for change and to build the capacity for improvement". As to distributed leadership, the principal should visit the classroom though it can be pressure for some teachers. "The focus moves from teacher actions to student learning and provides a good entry to discussions around next steps in teacher learning", said Principal Darlene. She further added,

> The support from the principal as an administrator and the principal as a lead learner and co-learner is quite different. A respectable leader can always find a way such as a relationship-building and monitoring while co-learning to help their staff.

From Principal Darlene's narratives, we see the relationships that form between her and her teachers are profession-centered relationship. They build relationships around teaching and learning improvement. Profession-centered leadership keeps a target in mind while concurrently maintaining relationships. As Principal Darlene stressed many times in her narratives that "it [profession-centered leadership] is important in the successful implementation of initiatives". In other words, Principal Darlene manages her relationship with her teachers mostly in terms of working relationships.

8.5 Cultural Comparison and Analysis on Sister School Principal's Teacher Leadership

Through the story constellations of Principal Ting and Principal Darlene "stories to live by" (D. J. Clandinin and Connelly 2000), we can interpret the images of Principal Ting as *a big sister (parent)* and *teacher master* and the image of Principal Darlene as *a lead learner and co-learner*. Taken these images and their cultural and theoretical background together, we can provide an in-depth look at the cultural difference in teacher leadership between China and Canada. The leadership to some extent is the relationship between leader and follower (Grint 2005; Bryman et al. 2010; Grint 2010). Thus we focus on the principal-teacher relationship in principal images.

8.5.1 Family Culture and the Power Structure Behind the Principal Images

With the family culture embedded deeply in every Chinese people's blood, the principal in school has a grand space to implement her leadership. In Principal Ting's living story, her predecessor, Principal Guo is frequently compared with Principal Ting. It is clear that Principal Ting and Principal Guo have distinct leadership style, which can be respectively described in Western terms as "Egalitarianism-Meeting" (Principal Ting) and "Hierarchy-Military" (Principal Guo) (Grint 2010). However, these two very different leadership practices in the same school occurred during a flourishing period of school development. Because of the strong family culture (filial piety) tradition, centralized power lies in the hands of the principal. Even though Principal Ting respects every teacher and allows them to develop freely" the "top-down" power structure remains. All the freedom that teachers have in MPS that was once withdrawn by Principal Guo is now endowed by Principal Ting.

Therefore, though Principal Ting and Principal Darlene both build up a trust relationship with teachers, the relationships are inherently different. The family culture nests Principal Ting and her teachers in a centralized power structure. Principal Ting has the natural supreme power in school. For her, being an amiable sister(and parent) and presenting teacher leadership are "the cherry on the top". There is no doubt that she still can implement the plans that she wants when she uses Principal Guo's way. What is interesting is that in the MPS school systems that promote teachers, we can see the distributed leadership in it. The MPS school system portfolios empower and engage the teachers to achieve their development through enacting certain education reform projects, initiatives, and so on. Is the distributed leadership in MPS the same as that in BSS? The answer is no. In BSS, Principal Darlene doesn't have the same ultimate authority like that of Principal Ting. As one of the BSS teachers participating in the project and visited MPS several times said, "She (Principal Darlene) is not as powerful as Principal Ting. We can choose to use a different strategy than our P[principal] is suggesting, if we believe it is more appropriate in this situation". In this context, teachers' power in BSS is "aroused" rather than given by principals because they own the leadership originally. The distributed leadership in BSS is a way for the principal to help teachers to use their power and to motivate teachers to successfully enact change initiatives.

8.5.2 Principal Appointment System and the Principal-Teacher Relationship

Besides the power structure in principal-teacher relationship, the family culture also makes a different type of interpersonal relationship in MPS than that of BSS. In the discourse of image as sister (parent), the expansion of family culture in school institutions creates the kinship-like interpersonal relationship in MPS and transfers the school to an "expanded family" (Fei 2011). In kinship-like relationship, people are more likely to trust each other and are more willing to live with contradictions. However, in BSS, the trust relationship is transactional rather than being kinship-like. "My P (Principal Darlene) represents my employer. It feels like she is the boss", as one BSS teacher said. It is more difficult to build the trust relationship in BSS. It is not just because of the culture but also because of the principal appointment system. Principal Ting spent all her education career life in MPS. She has been the principal in MPS for almost 20 years. But in Canada, principals change campuses frequently. Principal Darlene is the fourth principal of BSS since 2008, and she herself has been principal in other four schools in the past. The frequent change of principals in Toronto determines that principals are not able to build so-called strong school cultures and cultivate school traditions as Chinese principal does. But the frequent change works well because it is in accordance with the principalship in OLF. Different from Principal Ting who is responsible for all school affairs planning and launching, Principal Darlene is more like a change initiator. As she explained, "Cyclical changes in provincial governments and their priorities and policy directions result in a continuous stream of initiatives in schools. Principals play a key role in implementing new initiatives through the setting of direction in their schools". In this case, it is unnecessary for principals in Toronto to stay in the same school for a long time because they develop the school according to the requirements of Ontario Education Ministry and Toronto District School Board. The different relationship between principal and upper administration hugely affects the relationship between principal and their teachers.

8.5.3 "Life Consciousness" Encounter Teacher Professional Development

Both Principal Ting and Principal Darlene illustrate their proficiency in teaching and education through their respective images of *teacher master* and *lead learner and co-learner*. They win teachers' respect by showing their knowledge about new initiatives and real teaching context. However, rooted in different philosophies background, the *teacher master* and the *lead learner and co-learner* focus on different objectives.

Hugely influenced by "Life-Practice" Educology, Principal Ting pays more attention to achieving a teacher's life consciousness. As Zhengtao Li points out (Z. Li 2010), "The essential task of the contemporary educator is cultivating life consciousness. The task should not only be implemented for students, but also the educator's self". Standing at the nexus between Western philosophy and Chinese philosophy, Professor Lan Ye finds the lack of respect and cultivation of individuality in Chinese traditions and urges to enlarge the space and possibilities for individuals to achieve their development (Bu and Liu 2017; Ye 2014; Z. Li 2012). The *development* that "Life-Practice" Educology emphasize is more than teachers' professional development. Inherited from the traditional Chinese education ideal, its aim is to fuel people's self-realization, to empower them to significantly achieve their potentials and then make contributions to politics and education (Qian 1976), "Life-Practice" Educology further proposes that life consciousness should surpass its tradition of being stuck in politics and education and focus on all-round life development (Ye 2014).

Compared to the life conscientious in Principal Ting's image, Principal Darlene's image as lead learner and co-learner mainly pays attention to teachers' professional development. Principal Darlene and her teachers will share their knowledge landscape and Principal Darlene will try her best to distribute leadership with her teachers to support them in curriculum implementing and making. Besides support on the teaching knowledge landscape, guided by OLF, Principal Darlene also keeps a watchful eye on teachers' emotions and cooperate with teachers in appropriate ways.

8.6   Discussion: What Can We Learn from Each Other?

The principal is the spirit of the school. If you want to judge a school, assess its principal firstly. (X. Tao 2008)

The idiom mentioned above is wildly known and recognized in China as the principal responsibility system being established and improved in basic education school since *the Outline of Chinese Education Reform and Development* and *Education Law of the People's Republic of China* were released respectively in 1993 and 1995. Supported by state policy, principals are legally granted the right of final decision on all school affairs. But it does not mean the school development only needs a single principal's effort. In highlighting principal leadership, Grint refers to *leadership* as "a ship loading leader and his/her followers" (Grint 2010). We believe that the emphasis on principal leadership works this way as well in the Western world (Pollock and Hauseman 2015; Fullan 2008, 1995; Leithwood and Montgomery 1982).

In this chapter, the principal teacher leadership images from Shanghai and Toronto were compared and contrasted. However, presentation and interpretation are not our ultimate aims. The concept *reciprocal learning* underpins our project. It was first proposed by S. Shijing Xu (2017) in her four-year study of new immigrating Chinese families' living experiences in Toronto. In her study, the intersection of Confucian and Dewey's education philosophy encountered each other when Chinese immigrant families arrived in Toronto with their own historical and cultural background. The context indicates the cross-cultural dimension of *reciprocal learning*, which includes the prior views that *reciprocal learning* as comparative education/comparative achievement/comparative values/comparative pedagogy (S. Xu and F. M. Connelly 2017). However, the comparison is not all about reciprocal learning, which essentially is a collaborative partnership.

The term proposed by Lugones can convey our aims of the collaborative partnership's technological aspect. Lugones (1987) proposed the term "world traveling" to emphasize that mutual learning between people from different worlds is a way to learn "how to be through loving each other". Sponsored by Canada-China SSHRC Partnership Grant Project, the principals, teachers, and researchers all complete the "world traveling" through observing, listening, communicating, and reflecting which are done by sister school principals and teachers. However, does *reciprocal learning* happen in this "world traveling" process? As the sister school principal communication has processed just for three years, we need more evidence to examine it though both principals admit that they "do learn something from the other". Reaching back to the notion of collaborative partnership, we not only care about the lived and living experiences but also look forward to unpacking forthcoming lived experiences. In this collaborative partnership, new stories will go on, new feelings will be expressed, and new living experiences will unfold between different education practices (Q. Yang 2017). The narratives have been written, but life is a "continual unfolding" (F. Michael Connelly and D. Jean Clandinin 1990).

Therefore, instead of examining the question of what have the principals reciprocally learned, it is perhaps more important to explore what *can* they learn from each other. Answering this question is helpful to guide the principal's further exchange and provides us an in-depth perspective on the possibilities of mutual learning between two education practitioners from different cultural backgrounds and system bases. In next section, I will focus on moral leadership lighten the part which is examined to be effective in both countries and see what can we learn from each other in these commonplaces.

8.6.1   Moral Leadership: Intersection of the East and the West

While most of the leadership theories like distributed leadership, instructional leadership, transformational leadership, and so on are "1980s imported goods" for Chinese education (Mingzheng and Xinhui 2014), the moral leadership has traditions and roots in Chinese culture, though the term *moral leadership* is not proposed by Chinese, it still shares the most commonplaces with Confucian values that centered in the Chinese leadership (W. O. Lee 2012; Bush and Haiyan 2000).

We mainly understand moral leadership in the Western context through Sergiovanni's work (1992). He sheds light on moral authority in comparison with the bureaucratic authority, psychological authority, technical-rational authority, and professional authority. Sergiovanni (1992) puts the moral authority as the highest authority. In his view, moral leadership is helpful to make teachers feel the obligation and duties that co-shared in the school community and to build the school as a professional learning community centered with shared faith, beliefs, and commitments. Principal and teachers are nested in the same moral commitment which motivates them to practice their beliefs. In Principal Darlene's narratives, she presents herself as an exemplar in learning and practices new initiatives to inspire and motivate her teachers. She learns and launches the new initiatives together with her teachers to make them feel supported and "like a target on the back".

In Chinese culture, hugely influenced by Confucianism, Taoism, and other ancient Chinese philosophies, morality plays a key role in people's everyday life. It is wildly recognized that Chinese philosophies are nearly equal to the moral philosophy (Chan 1963). In Confucian thought, a qualified leader always set themselves as an example to influence and lead his/her people. Confucius urged the leader to be *Zheng* (正) (rectitudinous in Western context), which means people's minds and actions correspond to the requirements of Ren (仁) and Li (礼). As he said, *"Politicians should be of rectitude (政者, 正也。)"*.

> If the leader is personally of rectitude, all will go well though he doesn't give any order. On the contrary, even though he gives orders, one will obey. (其身正, 不令而行; 其身不正, 虽令不从.)

The featured Chinese principal's moral leadership can also be found in Craig and her partners' work (Zou et al. 2016) in which she cited "teaching without words" from a TEDx lecture to interpret what she observed in a Chinese literacy class. In that class, the teacher used his facial expression and body movement instead of verbal expressions to motivate his students' deep thinking. While coming to the principal leadership context, we can transform "teaching without words" to "leading without words". As a matter of fact, "teaching/leading without words" is Taoism theory. As Lao Tzu said in *Tao Te Ching* (《道德经》),

> The saint treats the world with an inactive attitude and does things without words. (圣人处无为之事,行不言之教)

Saint, in Taoism, is described as the perfect governor. Therefore, *Tao Te Ching* is not only regarded as a philosophy book but also a book for leaders. *Doing things without words* aims to lead people by Tao rather than preaching. And Tao is presented in Saint's actions. As seen, both Confucianism and Taoism which are two strong components of Chinese culture put the leaders setting themselves as an example and then leading the followers at the first place of leadership practice.

As seen, though *moral leadership as a theory* is firstly proposed in the Western world, *moral leadership as the practice* has already been enacted in China thousands of years ago. The flow of Western wisdom and ancient Chinese wisdom joins each other in cross-cultural context in the era of globalization and becomes represented in the bond of Principal Ting and Principal Darlene's living stories and creates new stories as sister school principals' living stories continue to flow forward.

8.6.2   The Integration of Technology and Technique Matters

Although the West and the East share the wisdom of moral philosophy as we mentioned above, they still practice the moral leadership differently, which can be analog as the difference between the *technology* and *technique*. In the Western world, the widely recognized distinction between technology and technique can be concluded as the following: the former applies to phenomena that are modern and knowledge-based, and the latter refers to phenomena that are traditional and experience-based (Mauss and Schlanger 2006).

Respectively abiding by Ontario Leadership Framework and "Life-Practice" Educology (LPE) teacher leadership theory, Principal Darlene and Principal Ting's teacher leadership represents the features of leading technology and leading technique. *Ontario Leadership Framework*, the practice guideline frequently mentioned in Principal Darlene's narratives is perfectly implemented by Principal Darlene in her teacher leadership practice, while the LPE teacher leadership is applied wholly in Principal Ting's practice too. Respectively deriving power and vitality from the modern experimental research in the Western context and the revived and modified traditional moral philosophy, OLF and LPE provide different support which to some extent can be featured as technology and technique to their principals.

With respect to LPE, the teacher leadership theory is built and improved in the pathway of reciprocal transformation between practice and theory in cooperation among researchers, frontline principals, and teachers. In other words, the teacher leadership theory is the fruit of researchers, teachers, and principals' education practice and experiences. It contains the wisdom grown up in "soil of practice" (Ye 2013, 1997) and is refined and revised in millions of encounters of theory and practice, and utilized in principal and teachers' practical knowledge landscape.

The leadership theory in OLF is to build in the way of "hypothesis-examination-theory"—scholars collect data from the education field, analyze the existed problems, and provide their theory as a prescription which will be the action guide for all staff in the education field. Though the ways of building theories are different, there are more similarities between the OLF technology and LPE technique if we abandon the old-fashioned stereotype of the dual opposition of technology and technique. It is not just because of the ambiguity of the concept *technology* and *technique* but also because of the fact that there is a technique in OLF technology and there is technology in the LPE technique. And neglecting the traditional Western context that distinguishes *technology* and *technique*, both OLF and LPE teacher leadership theory is a kind of technology and the principal's leadership practice is the technique. In this way, the integration point of both emerges as we put our eyes on principals' leadership practice knowledge. It's easy to see that both Principal Ting and Principal Darlene flexibly adjust their leadership strategies in specific situations based on their practical wisdom/experiences. And it is in the principals' leadership practice knowledge, the channels between theory and practice are opened.

8.6.3   Autocracy or Democracy? From Dualism Misunderstanding to Cosmopolitan Learning Community

They (MPS) are autocratic. Do you (BSS) take our democracy to them?—One scholar in CSSE 2017

The text cited above is one scholar's challenge to us in the Canadian Society for the Study of Education (CSSE) 2017. We can understand that Principal Ting's image as *the big sister* and Principal Darlene's image as *lead learner* and *co-learner* is easy to make people have the illusion that they are respectively corresponding to the autocracy image and democracy image. In this section, we are not going to give *autocracy* and *democracy* a definition philosophically like John Mill, Isaiah Berlin, and so on. We mainly draw our research participants' understanding of *autocracy* and *democracy* which play a more important role in their life world than the theoretical literature play.

Accompanying the MPS school principals and teachers, especially in those days visiting BSS, the saying "We are different. They are more democratic" was heard frequently. When asked the reason for considering BSS school leadership being more democratic, one of the MPS teachers said, "The teacher and principal in BSS can communicate with each other equally". He added, "They don't have the same reservations as us when suggesting and negotiating with the principal". Another MPS teacher went straight to the heart of the matter without hesitation, "It's quite clear. Democracy is saying no to your principal". Then what is their knowledge on *autocracy*? MPS teachers commonly agree that *autocracy* means that all power belongs to one leader, and everyone should only follow and obey the leader. Combining MPS teachers' understanding of *autocracy* and *dictatorship*, we can conclude that the criteria for democracy and dictatorship have to do with the equality between principals and teachers.

As the research progressed, we found the same mistake we made in the interviews as the scholar in CSSE 2017. We both assumed a dualism framework while the MPS teachers said "they are more democratic", they were silently referring that MPS is a autocratic. On the contrary, in further inquiries, MPS teachers showed us the third way that surpasses the dualism of democracy and autocracy. MPS teachers think that though Principal Ting has more power, they still can freely negotiate and equally communicate with her. Meanwhile, they also admit that they "will show more respect to Principal Ting in the manner of treating eldership", which is acutely known by the BSS teachers when they visited MPS. The dialogue is recollected below:

> BSS-T: I find something interesting. When Principal Ting is going to stand up, you and the teachers will stand up too. When she sits down, you still stand up.
> Cheng: (surprised) I have never been conscious of it.
> BSS-T: Yes, we understand. But you can sit, right?
> Cheng: Yes, we will sit after the eldership sits.

As seen, the "reservations" and "being not easy to say no to principal" in MPS teachers' narratives are not caused by the autocracy but by the cultural tradition of respecting people of high status, which is easily mistaken as Chinese teachers' lack of equality and liberty. Besides the cultural side, the contemporary situation that almost all the basic education schools in China meet is the large scale and the almost motionless position changing of teaching staff provide a steady ballast stone for building a close relationship, but expose the school community to the risk of internal division into contradictory small groups. Therefore, strong glue is indeed needed. Principal Ting is the most appropriate person to play the role without a doubt.

In conclusion, the dualism framework of dictatorship and democracy is not suitable to understand the sister school principals' teacher leadership images. It diminishes the possibilities and richness of reciprocal learning and traps everyone in ideological biases. In other words, the reciprocal learning between sister schools is never a mutual learning between democracy and dictatorship, which is impossible for the lack of co-shared communicating space, but between two education cultures and practices with their own unique historical, cultural, and realistic genes. Principal Ting admires that Principal Darlene can remember every teacher and every students' name, while Principal Darlene admires that Principal Ting has the mettle and power to gather all people in the school to achieve their co-shared aims. Principal Ting admires that Principal Darlene has institutionalized various comprehensive curriculum in BSS, while Principal Darlene admires that Principal Ting set up an effective teaching and research group for her teachers. Sister school principals build the cosmopolitan learning community (KHOO 2017) together with their teachers. Exchanges bring advantages from each side and encourage both to reflect on shortcomings on their own for and to engage in inquiry so as to find better ways to move forward.

REFERENCES

Blofeld, J., & Calthorpe, E. (1965). *The Book of Change: A New Translation of the Ancient Chinese I Ching (Yi King) with Detailed Instruction for Its Practical Use in Divination*. New York: E. P. Dutton.

Bryman, A., Collinson, D. L., Grint, K., Jackson, B., & Uhl-Bien, M. (2010). *SAGE Handbook of Leadership*. London: Sage.

Bu, Y., & Liu, A. (2017). Lun "Yushengmingzijue" de Duochong Neihan 论"育生命自觉"的多重内涵 (The Multiple Connotation of "Cultivating Life consciousness"). *Journal of Educational Studies, 13*(1), 10–15.

Bu, Y., & Zhong, C. (2017). *Promote the Sustainable Development of School Communities Through the "Model of School Community"*. Paper Presented at the Canadian Education Research Annual Meeting 2017, Toronto.

Bu, Y., Yang, Q., & Lu, Y. (2016). Xiaoji Hezuo Zhong De "Xuexiao Shengtaiqun" Jianshe Zhi Yanjiu 校际合作中的"学校生态群"建设之研究 (Research on "School ecological community" in Interschool Cooperation). *Educational Science Research, 7*, 66–71.

Bush, T., & Haiyan, Q. (2000). Leadership and Culture in Chinese Education. *Asia Pacific Journal of Education, 20*(2), 58–67. https://doi.org/10.108 0/02188791.2000.10600183.

Caine, V., Murphy, M., Estefan, A., Clandinin, D. J., Steeves, P., & Huber, J. (2016). Exploring the Purposes of Fictionalization in Narrative Inquiry. *Qualitative Inquiry, 23*(3), 215–221.

Chan, W. T. (1963). *Source Book in Chinese Philosophy*. Princeton, NJ: Princeton University Press.

Charmaz, K. (2009). Shifting the Grounds: Constructivist Grounded Theory Methods. In J. M. Morse, P. N. Stern, J. M. Corbin, B. Bowers, & A. E. Clarke (Eds.), *Developing Grounded Theory: The Second Generation*. Walnut Creek, CA: University of Arizona Press.

Charmaz, K. (2014). *Constructing Grounded Theory*. London: SAGE.

City, E. A., Elmore, R. F., Fiarman, S. E., & Teitel, L. (2009). *Instructional Rounds in Education: A Network Approach to Improving Teaching and Learning*. Cambridge, MA: Harvard Education Press.

Clandinin, D. J. (1986). *Classroom Practice: Teacher Images in Action*. Philadelphia, PA: The Falmer Press.

Clandinin, D. J., & Connelly, F. M. (1992). Teacher as Curriculum Maker. In P. Jackson (Ed.), *Handbook of Curriculum* (pp. 363–461). New York, NY: Macmillan.

Clandinin, D. J., & Connelly, F. M. (1996). Teachers' Professional Knowledge Landscapes: Teacher Stories – Stories of Teachers – School Stories – Stories of Schools. *Educational Researcher, 25*(5), 24–30. https://doi.org/10.310 2/0013189X025003024.

Clandinin, D. J., & Connelly, F. M. (2000). *Narrative Inquiry: Experience and Story in Qualitative Research*. San Francisco: CA: Jossey-Bass.

Clandinin, D. J., & Rosiek, J. (2007). Mapping a Landscape of Narrative Inquiry: Borderland Spaces and Tensions. In D. J. Clandinin (Ed.), *Handbook of Narrative Inquiry: Mapping a Methodology* (pp. 35–37). Thousand Oaks, CA: Sage Publications.

Connelly, F. M., & Clandinin, D. J. (1988). *Teachers as Curriculum Planners: Narratives of Experience*. New York, NY: Teachers College Press.

Connelly, F. M., & Clandinin, D. J. (1990). Stories of Experience and Narrative Inquiry. *Educational Researcher, 19*(5), 2–14. https://doi.org/10.2307/1176100.

Connelly, F. M., & Clandinin, D. J. (2006). Narrative Inquiry. In J. L. Green, G. Camilli, & P. Elmore (Eds.), *Complementary Methods for Research in*

Education (pp. 477–488). Washington, DC: American Educational Research Association.

Craig, C. J. (1999). Parallel Stories: A Way of Contextualizing Teacher Knowledge. *Teaching and Teacher Education, 15*(4), 397–411. https://doi.org/10.1016/S0742-051X(98)00062-6.

Craig, C. (2004). The Dragon in School Backyards: The Influence of Mandated Testing on School Contexts and Educators' Narrative Knowing. *Teachers College Record – TEACH COLL REC, 106*, 1229–1257. https://doi.org/10.1111/j.1467-9620.2004.00378.x.

Craig, C. (2005). The Epistemic Role of Novel Metaphors in Teachers' Knowledge Constructions of School Reform. *Teachers and Teaching, 11*, 195–208. https://doi.org/10.1080/13450600500083972.

Craig, C. J. (2007). Story Constellations: A Narrative Approach to Contextualizing Teachers' Knowledge of School Reform. *Teaching and Teacher Education, 23*(2), 173–188. https://doi.org/10.1016/j.tate.2006.04.014.

Craig, C. J. (2012). "Butterfly Under a Pin": An Emergent Teacher Image Amid Mandated Curriculum Reform. *The Journal of Educational Research, 105*(2), 90–101. https://doi.org/10.1080/00220671.2010.519411.

Craig, C. (2018). Metaphors of Knowing, Doing and Being: Capturing Experience in Teaching and Teacher Education. *Teaching and Teacher Education, 69*. https://doi.org/10.1016/j.tate.2017.09.011.

Craig, C. J., & Ross, V. (2008). Cultivating Teachers as Curriculum Makers. In F. M. Connelly (Ed.), *Sage Handbook of Curriculum and Instruction*. Thousand Oaks, CA: Sage.

Craig, C. J., Zou, Y., & Poimbeauf, R. P. (2015). A Narrative Inquiry into Schooling in China: Three Images of the Principalship. *Journal of Curriculum Studies, 47*(1), 141–169. https://doi.org/10.1080/00220272.2014.957243.

Crites, S. (1971). The Narrative Quality of Experience. *Journal of the American Academy of Religion, 39*(3), 397–411.

Crites, S. (1975). Angels We Have Heard. In J. B. Wiggins (Ed.), *Religion as Story* (pp. 23–63). Lanham: University Press of America.

Dewey, J. (1938). *Experience and Education*. New York: Collier Books.

Douglas, M. (1996). *Natural Symbols: Explorations in Cosmology*. London; New York: Routledge.

Elmore, R. (2006). Leadership as the Practice of Improvement. In B. Pont, D. Nusche, & D. Hopkins (Eds.), *Improving School Leadership: Volume 2: Case Studies on System Leadership* (Vol. 2, p. 275). Paris: Organization for Economic Cooperation and Development (OECD).

Fei, X. (2011). 乡土中国·生育制度·乡土重建 *Xiangtu Zhongguo-Shengyu Zhidu-Xiangtu Chongjian*. Beijing: The Commercial Press.

Feng, M. (2002). *Goutong Yu Fenxiang: Zhongxi Jiaoyu Guanli Linxian Xuezhe Shiji Huitan* 沟通与分享:中西教育管理领衔学者世纪汇谈 (*Communication and Sharing: Debates Among Leading Education Management Scholars from the West and the East)*. Shanghai: Shanghai Educational Publishing House.

Fullan, M. (1995). The Evolution of Change and the New Work of the Educational Leader. In K. Wong & K. Cheng (Eds.), *Educational Leadership and Change: An International Perspective* (pp. 15–28). Hong Kong: Hong Kong University Press.

Fullan, M. (2008). *The Six Secrets of Change: What the Best Leaders Do to Help Their Organizations Survive and Thrive*. San Francisco, CA: Jossey-Bass.

Grint, K. (2005). *Leadership: Limits and Possibilities (Management, Work and Organisations)*. Houndmills, Basingstoke, Hampshire; New York: Palgrave Macmillan.

Grint, K. (2010). *Leadership: A Very Short Introduction (Very Short Introductions, Vol. 237)*. New York: Oxford University Press.

Hallinger, P. (2011). Leadership for Learning: Lessons from 40 Years of Empirical Research. *Journal of Educational Administration, 49*(2), 125–142. https://doi.org/10.1108/09578231111116699.

Hallinger, P., & Heck, R. H. (1996). Reassessing The Principal's Role in School Effectiveness: A Review of Empirical Research, 1980–1995. *Educational Administration Quarterly, 32*(1), 5–44. https://doi.org/10.1177/0013161X96032001002.

Hoy, W. K., & G, M. C. (1987). *Educational Administration: Theory, Research, and Practice*. New York: Random House Trade.

Huang, Z. (2009). Xuexiao Lingdao Ruhe Yinling Xuexiao Biange 学校领导如何引领学校变革 (How School Leader Leads School to Reform). *Research in Educational Development, 18*, 70–73.

Huang, Z. (2010). Woguo Xuexiao Biange De Zhengce Zouxiang 我国学校变革的政策走向 (The Policy Trends of School Change in China). *Journal of Schooling Studies, 7*(7).

Huang, X. (2017). How Teachers Learn and Change in Reciprocal Learning Space. *Frontiers of Education in China, 12*(2), 151–179. https://doi.org/10.1007/s11516-017-0014-5.

Khoo, Y. (2017). Regenerating Narrative Inquiry for Teacher Growth on a Toronto-Shanghai Sister School Partnership Landscape. *Frontiers of Education in China, 12*(2), 180–199. https://doi.org/10.1007/s11516-017-0015-4.

Lakoff, G. (1990). The Invariance Hypothesis: Is Abstract Reason Based on Image-Schemas? *Cognitive Linguistics, 1*, 39–74.

Lakoff, G. (1993). The Contemporary Theory of Metaphor. In A. Ortony (Ed.), *Metaphor and Thought* (pp. 202–251). Cambridge, UK: Cambridge University Press.

Lakoff, G., & Johnson, M. (1980). *Metaphors We Live By*. Chicago, IL: University of Chicago Press.

Lambersky, J. (2016). Understanding the Human Side of School Leadership: Principals' Impact on Teachers' Morale, Self-Efficacy, Stress, and Commitment.

Leadership and Policy in Schools, 15(4), 379–405. https://doi.org/10.108
0/15700763.2016.1181188.

Lee, W. O. (2012). Moral Leadership: Where the East Meets the West. *Multicultural Education Review, 4*(1), 29–50. https://doi.org/10.108
0/23770031.2009.11102888.

Leithwood, K. (2012). The Ontario Leadership Framework 2012, with a Discussion of the Research Foundations.

Leithwood, K., & Azah, V. N. (2014). Elementary Principals and Vice-Principals' Workload Study: Final Report.

Leithwood, K., & Jantzi, D. (2005). A Review of Transformational School Leadership Research, 1996–2005. *Leadership and Policy in Schools, 4*(3), 177–199. https://doi.org/10.1080/15700760500244769.

Leithwood, K., & Louis, K. S. (2012). *Linking Leadership to Learning.* San Francisco: Jossey-Bass.

Leithwood, K., & Montgomery, D. (1982). The Role of the Elementary School Principal in Program Improvement. *Review of Educational Research, 52,* 309–339.

Leithwood, K., Harris, A., & Hopkins, D. (2008). Seven Strong Claims About Successful School Leadership. *School Leadership and Management, 28*(1), 27–42.

Li, Z. (2010). Shengming Zijue yu Jiaoyuxue Zijue 生命自觉与教育学自觉 (生命自觉与教育学自觉). *Educational Research, 31*(4), 5–11.

Li, Z. (2012). Zhongguo Shehui Fazhan de "Jiangyu Chidu" yu Jiaoyu Jichu 中国社会发展的"教育尺度"与教育基础 ("Educational Dimension" and Educational Basis of the Social Development in China). *Educational Research, 33*(3), 4–11+34.

Li, Z. (2013). Xiaozhang de "XianChang Xuexi Lingdaoli" 校长的"现场学习领导力"(On-Site Learning Leadership of Principal). *Management of Primary and Secondary School, 3,* 4–5.

Liu, L. (2013). Zhongxiaoxue Xiaozhang fuzezhi Sanshinian Huigu Yu Xianshi Wenti Fenxi 中小学校长负责制三十年回顾与现实问题分析 (Review and Analyse Real Issues on the Course of Headmaster Responsibility System in Middle and Primary Schools). *Modern Education Management, 7,* 66–70.

Lugones, M. (1987). Playfulness, "world"-Travelling, and Loving Perception. *Hypatia, 2,* 3–19.

Lyons, N. P. (2007). Narrative Inquiry What Possible Future Influence on Policy or Practice.

Marzano, R. J., Waters, T., McNulty, B. A., & ebrary Inc. (2005). School Leadership That Works from Research to Results. (pp. vi, 194 p.). Alexandria, Va Aurora, CO: Association for Supervision and Curriculum Development; Mid-continent Research for Education and Learning.

Mauss, M., & Schlanger, N. (2006). *Techniques, Technology, and Civilization.* New York: Durkheim Press/Berghahn Books.

Mingzheng, X., & Xinhui, W. (2014). Chinese Leadership. *Public Integrity, 16*(2), 165–172. https://doi.org/10.2753/PIN1099-9922160204.

Okri, B. (1997). *A Way of Being Free*. London, UK: Phoenix House.

Polkinghorne, D. E. (1995). Narrative Configuration in Qualitative Analysis. *International Journal of Qualitative Studies in Education, 8*(1), 5–23. https://doi.org/10.1080/0951839950080103.

Pollock, K. (2016). Principals' Work in Ontario, Canada: Changing Demographics, Advancements in Information Communication Technology and Health and Wellbeing. *International Studies in Educational Administration Quarterly, 44*, 53–73.

Pollock, K., & Hauseman, C. (2015). *Principals' Work in Contemporary Times: Final Report*. The University of Western Ontario Faculty of Education.

Qian, M. (1976). *Zhongguo Xueshu Tongyi* 中国学术通义 *(Introduction on Chinese Academic)*. Taipei: Student Book Co., Ltd.

Rintoul, H., & Bishop, P. (2019). Principals and Vice-Principals: Exploring the History of Leading and Managing Public Schools in Ontario, Canada. *Journal of Educational Administration and History, 51*(1), 15–26. https://doi.org/10.1080/00220620.2018.1513913.

Schwab, J. J. (1954/1978). Eros and Education: A Discussion of One Aspect of Discussion. In I. Westbury & N. Wilkof (Eds.), *Science, Curriculum and Liberal Education: Selected Essays*. Chicago, IL: University of Chicago Press.

Schwab, J. J. (1969). The Practical: A Language for Curriculum. *School Review, 78*(1), 1–23.

Sergiovanni, T. (1992). *Reinventing Leadership. Getting into the Heart of School Improvement*. San Francisco, CA: Jossey-Bass.

Steen, G. (2008). The Paradox of Metaphor: Why We Need a Three-Dimensional Model of Metaphor. *Metaphor and Symbol, 23*(4), 213–241. https://doi.org/10.1080/10926480802426753.

Sun, J. (2009). *Zhongxue Xiaozhang Lingdaoli Yanjiu* 中学校长领导力研究 *(A Study on Principal Leadership in Middle Schools)*. Shanghai: East China Normal University.

Tao, X. (2008). *Tao Xingzhi Wenji* 陶行知文集 *(Collections of Tao Xingzhi's Works)*. Nanjing: Jiangsu Education Publishing House.

The Ministry of Education, M. o. E. (1985). Zhonggong Zhongyang Guanyu Jiaoyu Tizhi Gaige de Jueding 中共中央关于教育体制改革的决定 (The CPC Central Committee Decision on the Reform of Educational System).

The State Council of PRC, S. C. o. P. (1958). Guanyu Jiaoyu Gongzuo de Zhishi 关于教育工作的指示 (Instructions on Education).

Vitaska, S. (2008). *Strong Leaders, Strong Schools: 2007 State Laws*. Denver, CO: National Conference of State Legislatures.

Wallace, J. (2001). *The Work of School Administrators in Changing Times*. Paper Presented at the AARE Annual Conference, Freemantle, Western Australia.

Wang, T. (2016). School Leadership and Professional Learning Community: Case Study of Two Senior High Schools in Northeast China. *Asia Pacific Journal of Education*, *36*(2), 202–216. https://doi.org/10.1080/0218879 1.2016.1148849.

Wang, Y. (2017). Dazao Quanquan Liandong De "Qunyanjiu": "Xinjichu Jiaoyu" Huaping Shnegtaiqu Jianshe 打造圈圈联动的"群研究" – "新基础教育"华坪生态区建设 (Building the Inter-connected "group research": Construction of "New Basic Education" Minzhu Ecological Community). *Journal of Shanghai Educational Research*, *6*, 87–90.

Witziers, B., Bosker, R. J., & Kruger, M. L. (2003). Educational Leadership and Student Achievement: The Elusive Search for an Association. *Educational Administration Quarterly*, *39*(3), 398–425. https://doi.org/10.117 7/0013161X03253411.

Wu, Z., & Li, J. (2007). *Xueixao Zhuanxingzhong De Guanli Biange* 学校转型中的管理变革 *(The Management Reform in School Transformation: The Construction of New Chinese School Management Theory in 21st Century)*. Beijing: Educational Science Publishing House.

Xu, S. (2017). *Cross-Cultural Schooling Experiences of Chinese Immigrant Families: In Search of Home in Times of Transition*. New York, NY: Palgrave Macmillan.

Xu, S., & Connelly, M. (2010). Narrative Inquiry for School-Based Research. *Narrative Inquiry, 20*, 349–370. https://doi.org/10.1075/ni.20.2.06xu.

Xu, S., & Connelly, F. M. (2017). Reciprocal Learning Between Canada and China in Teacher Education and School Education: Partnership Studies of Practice in Cultural Context. *Frontiers of Education in China, 12*(2), 135–150. https://doi.org/10.1007/s11516-017-0013-6.

Yang, Q. (2016). Jiaoyu Shengtaixue Shiyuxia Jiaoshi Shengming Chengzhang Tanxi 教育生态学视域下教师生命成长探析 (Exploring Teachers' Life Development from the Perspective of Educational Ecology: Based on the Knowledge of School Ecological Community). *The Inservice Education and Training of School Teachers, 2*, 5–9.

Yang, Q. (2017). Intercultural Communication in the Context of a Canada–China Sister School Partnership: The Experience of one New Basic Education School. *Frontiers of Education in China, 12*(2), 200–218. https://doi.org/10.1007/ s11516-017-0016-3.

Ye, L. (1997). RangKetang Huangfachu Shengming Huoli 让课堂焕发出生命活力—论中小学教学改革的深化 (Rejuvenate the Class Teaching: Deepen Primary and Secondary School Teaching Reform). *Educational Research, 9*.

Ye, L. (2005). 21 Shiji Shehui Fazhan Yu ZHongguo Jichu Jiaoyu Gaige 21世纪社会发展与中国基础教育改革 (The Development of Society and Chinese Basic Education Reform in 21st Century). *Journal of the Chinese Society of Education, 1*, 2–11.

Ye, L. (2009a). Zai Xianshi Zhong Xieshou Zouchu Jianshe Xinxing Xuexiao De Chuangyezhilu 在现实中携手走出建设新型学校的创业之路 (Building New School in Reality: General Report on "New basic Education" Moulding Researches). In L. Ye (Ed.), *"Xinjichu Jiaoyu" Chengxingxing Yanjiu Baogaoji* "新基础教育"成型性研究报告集 *Collections of "New basic Education" Moulding Researches* (pp. 1–82). Guilin: Guangxi Normal University Press.

Ye, L. (Ed.). (2009b). *Zhongguo Jichu Jiaoyu Gaige Fazhan Yanjiu* 中国基础教育改革发展研究 *(Research on Chinese Basic Education Reform and Development) (New Historical Startpoint)*. Beijing: Chinese Renmin University Press.

Ye, L. (2013). "'Shengming-Shijian' Jiaoyu Xuepai: Zai Huigui Yu Tupo Zhong Shengcheng" 生命·实践"教育学派 – 在回归与突破中生成 (School of Life-Practice Pedagogy: Creation in Return and Breakthrough). *Journal of Educational Studies, 9*(5).

Ye, L. (2014). *Huigui Tupo: "Shengming-Shijiang" Jiaoyuxue Lungang* 回归突破: "生命·实践"教育学论纲 *(Life-Practice Educology: A Contemporary Chinese Theory of Education)*. Shanghai: East China Normal University Press.

Ye, L., & Li, Z. (Eds.). (2010/2011). *"Xinjichu Jiaoyu" Yanjiushi* "新基础教育" 研究史 *The History of "New Basic Education" Research*. Beijing: Educational Science Publishing House.

Ye, L., Luo, W., & Pang, Q. (2019). Zhongguo Wenhua Chuantong Yu Jiaoyuxue Zhongguo Huayu Tixi De Jianshe 中国文化传统与教育学中国话语体系的建设 – 叶澜教授专访 (Chinese Cultural Tradition and the Construction of Chinese Discourse System in Educology: An Interview with Professor Ye Lan). *Journal of Soochow University (Educational Science Edition)*, (3). https://doi.org/10.19563/j.cnki.sdjk.2019.03.007.

Yukl, G. (2002). *Leadership in Organizations* (5th ed.). NJ: Prentice-Hall.

Zhang, X., & Ye, L. (2015). *"Xinjichu Jiaoyu" Yanjiu Shouce* "新基础教育"研究手册 *Handbook of "New Basic Education" Research*. Fuzhou: Fujian Education Press.

Zou, Y., Craig, C. J., & Poimbeauf, R. P. (2016). What the West Could Learn from the East: A Reflective Analysis. *Teachers and Teaching, 22*(7), 842–857. https://doi.org/10.1080/13540602.2016.1185820.

CHAPTER 9

Faith and Action

Yuhua Bu

The central topic we will address here is how, after more than a decade of cross-cultural reciprocal learning, the two sister schools understand themselves and each other, what the deepest cultural differences are behind this understanding, and what each learns from the other. This chapter first analyzes the understandings of Minzhu Primary School (MPS) and Bay Street School (BSS) of themselves and each other, then focuses on the issue of the social identity of the sister schools, and finally discusses possible future directions for each school in their respective countries.

Y. Bu (✉)
East China Normal University, Shanghai, China
e-mail: yhbo@dedu.ecnu.edu.cn

© The Author(s), under exclusive license to Springer Nature
Switzerland AG 2021
Y. Bu (ed.), *Narrative Inquiry into Reciprocal Learning Between
Canada-China Sister Schools*, Intercultural Reciprocal Learning in
Chinese and Western Education,
https://doi.org/10.1007/978-3-030-61085-2_9

259

9.1 How China-Canada Sister Schools Understand and Locate Themselves and Each Other

9.1.1 The Understanding of MPS about Itself and MPS in the Eyes of BSS

The history of schooling in China is long, and is recorded from the sixteenth to the eleventh century BC during the Yin Dynasty (14B.C–11.B.C.), when schools were called "xiáng (庠)" or "xù (序)." However, schools with the class teaching system as the main form of educational organization and modern school subjects as the main content of education were established in the late Qing Dynasty, which existed only 100 years ago, and to a large extent they were established by borrowing Western educational ideas and practice models from Europe and America. However, this does not mean that Chinese schools are replicas of European and American schools. The story of the two sister schools meeting in the twenty-first century, as explored in this book, can shed light on several differences in school education between Canada and China.

9.1.1.1 Positioning of MPS on Itself

MPS Is a Place Where Children Can Be Happy, Healthy and Active in Their Development

People who have been to MPS will always leave with a "happy" impression of this school; when you talk to the principal and teachers at MPS about the children's education, the word they use most often is "happy." Principal Ting of MPS states:

> We cultivate a happy, healthy, active development of 21st century youth, not only to learn written knowledge, but also to have the desire to use their intelligence and hands to explore the world. Therefore, our school carries out 'water science and technology education'... Nowadays, it is useless to know only the written knowledge, but we have to compound the talents of youths who are creative, hands-on and intelligent according to the new era and the characteristics of Minzhu district, so that the school can become a place for the healthy growth of children. (Interview, May 2018)

If you are visiting this school for the first time, the moment you walk through the doors of MPS, your first impression is that the campus is a place where children can happily grow up. If you stand at the front of the school and look straight ahead, you can see a landscaped pool 20 meters away from the school gate, with a pair of statues of schoolchildren: a pink girl and a light blue boy. Looking further to the left from the school gate, you will find a teaching building and a picture on the wall of the building of a group of children running merrily through flowers and green grass. When you look to the right, you will find a long row of bulletin boards with all kinds of information, most of it about children's everyday life activities. Then, walking further into the four-story teaching building, you will find that each step of the stairs is decorated with red, green, yellow, blue and other colors, on which are written the English numbers one, two, three and so on. Each English number represents a step. Upon entering each floor, you will also find colorful pictures of children's activities or art work posted on the walls on either side of each hallway. All of these scenes leave you with the impression that this is a caring school with a rich and varied life that children thrive in.

MPS Is a "Good School Close to Home" that Satisfies Residents

In 2014, the Shanghai Municipal Education Commission proposed a program called "good schools close to home" to satisfy residents, and MPS was one of the first schools to participate. What is a "good school close to home"? Until the 1990s, MPS was not recognized by the residents of the surrounding communities, but it gradually gained the trust of its neighboring residents when it received a number of distinctive student achievement awards, as well as recognition from the Shanghai Municipal Government. Hence, our understanding based on the experience of MPS is that, on one hand, schools should be able to keep children happy and healthy and active in their development, and on the other hand, they should be competitive in the community. At the entrance of MPS, visitors can see various signs representing the school's honors: National Green School,[1] Shanghai Advanced Collective of Moral Education Award, Shanghai Model School of Science and Technology Education, Shanghai Model School of Environmental Education, Shanghai Model School of Behavior Criterion Education, and so on. At the same time, similar information can be found on the website of MPS, such as announcements of students

---

[1] Note: The Ministry of Ecology and Environment of the People's Republic of China recognizes schools with outstanding performance in campus landscaping, environmental education, environmental protection practices and so on.

winning first, second and third prizes in many prestigious national and municipal writing and mathematics competitions.

The general consensus of all MPS personnel is that schools must win awards in order to gain a place in the region. For example, the science teacher in this project, Mr Zhiguo, after reviewing his experience at MPS, believed that it was because of the awards that he and the science and technology education of MPS were recognized:

> When I first came to MPS to do science and technology education, I wanted MPS to gain fame in this field. So, through a year of hard work, the students on my team have won awards by participating in several competitions, which has set a good sign in the district. After that, we gradually achieved more and more, and the fame grew. The school and parents support us in taking our students out to technology events and competitions, winning makes them happy, and the school gets honors. (Interview, April 2017)

So, do residents really care about the school's awards? Our interview with the head of the Office of Community Education Funding seems to have been tempered by this. We asked the director to evaluate how MPS is faring throughout the district's educational system, and the director's response was as follows:

> MPS is the first level school in our district. Our district's schools are divided into one, two and three levels. The first level is the best. MPS used to be a very common school. Now it is not the same as before. It has become the first level school and won many awards. Residents trust MPS very much. (Interview, April 2018)

As far as we know, the reason why MPS attaches so much importance to competition and external performance is due to the need to survive in the competitive pattern of its region.

Ms Barton of BSS probably has vivid memories of researching science and technology projects at MPS for the purpose of winning awards. In March 2017, Ms Barton and Mr Zhiguo discussed carrying out research for a water project around "World Water Day" in the new semester. Ms Barton suggested that students from both schools should conduct research on the use of water resources in their communities, but this initiative did not get Mr Zhiguo's fully agreement. Mr Zhiguo said he was going to take the students to the Shanghai Science, Technology and Innovation Project Competition in May and wanted some advice from Ms Barton. Ms Barton could not understand it, and the collaborative research never came to fruition. But now everything seems to be quietly changing: a year later, in September 2018, Mr Zhiguo's understanding of students' scientific learning altered. He states:

> I started to think about the reciprocal learning that has been going on for years, mainly in the exchange between teachers, which is more helpful to teachers, but, can it be implemented to the students? The ultimate goal is the development of the students. Therefore, I plan to make it a priority to facilitate daily communication between students of both schools from September 2018 onward, and track their growth and take literacy evaluation at the appropriate time (e.g. a year later) to see how students develop in terms of communication, hobbies, international outlook, learning ability, etc. (Interview, April 2018).

MPS Is an Open Model School
Although MPS is focused on inter-school competition and award-winning rates, the campus is not narrow-minded. In 2013, after being named the "New Basic Education" model school, its faculty mentored more than 10 mainstream schools in the surrounding area. At the same time, MPS's teachers and administrators have joined hands with schools in the educationally underserved provinces of Xinjiang, Qinghai and Sichuan in western China and formed sister schools with some of them, where teachers meet every semester to exchange educational experiences. In addition, MPS has opened its doors to principals and teachers from all over the country, presenting demonstration lessons, holding seminars and giving presentations. MPS believes that "basic education is about raising children for the country, and ... treat[s] them the same no matter what school they come from or where they come from. We are willing to contribute experience."

9.1.1.2 The Understanding of BSS about MPS

Overall, our understanding of how BSS understands MPS is not very comprehensive or accurate, and while we tried to take advantage of every face-to-face collaboration and every meeting, even over dinner, to talk to them about what they thought about MPS, perhaps out of their tolerance for differences, the answers we got are usually along the lines of "We have a lot of similarities, we both care about students, although we do it a little differently; we learn a lot from each other." In the following sections, we have attempted to summarize these responses based on the available research data.

MPS Focuses on Teacher Community and Professional Sharing

This evaluation is based on the motivation of Ms Barton and Ms Hanny to participate in the sister-school cooperation. Ms Barton was part of our reception in Canada and we watched her math lesson together back in 2008, when MPS first visited BSS. In 2013, Ms Barton joined the program again, as she herself says, when she was preparing to leave BSS, for two main reasons. One was that under the Canadian teacher recruitment and appointment system, a teacher who has been able to teach in more than one school indicates that he or she has a rich educational experience and can be recognized by multiple schools. She believes that after nearly 20 years at BSS, it was time for a change. Second, she felt lonely, as the teachers at BSS were only responsible for their own classes and did not interact with each other, and even when she had difficulties or new ideas, it was difficult to get help or recognition from her colleagues. Coupled with her excellent teaching, she had planned to apply to work at the Ontario Institute for Studies in Education (OISE) to enhance her research. But the reciprocal learning project opened her eyes to new possibilities, namely that she felt it would be a joy to have a group of teachers on the other side of the ocean with her, sharing the fruits of her education. Here is what Ms Barton originally thought:

> 'I am having an amazing year,' said Barton, 'Even my husband noticed it. He was asking me if I would leave Bay Street School this coming year because every year in the past, I have told him that I would like to leave the school and get hired somewhere. This is the first year I am really not thinking about leaving.' (Khoo 2018)

On a visit to MPS in 2016, Ms Barton expressed envy when she further learned that teachers at MPS in almost every subject in addition to their day-to-day teaching were working together on weekly teaching seminars and wished she could be a part of it.

MPS Focuses on Harmony between Humans and Nature

In Ms Barton's view, MPS focuses on the harmonious coexistence of humans and nature, which is inseparable from traditional Chinese culture, expressed in such sayings as "heaven and man are united as one" and "the gentleman's nature is as inclusive and peaceful as water." She said to Dr. Yishin Khoo:

> All around the world there is water and we use it every single day. However, our earth is polluted; so are the lakes, oceans, rivers, seas, waterfalls, tidal pools, water in pipes, swamps, icebergs, sewage and ponds. We must have water to survive. Located close to the Huangpu River, Green Lotus School (MPS) values water and therefore has a water culture. (Khoo 2018)

Indeed, over nearly seven years of interaction and reciprocal learning among teachers at sister schools, the principal and teachers at MPS have begun to break away from their original awareness to only make their schools competitive, becoming increasingly aware of the significance of this work for the ecological well-being of the modern world. Principal Ting stated:

> The Water Science and Technology Museum of our school is not just a place for children to master the knowledge of water, we want them to truly realize the close relationship between water and the world and that water is the source of our life. Our museum is now also open to all schools and residents in the community to learn about the importance of water culture. (Fieldnotes, May 2019)

MPS Is also a Somewhat Confusing School

The teachers at BSS seem to be filled with more confusion about MPS after over seven years of reciprocal learning, especially in 2018–2019.

Confusion 1: Why are teachers afraid of students making mistakes in class?
I clearly remember that in May 2018, Ms Barton was going to work with the teachers at MPS to present their collaborative teaching to teachers in about 14 different regions of China. To this end, teachers from both schools prepared lessons together. One day at noon, I met Ms Barton in the first floor corridor of MPS and asked her if everything was going well. She shook her head and told me that she understood classroom teaching to be about giving students questions to think about, and that students may make mistakes and not be able to find the answers for the whole lesson, which is in line with their development, and teachers should not tell students the answers directly. I fully agreed with her and told her that this was the basic idea of the "New Basic Education." But she looked me in

the eye and said: "Isn't MPS a model school for NBE? Why don't some teachers understand it that way?" I told her that not all teachers were involved in NBE, just as she and Ms Hanny were the only ones involved in the project in BSS.

On top of that, something happened that made Ms Barton very angry. The class we mentioned above in relation to the demonstration lesson was supposed to have 40 students, but on the day of the demonstration, Ms Barton found that two students were absent. Later, she learned that the Class Supervisor thought the two students were poor in academic performance and discipline, which led them to cause trouble in class. Therefore, the two students were not allowed to participate in the demonstration. Ms Barton grew angry when she heard about this. "That's not fair," she told me. This is hurting children! She kept asking me, "Why are they doing this? Is it fair?" I was also very shocked to hear about it afterwards. Perhaps because of this, there was a time when Ms Barton began to alienate Mr Zhiguo, which I guess it's the last thing she can tolerate.

Confusion 2: Why don't mentors respect the ideas of young teachers?
In 2018, at a national teaching seminar, Ms Barton and Ms Liu had a class on scientific inquiry. For this reason, they spent a whole day together in teaching design. Mr Zhiguo, Ms Liu's mentor, was not initially involved in the preparation, but the day before the class, Mr Zhiguo asked Ms Liu to modify their teaching design and follow his advice. Ms Barton was shocked and confused as to how Mr Zhiguo could interfere and discount their ideas; at the same time, she was shocked that Ms Liu accepted Mr Zhiguo's opinion so easily.

Here is another example. Ms Hanny and Ms Dongmei were co-teaching partners, holding a class meeting session together. The two of them had already discussed their ideas. But for some reason, one day, Principal Ting invited Ms Lu from Minzhu district to guide them, and Ms Lu overturned almost all their ideas. Ms Hanny was very confused as to why Principal Ting had asked Ms Lu to guide them, and why Ms Lu dismissed their ideas without giving a convincing reason. And Ms. Dongmei Wang didn't seem to have any counter-arguments...

Confusion 3: Why do you understand the research differently than we do?
Ms Barton has been in contact with MPS for many years, and she is increasingly aware of the relationship between MPS and the East China Normal University research team, namely that MPS is a school engaged in NBE research. However, she was always confused that every study always has to have a problem and then apply the research method to find the

cause and a solution to the problem, but it seemed to her that the teachers at MPS did not seem to have problem awareness and did not apply a certain research method to the study. So how can we confirm that MPS is a school that does NBE research? In response, Ms Barton was curious to learn how MPS conducts its NBE research. Later, she found that teachers at MPS were constantly looking for breakthroughs in their daily educational practices, hoping that their classroom teaching or classroom management would continue to meet the requirements of equity, quality and students' active engagement. What she cannot understand, therefore, is how the philosophy of NBE relates to the Chinese government's educational advocacy. And if the teachers at MPS are inclined to adopt the NBE philosophy, then why does the Chinese government not allow it? But she thinks that MPS teachers not only seem to be insensitive to research questions, but also do not know how to apply research methods to conducting research. These questions were puzzling to Ms Barton and Ms Hanny.

9.1.2 The Understanding of BSS about Itself and BSS in the Eyes of MPS

9.1.2.1 The Understanding of BSS about Itself

BSS Is Based on the Principle of Academic Success and Happiness for every Child

On the school's official website, we see that the goals of BSS are as follows:

> We are committed to ensuring that every student succeeds academically and develops a positive sense of well-being; The Model Schools program is committed to nurturing the individual and collective strengths of students, families and communities. By recognizing and honoring students' identities and lived experiences in the classroom and larger school community, we can enhance equity, student achievement and well-being for all students. (https://www.tdsb.on.ca/Community/Model-Schools-for-Inner-Cities.)
>
> As a Model School, BSS is committed to: (1) Innovative teaching and learning practices; (2) Providing support services to meet social, emotional and physical well-being of students; (3) Researching, reviewing and evaluating students and programs; (4) An ongoing commitment to share successful practice. (BSS 2014)

So how does BSS implement its goals? We now take a cursory look at the work plan of BSS from 2018 to 2019. During the school year, BSS divided their educational goals or tasks into three sections: reading, writing and mathematical literacy. Here is a specific example of reading literacy.

The goal of reading is to: (1) Increase reading scores in grades 3 and 6 by 5% each year in the next two years; (2) Increase Grade 1 at the expected level in June 2018 to 1/5 of students (we have about 60 students, so approximately 12).

The corresponding educational actions are:

- Guided Reading Professional Development (PD) for all grade levels by December 2018 in order to ensure guided reading in each classroom three times per week;
- Reading coach to work with Grade 1 and Kindergarten teachers to build further capacity in integrating a comprehensive literacy model and guided reading program;
- Data tracking in Grade 1 to monitor progress (data wall)—to be increased to grades 2 and 3 in 2019;
- Empower reading program for those students most at risk in primary/junior grades (12 students this year—2 groups at max);
- Wilson Reading Program for intermediate students in Hearing Service Program (HSP) program.

Ways of Monitoring: Admin walks through to observe guided reading; data meetings with grade 1 staff and reading coach to track reading progress and revise strategies; more students graduating grade 1 at the expected level; increase in reading scores in grades 3 and 6; meet with resource teachers to note progress in Empower and Wilson programs for each student (through reading assessment).

How does BSS understand the students' healthy and happy life? This can be learned from the school culture section. Schools still focus on equality. Equity Learning Focus states further that staff must learn to identify bias and barriers to promote inclusion and greater engagement in our learning community. Some educational actions will continue in order to provide opportunities for staff to learn about being culturally competent at staff meetings, providing them with resources (texts, videos, activities, websites) and ensuring they are aware of PD provided within Toronto District School Board (TDSB). These will continue to encourage staff to include culturally relevant images, resources and sources in their classrooms. Reading materials are purchased for the library that are culturally relevant. Ways of Monitoring are administrators' walk-through images, learning tasks, work samples, open-ended questions and student surveys.

Likewise, in many classrooms at BSS, we can see the presence of slogans expressing equal treatment of differences, such as "BULLYING IS NEVER OK" and "ANGER IS ONLY ONE LETTER SHORT OF DANGER." In addition, there are some classroom rules that express the same meaning, such as 'Laugh,' 'Be yourself,' 'Love your family,' 'Respect each other' and 'Be grateful.'

Our findings are broadly consistent with those of the Canadian project team's researchers. As Yishin says (Khoo 2017):

> Overall, Ann's curricula-making around the mental health unit reflects her rhythm of building a classroom community that reflects Dewey's ideal of a moral and intelligent community and that provides students with continuous new experiences for further growth and democratic learning. This rhythm of Ann's, as it beat through the school year, made possible a citizenship educational environment that prepared her students to become democratic citizens on the broader political landscape of Canada, a country of immigrants that generally defines itself—on the premises of its Constitution 1982 Canadian Charter of Rights and Freedoms, and the 1988 Canadian Multiculturalism Act—as a democratic country that strives to ensure the equality and freedom of all individuals while focusing on the common good. (Khoo 2017)

Establishing Schools as the Heart of the Community
The schools as community heart approach has been shown to improve attendance rates, parent engagement and encourage of different ways to meet the complex and changing needs of students. The goal is to build a community where children, young people, teachers, parents and community members work together interactively, recognizing that children and young people learn best through real-life situations and hands-on activities. This is most evident in the childcare center of BSS, which was the aspect of this school that impressed us most. We were surprised to find that BSS not only provides a safe, warm, toy-rich space for the young children of the community, but also professional guidance to parents at no cost. Some of the newcomers have just arrived in the community and have not yet made many friends, and often stay at the center for a full day, and it thus becomes a psychologically safe space for them.

Of course, BSS understands the concept of the school as the heart of the community, and this does not just mean that the school is the hub that connects children, families and communities, and that all forces in the community should do their best to support the school. During their visit to BSS, we believe this was deeply felt by the principal and teachers at MPS:

> When I first visited BSS in 2008, I saw what a great community they had, children could go straight to the community center when they got enrollment of school, not only were there free snacks to eat, but they could also study in the library, and the librarians helped each child choose books that matched their reading level and sometimes tutored them in reading. It was great! when I visited BSS in 2017, Ms. Hanny and I took the kids to the community centre for swimming lessons, where there are dedicated swimming facilities and a dedicated swim coach to train the kids. This again makes me think that while BSS is not as big as our school and seems to have outdated facilities and not as modern as our school, their educational resources are not limited to the school and the entire community can be said to have resources for the school! (October 2019)

BSS Is a School that Operates at the Request of the Government and Has a Constant Need to Defend Its Rights with the Government

Without knowing as much as we would like about BSS, our understanding of the school—government relationship in Canada is that if Canada is a free country, then schools should also have more autonomy and the government should play a greater mentor and supporter role. But as we went deeper and deeper, our understanding of the relationship between the two changed. We found that BSS has been pursuing an educational strategy based on curriculum standards for the last decade or so. This is how the most recent principal, Principal Green, made sense of Principal Ting's and her roles:

> Educational priorities change with each new government. Every government starts a new education reform every four years. Principals are responsible for establishing these initiatives in the school. The principal of MPS school can work with the teachers to plan the school's direction, to develop and modify the school's internal policies, and to reform the evaluation of teachers. But I can't. I'm a teacher leader. Important for principals is to be involved in the learning with the staff, to develop a deep understanding of the reform and principals are the lead learner. Important for principals is to

9 FAITH AND ACTION 271

build relationships and capacity with staff through distributed leadership. (Fieldnotes, October 2019)

Because the government appears to have been cutting back on educational spending in recent years, it may be increasing class sizes. This is why teachers at BSS have been on strike almost every year since the sister-schools program was established. When we visited BSS in October 2019, the school was in the middle of a strike. However, the teachers did not let it affect their normal teaching and learning. Ms Barton explained that the reason she joined the protest organized by the Ontario Teachers' Federation was mainly to defend the rights of students, not her own rights. We were all moved to hear that; we felt the love teachers had for children.

9.1.2.2 BSS in the Eyes of MPS

BSS Truly Respects and Loves Children Everywhere and at All Times

The initial understanding of MPS's attitude toward BSS began in 2008. That year, Principal Ting visited BSS and formed a sister-principal bond with the then principal. At the time, Principal Ting was most impressed by the fact that BSS has great respect for children and treats them as equals, no matter what country they come from.

> At BSS, you can feel that every child is respected and that everything on campus expresses the sense of equality. They express the same meaning in different languages, they put their palms together with different skin colors, expressing both equality and unity of trust. (Interview, April 2017)

When Principal Ting revisited this school in 2017, she expressed this sentiment once again:

> Most of the children at BSS come from lower-middle class families in the community and their families are of average financial status, but the school is caring and treats each child equally, which is very similar to us. Most of our students are also from ordinary families in the community, but we want to give them the best and most equal education (Interview, April 2017).

When Ms Barton and Ms Hanny visited MPS for the first time in April 2016, the faculty and students further appreciated the notions of the true student position held by BSS. In the classroom, the teachers at MPS saw that:

- When the two BSS teachers talk to their students, they always habitually crouch down or kneel directly on the floor with both legs, with both hands on the corners of the student's desk, to communicate with the student up close. This is largely impossible to do in a Chinese classroom. Because traditional Chinese culture considers teachers to be elders, and kneeling is a gesture of interaction from junior to elder, it is unlikely that teachers would disturb this hierarchical relationship.
- In the teacher-student dialogue, if Ms Barton or Ms Hanny wants a student to answer a question, they always say, "____, please share your opinion!" After the student answers the question, they always say "Thanks!" If the students misunderstand, or the ideas expressed are not correct, the two teachers always respond: "Your ideas are very interesting, something which I did not expect. Thank you!" The children are not embarrassed or nervous at this time because of their inaccuracy. In short, the teachers use students' names and they praise them, even when their answers are incorrect.
- In terms of classroom organization, the teacher usually forms a small group sitting around the teacher or the teacher moves back and forth and left and right in the classroom to capture each child's attention.
- In the classroom, children can express their individual needs. If a child says to a teacher that they would like to go away for a while and think on their own, the teacher is usually supportive. Thus, their classrooms look and feel less tidy than Chinese classrooms but the teachers at MPS know that it is because they respect the individual needs of the child and where he/she would like to sit.

At the end of class, teachers at MPS noticed that Ms Barton would often walk quickly to the classroom door and greet each student who left the classroom, sometimes with a thumbs up to praise them; the children also responded to Ms Barton in a polite manner.

The Vice Principal of MPS put it this way: "They are genuinely respectful of children, and that is something we must learn seriously. Although our class sizes are large, that's not really a reason to stop us from making a change, we need to explore new possibilities."

Most importantly, teachers at MPS felt that Ms Barton and Ms Hanny's love for the children was not limited to their own classes and that they seemed to extend love for all the children in the world sincerely and deeply. The MPS teachers were touched when Ms Barton, who was standing at the back of the class, burst into tears as she listened to a Chinese class supervisor's lively conversation with the children on how to understand their parents. The MPS children came up to hug Ms Barton after class. The Chinese teachers who listened to the class found it strange and slightly embarrassing. However, they too were moved by her love of being a teacher, regardless of borders or race dividing students and teacher.

BSS Prioritizes Student Character and Comprehensive Literacy over Knowledge Acquisition

On her first visit to BSS in 2008, Principal Ting, who is also a mathematics teacher, felt that the targeting of mathematics teaching at BSS was a bit low, as it seemed that what could be learned by primary school students in the third grade in China was not taught until the fifth grade in BSS. In the interactions that followed, there were many scenes that left this impression on Principal Ting.

A. Impressions of Ms Hanny's English Teaching at MPS
In 2016, the principal and teachers at MPS observed Ms Hanny and Ms Ding co-teaching English. If we follow the teachers' habit of China, the teaching goal is relatively simple and clear, as long as the students are taught to flexibly use the words grass, bench, hill and flower, for example, in combination with a few imperative sentences. However, in Ms Hanny's classroom, the teachers at MPS saw that instead of directly testing whether students had mastered the four words, as Chinese teachers usually do, she took the words and made them into vocabulary and pictures, 20 of each, and randomly distributed them to the students in her class, who then broke the pattern of peer cooperation and established new learning friends based on word-to-sense matches. As a result, two students came up to Ms Hanny and one girl started to complain that she hadn't found a friend. Ms Hanny pointed to the boy next to the girl, but the girl was dismissive and said that this boy was not her friend and she wanted her teacher to help her find another friend. At this point, Ms Hanny said to the girl with a serious expression on her face, "Did you know that even though many people in life are not our friends, we have to learn to be friends with them because of the need to work together, so that things can be done smoothly.

Good at working with others, and although we may not like the person, we have a responsibility to treat them as friends for the sake of getting things done, and at the same time, we have to learn to respect others." The girl didn't quite understand this but nevertheless she reluctantly completed the cooperative task. Afterwards, one of the class supervisors of MPS said she was deeply impressed by what Ms Hanny had said and done and she felt that it was worth learning. She thought Ms Hanny could always use what was happening in her classroom as a resource for character education.

Next, Ms Hanny had the class work in pairs to create a small science experiment on "light and shadow" using paper, scissors, flashlights and other tools to discover the relationship between the angle at which light moves and the change in shadow length. The children's interest was so high that the experiment lasted nearly 12 minutes. After the students had finished, Ms Hanny asked them to describe the process of their experiment. Following the students' answers, she guided them on the board to describe the experiment in an orderly manner using first, second, third....

After the lesson, Principal Ting exclaimed, "Such lesson was a joy to learn, and the children had a lot to gain: they mastered science, experienced experiments, and learned to express English in order with ordinal words. That's amazing!"

Ms Ding, with whom she co-taught, explained that:

> In China, most of the time, a teaching unit has only one week to complete and it is not possible to have students do hands-on experiments in the language class, which would leave out some of the teaching tasks, but there is no set material in Canada ... so the difference in teaching materials, the difference in the teaching system, the difference in the way we teach. (Interview, May 2017)

B. Impressions of Ms Barton's science class

In May 2018, Ms Barton taught a physics class on "Fixed Pulleys." In the first lesson, she started by putting a set of pictures on the PPT of Chinese workers working on the railway around 100 years ago. She began by telling the students that China has made important contributions to Canada's development history, and that some Chinese participated in the construction of Canada's railways under very difficult conditions, some dying of illness as a consequence of their efforts. She then asked the students how they felt about this, and the children agreed that they should remember everyone who has contributed to Canada and be grateful for their contributions; some said they had Chinese friends and felt that the Chinese were friendly. Next, Ms Barton put up a picture of Chinese workers carrying heavy sandbags to repair the railway and a picture of a crane and asked the students, "If Chinese workers were building railroads today maybe they wouldn't be working so hard, because the work they did then could be done today with machines. But what is the principle of this crane?" The students indicated that they did not know, so Ms Barton asked them to read the article and first identify two types of words, one that indicated something scientific and one that was new to the students, and to sort them out. Before that, she asked the students what kind of approach would help with classification. Some students said that it was a cross-coordinate diagram while others said it was a Venn diagram. Finally, with about three minutes left in the first session, the students hadn't finished reading the text and hurriedly ended up in another classroom for their French lesson.

Seeing this, Principal Ting and her fellow teachers felt that the class was too comprehensive, resembling both a history lesson and a character lesson, but there seemed to be no trace of physics. Mr. Zhiguo stated:

I couldn't learn from her, my science classes were in the last part of the afternoon, each session was only 20 minutes long, and the number of students was so large that I estimated I wouldn't be able to finish teaching for a semester if I was like them (Interview, May 2018).

In this regard, Principal Ting was deeply touched by the fact that Ms Barton assumed that students should be given sufficient time to explore and think, rather than focusing on the transfer of knowledge. She also said that with the start of the new semester, she hoped to combine some of the classes into 80-minute blocks to allow students ample time to explore.

BSS Doesn't Seem to Have Its Own School Culture
The formation of this impression began in 2018 when Principal Ting visited BSS. At the exchange meeting between the two schools, Principal Ting introduced the school culture of MPS to the principal and teachers at BSS, professors from the Ontario Institute for Studies in Education, University of Toronto, and a district head from the Toronto School Board who were present at the time, which generated a great deal of interest from these audiences. They found it incredible that MPS has such a clear

and deep school culture over its 60 years of existence, and asked many questions during the discussion session about school culture building. During the exchange, Principal Ting was surprised to realize for the first time that although BSS has a history of more than 200 years, the school does not highlight cultural traditions and seems to have no cultural characteristics of its own, which is a theme that most schools in China have been working on for the last 30 years.

After that, MPS began trying to understand the reasons for this situation. They supposed this had more to do with the frequent change of principals at BSS. Another thing that impressed MPS about BSS was the difference in the roles of principals and teachers. In the almost 10 years of its relationship with BSS, the school has had 6 principals, each of whom stayed at BSS for almost 2 years, while the teachers have been relatively stable, such as Ms Barton who has been with the school for almost 20 years.

Of course, as our understandings deepened, we saw that BSS teachers knew why BSS does not have its own culture. It boils down to the concept of schools being different between China and Canada. Where MPS is concerned, the school is more like a spiritual organism; the principal is the spiritual leader, who has a holistic grasp of the school philosophy and the direction of development of the campus, and the teachers work together to achieve the overall goal. Moreover, the Chinese teachers work in a subject group, that is, mathematics teachers belong to the mathematics subject group and science teachers belong to the science teachers group, and teachers from different subjects collaborate to teach students in the same class, so a subject group becomes a spiritual home where teachers work together on a daily basis to conduct research. For BSS, however, the school is more like an archipelago of islands, where each teacher's own class is a separate kingdom, with little opportunity for teachers to interact with each other. Also, they are less constrained by the school philosophy, and the principal's role is more that of professional supporter and facilitator of school life.

9.2   The Social Identity of Sister Schools Between Canada and China

So far, we have stated the understandings and positioning of the two schools from a cross-cultural perspective. It is clear that both schools emphasize the active and healthy development of children as a core tenet in contemporary society, and strive to achieve a harmonious relationship with the community. However, we also found that they differed considerably on what a good school is, what the mission of a good school is, and how to understand the identity of the school. Therefore, we will mainly discuss the question of school identity, that is: Who does a school belong to? This question includes two more questions: What is the school's mission in society? And what is the relationship between the school and the individual? For the latter question, both MPS and BSS advocate the basic principles of inclusion, equity and quality, and have greater similarity, so we will not discuss it again, and will focus on the first question.

9.2.1 The Social Mission of Schools in Canada

9.2.1.1 Positioning the Social Identity of Schools in Canada: Schools Are the Heart of the Community

As noted, what MPS most admires and appreciates about BSS is the mutually supportive relationship between the school and the community; at the same time, MPS was surprised to learn that BSS has a history of more than 250 years, but seems to have no cultural heritage of its own, and that the principal has very limited administrative authority, having been relegated to a curriculum leader. So, is there really no cultural tradition in BSS? Where did the power of the principal go? As researchers on the project, we were actually somewhat surprised by this positioning in the development of BSS. As we dug deeper into the educational literature in Canada and the United States, we found that Ms Barton and Ms Hanny were not the only two teachers who cared about what schools meant to their communities and the human world. For example, in reading Oakes and Lipton, we found that many teachers mentioned in their book had such a professional vision (Oakes and Lipton 1999). One first-time sixth-grade teacher, Janine Ashford, put it this way:

> I encourage my students to be active intellectual inquirers and knowledge constructors, rather than negative, submissive participants... In order to transcend inequality and transform society, my students must enter a world in which the nation understands established social, political, and economic realities. (p. 35)

Kelly Genzel, a beginning high school English teacher, said: "The need to pay attention to every student who enters my classroom drives me to seek socially just education that will help them become transformative citizens in our society, freeing their minds to soar above their racial, ethnic and social status…" (p. 35).

Such a vision of the teaching profession is something we rarely find among contemporary Chinese teachers. Chinese teachers are more concerned about the happy growth and academic achievement of the students they teach, and few of them mention whether or not their students will contribute to society in the future. Of course, this is not to say that Chinese teachers are not concerned about their students' contribution to society, but it is rare for them to express their vision so clearly.

In fact, we also find that not only are the parents of BSS students regularly involved in the educational life of their children, but the community in which BSS is located also shares many educational responsibilities. BSS is not the only institution in the community with educational responsibilities, as the community library provides not only reading materials but also instruction on how to read; the community swimming pool is not only a place for children to swim, but also has specialized coaches to teach them swimming skills; the community children's study room is not only a place for children to do their homework after school, but also offers professional tutors; the community zoo is not only a place for children to observe animals, but also a place for teachers to teach about wildlife and conservation….

In terms of spatial relationships, BSS is fully integrated into the community, with no walls or gates; children have a deep sense of the school in the community, the swimming pool, the library, the zoo, the museum … all are places where they live and learn.

This reminds us of Boyer's understanding of what a school of excellence is (Boyer 1995):

> We found in our study that it is simply impossible to achieve educational excellence at a school where purposes are blurred, where teachers and students fail to communicate thoughtfully with each other, and where parents are uninvolved in the education of their children". (p. 1) … it is simply impossible to have an island of excellence in a sea of community indifference. (p. 3)

9.2.1.2 Why Canada Understands the Social Identity of Schools in this Way

First, learning is a kind of social and cultural activity.

In China, when we talk about learning theory, we always understand it in a cognitive sense, but perhaps because of cultural diversity and the quest for educational equity, scholars in North America have broken away from traditional cognitive learning theory, recognizing that human learning is a kind of social and cultural activity. The American educator Jerome Bruner has pointed out that "learning, remembering, talking, imagining, all of this is made possible by participating in a certain culture" (Bruner 1996), arguing that the mind creates culture as much as it creates for culture (p. 166). Oakes and Lipton also note that "students must be able to apply their own social and cultural thought processes to understand everything new, whether this knowledge comes from their 'family's' culture, the larger socio-cultural, or some combination of the two" (Oakes and Lipton 1999). Based on this understanding, Boyer (1995) asserted that "if we hope to achieve quality in the nation's schools, parents simply must become partners in the process." Dewey's empirical theory also influences this view of learning: "Children learn in the process of interacting with social situations, i.e. learning occurs not in interaction with knowledge but in interaction with culturally based uses" and "learning is becoming part of a community" (Oakes and Lipton 1999, p. 60).

For this reason, we can understand why teachers at BSS bring children to the community from time to time, and why they introduce the topic of history and culture in their physics or math lessons. In fact, the teaching methods that seem irrelevant to knowledge learning by Chinese teachers are exactly the inherent requirements of child learning. Perhaps it is only this kind of education that will truly break the mold of knowledge transfer and produce future citizens who will understand, relate to and integrate into Canadian society. At this point, we recalled what Professor Ma Yunpeng said about this project:

> My research is in math education. When I first visited the Canadian math lessons, my colleagues and I thought that there was no math feeling, and we just saw the children discussing this and that in an enjoyable way. Forty minutes later, they did not understand what they had learned. However, my opinion has changed now (Interview, Oct. 2019).

Professor Ma continued:

> One of my PhD students studied with them for a while and visited dozens of math classes every week, and made videos of them. She said to me: "Canadians think that learning math on a certain type of topic is a big concept, and the process of learning to understand that big concept is a longer process, and it takes three weeks for a student to master that topic. The teacher then looks at the student's mastery in three weeks as a whole, so they do not care as much about how well they master a particular lesson (Interview, Oct. 2019).

He concluded: "Their mathematical learning is not only mathematics, but how mathematics is closely related to people's lives, culture, so mathematics needs to be placed in the socio-cultural life of the people (Interview, October 2019).

Overall, schools in Canada deal with the relationship between knowledge, character and society in a way that not only focuses on knowledge, but also focuses on citizenship because they know—in the end result—that both rely on each other and should not be ripped away from one another because that would be unnatural for child development.

In addition, schools are "under community autonomy," not just "in the community."

In recent decades, Canada has been promoting the idea of distributed leadership, which requires principals to devolve leadership and empower teachers to recognize the value of "teachers personal practical knowledge" (Clandinin and Connelly 1992) and look at teachers as curriculum-makers (Craig and Ross 2008). Thus, a portion of principal leadership is transferred to teachers, but this is only an internal look at the distribution of school leadership. If viewed from outside the school, the principal's leadership itself is also very limited. This is closely related to the Canadian education system. Canada is heavily influenced by the Commonwealth system and has traditionally focused on local self-government, which is a concept wherein "the residents of a region decide and conduct public affairs of their own free will in relation to their own interests"(Huang 2019), and is closely related to freedom and democracy. John Mill (1806–1873) argued that the core issue of "liberty" is "the nature and limits of the power that society can legitimately exercise over individuals." Moreover, the Anglo-Saxon political tradition has always held that it is the combination of "self-government" and "democracy" that gives people the beliefs, ideals and institutional guarantees for "freedom" that is the appeal of "self-government."

In terms of political tradition, we can thus understand how the community has given BSS so much support. In addition, from the early 1990s, there was increased focus on reforms that aligned each level of the educational structure from the school, to the district, to the state (Smith and O'Day 1991). Some characteristics of successful districts in advancing achievement on standardized tests are the importance of a shared vision and clear leadership focus, evidence-informed decision-making, a strategy for implementation, capacity building at all levels, developing social networks and internal/external partnerships, and creating a culture of learning (p. 34). Put simply, in Canada, schools are under the control of local society or community autonomy, which is an important component of the development of local society. Therefore, local society is responsible for children by sharing responsibility for education, and schools have to feed back to local society and accept leadership from it.

9.2.2 Identity Orientation of Schools in China

9.2.2.1 Schools Are Community Partners in Fulfilling Government Requirements

While MPS also focuses on school—family interaction, the difference is that MPS runs a parents' school to teach them how to develop good learning habits in their children or to involve parents in school activities, unlike BSS, which invites parents to share their own educational ideas and cultural traditions in the sense of cultural equality. On the other hand, MPS largely regards the community as the background and service object of school development, and rarely sees the community as the subject of education; the community likewise sees the school as the only educational institution in the community and needs to support the school itself, but may not directly take on the educational function. Therefore, in the community where MPS is located, the zoo is available for students to visit, but not for the instructional function, and teachers do not think of involving students in the construction of the zoo or using the zoo as a place for direct instruction; the Natatorium is available for students to swim and there are coaches to provide technical instruction, but the purpose is not to share responsibility for swimming lessons, but for financial gain. In recent decades, Chinese communities have interacted more frequently with schools, not because of the need to support them, but because communities need the support of schools in order to complete the tasks assigned by higher authorities, such as community health promotion, fire safety promotion, traffic safety promotion, or anti-corruption promotion and the work against Pornography and Illegal Publication and so on, which need to be done better with schools as intermediaries. Therefore, Chinese communities are more like the background and cooperation units of schools, and schools are also only cooperation units of communities, and do not need schools as the cultural glue of community development, which is very different from Canada, where schools are the heart of community cultural integration.

In short, in Canada, public schools for basic education, such as BSS, are first schools of the community or local society, followed by schools of Ontario, and finally schools of Canada. In China, public schools for basic education, such as MPS, are first and foremost state schools, then schools of Shanghai, and finally schools for parents and children, and the identity of the local society or community in school development is obscure.

9.2.3 Why China Understands School Identity in this Way

In terms of the understanding of school—society relations, the Chinese educational academic circle was influenced in the 1990s by several concepts in *Learning to Be*, which was published by the United Nations Educational, Scientific and Cultural Organization (UNESCO), such as "education precedes" and "it is hard to conceive of society developing without a renewal in education"(Faure 1972). Therefore, in this sense, China takes the possible requirements and challenges of the future development of the society as the background, and meeting the challenges of society has become the basic goal of school development, without understanding society as a partner of the school or an important educational resource and position, as Canada does.

Moreover, this is also related to the characteristics of Chinese social structure. Traditional Chinese society is an ethical one in which members of society "value each other, and one person seems not to exist for himself, but as if he exists for others" (Liang 1990), and lacks the group life of Western society. Since ancient times, China has emphasized the "homogeneous structure of the family and the state," and the realization of centralism. Therefore, traditional Chinese society has always been immature, and has remained underdeveloped until modern times. Schools in China generally understand society as an umbrella term for the political, economic and cultural spheres, rather than the spatially conceptualized society of Canada in the sense of local autonomy. So when the Chinese talk about school and society, they rarely understand the relationship between the two in terms of school and community relations.

9.3 Discussion

9.3.1 Do Chinese Schools Need to Learn from Canada and Re-understand the Relationship between Schools and Society in the Future?

This issue can be approached from two perspectives. One is the logic inherent in the development of Chinese schools over the last 40 years, and the other is that Chinese education has entered the stage of modernizing governance.

After the founding of the People's Republic of China in 1949, the educational function of Chinese schools was replaced or suppressed by political function, and after the reform and opening up of the country in 1978, the educational function of schools was replaced by the economic function, with an emphasis on schools to provide society with all kinds of technical talents and gradually embark on the path of examination-oriented education. In 1993, the Chinese government promulgated the Programme for the Reform and Development of Education in China, which marked the beginning of the transformation of Chinese schools into educational functions. In 2005, the Chinese educational academic circle generally agreed that the main goal of school development should be "connotation development" (Fang 2006), which means that schools should "shift from the main direct goal of transferring knowledge to the main direct goal of cultivating people, who have the consciousness and ability to develop actively through various means, including knowledge education, and who can strive to develop their own potential in various different and changing specific scenarios," and that they should no longer just "reproduce social productivity and production relations. Schools should pursue the existence value of serving the renewal development of society and the lifelong development of individuals, so that education can become a renewal system of human society" (Ye 2006). The connotation development of school mainly includes professional development of teachers, principal leadership, and improvement of the quality of classroom teaching and learning, which the NBE describes as "nurturing of endogenous power in schools" (Ye 2019). Many schools like MPS have become Shanghai's "New Quality Schools" or model schools of group developing plans, indicating that the historical task of connotation development of schools in China has basically been completed. Therefore, the goal of the new historical period will become how to take the school as the core, to establish a virtuous interaction and to develop a relationship with society and give back to society, so as to promote the cultural construction of Chinese society.

In 2013, the Chinese government proposed the goal of "promoting the modernization of the national governance system and governance capacity," and in 2014, the Chinese Minister of Education Yuan Guiren proposed that education in China had also entered a new phase of modernization of education governance. Education governance is the process of pluralistic subjects jointly managing public affairs in education, the goal of which is to establish a new pattern of efficient, fair, free and orderly education, the core of which is to adjust and optimize the power-responsibility relationship of those who co-lead through both decentralization and centralization, and to solve the outstanding problems of insufficient social participation in education management, insufficient autonomy of schools, insufficient macro-management capacity of the government, and imperfect governance structure within schools (Chu 2014). This means that the relationship between schools and society in China will be rebuilt and society will necessarily be more involved in school work.

Of course, the reconstruction of school—society relations in China cannot simply replicate the model of BSS school—community relations, which is related to different cultural traditions, social institutions and political ideologies between China and Canada. However, there is one point we can learn from BSS, that is, education governance should not be understood only as multi-subject participation in education. Schools in China need to clarify their social functions, and further think about how to use school development to drive the cultural development of society, and conversely to use the cultural construction of society to promote school education. In fact, during periods of Chinese agrarian society, such as the Sui and Tang dynasties, schools and rural society were always in a symbiotic relationship, and the primary purpose of schooling was not for employment, but for the transmission and development of rural culture (Wang 2016). By the middle of the twentieth century, the symbiotic relationship between schools and rural areas had been severely damaged.

Liang Shuming was so worried about this that he began the rural construction campaign in Zouping County, Shandong Province, to rebuild rural culture through education (Liang 2006), but due to the limitations of the times and social conditions, he did not succeed. Modern China has entered the era of educational governance, and the conditions for strengthening the interactive development of schools and society have arrived.

9.3.2 Do Canadian Schools Need to Have Their Own Unique Culture?

This problem stems from the fact that MPS has its own school culture, something which BSS does not seem to have. To remedy this, we need to clarify two basic issues. First, why is MPS constantly talking about its own school culture and what is the social background in which it emerged? Second, why is it important and essential to build school culture? In the 1980s and 1990s, the Chinese government, in order to undo the devastation of school education caused by the Cultural Revolution, built a number of key schools in various provinces, cities and counties in the shortest time to lead the development of other schools. The government invested heavily in their construction, with relatively obvious results. In the follow-up development, more and more schools joined the ranks of those vying for government resources. One of the most important ways was to flaunt their uniqueness and cultural characteristics to construct strong school cultures. In this environment, this is what MPS did to distinguish itself. Schools in China generally are similar to the traditional Chinese family, a relatively stable and closed structural system. In schools, principals and teachers remain largely unchanged for many years and get along like a family. Therefore, schools in China need cultural and inspirational leadership to promote the identity of teachers, which leads to the formation of a spiritual community and basic value principles for members to live together within the school. Thus, school culture building itself can also promote positive cultural identity. In this regard, BSS, as a public school with a history of over 200 years, needs to sort out the internal cultural spirit that has been running through the school for over 200 years, whether this spirit has changed in modern society, why it should change and where it should go. Once these new ideas are clear, it will be easy to reposition the direction of BSS and help the campus to gain new growth and assume new powers.

But, on the other hand, we also have to see the relatively narrow aspects of cultural construction of schools in China. From the inside of the school, although it is easy to encourage cooperation among teachers, it is also easy to produce homogenization, which may suppress the autonomy of individual teachers. In terms of the school's relationship with the outside world, it tends to generalize the work of the school, overlooking the fact that basic education schools should emphasize first and foremost their common and fundamental educational tasks. Therefore, because of the different systems and conditions of school development in different countries, BSS needs to approach the issue of school culture carefully and not deliberately pursue uniqueness for uniqueness's sake.

REFERENCES

Boyer, E. L. (1995). The Basic School: A Community for Learning. Princeton, NJ: Carnegie Foundation for the Advancement of Teaching.

Bruner, J. (1996). *Culture and Education*. Cambridge: Harvard University Press.

BSS. (2014). Toronto District School: Model Schools for Inner Cities. Accessed 22 July 2019.

Chu, H. (2014). Jiaoyu Zhili: Yi Gongzhi Qiu Shanzhi 教育治理: 以共治求善治 (Education Governance: Seeking Good Governance by Co-governance). *Education Research, 35*(10), 4–11.

Clandinin, D. J., & Connelly, F. M. (1992). Teacher as Curriculum Maker. In P. Jackson (Ed.), *Handbook of Curriculum* (pp. 363–461). New York, NY: Macmillan.

Craig, C. J., & Ross, V. (2008). Cultivating Teachers as Curriculum Makers. In F. M. Connelly (Ed.), *Sage Handbook of Curriculum and Instruction*. Thousand Oaks, CA: Sage.

Fang, T. (2006). Cujin Xuexiao Neihan Fazhan: Zhongguo Jiaoyuxuehui Di 18 ci Xueshu Nianhui Zongshu 促进学校内涵发展—中国教育学会第18次学术年会综述 (Promoting Connotation Development in Schools—A Summary of the 18th Annual Meeting of the Chinese Society of Educational). *Journal of the Chinese Society of Education, 3*, 77–78.

Faure, E. (1972). *Learning to Be: The World of Education Today and Tomorrow*. Paris: Unesco.

Huang, D. (2019). Kua Yujing de "Zizhi" Gainian: Xifang-Riben-Zhongguo 跨语境的"自治"概念——西方·日本·中国 (The Concept of "Autonomy" across Contexts: The Western World - Japan - China). *Jianghai Academic Journal, 1*, 191–202.

Khoo, Y. (2017). Regenerating Narrative Inquiry for Teacher Growth on a Toronto-Shanghai Sister School Partnership Landscape. *Frontiers of Education in China, 12*(2), 180–199. https://doi.org/10.1007/s11516-017-0015-4.

Khoo, Y. (2018). *River Flowing and Fire Burning: A Narrative Inquiry into a Teacher's Experience of Learning to Educate for Citizenship—from the Local to the Global—Through a Shifting Canada-China Inter-school Reciprocal Professional Learning Landscape*. University Toronto.

Liang, S. (1990). *The Complete Works of Liang Shuming (The Complete Works of Liang Shuming)*. Jinan: Shandong People's Press.

Liang, S. (2006). *Xiangcun Jianshe Lilun* 乡村建设理论 *(Rural Construction Theory)*. Shanghai Shanghai People's Press.

Oakes, J., & Lipton, M. (1999). *Jiaoxue yu Shehui Biange* 教学与社会变革 *(Teaching to Change the World)* (L. Cheng & J. F. et al., Trans). Shanghai: East China Normal University Press.

Smith, M. S., & O'Day, J. (1991). *Putting the Pieces Together: Systemic School Reform* (CPRE Policy Briefs) (p. 13). New Brunswick, NJ: Consortium for Policy Research in Education.

Wang, L. (2016). Cunluo Wenhua de Chuancheng yu Xiangcun Xuexiao de Shiming 村落文化的传承与乡村学校的使命 (The Inheritance of Village Culture and the Mission of Rural School). *Journal of Education Science of Hunan Normal University, 15*(6), 26–32.

Ye, L. (2006). *"Xinjichu Jiaoyu" Lun: Guanyu Dangdai Zhongguo Xuexiao Biange de Tanjiu Yu Renshi* "新基础教育"论—关于当代中国学校变革的探究与认识 *("New Basic Education" Theory: Exploration and Understanding on Contemporary Chinese School Reform)*. Beijing: Educational Science Publishing House.

Ye, L. (2019). "Xin Jichu Jiaoyu" Neishnegli Jiedu "新基础教育"内生力的深度解读 (An In-depth Reading of the Endogenous Power of the "New Basic Education"). In *Biange zhong Shengcheng: Yelan Jiaoyu Baogaoji* 变革中生成: 叶澜教育报告集 *(Generated Through Change: Ye Lan Education Report Collection)* (pp. 234–247). Beijing: China Renmin University Press.

CHAPTER 10

Future

Yuhua Bu

To end this book, we discuss three basic questions. (1) Will the sister schools continue their reciprocal learning after the project funding ceases and everything returns to normal? (2) What should MPS learn from BSS through the project? (3) What positive experience has the sister schools accumulated in reciprocal learning and what needs to be improved for the future we expect?

10.1 WILL THE SISTER SCHOOLS CONTINUE THEIR COOPERATION AFTER THE PROJECT?

To answer this question, two related sub-questions need to be considered. Broadly speaking, do the teachers recognize that they have reciprocally learned from the project? If the answer is no, then there is only a slight possibility that the cooperation will continue. From an objective

---

Y. Bu (✉)
East China Normal University, Shanghai, China
e-mail: yhbo@dedu.ecnu.edu.cn

© The Author(s), under exclusive license to Springer Nature Switzerland AG 2021
Y. Bu (ed.), *Narrative Inquiry into Reciprocal Learning Between Canada-China Sister Schools*, Intercultural Reciprocal Learning in Chinese and Western Education,
https://doi.org/10.1007/978-3-030-61085-2_10

point of view, are the conditions suitable for their further communication and cooperation?

To solve these questions, we can rely on the last academic annual conference held by the project team in 2019. This provides the best material for analysis as it is not only a conclusive review and reflection on the research process and the results for the past six years, but also the place where a discussion about the prospects for future development took place.

The sixth international academic conference of the project was held from October 1 to 3 in 2019 in Windsor, Canada, the theme of which was "The 6th Annual International Conference on West-East Reciprocal Learning in Education, Reciprocal Learning as Collaborative Partnership: Global Visions, Local Practices in Education". Principal Ting, Ms. Ding, and Ms. Dongmei from MPS and Ms. Barton and Ms. Hanny from BBS attended the two-day conference. The sister teachers carefully prepared for the conference by co-authoring a conference report and created a PPT presentation. As this was the last project conference, all the attendees exchanged their own learning and even used the breaks and meal time to make full use of the time. All these interactions produced material for us to analyze whether the sister schools' project will continue to cooperate.

The conference also symbolized the beginning of another new project, which also made it unique. When this seven-year project finishes, Professors Xu Shijing and Connelly hope to plan a new project, which aims at carrying out interdisciplinary and cross-cultural research on the theme of freshwater conservation and education in cooperation with the Great Lakes Research Center in Canada. Therefore, on the last afternoon of the conference, the principals and teachers of the sister schools all participated in the planning part.

10.1.1 Do Teachers Think the Project Beneficial? Will They Continue to Cooperate?

The sister schools basically cooperated in pairs, which not only reflected the friendship between the two schools but also represented the recognition and respect that exists among the teachers.

10.1.1.1 Group 1: Science Teachers—Ms. Barton and Mr. ZhiGuo
First, let's look at Ms. Barton and Mr. ZhiGuo, the science teachers, both of whom are mentor teachers in their own schools in terms of identity.

Ms. Barton

Ms. Barton plays a crucial part in determining whether the two schools will continue to cooperate in the future. As the principals of BSS change every two to three years, they do not know much about the sister schools nor have deep feelings about the project. They can choose to cooperate or not at any time. However, Ms. Barton is different, as she is over 50 years old and has no intention of leaving BSS. Moreover, she has also been invited to participate as an important member in the environmental education project of the University of Toronto and the social education project of the Great Lakes Research Center due to her excellence in water and environment education and her research acumen. Therefore, although the reciprocal learning project will end, Ms. Barton will become more important and play diverse roles. As the most soul-stirring key figure in the sister-school cooperation, her willingness to continue is obvious and strong. Of course, this is closely related to her recognition of her own learning from the project, as she has said:

> My sister teachers and I, we are not only getting closer to each other, becoming more and more like each other, we are growing and improving together! We have many similarities, we have a common water culture, but we also have our own ways of applying it. We have worked together, but we have also designed teaching independently of each other. (Interview, Oct. 2019)

Ms. Barton continued:

> I am no longer the person I was when I first took part in the project. I have become a completely new person ... although I cannot say that I have become a better teacher, I undoubtedly prefer my present state. The cooperation with sister teachers and other members of the project has brought me a lot of fun. (Interview, Oct. 2019)

Therefore, Ms. Barton can be regarded as a firm future cooperator, which is reflected not only in how she expressed her achievement but also in the following events during the conference. In the last half-day of the conference, when the project members discussed further cooperation and communication in the future, Ms. Barton promised on behalf of BSS that she would firmly participate in the new project and continue to cooperate with MPS. Shortly after the conference, she still shared the initiative to share her educational information in the WeChat group of the sister schools. It is said that she is also preparing a paper with the theme of the sister-school cooperation between China and Canada for the 2020 International Conference on Comparative Education, despite COVID-19 in early 2020.

Mr. ZhiGuo: "I Have Decided to Return to the Purpose of Science Education Itself"

Mr. ZhiGuo is an assistant to the principal of MPS and has been working hard. He did not attend the sixth annual academic conference due to family issues. Mr. ZhiGuo is a man who has a calm and gentle personality; he never boasts about himself. Although MPS allows him to engage in many scientific education research and activities independently, he still respects and accepts Principal Ting's decision. As he is responsible for science education in MPS, his attitude and enthusiasm can influence the cooperation between the two schools.

However, Mr. ZhiGuo has not been very active recently. The reason might be that he is too busy as he plays too many roles at the same time. In MPS, he is the leader of the teaching team in the subject group and assistant to principal. Outside the school, he is the training director of science teachers in Minzhu district. Family issues also disturb him. All these circumstances drain him of his vitality and make him unable to devote much time to the cooperation between the sister schools. Therefore, keeping silent for most of the time, Mr. ZhiGuo only occasionally responds to Ms. Barton's remarks in the WeChat group. It shows that although Mr. ZhiGuo is still concerned about the cooperation, he does not seem to be involved like before. However, now their understanding of the purpose or value of science education has changed to some extent, he said:

> In the past, when I was conducting science education projects, I always wanted to win prizes. At that time, the surrounding schools did not attach importance to science education and there was little competition. Our children in Minzhu Primary School often won many prizes. But now, many schools have begun to attach importance to science education competition. For example, many parents of students in the primary school affiliated to Jiaotong University are professors or scientists who can guide children to do more creative experiments. However, parents of children in Minzhu Primary School do not have the strength in this field and have no advantage in science competitions. However, now my ideas are beginning to change. I hope

to learn from Ms. Barton and return to science education itself, so that Minzhu primary school students can truly learn to love science through water projects and develop the concept and basic knowledge of loving the water environment. (Interview, May 2019)

Therefore, it is possible for Mr. ZhiGuo to continue to participate in sister-school interaction, but he will remain relatively passive due to his personal and professional circumstances.

During my visit to BSS, I asked Ms. Barton what she learned from her sister teacher. Since teacher Mr. ZhiGuo was not present, she politely said it was not very polite to talk about him without him being present. However, she thought that Mr. ZhiGuo did a lot for students and science classes, and she appreciated this spirit very much. Moreover, she hoped to increase her interactions with Mr. ZhiGuo concerning the school curriculum, not the competitions.

Realizing that Ms. Barton indicated that Mr. ZhiGuo was not as actively cooperating and that he was not as concerned as before about their growth as teachers, I turned to Principal Ting of Minzhu Primary School for an added explanation:

Our primary school is an excellent demonstration school in Shanghai specializing in science and technology, and Mr. ZhiGuo is the school's lead teacher in science education. However, as more and more schools pay attention to science and technology in recent years, our school and Mr. ZhiGuo are under great pressure to compete for honors. In particular, the parents of many primary school students may be experts and professors in science, who can help their children greatly. Mr. ZhiGuo has gradually lost his advantage in the competition. Mr. ZhiGuo and the whole school are making great efforts to maintain the honor of the school, and thus he lacks energy for reciprocal learning. (Interview, Oct. 2019)

Ms. Barton repeatedly clarified that she did not blame Mr. ZhiGuo. In her words, "Mr. ZhiGuo is very good in professional field, and being able to cooperate with him is like winning the lottery". They have since decided to cooperate in student activities. When Principal Ting stressed the importance of school honors, Ms. Barton asked whether Minzhu Primary School would be closed if it lost its lead position in science and technology and whether receiving honors brings money. Principal Ting denied that the school would be closed, but underscored the fact that bringing honors to

MPS was very important to the campus. Due to cultural differences, Ms. Barton did not seek school honors like the teachers at MPS.

10.1.1.2 Group 2: Language Teachers—Ms. Hanny and Ms. Ding

This pair of teachers was involved from the beginning of the project. The two of them are gentle in temperament, open-minded, and friendly in their relationship. During the more than six years of cooperation, the two seemed to get closer and closer, and their friendship deepened.

Ms. Hanny is the youngest teacher at BSS. Although young, she is filled with educational ideas and strategies, as she always finds many creative teaching methods for her class. Ms. Hanny has always had a friendly and sincere attitude toward Ms. Ding. Therefore, as long as conditions permit, she will continue to cooperate and communicate.

During the conference, I asked Ms. Hanny why she joined the reciprocal learning project and whether she would continue to cooperate. Ms. Hanny smiled wittily and gave a "simple but sweet" answer. At the beginning, she hoped to know her Chinese students better and give them more opportunities to express themselves. At the same time, she hoped to learn about the similarities and differences between the two countries. She said: "I think I will continue to participate. I have gained a lot; reciprocal learning has enriched my life a lot".

Ms. Ding is a teacher who keeps a low profile, but works seriously and has excellent educational ability. During the New Basic Education (NBE) research, her excellent classroom teaching ability won much recognition. After taking part in the sister-school project, Ms. Ding still maintains her original style, participating in practical and earnest manner throughout all the activities of the project, thus winning Ms. Hanny's friendship. At the beginning of the project, the cooperation between the two people was confusing and no one knew what to do. However, with sincere communications and attempts, the direction of cooperation became clearer and clearer. At the beginning of 2018, Ms. Ding began to teach the first grade of primary school, so she proposed the idea of making letter books according to characteristics of the students in order to cooperate with Ms. Hanny, who responded in the affirmative. We clearly remember that in May 2018, when Minzhu Primary School held a national meeting, the two teachers co-taught a demonstration lesson. After the class, Ms. Ding proudly said: "It only took us half an hour to reach a consensus, and soon we had a clear idea". In October 2019, when the two of them prepared a class together for the next day's cooperative teaching in BSS again, Ms. Ding again happily said to me: "It only took us half an hour to reach a consensus, we developed a clear vision soon". Therefore, the friendship between the two teachers is stable and their continued cooperation is also possible.

10.1.1.3 Group 3: Class Meeting Teachers—Ms. Hanny and Ms. Dongmei

Ms. Dongmei started to cooperate with Ms. Hanny in class meeting research in March 2018. They focused on teaching methods having to do with story picture books. It was at the on-the-spot meeting held in Minzhu Primary School in May 2018 that the two teachers cooperated in picture book teaching for the first time. The picture book they taught is "Ducks on Bicycles" with the theme being one of encouraging students to have the courage to try new things. In fact, the two teachers began to learn from each other since the first cooperative teaching.

I clearly remember some details of the class at the national meeting. Ms. Dongmei first introduced to the students that there would be two teachers teaching together in today's class. She introduced Ms. Hanny to the students, and the children all welcomed Ms. Hanny. Then, Ms. Dongmei explained the theme of the class and the first paragraph of the picture book story. After explaining the first story, Ms. Dongmei asked the students to predict the development of the story and the mood of the duck. We observed that when the students discussed in pairs, Ms. Dongmei stood at the front of the classroom waiting for the students to finish, without joining the students to listen, guide, or participate in their discussion. Next, Ms. Hanny went on with the second part of the story and communicated with the students whether their predictions were accurate and reasonable. She asked the students to talk about how the ducks felt after falling into the water. At this time, we discovered that Ms. Hanny walked among the students. Sometimes she crouched down to communicate with them, and sometimes she went to another group of students and knelt on the ground to listen to the students' discussion. When giving feedback, every time the students spoke, she would thank them! When it was Ms. Dongmei's turn to teach again, we noticed a remarkable change. When the students discussed with each other again, Ms. Dongmei no longer stood in front of the classroom waiting for the students to give answers. Instead, she walked among the students, leaned down to listen to the students' discussion, and sometimes she also participated in the discussion! This was obviously reciprocal learning taking place on the spot!

After teaching, both teachers realized the difference between them. Ms. Hanny thought that Ms. Dongmei's class was more specific and concrete. Ms. Hanny stated:

> "The details of Dongmei's class were very specific, and even scripts were designed for each activity, but the class did not seem to give students much room to learn independently." Ms. Dongmei also recognized the flexibility of Ms. Hanny class. She noted—"Ms. Hanny's class had a clear focus, but it was more flexible in structure and activities, and the students were very lively." Perhaps it is this difference that makes the two teachers—one from Canada; the other from China—want to know more about each other's teaching. (Fieldnote, Oct. 2019)

From this starting point, the two teachers planned lessons with picture book stories around the theme of "self-awareness". At the project's last international conference in October 2019, the two teachers reported to the attendees their stories and experiences of cooperating in picture book teaching.

When we visited BSS after the conference, the two teachers conducted a face-to-face picture book lesson again. This time, we were pleasantly surprised to find that although Ms. Dongmei taught Chinese in China, she could calmly and effectively interact with BSS children in English! The theme of the class is "my school", which was creatively carried out by the three sister teachers, Ms. Hanny, Ms. Ding, and Ms. Dongmei. The teaching went smoothly and the cooperation was very pleasant. The three teachers also agreed to continue the topic of "My School" after the conference to guide students to discuss the following questions: What is my favorite school? What do I think the school needs to improve most? What actions should I take to change the school? Therefore, in November 2019, all three teachers started teaching the remaining part of "my school" and shared it with each other.

In this regard, the cooperation of the three teachers might continue. In January 2020, Ms. Hanny became a mother to a lovely little boy, which temporarily interrupted her communication. Still, she is willing to cooperate and will communicate when she returns to her school.

Therefore, overall, the possibility of further cooperation between teachers in the sister schools is relatively high. Not only have they forged a deep sense of trust and friendship, but they all feel that they have gained and grown through working together. They have expressed their willingness to continue their cooperation, and their actions have proved it.

10.1.2 Are There Conditions for Further Cooperation?

Although teachers are willing to continue the cooperation, it is, after all, cooperation in a cross-cultural sense and needs external support. Experience has also proven that in the first six years of cooperation, face-to-face communication plays an irreplaceable role in establishing friendship and understanding the characteristics of the two kinds of education directly. However, face-to-face communication involves finances, time, and manpower: that is, the communication between teachers involves not only individual teachers but also schools, which makes the support of schools necessary. Therefore, what is the attitude of principals of the two schools?

10.1.2.1 Attitude of Principals of the Sister Schools

Let's start with Principal Ting of MPS, a principal who is far-sighted and dares to break through status quo thinking. She has not only given strong support for the cooperation throughout the whole project but also participated in every key activity in person. As for the situation after the end of the project, she has always said that she would insist on sister-school cooperation. She believes that the construction of sister schools has set up a platform for international communication between teachers from different cultures. The cooperation and exchange between teachers not only bring more ideas on educational concepts and teaching methods to MPS, but also improve teachers' independent learning abilities and cultural understandings. In the interaction between the two schools, Minzhu Primary School has continuously clarified its traditional Chinese educational culture and the current situation of the times in which the school is rooted, thus enhancing its recognition and confidence in the uniqueness of its own educational culture. At the same time, Principal Ting believes that the cooperation of the sister schools has promoted the development of Minzhu Primary School in many ways (Wang and Zhang 2019). In terms of student activities, she added: "After conducting reciprocal learning, Minzhu Primary School has created more student activities that reflect the characteristics of an intercultural collaboration".

In terms of curriculum adjustments influenced by the sister-school project, Principal Ting had the following to say:

> Before we joined the reciprocal learning project, the curriculum of our school was mainly based on different specific subjects, divided into three kinds including basic courses, extended courses, and inquiry courses. The advantage of such a pattern is that it helps to transfer systematic knowledge to students, because the unique educational value of each subject and field is clear and easy to locate. Its deficiency, however, is that it is not conducive to integration. Through reciprocal learning, we have selectively drawn lessons from the comprehensive curriculum of BSS and gradually explored how to integrate the existing curriculum without losing the advantages of different subject areas. At present, we have developed water culture courses, four seasons courses, and STEM courses, all of which reflect the characteristics of integrated courses. (Interview, Oct. 2019)

Principal Ting continued by discussing the progress of the reciprocal learning concept and practice as follows:

> After years of practice and exploration, our school has formed a "double-subject interactive" teaching mode with "open process interaction-feedback recovery" as its main characteristic. This mode focuses on open interactions and structured advancements in teaching and learning, which is helpful to stimulate students' enthusiasm for participation and the timely guidance of teachers. But there is still insufficient space for students to explore independently. With the deepening of the communication, especially the cooperation via the tangram course, the communication between the two schools dug deeply into the curriculum level and realized the mutual promotion of "dialogue-teaching-curriculum development". (Interview, Oct. 2019)

Through much teaching cooperation and discussion, Minzhu Primary School has not only retained its own teaching advantages but also absorbed the sister school's advantages in students' independent inquiry, forming a "double-subject interactive" teaching mode with students' independent inquiry as the core.

Therefore, Principal Ting hopes that Minzhu Primary School will continue to participate if the second phase of China-Canada project focusing on environmental education is established.

As for Principal Green, the current principal of BBS, she only joined the school about a year ago. She is very communicative and cooperative and treats people sincerely. Principal Green has always supported the cooperation between the sister schools. In the first half of 2019, a new school was built near BSS, so some teachers in BSS had to teach in the new building. According to the rules, Ms. Hanny should have taken up her post in the new school in September 2019. However, considering that Ms. Hanny played an important role in the sister-school cooperation, Principal Green personally negotiated with the district manager and Ms. Hanny will remain at BSS. In October 2019, when we visited BSS, local teachers were on strike for the rights and interests of students. In order to ensure the quality of our visit, Principal Green kept the whole school as normal as possible. During the visit, she not only participated in our discussion and activities but also provided us with a delicious lunch. All of this proves Principal Green's sincerity. However, when it comes to chances of future cooperation, she said with a forced smile that she envied Principal Ting being able to stay in MPS for such a long time, while her future was not in her hands, since she would probably have to leave BSS a year later as was stipulated by the Toronto education system. As a result, we could see the possibility of further cooperation, which is of course fraught with uncertainty.

10.1.2.2 Is the Support Provided by the Project Crucial for the Cooperation Between the Sister Schools?

We know that MPS and BSS have been sister schools since 2007. Gifts were given to each other on important holidays to express friendship, but deep and frequent communications were rare. Only after 2013 did the two schools gradually establish formal and professional cooperation. During this period, in accordance with the basic requirements of the project, university researchers did not interfere with the communication between the two schools, giving sister schools more space for autonomous communication. Researchers only participated in the project as supporters and helpers. For example, in the past six years, East China Normal University (ECNU) and University of Toronto have sent more than 20 graduate students to participate in project as volunteers to provide language and content support to the sister schools. However, the process of offering support was not smooth. Although BSS teachers were more open-minded, and graduate students could enter the school at any time for field research, MPS teachers were relatively closed, so that student assistants needed to make an appointment with teachers a long time in advance before they would be granted the opportunity to enter the classes. The impression was left that MPS teachers were completing the tasks set by the school rather than motivated by their own learning needs. Moreover, when the sister teachers reached an agreement about the theme for teaching, the exchange of teaching content was always delayed. Usually, a teacher from one school would provide his or her lesson first, while the corresponding sister teacher might take a long time to reply—and only after the graduate students constantly asked and pushed for feedback.

Additionally, the annual conference of the project has played a key role in promoting the communication between the two schools. It provided an important opportunity for the members of the two schools to write, report, and teach together. At the same time, the participation of many teachers from other places in the conference has also provided rich resources for sister-school teachers to learn and improve. The change of conference places has also attracted the sister-school teachers to participate enthusiastically. Therefore, overall, the project has given a lot of support to the sister-school cooperation. However, the end of the project means that such support will no longer exist. Without an organized structure, will teachers continue to cooperate with each other? Is there sufficient power to make this further cooperation happen? The answer will only be revealed with time.

Of course, we know that as the China-Canada reciprocal project comes to an end, the project directors, Professor Xu Shijing and Professor Connelly, are jointly applying with the Great Lakes Research Center of Canada for a new project with the theme of environmental education. If the new project is successfully granted, it will continue to provide financial and visionary support for further cooperation between the sister schools, which will be the best result we can expect.

10.2   What Should MPS Learn from BSS if the Cooperation Continues?

We comparatively took up this question in Chap. 8. The first response to this query has to do with the identity of the school in its relation with the society. BSS excels in community education, but there is still much room for MPS to improve in this aspect, as we have already discussed. Hence, this should be one of the inevitable directions of development of modern Chinese society toward civil society. Two aspects will now be brought forward for analysis here.

Since China entered the market economy in the 1990s, education for human consciousness has been a concern of the Chinese educational establishment (W. Huang 1994; Sun et al. 1995). It was only at the beginning of the twenty-first century that the issue of children's position or students' position in education gradually entered the horizon of Chinese education (Bu 2000; Li 2006; Yang 2008), and became an important value orientation for school reform in contemporary China. However, this issue is usually understood as the subjectivity of students in the teacher-student relationship rather than from the school reform perspective. For example, in order to highlight students' subjective views, NBE has proposed that teachers should "return the classroom to the students and make the classroom full of vitality" and "give the class back to the students so that the class will be filled with vigor". Minzhu Primary School has been pursuing children's positioning in the educational act for many years. However, due to the large class sizes in China (usually about 40–50 students), teachers often see students as an abstracted group leaving little room for students' individualized growth. Therefore, in teaching or class meeting activities in MPS, teachers usually pay less attention to individual students. Therefore, MPS can learn from BSS from the following aspects: (1) leaving more space for children's individualized growth and (2) learning to provide students with a structured framework of thinking to support independent learning. In the following sections, I share more about each sub-point.

10.2.1 Learn to Leave More Space for Children's Individualized Growth

In BSS, we can see that there is a lot of space for children's individualized growth, which can help students with self-awareness, such as the following:

- During morning reading, each BSS student chooses a book that he or she likes or is recommended by a teacher, which need not be consistent with their peers. BSS would not ask all the students to do the same thing at the same time like MPS.
- In classroom teaching, teachers encourage students to ask personally generated questions. Teachers usually write the questions on the board and mark each question with the name of the student who asked it.

- In group activities, BSS teachers will assign different tasks to students in the same group so that each student has an active role to play and is irreplaceable.
- When it comes to learning content, teachers will choose content that can promote students' self-awareness or personal awareness, for example, the series of picture books selected by Ms. Hanny for class.
- When the students are learning in the classroom, teachers do not require them to maintain a certain sitting position, and students can sit, stand, or otherwise move around as they wish, as long as it does not interfere with the order of the class.
- In educational activities, teachers provide students with a selection of assignment questions from which to choose.

Moreover, BSS not only provides space for students' individual development but also gives students a clear idea of the importance of individuality and how to treat differences. Individuality can be regarded as difference; that is, the difference that distinguishes me from you and him. For example, we have found that in the BSS classrooms, teachers have put up posters that encourage individualized growth and that encourage treating differences with acceptance, such as "Our differences make us unique. You don't have to be handicapped to be different. Everyone is different. Be considerate of the feelings of others".

Here are two more examples of children who have their own characteristics that we found during our visits to BSS and who are in a psychologically safe space:

Principal Luu showed us around BBS, and as we passed a first-grade classroom, we noticed that there were only 3–5 students and one teacher inside. A child was lying on the floor at the entrance of the classroom, absorbed in writing something. Although several of us came in, and the principal was still introducing the layout of the classroom to us in a not-so-small voice, the child was not affected by us, and remained motionless, writing something. The teacher nearby found us staring at the little child and said that he was composing a script. On the left side of the classroom, there were two other children around the teacher, listening quietly to what the teacher was saying and not turning back or greeting us as we arrived. On the right side of the classroom, a child was reading quietly and did not look up at our presence. It reminded us of the daily scene of Chinese children in China on this occasion: they would immediately stand up, salute politely and say loudly, "Hello teacher!" Then, they might choose to dodge the teachers quickly. (Fieldnotes, May 2017)

Which kind of children do we want to cultivate most? Is the child in the BSS who is preoccupied with interests and explorative delight? or Is it the child who is always only well-mannered according to the politeness of the adult world? In our view, the child who is preoccupied with his own interests may not be impolite, and a polite child may not be able to be fully absorbed in exploring the world. Therefore, MPS students or Chinese students have much to learn from BSS students in terms of exploring personal interests.

What we see in MPS are ways of a practice that encourage homogeneous development. Students read the same content in the morning. In classroom teaching, teachers often regard the ideals of a few students as the thinking of all students, understanding them as a group rather than as individuals. In group activities, the tasks of the four students are the same and can be replaced by each other. When it comes to sitting in class, everyone maintains the same posture, otherwise they will be criticized, and so on.

It is true that BSS is concerned with the individualized education of students, not only due to Western culture's emphasis on individual freedom but also due to the multicultural context in which there are different races, colors, languages, and cultural habits, and in which harmonious coexistence requires understanding differences and individuality as important educational themes. However, this does not mean that there is no difference in modern Chinese society and in individual development. First, it is harmful to understand people from an abstract perspective in terms of education. French educator Paul Legrand has pointed this out poignantly: "Modern people are victims of abstraction. All kinds of factors can divide people and destroy their unity" (Legrand. 1985). He therefore appealed: "The real object of education is the whole person, the person living in various environments, the person with all responsibilities, in short, the concrete person" "and education should have all aspects and spheres of being as a material, rational, emotional, gender, social and spiritual being". All these compositions cannot be and shall not be separated. They depend on each other" (Legrand 1985). Second, each individual is both unique and distinctive and embodies the universality and commonality of human being. Each individual is a specific unity of uniqueness and group commonality and therefore needs to be respected. Third, although the Chinese cultural tradition emphasizes collectivity, it does not mean that there is no difference between individuals, especially in contemporary China, where there are differences in children's family backgrounds, personal characters, scores and achievement, ways of doing things, growing experience, and so on. Therefore, it is also necessary to pay attention to children's individuality.

If MPS focuses on individualizing students, it means that personal differences are no longer a problem. For example, MPS would no longer exclude children with special needs from public classes, but consider the uniqueness of the child as valuable resources for education. It also means that children's present is no longer judged based on their past, much less their future based on their present, and that each child's daily growth is concrete and vivid. Instead of simply setting goals and providing content, education is about providing students with more personalized content and educational methods based on their individual needs. Teachers are pleasantly surprised and excited by the different voices children make, rather than dismissing students or getting irritated because students are so different from the teachers themselves.

10.2.2 Learn to Provide Students with the Structured Framework of Thinking to Support Independent Learning

NBE teaching has always advocated for "structured teaching" to develop children's thinking. Recently, the concept of high level thinking from the OECD has attracted the attention of the Chinese education academia. MPS has been exploring it for years. However, in BSS we see a better understanding and approach to it that is worth learning by MPS. During the visit of Ms. Hanny's class, we have found that for children in grades 2–3, she focused a lot on providing the students with the framework of thinking. This excerpt forms an apt exemplar:

Today, Ms. Hanny continued the story of lion and mouse for grade 1–2. Yesterday, the children already knew the outline of the story and today's assignment was to retell the story. The target of this lesson is: "*I used this story to let students to retell characters, setting, problems and solutions and more of the story.*" Obviously, this is a structure-conscious target, and how to help students have this consciousness is also very important. As can be seen in this example, Ms. Hanny used dialogue and writing to show how to retell the story structurally with the framework of thinking. At the beginning of the story, the characters and the place of the story should be explained clearly. In the process of unfolding the story, "first, next, then, finally" and other words can be used to narrate the story in an orderly way. Finally, how to solve the contradiction in the story should be revealed. (Fieldnotes, November 2017)

Moreover, we have found in Ms. Hanny's class that she spent a lot of effort to cultivate students' real curiosity. In May 2017, we visited BSS. That semester, Ms. Hanny was preparing to teach students about the butterfly growth cycle. For this reason, she had kept butterflies in her classroom since March, so that the students could experience the growth of butterflies from eggs to larvae and finally into butterflies. When we visited her class that day, she took the butterflies with the students to the garden beside the school playground and let them fly away. Then, she buried two dead butterflies with the children and put a small flower on the butterflies' tiny grave, and the children and teachers prayed three minutes together. The students were serious the whole time. When they returned to the classroom, Ms. Hanny sat on the carpet with the children, and she first asked the students to observe the cocoon of the butterfly in her hand, then asked the students to recall their observation of the butterfly's growth, and finally asked them if they had any questions. All the children thought carefully together.

Student 1: I find that the cocoon of the butterfly is very clean, doesn't the butterfly have poop in it?

Student 2: The butterfly's cocoon is closed. And how does it breathe before it comes out?

Student 3: I find that the butterfly's egg is very, very small, and then it lives inside a cocoon with no door, and I wonder how it can grow so big without eating any food.

Student 4: Ms. Hanny, my mother said it might be windy and rainy tomorrow. So, where are butterflies' homes? Will they die?

Student 5: If a butterfly gives birth to a baby, does her baby have to go through the same process of growth? But it needs proper temperature. If it is winter, will their eggs freeze to death?

Student 6: Does the butterfly have memory? If so, I will be sure to invite it to our classroom again if it returns this afternoon.

...

The children asked questions like that while Ms. Hanny listened and took notes, discussed the possibilities with the children, and asked the children to try to answer various questions. At the same time, she would occasionally stick some note marks on a board painted rose, green, yellow, and blue behind her. Later, we learned that it was a question assessment board and that the different shades corresponded to the level of thinking where the students belonged. Only later did it gradually become clear why Ms. Hanny had taken such a long time to carry out this kind of teaching. She was trying to diagnose the thinking level of her students in this way.

Isn't this commendable? The children gained not only training on thinking but also an understanding of the life cycle of butterflies, awe of life, and the value of observation. Similarly, we have found Ms. Barton's structured teaching in her science and math classes as well as in her writing classes.

10.2.3 *Learn to Provide Special Students with More Professional and Inclusive Education*

MPS has another identity in its midst: the special education center in the Minzhu district. Its presence is related to China's policy of inclusive education for special children in recent years, which allows special children to attend normal classes. In 2010, Shanghai issued the Outline of Medium- and Long-Term Education Reform and Development Plan for Shanghai (2010–2020), which puts forward the concept of "lifelong development for every student" and takes all students, including students with disabilities, to enjoy equal educational opportunities and high-quality educational resources as development goals. Since then, Shanghai's special education has entered the track of rapid development. In 2017, seven ministries, including the Ministry of Education, issued the "Second Special Education Promotion Plan (2017–2020)", and in 2018, Shanghai issued the "Shanghai Special Education Three-Year Action Plan (2018–2020)", proposing to actively provide diversified and individualized special education services for disabled students and promote the development of special education. At present, Shanghai has formed an operational mechanism led by the municipal and district governments, with education, health, civil affairs, disability federations, and other departments working together.

MPS is now actively participating in the inclusive education policy as a high-quality local school. The director of special education at MPS says that almost every course has both general education objectives and special education objectives, which are inspected by the relevant government department every term. These are brilliant changes. When listening to lectures in MPS, I can see the presence of these special children in almost every class, and notice their difficulties in school life. I often find that they do not really understand what the teacher explains for normal children. They are usually relatively quiet, sitting at their seats instead of making trouble everywhere. However, their facial expression is often blank and bored, as the passionate and chaotic life of others is often beyond their comprehension. Whenever this happens, I feel so sorry for these children, and the ideal emerges that maybe it would be better for them to study in specialized schools. The preparation that Chinese teachers receive in special education is limited, and even if some training is given, it is often abstract and theoretical, and difficult to integrate with the specific situation of each special child in reality. What teachers can do is lower the instructional requirements and increase the amount of time for individualized instruction, but it is doubtful whether such instruction is effective.

In some schools in Windsor, and in BSS, we have learned about the special education provided. Two experiences were very impressive: one was a high school in Windsor, which had a rehabilitation physiotherapy room for a special student with a physical disability, and two nursing staff, a doctor, and teachers in charge of teaching, at least five or six of whom were working this special student. At that time, we felt that the special student was happy and that his family should be satisfied and at ease. However, in terms of equipment and personnel, China does not yet have the conditions and will to do so. The other example is in BSS, where we met a special education teacher who worked not only in BSS but also with special children in about four to five schools around BSS. His salary was also not borne by BSS, but was paid by the Toronto School Board. He introduced us to some of the diagnostics for children with dyslexia and gave us a story-based language class. In class, he was like a comedian, whose tone and body movements were extremely exaggerated. The children were attracted to him and responded to his questions during the performance from time to time. At this time, we did not feel that these children were special children because they were attracted by the special teacher, their eyes were very focused, and they laughed from time to time. Through this example, we can see the necessity of professional guidance. In MPS, however, there are few teachers with such expertise, and it seems that there are very few special teachers in Minzhu District who can work

308   Y. BU

in several schools at the same time and in the same way. Therefore, if MPS truly assumes the responsibility for special education, it is necessary to strengthen its faculty with specialized training.

Of course, in the classroom of BSS, we have also discovered that children who came to school with trouble paying attention who could barely learn anything and would even dance around the classroom when the teacher was giving the lesson. Other children seemed to be accustomed to such student behaviors, and they participated in the teacher's teaching activities almost undisturbed. To some extent, it indicates that inclusive education in BSS is successful. Teachers at MPS have also taught children to be tolerant of children with special needs. However, perhaps because of the face-saving tradition rooted in Chinese culture, teachers choose to exclude children with special needs from activities on special public occasions, which needs to be reflected on and firmly discarded.

10.2.4   *Learn to Become More Open-Minded and Positive in Reciprocal Learning*

Here, we would like to pay tribute to Ms. Barton and Ms. Hanny, the two sincere and open-minded teachers! Under the circumstance that the principals changed frequently and the full support of the school could not be guaranteed, they insisted on cooperating with MPS. In fact, without the two of them, the cooperation between the sister schools could not have been established. During the communication, we believe they have also encountered many difficulties.

Let's look at their own lives. As far as we know, according to the provisions of Canada's teacher work system, if the two of them want to go out to communicate during their working hours, they have to ask another teacher to teach for them and transfer all their remuneration to the substitute teacher, so there is no money left for themselves. However, they don't care about it. It was their first visit to MPS in 2016 that made the cooperation and communication between the sister schools smoother. They did that voluntarily. In 2017, we visited BSS and experienced the daily school life of the two teachers all day long. We directly understood their business and hard work. They worked much harder than the Chinese teachers. As they did not have fixed textbooks and needed to prepare learning materials for many courses, they just paid themselves for some learning materials. Their workplace was always their classrooms, and they would stay with students almost all day long, with little time to rest. They not only had to give classes but also were responsible for the daily sanitation and arrangement of classrooms. Although we have just experienced only one day of their daily life as mere onlookers, we have already had the feeling of tiredness. However, the teachers have worked in the same way day-by-day.

In addition, there are also difficulties in the communication between the sister schools. Although the teachers in the sister schools have always been friendly and open-minded and have kept sincere friendship, they have also encountered some conflicts in the process of communication, because of cultural differences or the dilemmas in daily life. As a "window school", MPS needs to open its school life to the public, receive visitors, and deal with all kinds of daily affairs required by the government almost every month and every week. Teachers are very busy and sometimes have no time to pay attention to the communications between the sister schools. However, the two BSS teachers did not complain much about it. Moreover, other things mentioned in Chaps. 6 and 8 that made the two teachers feel confused have not prevented their sincere cooperation with MPS

In contrast, the teachers of MPS have less initiative, as they always regard the cooperation as the project team's business or the school's business, which has little to do with themselves. Therefore, in the future, the teachers of MPS need to learn from the professionalism of the teachers of BSS, their active and open learning attitude, and their ability to transform external requirements into internal motivation!

10.3 What Should MPS Stick To?

As a high-quality school in Shanghai and a cooperative demonstration school of NBE, after years of development and more than 20 years of active reform and exploration, MPS has gained many positive experiences, which need to be adhered to in cross-cultural reciprocal learning. Here are the main points:

First, we should stick to the idea of creating our own school culture. For MPS, the school is no longer just a place for children to go to school nor a place for teachers to give classes, but also a mutual spiritual home for all teachers and students. In MPS, the school culture includes cooperation, unity, innovation and exploration, mutual love, and common endeavor. The school culture is the spiritual motivation for every teacher and student in MPS to work hard.

Second, we should stick to teaching of different subjects as the core, supplemented by comprehensive courses. The curriculum with different subjects is the main feature of China's basic education and an essential carrier for children to contact with the world of human culture. Containing rich educational value, it is also what China's teacher education has insisted on for many years and what Chinese teachers are used to and good at. MPS has accumulated rich experience in exploring the educational value in subjects like Chinese, mathematics, foreign languages, and science in recent ten years, and has effectively improved the effectiveness of classroom teaching. Therefore, MPS should insist on teaching based on different subjects as the core.

Third, we must stick to helping the surrounding schools and serving our country. Although MPS is an ordinary public school, since 2013, it has been adhering to the principle of the development of school eco-community by sharing experience, co-researching, and developing together with more than ten surrounding schools, which has effectively helped the surrounding schools to successfully improve the quality of education. Additionally, MPS has been maintaining a helping relation with schools in underdeveloped areas in the country, passing on its own school-running experience to local schools, which has not only helped to improve the quality of school education in these areas but also made MPS teachers enjoy a sense of accomplishment brought by their professionalism. Moreover, every communication is also a chance for learning, which effectively promotes teachers' self-awareness of professional growth.

Fourth, we must stick to the promise of running "a good school at home that satisfies the people". Minzhu Primary School was founded as a private primary school, shouldering the educational mission of providing opportunities for children who did not have the opportunity to enter public schools. More than 60 years have passed and Minzhu Primary School has made great efforts to run the school and experience progress in the reform. It has turned from a private primary school to a local demonstration school. However, the background of students in Minzhu Primary School has not changed much. Most of the students still come from working families in the old industrial age, whose parents are neither rich nor highly educated. Besides, as their communities can provide few educational resources, these students still rely on MPS to a large extent in terms of education. In the future, with the relocation of Minzhu district's economic and technological center to the north and the south, some students from better family backgrounds in Minzhu Primary School will move out, and more children from migrant families will probably flow into Minzhu Primary School, meaning that the migrant students will have less support from their families compared with other students. Therefore, MPS will need to stick to its original intention, adhere to the idea of "no discrimination among the students", and provide education of the highest quality for the children from typical Chinese families.

10.4 What Positive and Negative Experiences Has the Sister-School Cooperation Provided for Cross-Cultural Reciprocal Learning?

10.4.1 Positive Experience in Sister Schools' Reciprocal Learning

Over the past six years, the sister schools have accumulated many positive experiences of cooperation through reciprocal learning. Here are three main points:

First of all, the non-utilitarian principle of sincere communication. The establishment of the friendship between MPS and BSS is quite special. The two schools learn from each other on a voluntary basis, as there is neither administrative support or requirements nor external financial or reputational benefits. Everyone interacts with each other out of a sincere friendship between "I-You" as opposed to "I-It", as Martin Buber (1986) put it. It is also this kind of relationship that makes the two schools more and more trustful and intimate after experiencing various contradictions such as differences in time and space, cultural differences, system barriers, and so on. Therefore, this is one of the most valuable experiences accumulated by the sister schools in cross-cultural cooperation.

Second, the most comfortable way of reciprocal learning is the combination of daily online interaction and face-to-face communication. In the more than six years of reciprocal cooperation between the sister schools, teachers were always very busy, but they still insisted on making full use of modern technology for daily online communication and transmitting their daily work information to each other, which helped to maintain friendships without adding burden. Face-to-face communication refers to the activities at the annual academic conference once a year. The close contact has not only promoted friendship but also offered a more comprehensive understanding of each other.

Overall, the frequency of daily communication between the sister teachers in the sister schools is not very high, usually one to two reciprocal learning cycles, because every complete cycle of cross-cultural learning activity needs many actions. For example, if an activity is initiated by the Canadian teacher, then this cycle of reciprocal learning activity usually consists of the following steps: (1) the Canadian teacher arranges time to complete the task they wish to cooperate with the sister teacher; (2) Canadian graduate students record the activity in field notes; (3) the field notes need to be confirmed by the Canadian teacher; (4) then it will be transmitted to the Chinese partners; (5) after receiving the field notes, the Chinese graduate students need to translate them into Chinese before transmitting them to the Chinese teachers; (6) the Chinese teacher need to find time to read and understand; (7) the Chinese teacher needs more time to conceive of the corresponding work plan; (8) then the Chinese teacher finishes the plan; (9) next, the Chinese graduate students need to write field notes of the Chinese teacher's activity; (10) the field notes need to be reviewed by the Chinese teacher; (11) then, the field notes are sent to the Canadian teacher; (12) the Canadian postgraduates translate them into English and pass it to the Canadian teacher; (13) the Canadian teacher will read them and give feedback to the Chinese teacher. This 13-step cross-cultural interaction is a complete cycle of reciprocal learning activity. Each step requires a certain amount of time. Teachers usually forget about the reciprocal learning if there is no reminder from graduate students due to their busy daily work, which will delay the feedback for a long time. Therefore, it is most convenient and appropriate for each pair of sister teachers to complete one reciprocal learning cycle every semester, occasionally twice a semester, but no more. Otherwise, the teachers' daily work will be disturbed.

Third, continuous cross-border learning and far-sighted project aims are important motivations for the sister schools to overcome difficulties and persist in reciprocal learning. The sister schools of Shanghai and Toronto were founded out of friendship. They have solved many difficulties and kept cooperation because everyone has gone beyond the role given by work and cooperated out of sincerity based on common human feelings, educational visions, and friendship without utilitarian intentions. Especially after contact with the two selfless teachers, Ms. Barton and Ms. Hanny, the MPS principal and teachers have developed a broader vision. The educational concepts of globalization and world citizenship have entered their vision, making them realize that education under the background of globalization needs a broader educational mission! Xu and

Connelly (2013) underscore the value and impact on behavior when individuals have the experience of varied learning situations in different learning spaces (Shijing Xu and Connelly 2013).

Moreover, the project holds conferences in different places once a year, so that principals and teachers can be exposed to the history, society, and culture of different places and participate in academic activities organized by university scholars, doing such things as making reports, participating in discussions, and planning projects. This kind of cross-border learning itself is a kind of self-transcendence.

Therefore, the real motivation of MPS to participate in the sister-school cooperation is the call of educational mission, which helps them become better friends and achieve better selves at the same time! Isn't it wonderful to enjoy life like this?

10.4.2 Reciprocal Learning Between Sister Schools Needs Further Improvement

Liu Luxia, a graduate student assistant at ECNU, has analyzed how to improve the reciprocal learning between the sister schools in her thesis, which has comprehensively reviewed and reflected on the difficulties of reciprocal learning and teacher growth in the sister schools, in the context of the last international conference in October 2019. At the end of the thesis, she pointed out the shortcomings of the sister teachers in reciprocal learning and what to be strengthened in the future (Liu 2020).

First of all, it is necessary to promote teachers' reflection on the internal driving force of their own development and to truly clarify the external motivation and internal motivation of their participation in the project. As teacher participation is essential in cross-cultural communication, only internal motivation can ensure high-quality reciprocal learning. During the whole process of the project, we have discovered that the motivation of the MPS teachers was always external, which has hindered the advancement of the cooperation between the sister teachers from time-to-time. Therefore, we should highlight the reflection on the internal driving force of the teachers' own development, find out the conflicts the teachers are facing, thus enhancing the internal needs of participating in the project by connecting the realization of teachers' professional development and personal growth with cross-cultural reciprocal learning. Therefore, the teachers will seize the opportunities actively and cooperate.

In terms of specific measures, "teachers need to regularly reflect on the results of cross-cultural reciprocal learning from multiple perspectives, clarify their own gains in teaching consciousness, knowledge and practice, strengthen their confidence in cross-cultural learning, stimulate their motivation for cross-cultural learning, and sum up experiences for further cooperation" (Liu 2020).

In addition, it is crucial to provide sufficient support and supervision mechanism for the reciprocal learning cooperation between the sister schools. First, social software and network media can be used to facilitate communication to overcome obstacles in time and space. When necessary, the sister schools can even build their own network platform, which not only helps teachers communicate but also provides a platform for both sides to store and exchange data, carry out curriculum co-designing activities, and record student activities. Second, the project should improve the supervision and reward mechanism. At the project level, it is important to improve the management of participating schools and teachers, to clarify the responsibilities and obligations to be undertaken by participants in the project, to set up a special agency to be responsible for supervision, to collect periodical summary reports, and to reward the participants according to their accomplishments. At the school level, it is necessary to provide support for participating teachers, make corresponding resource inclinations and auxiliary arrangements, reward outstanding teachers, and even incorporate reciprocal learning into the school's performance evaluation of teachers.

Finally, it is important to ensure the independent cooperation between the sister schools by clarifying whens and how the research team should stop providing support. The research team has played a great supporting role in the early stage of the cooperation, by not only providing a guarantee for the communication between the teachers but also promoting the cross-cultural harmonious coexistence of the teachers, and even helping the growth of the teachers to some extent. However, the long-term cooperation between the two schools requires them to reach a state of independent communication. Therefore, the research team should clearly define their own responsibilities, cultivate the teachers' ability of independent cooperation and cross-cultural communication at the beginning of the project, and then gradually stop interfering with the sister schools.

10.5 Expectations: What Kind of Future Do We Expect?

Martin Buber once pointed out that there are two kinds of relations between people, one is the "I-it" relation and the other is the "I-you" relation. The "I-it" relation is not a real relation in essence, which only reveals the experience and utilization between subjects and objects, as "I" is the center of the world, "I" perceive the world, and the surrounding world is only a sensory object (Buber 1986). My experience of "it" shows that I only perceive the world outside the world, showing that I and the world are opposite, not blending with one another. In addition, this kind of relationship is also unequal, because "I" is the subject, "it" is the object determined passively. "I" is experiencing "it" and using "it" as the dominator.

"I", the subject, has the ability of objectification, while "it" is just an object. Moreover, the "I-it" relationship needs to be established through intermediary tools, which weaken the intimate relationship that can exist between "I" and "it". Contrary to the "I-it" relation, Buber has stressed that "I-you" is a real close relation, a direct and mutual relation. The directness of the relation means that the mutual understanding between "I and you" does not need an intermediary, which can make us lose our sincerity due to the pursuit of power, recognition, and honor. Reciprocity means that the meaning of my existence is neither in me nor in you. It is our communication that brings about meaning. In this way, you and I can not only maintain our own characteristics but also link together, as there is always a tension between us. So, how do we become "I" in the "I-you" relation? Buber has said that I can become "I" (Buber 1986) through "you". In other words, the relation appears before "I", and the concept of "I" as "entity" comes after the "I-you" relation.

According to Buber, we can therefore expect the sister schools to adhere to the "I-you" relation in further cooperation, so that they can continuously achieve the best of themselves in this relationship. We also expect that Professor Connelly of the University of Toronto, Professor Xu Shijing of the University of Windsor, and all those who are willing to cooperate with us in the future will be able to get along with each other in the "I-You" relation and make the human world more and more "harmonious and different, and enjoy the common good" due to our shared existence!

REFERENCES

Bu, Y. (2000). Fansi "Erton Zhongxin" de Jiaoyu Mudi Guan. 反思"儿童中心"的教育目的观 (Rethinking the Educational Purpose of "Children's Center"). *Shanghai Research on Education, 3*, 24–27.

Buber, M. (1986). *Wo Yu Ni*我与你 *(I and You)* (W. Chen, Trans.). Beijing: Joint Publishing House.

Huang, W. (1994). Zhuti Xing·Zhutixing Jiaoyu·Shehui Fazhan. 主体性·主体性教育·社会发展 (Subjectivity. Subjectivity Education. Social Development). *Future and Development, 4*, 30–33.

Legrand, P. (1985). *Zhongshen JiaoyuYinlun*终身教育引论. *(Introduction to Lifelong Education)* (N. Zhou & S. Chen, Trans.). Beijing: China Foreign Translation and Publishing Corporation.

Li, W. (2006). Jiaoyu Yao Queli "Ertong Lichang" 教育要确立 "儿童立场" (Education Should Establish "Children's Standpoint"). *Jiangsu Education Research, 6*, 1.

Liu, L. (2020). *TuoZhanXingXuXi Shijiao Xia Jiaoshi Chengzhang De Xushi Tanjiu.* 拓展性学习视角下教师成长的叙事探究:—基于"中-加跨文化互惠学习项目"的研究. *(Narrative Inquiry of Teachers' Growth from the Perspective of Expansive Learning: Research Based on the Inter-cultural Reciprocal Learning Project between China and Canada.).* Shanghai: East China Normal University.

Sun, X., Cheng, X., Chu, H., Huang, W., Tian, H., & Chen, J. (1995). Ren de Zhutixing Neihan Yu Ren de Zhutixing Jiaoyu人的主体性内涵与人的主体性教育 (Connotation of Human Subjectivity and Human Subjectivity Education). *Educational Researcher, 10*, 34–39.

Wang, Y., & Zhang, X. (2019). Jiyu Kuaguo Jiaoliu Chonggou Xiaoyuan Shenghuo. 基于跨国交流重构校园生活 (Reconstruction of campus life based on transnational communication). *Jiangsu Education, 1242*(7), 23–25.

Xu, S., & Connelly, F. M. (2013). Reciprocal Learning in Teacher Education and School Education between Canada and China.

Yang, X. (2008). Dangdai Jiaoshi Yaoyou Jianding de Xuesheng Lichang. 当代教师要有坚定的学生立场 (Contemporary Teachers Should Have a Firm Student Position). *Research in Educational Development, 4*, 6.

Index[1]

B

Banhui lesson, 146, 153, 155, 157, 158, 160, 162, 163, 166, 167

Basic education, 13, 14, 40, 53, 66, 90, 91, 113, 120, 143, 176, 222, 228, 237, 244, 249, 263, 282, 286, 310

Bay Street School (BSS), 1–3, 6, 7, 11–13, 73, 96, 98, 100, 102, 103, 105, 111, 114–126, 128, 129, 131, 132, 134, 136, 141–143, 145–148, 158, 181, 182, 193, 197, 198, 206, 213, 214, 218–223, 226, 242, 248–250, 259, 260, 262–265, 267–282, 284–286, 289, 291, 293, 294, 296, 298–309, 311

C

Canada-China, v, 38, 245

Chinese education, v, 8–11, 30, 32, 54–77, 79, 103, 105, 140, 169, 205, 243–245, 283, 301, 304

Clandinin, Jean, 4, 10, 19, 34, 36–38, 91, 92, 95, 105, 143, 144, 148, 180, 214, 221, 222, 224, 232, 233, 241, 245, 280

Classroom teaching, 6, 12, 22, 41–43, 64, 66, 140–141, 145, 165, 169, 176, 179, 183–198, 208, 228, 265, 267, 283, 294, 301, 303, 310

Communication, 3, 6–9, 11–13, 24, 28, 88–90, 93, 94, 96–100, 102, 104, 120–132, 137, 143, 145, 146, 155, 161, 167, 178, 182, 201, 213, 219, 245, 263, 290, 291, 294, 296–300, 308–315

[1] Note: Page numbers followed by 'n' refer to notes.

© The Author(s), under exclusive license to Springer Nature Switzerland AG 2021
Y. Bu (ed.), *Narrative Inquiry into Reciprocal Learning Between Canada-China Sister Schools*, Intercultural Reciprocal Learning in Chinese and Western Education,
https://doi.org/10.1007/978-3-030-61085-2

318 INDEX

Community, 10–12, 14, 18, 18n1,
26–28, 32, 35, 38, 43, 61, 89,
90, 94, 111, 113–115, 118, 122,
129, 141, 159, 166–167, 179,
217, 219, 225, 228, 231, 246,
248–250, 261, 262, 264, 265,
267–271, 277–285, 300, 310
Compound subject theory,
176, 179–180
Compulsory education, 44, 141, 169
Confucian culture, 10
Confucianism, v, 25, 28–30, 168,
246, 247
Connelly, Micheal, v–vii, 2–7, 9–11,
19, 28, 33–38, 53, 54, 64–71,
74, 79, 80, 80n2, 88, 91, 92,
95–97, 105, 121, 125, 142–144,
148, 178, 180, 214, 221–224,
232, 233, 241, 244, 245, 280,
290, 300, 313, 315
Craig, Cheryl, v, vii, 5, 7, 10, 19,
34–38, 46n7, 92, 95, 125, 144,
145, 181, 201, 214, 221,
223–225, 232, 246, 280
Cross-culture, 36
Cultural-historical activity theory, 12,
176, 179

D

Dewey, J., vi, 5, 9–11, 18, 30, 33–38,
53–80, 92, 94, 95, 105, 164,
180, 214, 221, 224, 244,
269, 279

E

East China Normal University
(ECNU), vii, 2, 4, 5, 13, 14, 32,
34, 38, 39, 41–43, 65, 92,
96–98, 113, 121, 122, 125–127,
130, 181, 218, 219, 223, 226,
238, 266, 299, 313

Education bureau, 41, 119, 120,
215, 239
Education Institute, 41
Education reform, 13, 14, 40,
44, 54, 56, 59, 63, 66, 72,
74, 79, 80, 113, 116, 142,
222, 226, 235, 242,
244, 270
Education researcher, 38, 41,
141, 169

F

Fire and water, 218–219

H

HE LE school culture, 214–223
Heterogeneous lesson, 148–153,
162, 164

K

Knowledge landscape, 243,
244, 248
Knowledge transfer, 37, 88,
206, 279

L

Lesson preparation and discussion,
139, 153–158
"Life-Practice" Educology (LPE), 12,
13, 19, 32, 34, 38–45, 53,
93–96, 214, 226–233, 243,
247, 248

M

Ministry of Education, 43, 115, 117,
206, 215, 229, 306
Minzhu District School Board
(MDSB), 194, 235

INDEX 319

Minzhu Primary School (MPS), 1, 7, 10, 41, 43, 44, 66, 97, 109–116, 120, 129, 130, 134, 141, 142, 145–148, 153, 157, 158, 162, 166, 168, 170, 176, 213–218, 222, 292–295, 297, 298, 301, 310, 311

N
Narrative inquiry (NI), v–vii, 3–9, 11, 36–38, 45, 65–67, 69–72, 91–96, 121, 143, 144, 176, 180, 181, 214, 221–225
New Basic Education (NBE), 2, 4, 6, 9–11, 13, 39–45, 46n7, 64–67, 102, 103, 113, 125, 141, 145, 146, 166, 176, 209, 218, 222, 223, 226, 228, 263, 265–267, 284, 294, 301, 304, 309
New curriculum reform, 113, 215

O
Ontario Education Ministry, 231, 243
Ontario Environmental Resources Bureau, 122
Ontario Institute for Studies in Education (OISE), 36, 65, 97, 182, 264, 275
Ontario Leadership Framework (OLF), 12, 214, 226, 228, 229, 231–233, 244, 247, 248
Ontario Leadership System, 12

P
Personal practical knowledge, 6, 38, 69–71, 143, 144, 224, 280
Practical knowledge, vii, 6, 68–70, 248
Professional development, 6, 14, 38, 101, 119, 120, 166, 167, 178, 182, 232, 243–244, 283, 313

Q
Quality-oriented education, 61, 63, 64, 113

R
Reciprocal learning project, v, vii, 7, 33, 38, 92, 122, 124, 131, 170, 176, 178, 190, 264, 291, 294, 298
Reciprocal Learning (RL), v–vii, 1–4, 7–14, 18, 28, 33, 36, 37, 45, 54, 67, 74, 77–80, 87–89, 91, 100, 102, 103, 109, 120–137, 139, 142, 143, 146, 147, 167, 184, 190–192, 202–203, 207, 213, 214, 218, 220, 222, 226, 244, 245, 250, 263, 265, 289, 290, 293–295, 297, 298, 308–309, 311–314

S
School Board, 116, 118
School ecological communities, 43, 44
School education, 2, 28, 36, 141, 175, 177, 199, 227, 260, 284, 285, 310
Shanghai education, 235
Sister school project (SSP), 7–11, 28, 90, 96–98, 102, 105, 114, 294, 297
Social Sciences and Humanities Research Council of Canada (SSHRC), 36, 38, 213, 222, 245

T
Teacher education, v, 13, 14, 35–38, 114, 217, 310
Teacher leadership, 12, 213, 214, 220, 221, 226–241, 244, 247, 248, 250

320 INDEX

Teacher learning, 14, 240
Teacher-student interaction, 12, 176, 179, 180, 182–206, 208, 209
Teacher-student relationship, 12, 94, 98, 175–178, 180, 185, 190, 196, 198, 201, 204–205
Toronto District School Board (TDSB), 117, 182, 243, 268

U
The University of Toronto (UT), 2, 5, 7, 32, 34, 36, 65, 67, 88, 96, 101, 120, 121, 125–127, 181, 182, 218, 223, 275, 291, 299, 315
The University of Windsor (UW), 2, 36, 38, 65, 67, 88, 218, 315

V
Videoconference, 127

W
Western culture, 21, 22, 303
Western education, 141

Y
Ye, Lan, vii, 2, 9–11, 13, 19, 29–34, 30n5, 31n6, 39–45, 53, 64–67, 78, 79, 93, 97, 113, 125, 140, 141, 165, 166, 175, 176, 179, 180, 205, 216, 218, 226–228, 243, 248, 283, 284